AN INTRODUCTION TO PROGRAMMING WITH

ActionScript 3.0

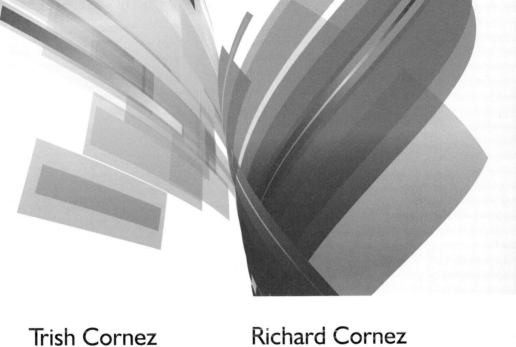

Trish Cornez
University of Redlands

Richard Cornez
University of Redlands

& BARTLETT
LEARNING

World Headquarters
Jones & Bartlett Learning
5 Wall Street
Burlington, MA 01803
978-443-5000
info@jblearning.com
www.jblearning.com

Jones & Bartlett Learning books and products are available through most bookstores and online booksellers. To contact Jones & Bartlett Learning directly, call 800-832-0034, fax 978-443-8000, or visit our website, www.jblearning.com.

Production Credits
Publisher: Cathleen Sether
Senior Acquisitions Editor: Timothy Anderson
Managing Editor: Amy Bloom
Director of Production: Amy Rose
Marketing Manager: Lindsay White
V.P., Manufacturing and Inventory Control: Therese Connell
Composition: Northeast Compositors, Inc.
Cover Design: Kristin E. Parker
Cover Image: © echo3005/ShutterStock, Inc.
Printing and Binding: Courier Kendallville
Cover Printing: Courier Kendallville

Library of Congress Cataloging-in-Publication Data
Cornez, Trish.
 An introduction to programming with ActionScript 3.0 / Trish Cornez, Richard Cornez. -- 1st ed.
     p. cm.
 Includes bibliographical references and index.
 ISBN 978-1-4496-0008-2 (pbk.) -- ISBN 1-4496-0008-5 (pbk.) 1. ActionScript (Computer program language) 2. Object-oriented programming (Computer science) 3. Flash (Computer file) I. Cornez, Richard. II. Title.
 QA76.73.A146C67 2011
 005.1'17--dc23
                                2011018737

6048

Printed in the United States of America
15 14 13 12 11   10 9 8 7 6 5 4 3 2 1

Contents

Preface

An Introduction to Programming with ActionScript 3.0 is an unabashed attempt to turn students on to the joys of programming. The "hook" we employ is interactive multimedia; the method is ActionScript 3.0, in concert with Flash. Although our particular experience is teaching at a liberal arts university, we do not feel our students are unique in their being acculturated in an exceedingly visual and interactive environment. Having taught C++ as our beginning course for a number of years, we accept its efficacy in selecting students who intend to continue on in computer science. But our recent switch to ActionScript 3.0 has enabled us to capture considerably more students, who may not have initially considered the idea of a career in computer science. We additionally have recognized the tremendous crossover potential for computer science and the arts—especially the visual arts and gaming community. This text is an effort to teach sound programming concepts to a wide variety of students.

Although C++ is a requirement for students majoring in CS, we feel, as a first course, it is unappealing to students who imagine studying CS to be the development of interactive multimedia applications like they see and use on their computers and mobile devices. ActionScript 3.0 allows them to make the connection between their studies and the world they are a part of much more effectively than a less graphically and less aurally enabled language such as C++. We've been encouraged by our introduction of ActionScript 3.0 in our classes at the University of Redlands.

The best students, of course, will always thrive. To our delight, we see a wider range of students eager to improve their programming skills using ActionScript 3.0 and Flash. If we introduce programming concepts that involve graphics, students excitedly want to animate their images, add sounds, and program more sophisticated interactivity. On several occasions we've been surprised to see students ignore the end of class and continue to work, so intent were they on improving their programs, both artistically and functionally.

We have designed the text to integrate key Object-Oriented Programming (OOP) concepts that relate to the world of computers students see daily in an easy to understand and straightforward approach. The development of games and web applications utilizing graphics, animation, and sound take center stage.

We cover the standard topics of any first course in a programming language: data types, selective and iterative control structures, functions, arrays, and classes, but additionally cover the basics of ActionScript 3.0 along with its powerful ability to construct complex and engaging interactive animations and web programs with a high degree of multimedia content. The coverage of the usual topics in a first programming course is tied to creating Internet applications that have a significant visual component and/or are highly interactive.

In addition to the programming focus, this book will help Flash users take their skills to a new level by merging their working knowledge of multimedia with OOP programming. New technologies and networked communications have created a demand for students who understand the multidisciplinary nature of information technology and multimedia. Through programming, this text exposes students to problem solving and critical thinking skills required for effective participation in the digital world.

Intended as a textbook, not a tutorial, with problems at the end of chapters dealing with software programming aspects and web-available solutions, this book could also be used by those who wish to teach themselves ActionScript 3.0. Programming examples from the text are included on the text website. This text is designed to satisfy ACM guidelines for a first course in programming for a computer science curriculum.

Book Objectives

This book was conceived with two types of individuals in mind: programming students and multimedia developers.

Those who teach a first course in computer programming are familiar with the problems encountered by beginning students. Students can be impatient for results and the language syntax and the structure of a program can be initially overwhelming. In addition, solving the most interesting problems requires a sound understanding of many programming concepts. Our experience has been that a visual payoff in the guise of even the simplest of animations or visual effects goes a long way toward motivating student interest.

By using the Flash environment, this book attempts to present programming concepts that are relevant to multimedia rich games and applications. With this in mind, we believe that a first course in programming should accomplish two goals:

1. Students should be introduced to the methodologies and techniques of programming using a modern visual programming language. The programming concepts mastered in ActionScript 3.0, independent of specific details involving move-

ment, sound, graphics, and interactivity, are easily transferable to other programming languages.

2. Students should be introduced to the breadth of the discipline and should learn the essential elements of problem solving in a world in which graphics, games, and multimedia are ubiquitous.

Skill Set and Software Requirements

This text is intended for anyone with an interest in learning computer programming, including a web designer or art student wishing to learn the programming side of interactive multimedia. This book could also be used for an additional course in Flash using Actionscript 3.0.

There are no prerequisites for students taking a course that uses this text. It is geared toward beginning programmers, particularly those individuals who are seeking a visual adjunct to their programming endeavors.

It does not presuppose awareness of OOP and does not operate on the assumption that one is already familiar with Adobe Flash CS5.5. There is a basic introduction to the rudiments of Flash, sufficient for students to develop their own graphic applications. It delves into the theory of programming for interactive games and multimedia experiences. Throughout the text, sets of examples and complete programs are used extensively to illustrate programming concepts, ActionScript 3.0 instructions, and interactive methods. They provide the reader with hands-on experience using ActionScript 3.0 with Flash CS5.5 (or CS4).

The software used for this text is Adobe Flash CS4 or CS5.5. ActionScript 3.0, along with its development environment, is built into Flash. These are available for download at http://www.adobe.com/products/flash.html.

Chapter Descriptions

Chapters 1–9 present a complete foundation to OOP programming.

Chapter 1 introduces Flash and ActionScript 3.0 to readers who have never used either of them before. This chapter contains a collection of step-by-step labs for a rudimentary introduction to Flash for a quick understanding of the fundamentals. The first ActionScript 3.0 program is constructed in the last tutorial of this chapter and must not be skipped.

Chapter 2 begins with the techniques of problem solving and application implementation. This discussion focuses on algorithm design and starts with simple problems that allow for easy translation to a final coded ActionScript 3.0 application. Traditional data types are treated as classes with constants and variables treated as objects of those classes. We begin integrating structured and object-oriented programming in this chapter. Full object-oriented concepts are covered in depth in Chapter 9.

Chapters 3–6 cover the foundations of programming, including branching and iteration. It is in these chapters that a student starts to acquire the skills necessary to construct useful programs. We incorporate easy-to-follow examples for building applications that use multimedia elements and XML data files. From a programming perspective, these chapters are essential to master.

Chapter 7 exposes readers to arrays and character strings and their manipulation. Syntax and usage are thoroughly covered. Several classic searching and sorting algorithms are presented along with an exposure to stacks and queues.

Chapter 8 introduces functions in depth. At this point students have the knowledge required to create solid applications. This chapter is important for understanding functions for both the structured and object-oriented paradigms. Since Chapter 2, readers will have seen structured programs using functional decomposition and observed the role of functions relative to object behavior. Our approach is to thoroughly explore functions with return values and parameter passing before passing by reference is considered. It is our experience that a student can best comprehend the concept of functions when learned in this sequence. The last section of this chapter discusses problem solving with recursion. Recursion is introduced via a fractal drawing example and includes an in-depth discussion of how recursion works and when it should be applied. Time spent in this chapter mastering functions lays an important foundation for understanding the object-oriented concepts presented in Chapter 9.

Chapter 9 introduces OOP concepts in greater detail. At this point the reader is prepared to learn about classes and objects more thoroughly. The transition should be straightforward since we have integrated these topics into the text since Chapter 1. The chapter begins with a discussion of inheritance and ends with polymorphism. The case studies in this chapter make these cornerstones of OOP relatively easy to cover at this point. At this stage, an appreciation of object-oriented programming is validated, since multimedia elements and animations are naturally implemented using ActionScript 3.0.

How to Use This Book

The first chapter contains four step-by-step labs that constitute a quick review of the workings of Flash. If students already feel comfortable with Flash, they may skip the first three labs. Lab 4 should be read since it introduces the single document class and ActionScript 3.0 file used by the ensuing chapters in the book.

The material in Chapters 2–9 is suitable for a one-semester introductory course in programming. Chapters 2 and 3 cover the key concepts for problem solving, designing, and constructing interactive programs.

Chapter 4 introduces multimedia programming and the event system. Chapters 5, 6, and 7 cover the important control structures, including selection and iteration.

The case studies used in the text are particular to the programming concepts being discussed and are designed to inspire projects for students to work on. All code is downloadable from the text website. Case studies are constructed in a way that matches the learning style of programmers, game developers, and multimedia developers. We encourage instructors to suggest that students experiment with the case study code.

The end of chapter projects and exercises should be assigned for homework. Some of the projects are quite involved, while some require careful reading of the provided programs, with simple modifications thereof.

We foresee faculty using this text in different guises, in addition to those we have explicitly outlined. We would be extravagantly grateful for any feedback from those using this text in any form and are inherently interested in conversations about pedagogical issues related to first courses in programming. We may be reached at Trish_Cornez@Redlands.edu and Richard_Cornez@Redlands.edu.

Instructor and Student Resource Material

The following ancillary materials are available on the text website:

go.jblearning.com/Cornez

- Student Programming files to case studies and examples from the text.
- Instructor's Manual containing solutions to end-of-chapter exercises.
- Instructor PowerPoint Lecture Outlines available to adopters of the book. These include figures, tables, and selected other material from the text.

Acknowledgments

We have received invaluable support from friends, students, and colleagues in the preparation of the book. The University of Redlands has provided the resources and means for us to complete the project. Jones & Bartlett Learning offered an excellent team of professionals who handled the book from manuscript to final production. We are especially grateful to Tim Anderson, Amy Rose, and Amy Bloom.

We are thankful to Pani Chakrapani for providing content input as well as Barbara Pflanz who gave us keen suggestions on readability. We are indebted to Stan

Schroeder who gave us invaluable technical support. Our reviewers—Dr. William E. J. Doane, Bennington College; Andrew R. Haas, PhD, University of Albany; Audrey St. John, Mount Holyoke College; and Jack A. Tompkins, University of North Carolina, Wilmington—offered us indispensable pedagogical and content guidance for revision.

And last but not least, thanks to our many students whose enthusiasm and comprehension, or lack thereof, made it abundantly clear which parts of our text worked and which missed the mark.

1 The Flash Interface and ActionScript 3.0

Introduction

ActionScript 3.0 is the programming language used in this book, and Flash is the multimedia environment that will be used with ActionScript 3.0. This chapter introduces Flash and examines the essential tools and visual components for building basic multimedia. It also takes a first look at the fundamental structure of an ActionScript 3.0 program.

Four tutorials appear in this chapter. The first three tutorials are designed for readers who have never used Flash and want to quickly get up to speed with the tools and features that Flash has to offer. The primary goal of these three tutorials is to highlight fundamental features and illustrate the processes of creating and working with vector graphics, constructing simple linear animations, and publishing a final product. In short, new Flash users will be up and running in the shortest possible time.

The fourth tutorial introduces the anatomy of an ActionScript 3.0 program. This tutorial illustrates the creation and execution of a complete Flash application containing simple multimedia objects controlled by an ActionScript 3.0 program. This tutorial is required for learning the essentials of working with both ActionScript 3.0 and Flash in a development environment.

1.1 What Are Flash and ActionScript 3.0?

Flash is a software application that is widely used for creating animations and eye-catching cross-platform web experiences. It is regarded as a powerhouse for multimedia creation due to its ability to seamlessly combine graphics, audio, and video with interactive content in the development of engaging applications such as online games, e-learning tools, and database driven web sites. Flash allows developers to build iPhone and other mobile applications directly in Flash Professional CS5.

ActionScript 3.0 (AS3) is the built-in programming language of Flash. This object-oriented programming (OOP) language performs at a high level with rich functionality.

Flash uses ActionScript 3.0 code to interact with its multimedia elements in the development of multifaceted applications. Several versions of ActionScript are available, with ActionScript 3.0 being the latest generation and the topic of this book.

Flash Player is a web browser plug-in that allows users to view Flash animations and applications distributed across the Internet.

This book focuses on using Flash and ActionScript 3.0 in cooperation to design and program multimedia applications that can be accessed over the Internet and as stand-alone applications that run on the desktop. The ActionScript 3.0 applications created in this textbook will be developed using the Flash CS5 Professional integrated development environment.

It is difficult to characterize Flash because it is used by such a diverse array of professionals. For example, cartoonists are attracted to Flash for its animation capabilities. Animation studios are drawn to the software's ability to construct and organize characters and scenes, build sophisticated animations, and reuse these elements again and again. Figure 1-1 shows a linear animation constructed in Flash and played as a movie with a controller bar in a web browser. For web programmers and game designers, the possibilities for interactive applications are enormous. Figure 1-2 shows applications that use ActionScript 3.0 and Flash, such as an online database XML site and an online game of billiards featuring collision detection and realistic physics.

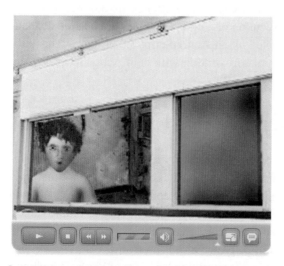

I FIGURE 1-1 An online Flash movie containing a playback controller bar.

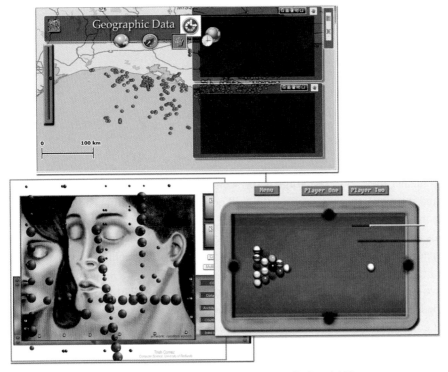

I FIGURE 1-2 Examples of online applications constructed using Flash and AS3.

■ 1.2 The Flash Interface: Terminology and Principal Components

In this textbook we will use AS3, along with Flash, to create interactive applications. Thus much of the development work hinges upon an understanding of the Flash visual environment. Designing and implementing applications that use both Flash and AS3 will require considerable switching back and forth between the visual side of Flash and ActionScript programming files.

We begin our tour of Flash by looking at the essential interface elements, which fortunately are few and remarkably intuitive. This section examines the five principal components and basic terminology that are essential to understanding the operational environment. Seasoned Flash users will use more than the five components described in this section to construct sophisticated animations and multimedia. Because this volume is primarily a programming textbook, we will restrict the animation and artwork skills covered here to unadorned basics. This will allow us to commence building visual applications without delay.

The five main interface elements are as follows:

1. Stage
2. Library
3. Timeline
4. Toolbar
5. Properties Inspector

1.2.1 The Stage

Using a theater metaphor, the **Stage** is the scene of action. All graphic content, movement, and interactivity—large or small—will occur on this two-dimensional rectangle. During the creation of a Flash document, the Stage represents the work area where graphics are placed, visual layouts are organized, and movement and interactivity are constructed. The Stage is the only window that end users will actually see.

In Figure 1-3, the Stage is shown as a white rectangle. The Stage uses the common two-dimensional top-left Cartesian coordinate system. This coordinate system is flipped upside down, so that content is contained in the +x and +y quadrant. The top-left corner, where the x-axis and the y-axis cross, is designated as the origin of the Stage with an x, y value of 0,0. Anything to the left of the origin is a negative x value and anything above it is a negative y value.

The x coordinate of the lower-right corner of the Stage is the width of the Stage. The y coordinate of the lower-right corner of the Stage is the height of the Stage.

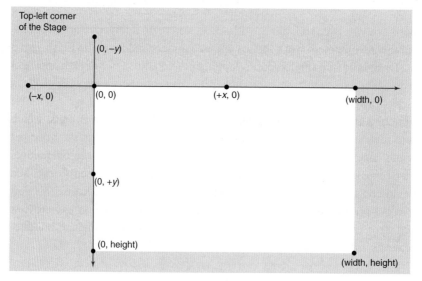

FIGURE 1-3 The Stage's coordinate system.

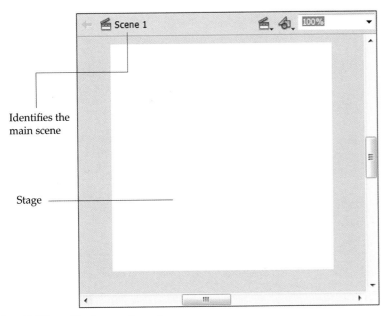

Identifies the
main scene

Stage

| FIGURE 1-4 The Stage at Scene 1.

The Stage in Figure 1-4 is labeled Scene 1 instead of Stage. This labeling system can be somewhat confusing to new users. Full-featured animations often have multiple scenes beginning with Scene 1. In this textbook, all our Flash applications will have exactly one scene.

1.2.2 The Library

In Flash animations and applications, most elements that are seen or heard must be represented in the **Library** as symbols. As a consequence, media assets, such as graphics, audio, video, and interactive elements used in the document, are stored as symbols in the Library. They are created once but can be reused multiple times. ActionScript can also dynamically add these assets to the content of the application.

A well-designed Flash program application will have an efficiently constructed and organized Library. One of the more impressive points about Flash is that it can handle almost any media in a range of types.

Figure 1-5 illustrates a Library panel for a Flash document containing an assortment of symbols. A symbol represents a multimedia element that can range from simple graphics, buttons, and sounds to more complex elements such as animations, digital video, and custom-made interface components. Folders can be added to the library to organize related multimedia elements. Library content is often constructed within the Flash environment, but it can also be created externally from third-party software tools and then imported into the Flash application.

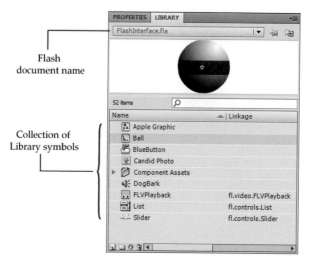

Flash
document name

Collection of
Library symbols

┃ FIGURE 1-5 The Library panel of a Flash document containing a collection of multimedia symbols.

1.2.3 The Timeline

The Timeline contains frames and layers. This Flash panel enables animators to create the illusion of movement by changing, organizing, and controlling the contents of the stage over time. A frame represents an instant of time, so an animation is simply a sequence of frames visited in a strict order. Figure 1-6 shows two examples of a Flash timeline. While a Flash animation plays, the playhead on the timeline moves through a series of frames. The playhead is used to identify the active frame currently visible on stage. As a default, the frames-per-second rate (fps) is set at 24; thus 24 frames represent 1 second. For application programmers and game designers, a frame represents a malleable stage at a given moment.

Layers, which are used less often by programmers than by animators, provide more flexibility to stage designs. They are similar to a collection of film strips stacked on top of one another, each containing a different image that appears on the stage. The second example in Figure 1-6 shows multiple layers used to hold a collection of multimedia elements.

1.2.4 The Toolbar and Vector Graphics

The Toolbar contains drawing tools for creating and editing **vector** images to be used in a Flash-produced application.

Unlike photographs, which are pixel-based images, vector images are created using mathematical formulae. Pixel is short for "picture element" and is literally a dot, many of which make up a digital photograph. Vectors, by comparison, take advantage of algebra and geometry. For example, rather than representing a circle as a set of dots, it is defined using the formula $x^2 + y^2 = radius^2$. Similarly, a line is stored as two loca-

Playhead   Frame 1   Frames per second

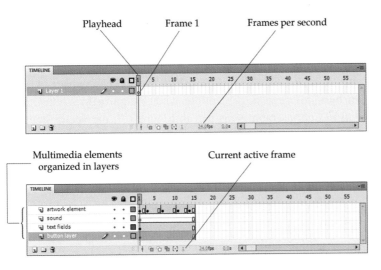

Multimedia elements   Current active frame
organized in layers

FIGURE 1-6 Two Timeline examples.

tions, one for each end of the line. Vector images are nothing more than mathematical constructs, with parameters stored for efficient re-creation.

JPEGs, PNGs, and GIFs are usually associated with photographs, web images, or nonvector illustrations. They are referred to as **bitmaps** because of their pixel-based image formats. The JPEG and PNG formats support millions of colors, whereas the GIF format supports 2^8 (256) colors—a small number compared to JPEG and PNG standards and, therefore, less visually rich. Consider a GIF image that is 100 pixels tall and 150 pixels wide. Any given pixel in this GIF image has exactly 256 (2^8) possibilities in terms of color. A one-color bitmap contains 2 (2^1) colors—specifically, black or white individual pixels.

JPEG is the standard compressed image format used for photos. Figure 1-7 shows a JPEG photograph with its pixel composition magnified at a high level. JPEG uses a

FIGURE 1-7 A JPEG image.

format known to as **lossy compression**, which compresses the final image, reducing its memory size but also decreasing data and quality from the original version. GIFs and PNGs, in contrast, use a lossless data compression format, which allows the exact original data to be reconstructed. JPEG, PNG, and GIF files can be imported into Flash.

Figure 1-8 shows a vector image constructed in Flash. The contrast between a vector image and a bitmap image is perceptible when magnified. While the pixel composition of the JPEG photograph is distinct in Figure 1-7, the vector image will reveal perfection at all levels of magnification.

The primary disadvantage of vectors is a restriction in drawing somewhat basic shapes. However, their advantages are enormous. Movement, real-time alterations, and animation will be very fast and uncomplicated with vectors mainly because changes can be made quickly to the underlying mathematical representation of the graphical image. Changes and movement are more problematic with pixel-based graphics.

The Toolbar panel contains all vector graphic tools provided by Flash. These tools, as shown in Figure 1-9, and listed in Tables 1-1 through 1-5, are categorized into the following five groups:

- Selection and Transform Tools: Used to select and or transform an existing vector drawing.
- Drawing Tools: Used to create lines, shapes, and text.
- Modification Tools: Used to make alterations to existing vector graphics.
- Viewing Tools: Used to pan or magnify a viewing area.
- Color and Brush Tools: Used to select brush color, shape, and size.

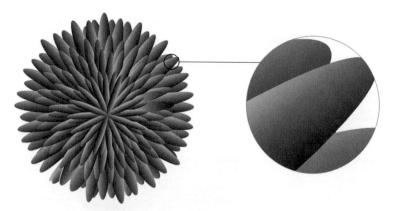

FIGURE 1-8 A vector image.

FIGURE 1-9 The Flash Toolbar.

TABLE 1-1 Selection and Transform Tools

Tool	Tool Name	Use
	Selection tool	Also called the Arrow tool; the most used tool in the entire toolbox. The Selection tool is used to select one or more objects on the Stage. Once an object has been selected, it can be named, repositioned, resized, and altered in other ways. This tool can also be used to add curvature to a vector line.
	Subselection tool	Used to adjust a straight or curved line segment that has been drawn with the Pen tool.
	Free Transform tool	Used to transform objects by rotating, scaling, skewing, and distorting them. The small triangle located at the lower right of the tool indicates a submenu.
	3D Rotation tool	Used to rotate and transform symbols along a three-dimensional axis.
	Lasso tool	Selects objects by drawing a freehand selection area.

TABLE 1-2 Drawing Tools

Tool	Tool Name	Use
	Pen tool	Draws precise lines and curves.
	Text tool	Used to create input/output text boxes and text labels.
	Line tool	Creates a straight vector line.
	Shapes tool	Creates basic shapes such as rectangles and oval vectors. These shapes can be filled or unfilled. This tool has a submenu containing other shapes, such as a rectangle and a polystar.
	Pencil tool	Draws free-form vector shapes.
	Brush tool	Creates free-form brush strokes.
	Deco tool	Used to create sophisticated patterns and fills, particularly a flower or leaf pattern.

TABLE 1-3 Modification Tools

Tool	Tool Name	Use
	Bone tool	Used for the construction of 3D animations.
	Paint Bucket tool	Used to fill any enclosed area with a fill color.
	Eyedropper tool	Used to pick up a color from another object and copy it to a color chip.
	Eraser tool	Erases vector drawings.

TABLE 1-4 Viewing Tools

Tool	Tool Name	Use
	Hand tool	Used in magnify mode to pan across the Stage.
	Zoom tool	Used to magnify an area of the Stage.

TABLE 1-5 Color and Brush Tools

Tool	Tool Name	Use
	Stroke Color	Used to select or change a color for the outline, or border, of a shape.
	Fill Color	Used to select or change a color for the fill area of a shape.
	Brush Size	Used to select the size of the Brush tool.
	Brush Shape	Used to select the shape of the Brush tool.

1.2.5 The Properties Inspector

Properties Inspector is one of the most versatile and valuable panels in Flash. This panel contains information about an active document or an object that has been selected. Its appearance and function change with every object or tool that is selected.

For example, each movie has a set of global properties that can be altered. To access these global properties, users can click on a blank part of the Stage. These properties initially share the same settings as those seen in the Preference dialog box.

The **Script** property identifies the version of ActionScript that will be utilized by the Flash document, and the **Class** property refers to the ActionScript document class that will control the movie. This document class is located in an ActionScript file and must be specified for Flash program applications. **FPS** is the number of frames shown per second, which determines the speed of the animation. The Size option has to do with the Stage size. The color chip next to the label Stage refers to the background color of the Stage. Figure 1-10 shows the properties of a Flash document named ballApp.

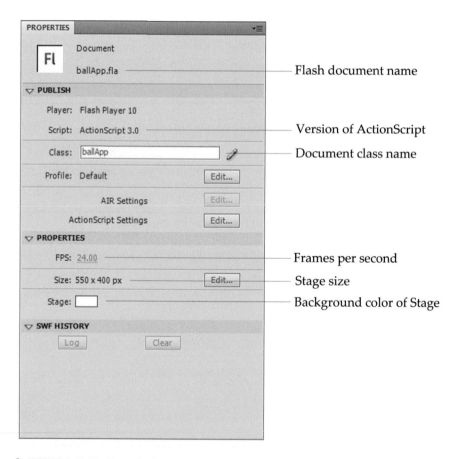

I FIGURE 1-10 The Properties Inspector for a Flash document.

The Properties Inspector reflects the changeable characteristics of any given object on the Stage or the document itself. As an example, Figure 1-11 shows the properties for two given visual elements placed on stage. The first Properties Inspector lists the attributes of an **instance** of a ball symbol. This Properties Inspector reveals

The name used to identify the specific ball object

Ball1 is an instance of the Ball symbol

The name used to identify the specific text field

The classic text field types:
• Static Text
• Input Text
• Dynamic Text

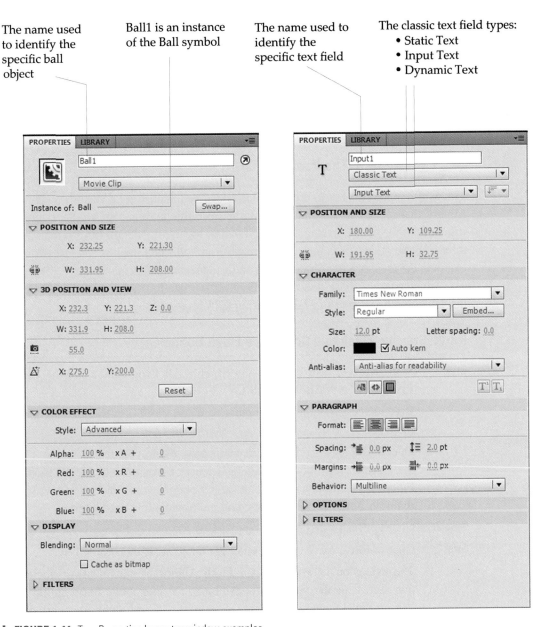

| FIGURE 1-11 Two Properties Inspector window examples.

that `Ball` is an instance of `Ball`. As an instance, `Ball` is simply a copy of its master symbol in the Library. The attributes of `Ball`, such as its name, position on stage (x and y locations), size (W: **Width** and H: **Height**), 3D position, and color effects can be easily altered using this panel.

The second Properties Inspector shown in Figure 1-11 lists the attributes peculiar to a text field placed on stage. Text fields must be identified as members of one of three types:

- Static Text: Text representing titles and labels.
- Dynamic Text: Interactive text fields that will change. Output text fields are dynamic text.
- Input Text: Interactive text fields used for input of data.

◼ 1.3 Tutorial 1: The Vector Artist

The goal for Tutorial 1 is to create a Flash document, construct a vector image in the Library that represents the master copy, and use this master copy to place multiple instances of the image on stage. The first part of the tutorial details how to manipulate a set of basic vector lines into a recognizable and polished image. The last two parts examine the idea of a master copy and an instance version of this copy.

Any version of Flash that uses AS3 is appropriate for these tutorials. All figures displayed in this chapter use Flash version CS5.

Part I: Starting Flash and Creating a Flash Document

Step 1:   Start **Adobe Flash** by choosing **Start > All Programs > Adobe Design Premium CS > Adobe Flash CS**.

If you have a Macintosh computer, you can start Flash by selecting it from the Dock.

Once Flash loads, a dialog screen appears giving you many options. Under the **Create New** column heading is a list of Flash file types. As shown in Figure 1-12, Flash works with a variety of documents, including JavaScript, multiple ActionScript 3.0 files, and multimedia for smart phones.

Step 2:   Choose **Flash File (ActionScript 3.0)**, as shown in Figure 1-12.

Step 3:   Choose **File > Save As**, and enter the name `Hello.fla`. Click **OK**.

The extension `.fla` refers to a **Flash Authoring** document—a document that represents the visual composition of the interactive Flash application. During development, the graphics, animations, and audio elements of the

Create a Flash file that uses ActionScript 3.0

FI

Adobe

ADOBE® FLASH® PROFESSIONAL CS5

Create from Template
- Advertising
- Animation
- Banners
- Media Playback
- Presentations
- Sample Files

Open a Recent Item
- ballApp.fla
- lecture3a.fla
- Open...

Create New
- ActionScript 3.0
- ActionScript 2.0
- Adobe AIR 2
- iPhone OS
- Flash Lite 4
- ActionScript File
- Flash JavaScript File
- Flash Project
- ActionScript 3.0 Class
- ActionScript 3.0 Interface

Extend
- Flash Exchange »

Learn
- 1. Introducing Flash »
- 2. Symbols »
- 3. Timelines and Animation »
- 4. Instance Names »
- 5. Simple Interactivity »
- 6. ActionScript »
- 7. Working with Data »
- 8. Building an Application »
- 9. Publishing for Mobile »
- 10. Publishing for AIR »
- 11. Adobe TV »

- Getting Started »
- New Features »
- Developers »
- Designers »

- Don't show again

FI   **Adobe® CS Live online services**
Simplify the review process, speed website compatibility testing, and more.

▌ FIGURE 1-12 Flash start screen.

application will be constructed and arranged in this file in a way that the AS3 code can access.

Part II: Creating a Vector Graphic as a Symbol in the Library

It is time for you to gain a first-hand acquaintance with the Flash workspace. Take a moment to examine the workspace and locate the Stage, Timeline, Library, Properties, and Toolbar.

Task 1: Understanding an Image

We are about to build a graphic of the apple shown in Figure 1-13. Before we can build this image, we must first understand its vector composition. The composition starts with identifying the curves. Vectors allow for the construction of complex lines and shapes that are really nothing more than one or more curves built around two or more points. Once they are built, vector graphics can be scaled, anti-aliased, and modified on the fly.

┃ FIGURE 1-13 Vector graphic symbol of an apple.

Take a moment to examine the outline of the final image of the apple, minus the stem. It may not be obvious, but the outline is composed of eight different arcs. In other words, eight lines with curvature applied to them can be used to represent an apple.

The following tools will be used in this construction:

- Tool 1: The **Line tool** will be used to create each line vector shape.
- Tool 2: The **Selection tool** will be used to select an individual line and then apply curvature. In addition, this same tool will be used to connect the curved lines, thereby forming the final image of an apple.
- Tool 3: The **Paint Bucket** will be used to dump color into the interior of the apple vector image.

Task 2: Creating a Vector Drawing and Storing It in the Library

As a general practice, the construction and organization of Library symbols are steps undertaken prior to writing code. This step-by-step development will be emphasized in the tutorials as well as the chapter case studies.

Step 1:   Choose **Insert > New Symbol. . . .**

A dialog box, such as the one shown in Figure 1-14, will appear.

FIGURE 1-14 New Symbol dialog box.

Step 2: Enter the name **Apple** in the **Create New Symbol** dialog box.

Also, choose **Movie Clip** from the Type drop-down menu. Click **OK**.

Note

MovieClips are versatile symbols. They can be simple vector graphics, bitmaps converted to vector graphics, or mini-animations. We will build most of our visual elements for applications as MovieClips because they are easily programmable.

Take a moment to examine the work area in Figure 1-15. Notice that a drawing canvas—rather than the Stage—is visible. A small symbol, very similar to a plus sign, appears on the canvas. This **registration point** determines where a symbol is positioned on the Stage. It is typically set in the center of an object that is symmetrical and at the top-left corner for text and other symbols.

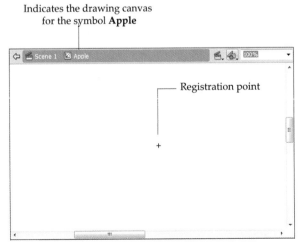

FIGURE 1-15 Blank canvas for drawing the apple vector symbol.

Step 3:   Choose the **Line tool** from the Toolbar.

Step 4:   Click the **Stroke Color** chip from the Toolbar. Select red from the color pop-up panel.

Use the image in Figure 1-16 as your guide and draw eight individual red lines on the canvas.

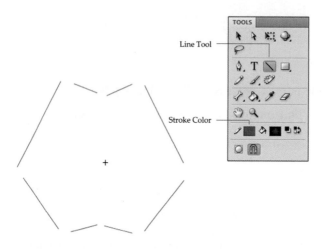

I FIGURE 1-16 The vector lines in the apple drawing.

Step 5:   Choose the **Selection tool** from the ToolBar. Click on a blank part of the canvas to make sure nothing is selected.

Step 6:   Guide the **Selection tool** close to the top left line. Notice that the tool now resembles an arrow with a curve. Drag the mouse until the vector line forms a curved shape as shown in Figure 1-17.

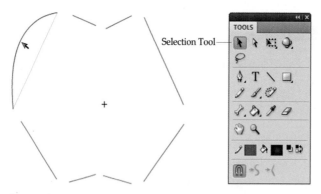

I FIGURE 1-17 Curvature applied to a vector line.

Step 7:   Apply curvature to each of the remaining lines as shown in Figure 1-18.

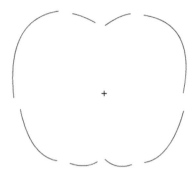

| **FIGURE 1-18** Curvature applied to all vector lines.

Step 8:   Make sure that no lines are selected (click on a blank part of the canvas to deselect a selected item). Guide the Selection tool to the bottom ending of the top-left line. Notice that the tool now resembles an arrow with a right angle. Drag the mouse until the vector curved line connects with the curved line just below it, as illustrated in Figure 1-19.

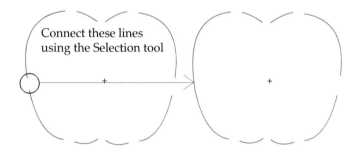

| **FIGURE 1-19** Connecting two vector lines.

Step 9:   Continue to use the Selection tool to make the remaining connections. Modify the curves and move the connections until your final image resembles an apple, as shown in Figure 1-20.

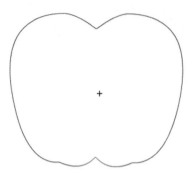

❙ FIGURE 1-20 Vector lines curved and connected to form an apple.

Step 10:   Draw the stem of the apple by creating three small vector lines near the top of the apple in a green stroke color (see Figure 1-21). Use the Selection tool to add curvature and connect the stem to the apple.

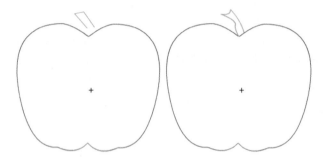

❙ FIGURE 1-21 The stem of the apple.

You have just created the outline for the vector apple. Now it is time to add a fill color to paint the apple, as shown in Figure 1-22.

Step 11:   Click the **Fill Color** chip from the Toolbar. Select a gradient red from the color pop-up panel.

Step 12:   Choose the **Paint Bucket tool**. Click in the interior of the apple.

Step 13:   Select a green color for the **Fill Color**. Using the Paint Bucket tool, click in the interior of the stem.

You have just completed the vector apple.

PaintBucket Tool

Fill Color

| FIGURE 1-22 A complete vector drawing named Apple.

Step 14: Once a vector drawing has been completed, we will move from the drawing canvas back to the main stage. The top of the canvas reads Scene 1 and Apple, as shown in Figure 1-23. Click **Scene 1** to close the drawing canvas. Once you have disengaged from the drawing canvas, you will find yourself back in Stage mode looking at Scene 1 and Apple will no longer appear.

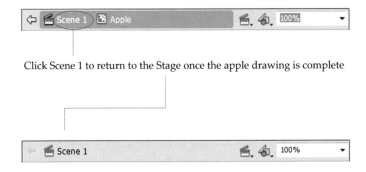

Click Scene 1 to return to the Stage once the apple drawing is complete

| FIGURE 1-23 The symbol name appears on the canvas while you are drawing the apple.

Part III: Creating an Instance of a Symbol

What Is an Instance of a Symbol? How Does It Work?

Once a symbol has been created and stored in the library, many instances of it can be placed on the stage. A symbol in the library, such as the Apple movie clip you just made, is nothing more than the original version, of which unlimited duplicates can be produced. All instances are linked to their original symbols, yet instance attributes, such as width, height, and color, can be modified to create variations of those symbols. This allows for a tremendous amount of flexibility.

Step 1:   Choose the **Selection tool**.

Step 2:   With the Library panel open, locate and drag an instance of the Apple symbol from the Library to the Stage. Remember, the Stage is labeled Scene 1. Figure 1-24 shows an instance of the library Apple symbol on stage.

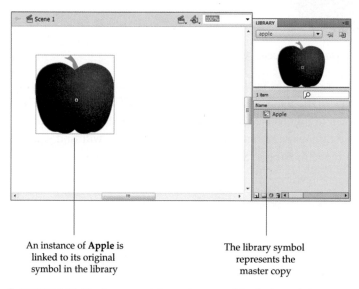

An instance of **Apple** is linked to its original symbol in the library

The library symbol represents the master copy

❙ FIGURE 1-24 The Stage containing an instance of the Apple symbol.

Step 3:   Drag another instance of the Apple symbol from the Library to the Stage. Place the second apple next to the first one on the Stage. At this point, two instances of the original Apple symbol appear on the Stage (Figure 1-25). We will now change one of them.

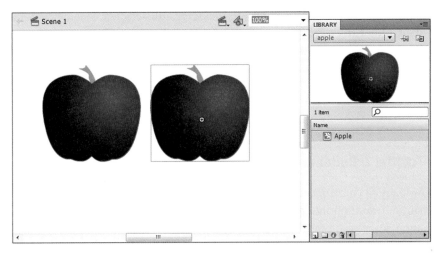

I FIGURE 1-25 The Stage containing two instances of the Apple symbol.

Step 4:   With the second Apple instance on the Stage selected, open the **Properties Inspector**.

Locate the name property and enter Apple2. Locate and change the properties for the attributes **W** (width) and **H** (height) to the values shown in Figure 1-26. Notice the size changes that occur in the second instance on the Stage. The original Apple symbol located in the Library, along with the first instance placed on the Stage, remain intact—they have not been changed.

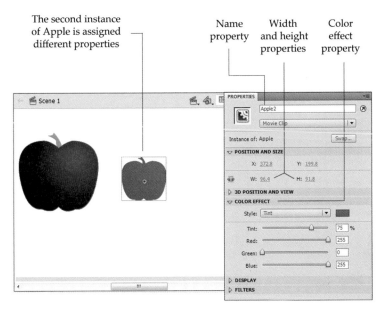

I FIGURE 1-26 The properties of the Apple instance.

With the second Apple instance on the Stage still selected, locate and click the **Color Effect** drop-down symbol from the Properties Inspector. Choose **Tint** from the **Style** drop-down menu. Click the color chip to the right of Tint and select a pink color. Change the **Tint %** to **75%**.

This completes a Stage layout consisting of two instances of the Apple MovieClip symbol.

▇ 1.4 Tutorial 2: Building a Frame-by-Frame Animation

We are now ready to construct an animation. Animation is at the core of Flash and will lead to a natural transition into programming with ActionScript 3.0.

Animation is the phenomenon of being able to perceive movement from a series of still images; it is based on perceptional illusion. Frame-by-frame animation is considered to be the most basic form of animation. It uses unique artwork in each frame and is ideal for complex animations such as facial expressions that require subtle changes.

The main goal for Tutorial 2 is to create and publish the frame-by-frame animated juggler shown in Figure 1-27 using six original JPEG images. The specific objectives are as follows:

1. Import external JPEG images into the library. These images will be used in the animation.

2. Understand and construct blank keyframes.

3. Add sounds to an animated movie.

4. Publish the final animated movie as an SWF file to be accessed over the Internet.

❙ FIGURE 1-27 The juggler linear animation.

Part I: Importing JPEG Images into the Library

Step 1:   Start **Adobe Flash**. Choose **Flash File (AS3)**. Save this new Flash document as **Juggler.fla**.

Step 2:   Choose **File > Import > Import to Library. . .** Use the dialog box to locate
the JPEG files J1, J2, J3, J4, J5, and J6 saved on the `Tutorial2Folder`. This
folder can be found at this book's companion website. These six images are
shown in Figure 1-28.

Step 3:   Select all six JPEG files by Shift-clicking each one in turn. Click **Open**.

Verify that all six JPEG files are stored as bitmap symbols in the Library.

I FIGURE 1-28 Six JPEG images used to construct the frame-by-frame juggler animation.

Part II: Constructing a Frame-by-Frame Animation Using Blank Keyframes

Before building the animation, it is necessary to make sure that the Stage is properly
sized to fit the images. Because the images themselves are all exactly 396 pixels in
height and 308 pixels in width, we will use these values for the Stage size.

Step 1:   Click on a blank part of the Stage. From the **Properties Inspector**, locate
Size and click **Edit**.

Change the Stage dimensions for the attributes **width** and **height** to **308** and **396**, respectively.

In frame-by-frame animations, each frame will hold a different image. In Flash, the insertion of a **blank keyframe** is the creation of a blank, or empty, frame in the Timeline. This tutorial uses six independent images, each placed in a strict sequence within a blank keyframe, to produce the final frame-by-frame animation. The first frame of any new Flash document is already created as a blank keyframe.

Step 2:   Select **frame 1** of **Layer 1** in the Timeline (it will appear highlighted). Drag the bitmap image named **J1** to the Stage.

Step 3:   Use the **Selection tool** to select the instance of the bitmap on the Stage. From the Properties Inspector, set the *x* and *y* positions to zero.

Step 4:   Select **frame 2** of **Layer 1** in the Timeline. Right-click and choose **Insert Blank Keyframe** to insert a new clean frame at this location in the Timeline. Drag the bitmap image named **J2** to the Stage. Set its *x* and *y* positions to zero.

Step 5:   Select **frame 3** of **Layer 1** in the Timeline. Right-click and choose **Insert Blank Keyframe**. Drag the bitmap image named **J3** to the Stage. Set its *x* and *y* positions to zero.

Follow this process three more times to place the remaining bitmap symbols **J4**, **J5**, and **J6** in frames 4, 5, and 6, respectively. Remember to set the *x* and *y* positions for each instance on the Stage.

At this point, the Timeline should contain six frames, as seen in Figure 1-29, each containing different images. Move the playhead across the Timeline to manually visualize the animation.

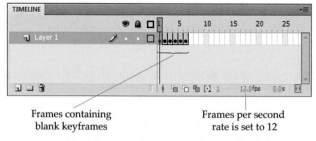

Frames containing   Frames per second
blank keyframes   rate is set to 12

❙ FIGURE 1-29 The Timeline containing a frame-by-frame animation.

Step 6:   Locate the **fps** (frames per second) setting at the bottom of the Timeline and change it to a slower speed of **12**, as shown in Figure 1-29.

Step 7:   To see your animation in action, choose **Control > Test Movie**.

Part III: Adding Sound to an Animation

Music, aural, and natural sounds occur frequently in our everyday lives. They often play a crucial role in understanding our experiences and encounters with a variety of communications media. In turn, adding sounds to a multimedia project can produce a richer effect.

In the following steps, we will add sounds to the juggler animation. Flash provides a collection of sounds built into its sound library. Most often, developers will create sound files using third-party software and then import them into Flash documents. For an easy demonstration, we will instead use the sounds built into Flash's sound library.

Step 1:   The sound instance in this animation will be placed on a separate layer.

Choose **Insert > Timeline > Layer**. A new layer named Layer 2 should appear in the Timeline.

Step 2:   Sounds, as with all instances, are placed on the Stage at a specific frame in the Timeline. Select **frame 4** of **Layer 2** in the Timeline and insert a blank keyframe.

Step 3:   Adobe Flash stores a collection of interesting sounds in its SOUNDS.FLA library, as shown in Figure 1-30.

Choose **Window > Common Libraries > Sounds**.

Once the library is displayed, locate and select the sound named **Sports Ball Basketball Caught With Hands 01.mp3**.

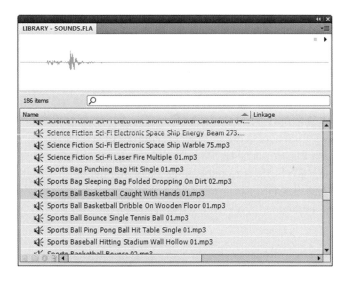

▌ FIGURE 1-30 The sound library provided by Flash.

Step 4:   With **frame 4** of **Layer 2** selected on the Timeline, drag the sound named **Sports Ball Basketball Caught With Hands 01.mp3** onto the stage. This sound has now been added to the Timeline as shown by the horizontal blue line in Layer 2 in Figure 1-31. It has also been copied to the Juggler.fla library.

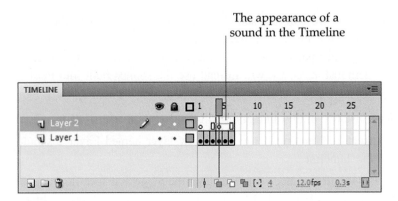

FIGURE 1-31 The Timeline showing sound in Layer 2.

Step 5:   Choose **File > Save**.

Step 6:   You have just created a simple frame-by-frame animation. Now it is time to test the animation.

Choose **Control > Test Movie**.

Notice the animation continues to loop over and over again. Unless it is forced to stop, the playhead will automatically loop back to frame 1 once it reaches the end of the Timeline.

Part IV: Publishing a Movie for Distribution over the Internet

At this point, you have tested the animated movie several times. Testing the movie generates an SWF file, which is simply a reduced-size Flash file format used to represent a movie that can be transported across the Internet and played by a browser using the Flash Player plug-in. Flash Player plays all SWF files generated by Flash.

The best way to generate a SWF file is to publish the FLA file. In addition to the SWF file, more options for publishing a Flash movie are available. One option is to create an HTML file with an embedded SWF file, which can be read and played by web browsers.

Step 1:   Choose **File > Publish Settings. . .**

Step 2:   Locate and check **Flash** (.swf) and **HTML** (.html).

Step 3: Click **Publish** and then **OK**.

In the next set of steps, you will create a stand-alone application for both Macintosh and Windows.

Additional Publishing Options

In addition to publishing files to be accessed over the Internet, options for generating stand-alone application programs are available. SWF files require a Flash plug-in to play them. Stand-alone applications contain the extensions .exe and .app and can play on computers without having Flash or Flash plug-ins.

If you are using an Apple computer, choose **Macintosh Projector** from the **Publish Settings**.

If you wish to generate a Windows stand-alone application, choose **Windows Projector** (.exe). Figure 1-32 shows relevant files generated after publishing juggler. fla.

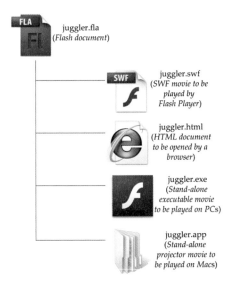

juggler.fla
(Flash document)

juggler.swf
*(SWF movie to be
played by
Flash Player)*

juggler.html
*(HTML document
to be opened by a
browser)*

juggler.exe
*(Stand-alone
executable movie
to be played on PCs)*

juggler.app
*(Stand-alone
projector movie to
be played on Macs)*

❙ **FIGURE 1-32** The files generated from juggler.fla by the Publish command.

1.5 Tutorial 3: Building a Motion Tween Animation

Tween is a common term used among animators that describes the process of creating movement by automatically filling in the successive frames between a starting frame and an ending frame. Flash is easily capable of performing this type of interpolated animation through the use of keyframes and motion tweens.

In this tutorial we will build an animation that utilizes both the motion tween and a keyframe. The goal is to animate a ball so that it travels from the lower-left corner of the Stage to the upper-right corner, as shown in Figure 1-33. We will also add a stop() action to the last frame in the Timeline. Instead of the animation looping endlessly, this action will be used to force the playhead to hold the frame once the ball reaches its destination.

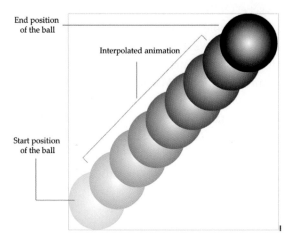

FIGURE 1-33 A ball travels in a diagonal line from the lower corner of the Stage to the upper corner.

The specific objectives for Tutorial 3 are as follows:

1. Build vector symbols that can be animated.
2. Understand and construct nonblank keyframes, referred to as **keyframes**.
3. Apply an interpolation technique called Tween to create motion animation.

| **Note** |

Tweens are an easy way to construct simple animations. Most of the animations in this text will be more sophisticated and will require the use of ActionScript 3.0 code to control motion and impart interactivity.

---

4. Explore the idea of stopping and holding an animation on a specific frame.

Part I: Creating an Object to Be Animated

Start **Adobe Flash.** Choose **Flash File (AS3)**. Save this new Flash document as **BallMove.fla**. Set the stage width and height to 300 (this was first done in Tutorial 2, Part II, Step 1).

Only one symbol will be required in the Library.

Step 1:   Choose **Insert > New Symbol. . . .**

The **Create New Symbol** dialog box will appear.

Step 2:   Enter the name **Ball**.

Step 3:   It is important that all animated symbols be created as MovieClip types rather than as Graphic types. MovieClip types are versatile and in later chapters we will use the fact that they can be programmed.

Choose **Movie Clip** from the **Type** drop-down menu.

The entry should look like Figure 1-34.

Click **OK**.

I FIGURE 1-34 The Create New Symbol dialog box.

Step 4:   Select the **Oval tool** from the Toolbar.

Step 5:   Click the **Fill Color** chip from the Toolbar. Select a gradient gray from the color pop-up panel.

Step 6:   Drag out a circular shape, as shown in Figure 1-35, and release the mouse.

Step 7:   Click **Scene 1** to close the **Ball** drawing canvas. Verify that Ball exists as a symbol in the Library.

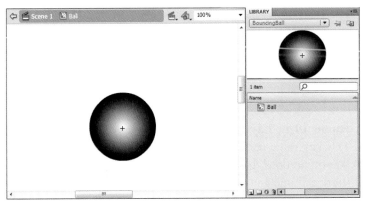

I FIGURE 1-35 Drawing canvas for Ball and Symbol Ball in the Library.

Part II: Constructing the Animation Using a Classic Motion Tween

In this part of the tutorial we build the animation using a Classic Motion Tween. An object that has a Classic Motion Tween applied to it must reside on a layer by itself. In other words, if the ball is to be animated, it cannot share the layer with other objects.

Task 1: Place the Ball on the Stage and Set Its Starting Position

Step 1:   Rename the Timeline layer as **Ball 1 Layer** by double-clicking **Layer 1** and retyping the name. Press **Enter** when done.

Step 2:   Choose the **Selection tool**. Click **frame 1** in **Layer 1**.

Step 3:   With the Library panel open, drag an instance of the Ball symbol from the Library to the Stage.

Step 4:   With the instance of the ball selected on the stage, position the ball in the lower-left corner of the Stage, as shown in Figure 1-36. This is the ball's starting position.

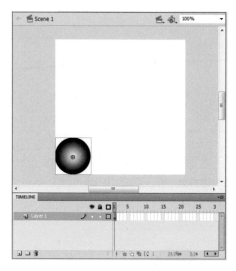

▌ FIGURE 1-36 Ball on the Stage.

Task 2: Create an Ending Position

Step 1:   Right-click **frame 10** in **Layer 1**. From the pop-up menu, select **Insert Keyframe**. This keyframe command will not clear out a frame in the way that a blank keyframe does. Instead, inserting a keyframe retains the contents of the starting frame and allows a change to its properties, such as its position, height, or color. In this tutorial we will change only the position.

Step 2: Using the Selection tool, position the ball so that it sits in the upper-right corner of the stage. At this point, the screen should look similar to Figure 1-37.

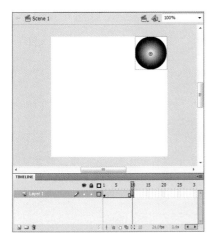

❙ **FIGURE 1-37** Keyframe added to frame 10.

Task 3: Apply a Classic Tween

Step 1: Right-click any frame between the start frame (frame 1) and the end frame (frame 10), such as frame 5, and select **Create Classic Tween** from the pop-up menu. Flash immediately fills in the successive frames between the first and final keyframes. See Figure 1-38.

Step 2: To see the animation so far, choose **Control > Test Movie**. Notice that once the ball moves to its final destination at the upper-right corner of the Stage, the animation repeats itself over and over again. In the next section of this tutorial, you will add a stop action to force the ball to remain at its final destination.

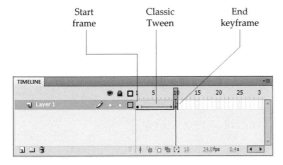

❙ **FIGURE 1-38** Classic Tween applied between keyframes.

Part III: Placing a Hold on the Animation Using a `stop()` Action

Oftentimes an animation is designed to loop endlessly. On occasion, however, it is necessary to force the animation to stop on a specific frame. This can be done by placing a stop action instruction on a new layer directly in the frame we wish to pause.

Step 1: Click **Layer 1** in the Timeline.

Step 2: From the Timeline panel, locate and click the icon to insert a new layer. This icon is shown in Figure 1-39. At this point, a new layer named Layer 2 will appear in the Timeline panel.

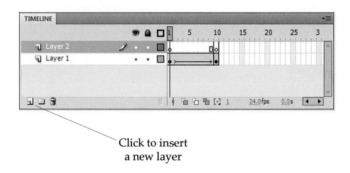

Click to insert
a new layer

❙ FIGURE 1-39 Timeline containing two layers.

Step 3: Right-click **frame 10** in **Layer 2**. From the pop-up menu, select **Blank Keyframe**. The `stop()` action will be placed in this blank keyframe in the next step.

Step 4: Choose **Windows > Actions**. A window labeled ACTIONS – FRAME will appear.

Step 5: Enter the instruction `stop();` in the window. Figure 1-40 shows the instruction in the Action window.

Step 6: Close the ACTIONS – FRAME window. Notice that an italicized *a* now appears in frame 10 of Layer 2.

Note

This textbook uses separate documents for ActionScript 3.0 code—the most straightforward and efficient way to program. On rare occasions, it is easier to place a simple instruction in the Timeline, as demonstrated in this example.

Step 7: Test the animation. Choose **Control > Test Movie**.

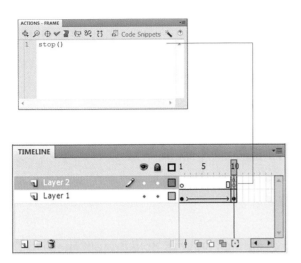

FIGURE 1-40 Action window for frame 10 of Layer 2 containing an ActionScript instruction.

1.6 Tutorial 4: Welcome to AS3—"Interactive Betty"

Since 1974, it has been a tradition that budding programmers write an introductory program that displays the greeting "Hello World." We will preserve that tradition in this tutorial with a slight modification. We will create a Flash application called "Interactive Betty," shown in Figure 1-41, to interactively display "Hello World" and "Goodbye World." The user will be presented with two buttons. When the user clicks a button, the application will respond by displaying the appropriate greeting or farewell in a dynamic text field.

This tutorial assumes that users have no previous experience with AS3 or computer programming. Our objectives for this tutorial are as follows:

1. Illustrate the process of constructing a simple Flash application from beginning to end in a short number of steps.

2. All Flash applications in this textbook will require two types of files—the Flash file that holds the multimedia elements and the ActionScript 3.0 program file that interacts with them. Both of these files will be constructed in this tutorial.

3. Discuss the idea and importance of the **document class** for a Flash application.

4. Introduce the basic anatomy of an AS3 program.

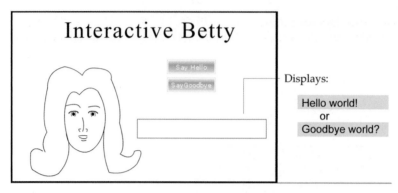

▌ FIGURE 1-41 The "Interactive Betty" application.

Part I: Creating an Application Program Folder to Hold Project Files

Application programs in Flash typically require many files. For easy navigation, we will place these files in a folder on the desktop.

Step 1: Create a folder on the desktop and name it BettyFolder.

Step 2: Start **Adobe Flash**. Choose **Flash File (AS3)**. Save this new Flash document as bettyApp.fla and locate it in BettyFolder.

Part II: Creating the Visual Elements for the Application in Flash

Before we do any programming, we must first create the visual elements. The visual elements of this application are the title for the application, a vector image of Betty, two interactive buttons, and an interactive dynamic text field, which will be used for output. The application title and the image of Betty have no functionality and exist solely for the purpose of making the application visually more pleasing.

Text elements are often created directly on the Stage, as will be done in this application. All other elements will be constructed as symbols in the Library.

Task 1: Add the Title "Interactive Betty" to the Top of the Stage
We will start with the title.

Step 1: Choose the **Text tool** from the Toolbar.

Step 2: Before typing any text, we will identify and set the characteristics for this title.

Open the **Properties Inspector** and use Figure 1-42 to guide your selections.

Choose **Static Text** as the text type from the first drop-down menu and set the remaining text properties for **Family**, **Style**, **Size**, **Letter spacing**, and **Color**.

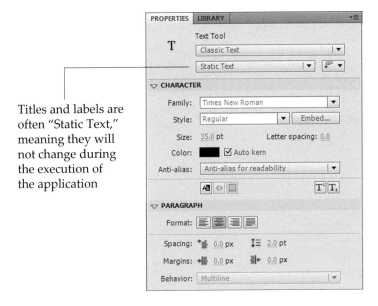

Titles and labels are often "Static Text," meaning they will not change during the execution of the application

❙ FIGURE 1-42 The text properties for the title.

Step 3: Click near the top part of the Stage where the title will go and drag the mouse to create a new text box covering almost the full width of the Stage. The text box will appear with a blinking cursor. Type the text **Interactive Betty** as appears in Figure 1-43.

Step 4: Choose **File > Save**. Save this file in `bettyFolder`.

❙ FIGURE 1-43 The title added to the Stage using the Text tool.

Task 2: Add a Dynamic Text Field for Displaying Betty's Greeting or Farewell

In many applications, it is required that information be displayed in a text field. In this task, an interactive text field of dynamic type will be added to the stage. In addition, we will give this text field a unique identifier name so that the ActionScript 3.0 program to be written in the final steps of this tutorial can access it.

Step 1:   Select the **Text tool** from the Toolbar. Open the **Properties Inspector** and choose **Dynamic Text** from the topmost drop-down menu.

Step 2:   Drag out the text field on the Stage as shown in Figure 1-44.

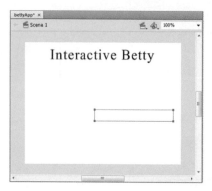

▌FIGURE 1-44 A dynamic text field created on the Stage.

Step 3:   With the Properties Inspector still open, as shown in Figure 1-45, specify its name as Output and make the necessary changes to the remaining text properties for **Family**, **Style**, **Size**, **Letter spacing**, and **Color**. Select the **Show border** icon.

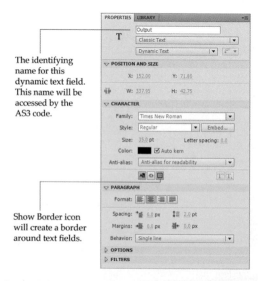

The identifying name for this dynamic text field. This name will be accessed by the AS3 code.

Show Border icon will create a border around text fields.

▌FIGURE 1-45 The properties for the text field on the Stage.

Step 4: Choose **File** > **Save**. Verify this file has been saved in `bettyFolder`.

Task 3: The Vector Drawing "Betty"

At the moment, the Library is empty. When you are finished with this task, the Library will contain the vector image of Betty as shown in Figure 1-47.

Step 1: Click the **New Symbol icon** in the Library panel.

Step 2: Enter the name `Betty`.

Step 3: Choose **Movie Clip** from the drop-down menu (see Figure 1-46). Click **OK**.

I FIGURE 1-46 Dialog box for the Betty symbol.

Step 4: Choose the Paint tools and color of choice to create a vector image of Betty, using Figure 1-47 as a guide.

Step 5: Once the drawing is complete, return to Scene 1.

Step 6: Choose **File** > **Save**. Verify this file has been saved in `bettyFolder`.

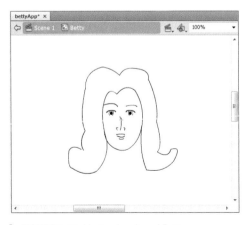

I FIGURE 1-47 Vector drawing of Betty.

Task 4: The Interactive Buttons

Buttons are important as interface elements and will be used often in the case studies in future chapters. Adobe Flash provides a collection of predesigned buttons. Instead of creating a button from start to finish, it will be easier to make alterations to an existing one.

Step 1:   Choose **Window > Common Libraries > Buttons**.

Step 2:   Locate and select the button named capped from the Buttons.fla library as in Figure 1-48. Drag this button into the bettyApp library.

Step 3:   Within the bettyApp library, rename this button SayHelloBtn. To do so, double-click its name. Drag over a second bar capped blue button and rename this second button SayGoodbyeBtn. Close the **Buttons.fla** library when you are done.

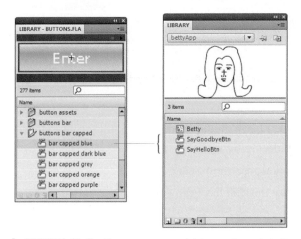

FIGURE 1-48 The library Buttons containing ready-made buttons.

In these next steps we will alter the existing text of the SayHelloBtn button by replacing it with "Say Hello."

Step 4:   Select the SayHelloBtn button from the bettyApp library. Double-click it to open it.

When the button appears on the Stage, notice as shown in Figure 1-49, the Timeline contains four frames corresponding to four possible states: **Up**, **Down**, **Over**, and **Hit**. Drag the Timeline playhead over each state to experience the different look of the button on each frame. The Up state appears when the user's mouse is not on the button; this is the normal state of the button. The Over state shows the appearance of the button when the user rolls the mouse over it. The Down state occurs when the user clicks the mouse while it is over the button. Finally, the Hit frame is a hotspot, the active area of the button that can trigger an action.

Step 5: Select the text layer in the button timeline and use the **Text tool** to replace its current contents with the text **Say Hello**.

Enter the text "Say Hello"

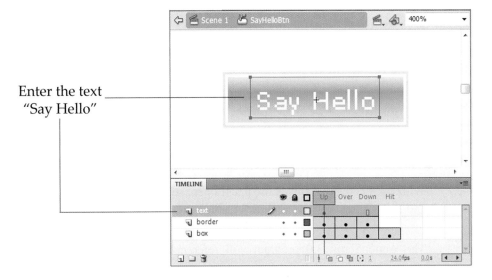

❙ **FIGURE 1-49** The button timeline.

Step 6: Return to Scene 1 and select the `SayGoodbyeBtn` button from the `bettyApp` library. Change its text to read **Say Goodbye**.

Step 7: Choose **File > Save**. Verify this file has been saved in `bettyFolder`.

Part III: Completing the Stage Design for Use with ActionScript 3.0

In this part of the tutorial, we will complete the visual composition for `bettyApp.fla`. At this point, the text elements have been placed on the stage and the dynamic text field has been named so the ActionScript 3.0 code can access it. Now it is time to complete the Stage design by placing the button instances on stage and give them names so that our ActionScript 3.0 code can work with them. Betty will also be added to the Stage for visual effect.

Step 1: Verify that Scene 1 is active. With the Library panel open, place an instance of each button on the Stage. Also place an instance of Betty on the Stage. Use Figure 1-50 as a guide for positioning these elements on the Stage.

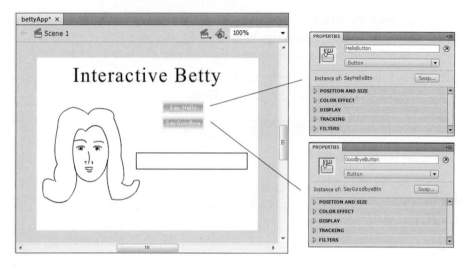

▌ FIGURE 1-50 Final Stage design with two buttons.

Step 2:   With the **Properties Inspector** panel open, select the first button instance and name it `HelloButton` as shown in Figure 1-50. Select the second button instance and name it `GoodbyeButton`.

The ActionScript 3.0 program will reference buttons by their instance names.

Step 3:   Choose **File > Save**.

Part IV: Specifying the Document Class

All applications created in this textbook will use a document class. The document class is the main ActionScript 3.0 program file that holds the ActionScript 3.0 code that executes as soon as the application starts. This file is linked to the Flash document and is the engine that drives the application.

As opposed to Flash documents, which have a **.fla** extension, ActionScript 3.0 program files have an **.as** extension. To specify the document class for an application, we simply provide the name of the ActionScript 3.0 program file without the .as extension.

Step 1:   With the **Properties Inspector** open, use the **Selection tool** to click on a blank part of the Stage.

Step 2:   Using Figure 1-51 as a guide, enter `bettyApp` for the **Class** property. This sets the document class to the file named `bettyApp.as`. Notice that the extension is not included in this name.

The Flash file `bettyApp.fla` is now linked to the document class `bettyApp`. The ActionScript 3.0 program file `bettyApp.as` will now be programmed.

Document class file linked to the Flash movie file

| **FIGURE 1-51** Document properties for `BettyApp`.

Part V: The Anatomy of an ActionScript 3.0 Program

Now we are ready to write the ActionScript code for `bettyApp.as`. All the applications written in this textbook will be composed of at least two files: the Flash document file and one or more ActionScript 3.0 program files. The complete application for Interactive Betty will consist of the following two files:

- `bettyApp.fla`
- `bettyApp.as`

Before we start, a few comments are in order:

1. To keep things simple, we will use a single class file for the first applications in this textbook. The document class will represent this class file.

2. The ActionScript 3.0 program file must be able to locate the Flash document file it will be controlling. For convenience, we will always place these files in the same directory.

3. The code in this part of the tutorial may look rather cryptic. We ask you to simply accept it for now, as some details will not be explained until later in the book.

Task 1: Creating an AS (ActionScript) File

Step 1: Choose **File > New**.

Step 2: Choose **ActionScript File** from the **New Document** dialog box, as shown in Figure 1-52.

Step 3: Choose **File > Save**. Save this file in the folder bettyFolder. Enter the name bettyApp.as. Click **OK**.

Verify that both bettyApp.as and bettyApp.fla are located in the same directory, bettyFolder.

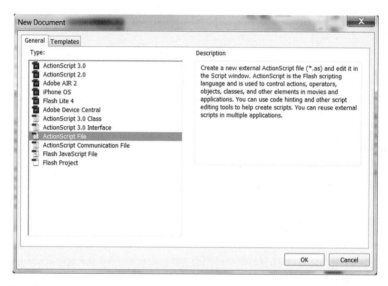

I FIGURE 1-52 Dialog box for the new AS3 document.

Task 2: Coding and Testing the Application

Step 1: The complete ActionScript 3.0 program file is shown in Figure 1-53. The code must be entered exactly as it appears. Each piece of the program is explained in the anatomy section that follows. Many terms and concepts will be skimmed over here in an attempt to provide you with the tools needed to write programs early in the process.

Step 2: Click the **Check syntax icon** to identify any errors. A window will appear indicating your syntax errors, if any. If syntax errors are present, carefully match the entered code with the code provided in Figure 1-53. Each time errors are corrected, check the syntax again until it is error free.

Step 3: Choose **File > Save** to save the bettyApp.as file.

Step 4: Choose **Control > Test Movie** to test the application.

Check
syntax

```
                                                    Target:  bettyApp.fla  ▼  ⑦
1    //PART I:  THE PACKAGE CONTAINING THE CLASS
2    package {
3
4        //PART II:  THE LIBRARY CLASSES NEEDED.
5        import flash.display.*;
6        import flash.events.*;
7
8        //PART III: THE CLASS DEFINITION
9        public class bettyApp extends MovieClip {
10
11           //PART IV: CLASS CONSTRUCTOR FUNCTION:  RUNS IMMEDIATELY UPON LAUNCH
12           function bettyApp() {
13               HelloButton.addEventListener(MouseEvent.CLICK, hello);
14               GoodbyeButton.addEventListener(MouseEvent.CLICK, goodbye);
15           }
16
17           //PART V: FUNCTION TO DISPLAY HELLO
18           function hello(event:MouseEvent) {
19               Output.text="Hello world!";
20           }
21           //PART VI: FUNCTION TO DISPLAY GOODBYE
22           function goodbye(event:MouseEvent) {
23               Output.text="Goodbye world!";
24           }
25      }
26   }
```

▌ FIGURE 1-53 AS3 code for Hello application.

The Anatomy of the `bettyApp.as` AS3 Program

I: AS3 files are class files. The term **class** will be discussed in the next chapter. A class file always begins with the declaration that it is a **package** containing a class.

```
2   package {
```

II: Inside the **package** is a list of the library classes that will be imported and used by the program. The first, `flash.display.*`, is required to display visual elements and text. The second library, `flash.events.*`, is needed for the use of interactive buttons. Buttons require an event that listens for the click of a mouse.

```
5   import flash.display.*;
6   import flash.events.*;
```

III: The `public class bettyApp extends MovieClip` line begins the `bettyApp` class definition. We are keeping matters very simple by using a single class definition for this tutorial, as well as for all case studies until Chapter 9. This class has been *extended* to work with MovieClips, which means that it will work not just with animations and visual graphics, but also, and more specifically, with our `Output` dynamic text field.

```
9  public class bettyApp extends MovieClip {
```

IV: Function `bettyApp()` is the first function in the program and is the **class constructor**. Later chapters of this book will take an in-depth look at class constructors. The only thing necessary to know at this stage is that this type of function executes automatically when the application runs.

Note three important details:

- A class constructor function should be given the same name as the document class, which is also the same name as the ActionScript file. For example, the name of the class constructor function is `bettyApp`, and the names of the ActionScript 3.0 file and document class are both `bettyApp`.
- On line 13, a listener event is initiated to listen for a mouse click of the `HelloButton` button. Once this button has been clicked, the function `displayHello()` is called.
- On line 14, a listener event is initiated to listen for a mouse click of the `GoodbyeButton` button. Once this button has been clicked, the function `displayGoodbye()` is called.

```
12  function bettyApp() {
13      HelloButton.addEventListener(MouseEvent.CLICK, displayHello);
14      GoodbyeButton.addEventListener(MouseEvent.CLICK, displayGoodbye);
15  }
```

V: The `displayHello()` function is a mouse event function. Once this function is called, it places the text "Hello world!" into the `Output` text box.

- On line 19, `Output.text` uses the dot notation for identifying the text property of the text field named `Output`. This line simply places the string "Hello world!" in the text box named `Output`.
- Line 20 has been purposely left blank. We will be adding a trace instruction on this line in the last task of this tutorial.

```
18  function displayHello(event:MouseEvent) {
19      Output.text="Hello world!";
20
21  }
```

VI: The `displayGoodbye()` function is a mouse event function. Once this function is called it places the text "Goodbye world!" into the Output text box.

- On line 23, the event that triggers the function is identified as a `MouseEvent`.
- On line 24, the string "Goodbye World!" is assigned to the text box named `output`.
- Line 25 contains a closed curly bracket required to end the `displayGoodbye()` function definition.

```
23  function displayGoodbye(event:MouseEvent) {
24      Output.text="Goodbye world!";
25  }
```

The last two lines of the program contain curly brackets. Curly brackets are used to begin and end function definitions, such as with the two functions `display-Hello()` and `displayGoodbye()`. On line 26, the closed curly bracket ends the `public class bettyApp`. The last curly bracket of the file closes the `package`.

```
26      }
27  }
```

Part VI: The `trace` Statement

Adding a `trace` statement to AS3 code is invaluable as a debugging tool during the development of ActionScript programs. The `trace` instruction, which is featured throughout this textbook, is used to display messages, as well as to evaluate and display expressions, in Flash's Output window. This statement will not affect the finished movie, as it is used only in testing, and the Output window will open only during testing.

In this task we will add a `trace` statement to display the message "HELLO BETTY" in Flash's Output window.

Step 1: Verify that you are working in the `bettyApp.as` document, which is the ActionScript code document. Select the blank line 20 and enter the following instruction:

```
trace("HELLO BETTY");
```

This line will activate the Output window during execution and then display the string "HELLO BETTY" to this window.

Step 2:   Execute the application. Click the `Say Hello` button and verify that two greetings are displayed—one in the `Output` text field on the Stage and the other in Flash's Output window.

◼ Review Questions

---

1. Describe the main components of the Flash environment.
2. What is the statement to display a string in a text box?
3. Explain the differences between a keyframe and a blank keyframe.
4. What is a stop action?
5. How does a vector graphic differ from a bitmap?
6. Define tween.
7. What do the extensions `.as` and `.fla` stand for?
8. What is a listener event?

◼ Exercises

---

1. Locate a picture of the Golden Gate Bridge and use the Flash tools to create a vector mock-up.
2. Create a movie clip containing a vector drawing of a coffee cup and saucer.
3. Create four movie clips, each containing a vector drawing of a human eye at a different stage of blinking. Using these movie clips, create a simple frame-by-frame animation of a blinking eye.
4. Create an interesting animation using six symbols from the library and Classic Motion Tweens.
5. Create an interactive movie that contains two buttons and one output text box. When clicked, the first button should display "Goodnight" in the text box. The second interactive button should display "Good morning."
6. Create a Classic Tween of a tree falling. You will need to rotate the tree you draw by using the **Modify > Transform** option on the menu. Insert a stop action unless you wish your tree to spring magically back to life.
7. Create an animation of a tree growing leaves by creating a tree trunk with bare branches symbol and a leaf symbol for the Library. Insert a keyframe for each leaf you add to your tree, and include a stop action to stop the animation from repeating. To add variety to your tree, you may change the properties of each leaf instance without adding new symbols to the Library.

8. Create an interactive movie that contains blue, purple, and salmon buttons from the "buttons circle flat"—Buttons.fla library. Each button will display the text "What color am I?" Include a static text box that displays the text "BLUE, PURPLE, or SALMON?" Modify the code from Tutorial 4 so that each color of button that is clicked displays the name of that color in a dynamic text box. Example: If you click the purple button, the text "PURPLE" appears in the output box.

2 Introduction to AS3 Programming

Introduction

Nicklaus Wirth, the developer of a number of seminal programming languages and a huge influence in the field of software engineering, summed up the heart of traditional programming as follows:

Algorithms + data structures = programs

Why is "Algorithms + data structure = programs" relevant to application programs created in Flash? The short answer is that the foundation of object-oriented programming (OOP) languages, such as AS3, solidly rests on the principles and concepts of traditional programming. All programming languages are made up of at least two basic types of statements: (1) those that define or manage data structures and (2) those that together form an algorithm, the step-by-step solution to a problem.

This chapter covers the basic elements of programming by beginning with a look at the process of program design. We explore both program instructions and data structures in general, and then examine the ways of combining them into a real program. Because Flash is highly visual, we also discuss the concept of storyboarding a visual solution.

Finally, this chapter examines the building blocks of the AS3 language. AS3 is both a structured and an object-oriented language. Structured programming is built around functions that perform various tasks, or actions—something you saw in Tutorial 4 in the previous chapter. Object-oriented programming is built around classes and objects. In this chapter you will be introduced to the concept of designing programs while at the same time exploring the basic idea of classes and objects.

2.1 The Basics of Designing and Building an Application

Being skilled in the workings of Flash and AS3 programming is one thing, but using these skills to build a robust, successful application is a skill in its own right. Whether the final application is to be a simple programmatic animation or a game with an elaborate responsive system, developers must plan ahead. Good planning is important not only for collaborations but also for individual projects.

A clear concept and a good flexible plan produce a better-quality application and help you to avoid unanticipated problems. In this section we examine five phases of software application development.

Phase 1: Problem Analysis: Brainstorming an Idea

Phase 2: Storyboarding the Visual Design

Phase 3: Algorithm Design

Phase 4: Physically Constructing the Application

Phase 5: Testing and Documentation

2.1.1 Phase 1: Problem Analysis: Brainstorming an Idea

Software design begins with a complete understanding of the problem at hand. Phase 1 is concerned with understanding the objectives of the application and the users who will be using it. It provides an opportunity to mull over ideas and flesh out goals and functionality.

Thinking technically is a requirement for this phase. The outcome should be a detailed list of the critical elements (including multimedia elements) and tasks performed in the application. If the application is a game, it must be visualized as a programming problem rather than as a segment of a story.

When analyzing how a complex application may be constructed, it is best to start with an abstract picture. It can be easy to get lost in complicated details. By comparison, by starting with a general and abstract understanding, we can be more flexible in our design. An important part of this phase is a consideration of the data requirements, calculations, and decisions that may be made during the execution of the application. General questions to ask are these:

1. Which information will be used and requested by the application? How is this information retrieved?

2. Which information will be produced by the application, and how will it be communicated to the user?

3. Which processing computations will be required?

As an understanding of the problem unfolds, details and refinements are gradually added in small steps until we have a comprehensive technical understanding of the application.

2.1.2 Phase 2: Design Storyboards and Navigation Maps for the Visual Design

During Phase 2, the interface and the visual elements of the application are investigated and designed. Specifically, it is important to explore not only the visual design, but also the physical and mental mechanisms that can affect the way users will intuitively respond to what they see. Oftentimes Phases 1 and 2 are performed in an overlapping fashion.

Planning the visual appearance of a software application can be accomplished through a technique called **storyboarding**. Storyboarding, in essence, answers the questions related to how a visual design will promote interaction, how information will be communicated, and how the visuals will affect playability and entertainment. Well-developed storyboards can range from sketches of screen layouts with navigation systems to elaborate designs of a menu system. A navigation map is often used to graph the logical flow of the interface from the user's perspective.

2.1.3 Phase 3: Algorithm Design

In Phase 3, a recipe detailing the code solution to the problem, or problems, is constructed. This program recipe, called an **algorithm**, is the blueprint that will be used to code the AS3 program for the application.

Designing the algorithm means identifying the necessary steps, or tasks required, to solve the problem and arranging them in a logical order. We will examine the concept of algorithm design in detail in the next section.

2.1.4 Phase 4: Physically Constructing the Application

Once the problem has been conceptually designed, the application can be physically built, which is simply a matter of following the outline of the storyboards and steps listed in the algorithms. In this textbook, constructing the application will involve building the interactive and graphic components, constructing a Flash timeline that represents the visual perspective of the user, and coding the algorithm in AS3.

2.1.5 Phase 5: Testing and Documentation

It is common knowledge that a thorough initial analysis of a problem and a good design will reduce the number of mistakes, or "bugs." However, there will undoubtedly be a few errors in an application. A good design means that the big errors will be avoided, but getting rid of program bugs (debugging) is still an expected part of software development.

The detection and correction of errors is an important part of developing an application. Testing is concerned with checking that the application works correctly, works efficiently, and is complete. Documenting programs makes them clear not only to you, but also to anyone else trying to read and understand them.

In the case study that follows, the first three phases of application development are explored in detail.

■ 2.2 Case Study 1: The Batting Average Calculator

Problem   Rodney is the coach of a local baseball team. He would like an uncomplicated application, such as the one shown in Figure 2-1, for his players to calculate their batting averages.

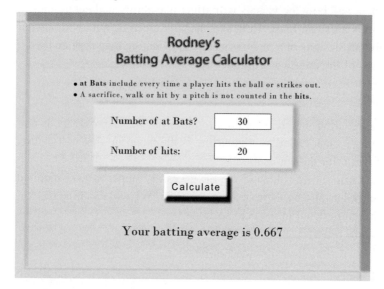

I FIGURE 2-1 Rodney's Batting Average Calculator.

Objectives of this case study are as follows:

1. Explore the process of conceptual design and physical implementation of a complete application.
2. Utilize **input text fields** for the user to enter values.
3. Program basic calculations.

Phase 1: Problem Analysis: Brainstorming the Idea   Although this application is rather elementary, the structure will serve as a model for more complicated examples.

At first glance, this application can be classified as data driven. In other words, the user enters data into input text fields and, after the user clicks a button, the application responds by displaying calculated data in an output text field. Because the primary objective is to calculate the batting average of a given baseball player, a general understanding of the application's data requirements can be accomplished by asking three questions.

Question 1: What data will be needed from the user?

Answer 1: For the application to compute the batting average for a given player, two input values are required by the user:

- **Number of at bats**—this number includes every time a player hits the ball or strikes out
- **Number of hits**

Question 2: Which data will be calculated and displayed by the application?

Answer 2: Displaying the computed **batting average** is the objective of the application and the only output requirement.

Question 3: How will data be computed by the application?

Answer 3: There is only one computational requirement for this application—calculating the batting average—which can be computed as follows:

Batting average = number of hits / number of at bats

The data objects required by this application are fairly basic, and with these questions answered we have a complete list necessary for solving this problem. The term **data object** is used throughout this text and refers to any data element that the program might perform operations on or manipulate.

Our list of data objects can now be fleshed out in more detail. Specifically, we must designate a unique name to identify each data object. This name, also called an **identifier**, should be meaningful and easy to understand. As shown in Table 2-1, the identifier names are single words. The rules that apply to identifier names are discussed in more detail in Section 2.4.

Finally, we must decide which type of data each data object will be allowed to store. This is a necessary step because application data may have some implicit structure that programmers must consider due to its possible effect on the construction of a solution. In this simple application, all the data objects are Number data types. Section 2.3 examines AS3 data types in more detail.

TABLE 2-1 Required Data Objects for Batting Average Calculator Application

Object Identifier	Description	Data Type
atBats	Data object that stores the number of times at bat.	Number
hits	Data object that stores the number of hits.	Number
battingAvg	Data object that stores the calculated batting average based on the ratio of hits over the number of times at bat. Computation: battingAvg = hits / atBats	Number

Phase 2: Analyzing the Visual Design and Constructing a Storyboard   The
Batting Average Calculator will utilize a single interactive screen containing text
fields for input, dynamic text fields for output, and static text fields for general titles
and labels. A button will also be placed on the screen so that the user may initiate the
batting average calculation. In terms of design, it is important that interactive screens
be readable, intuitive, and visually appealing. The primary source of interaction for
this application is textual, so labels must be worded carefully and easily understood.
For this example, text elements are organized from left to right and from top to bottom,
with input text fields grouped together for effective and quick navigation. The interactive button is graphically designed so that the user can reasonably understand what it
is and how to use it.

The storyboard for this example, as shown in Figure 2-2, is a sketch depicting
the visual layout of the interactive screen. All interactive components, such as text
fields and the button are identified by a unique name (Input1, Input2, and so on).
Once named, these visual elements can be utilized in an AS3 program by their valid
identifier names. Table 2-2 lists the details of the four interactive visual components
for this application.

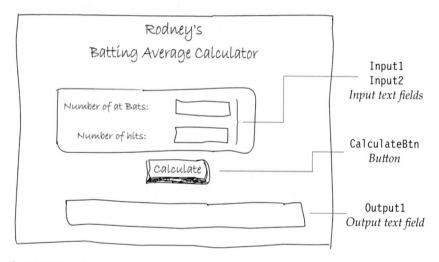

I FIGURE 2-2 Storyboard sketch showing the visual elements and interactive components.

TABLE 2-2 Interactive Visual Objects

Object Identifier	Description	Type of Object
Input1	Where the user inputs text that will eventually be translated and stored in the data object atBat	Input text field
Input2	Where the user inputs text that will be translated and stored in the data object hits	Input text field
CalculateBtn	Where the user activates the calculation and display process	Button
Output1	Used to display the batting average	Dynamic text field

Phase 3: The Algorithm Design   Now we begin with a model, or algorithm, of the program itself. The basic structure for an interactive program in Flash requires functionality for buttons. Therefore, this application will require two functions: (1) the main function and (2) a subfunction that computes the batting average when the button is clicked. The hierarchy of these functions is shown in Figure 2-3.

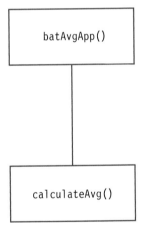

FIGURE 2-3 Functions used in the batting average application.

The main function, batAvgApp(), is given the same name as the class document and, therefore, is called a constructor function. As a constructor function, it will execute as soon as the application is launched; hence, it is regarded as the main function. The second function, calculateAvg(), performs the majority of the tasks, which include retrieving the input from text fields, calculating the batting average, and displaying the result in a text field.

The following discussion explains the algorithm design of the application, outlining and describing the tasks that will be performed by each of the functions. These tasks are derived directly from the problem analysis, as well as from the storyboard design.

The document class for this application will be named batAvgApp. It must be specified in the Properties Inspector. This also means that the AS3 filename will be batAvgApp.as.

Function batAvgApp() Design   As the main function, and constructor, batAvgApp() will begin once the batAvgApp application executes. Its sole task is to activate the calculate button on the Stage so that it will respond when the user clicks it.

> Task: Employ an addListener that will wait for the user to click the CalculateBtn button. Once the button is clicked, the function calculateAvg() will perform its set of tasks.

Function calculateAvg() Design   This function responds once the user has clicked the calculate button on stage. Its tasks are concerned with retrieving the input values supplied by the user, and calculating and displaying the batting average.

> Task 1: Create the data objects atBat, hits, and battingAvg, as identified in the problem analysis. These objects are required for storing the data that drives this application.
>
> Task 2: Read the text from text fields Input1 and Input2 and store them as numbers in the data objects named atBat and hits.
>
> Task 3: Compute battingAvg.
>
> Task 4: Display battingAvg in the dynamic text field named Output1.

Phase 4: Physically Construct the Application   The physical implementation of a Flash application can be subdivided into three parts.

Part A: Construct the Visual Part of the Application   Constructing the visual elements used by the application is the first step in the physical implementation process. Figure 2-4 shows a Timeline composition for the interactive screen that will be used in this application. The Timeline consists of multiple layers, each one containing visual elements, such as text fields, buttons, and graphics, used in the application. For readability, a layer can be renamed by simply double-clicking the name and entering a new one.

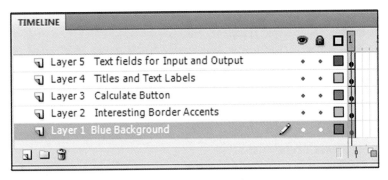

Part B: Specify the Document Class in the Flash .fla file   As demonstrated in Tutorial 4 of Chapter 1, the document class refers to the name of the AS3 program file that is used by the application. The document class name does not include the extension .as.

Document Class: `batAvgApp`

AS3 Program File: `batAvgApp.as`

Part C: Code the AS3 Program   The last part of the physical construction of an application is the writing of the code. The complete program solution for this case study is shown here. Much of the code you see will be unfamiliar at this point. A very brief explanation will follow, but most elements shown in the code will be discussed in the remaining chapter sections.

```
1   package {
2       import flash.display.*;
3       import flash.events.*;
4
5       public class batAvgApp extends MovieClip {
6
7           function batAvgApp() {
8               //TASK : ACTIVATE THE CALCULATE BUTTON
9               CalculateBtn.addEventListener(MouseEvent.CLICK, calculateAvg);
10          }
11
12          function calculateAvg (event:MouseEvent) {
13              //TASK 1: CREATE THE REQUIRED DATA OBJECTS
14              var atBats:Number;
15              var hits:Number;
16              var battingAvg:Number;
17
18              //TASK 2: GET DATA FROM THE INPUT TEXT FIELDS
```

```
19              atBats=Number(Input1.text);
20              hits=Number(Input2.text);
21
22              //TASK 3: COMPUTE THE BATTING AVERAGE
23              battingAvg = hits / atBats;
24
25              //TASK 4:  DISPLAY BATTING AVERAGE IN THE OUTPUT TEXT FIELD
26              Output1.text = battingAvg.toFixed(3);
27          }
28      } //END OF THE CLASS DEFINITION
29  }//END OF THE PACKAGE
```

Lines 1–3: The required class package and import library classes are placed at the beginning of the file. The flash.display library class is required for the visual elements and the flash.events library class is necessary for the button interactivity.

Line 5: This is the required class definition, which shares the same name as the document class and the constructor function.

Lines 7–10: The complete function batAvgApp().

Lines 12–27: The complete function calculateAvg().

Lines 28–29: The last two lines of all AS3 files contain closing curly brackets to close the document class and the package.

Phase 5: Testing   We have tested our program for errors. Thus the code provided here represents the final product of our labors.

■ 2.3 AS3 Data Types

AS3 is a structured language as well as an object-oriented language. It is structured because it is built around functions. For example, in the case study we just examined, the function calculateAvg() was used to perform the input of data, compute a batting average, and display the result. Programs consist of an assortment of functions that perform various tasks and collectively meet the objectives of the application.

As an object-oriented programming language, AS3 is built around classes and objects. Data identified for input, processing, and output will need to be stored as data objects. Classifying these objects is an important concept in programming. Before a program can process and manipulate data, it must know the data type, or class, it is dealing with. Fundamental to the concept of classification is the fact that the computer stores different entities in different ways. For instance, the string "banana" is stored differently than the number 3.1567. Both of these values are also stored differently than the whole number 2.

AS3 programs can process different types of data in different ways. For example, calculating wages earned by an employee requires numerical data, whereas sorting a list of employee names requires textual, or string, data. The goal of all programs is to process and manipulate data, be it numerical, textual, vector images, audio, or video. The types of information that can be represented in a programming language dictate to a great degree the type of programs that can be written.

Formally, a **data type** is defined as a type of data and a set of operations that can be performed on that data. AS3 categorizes data types into one of two fundamental groupings: primitive data types and class data types.

A **class data type**, which is referred to as a class, is a programmer-created data type. Thus the set of acceptable values and operations is defined by a programmer, using AS3 code. We will examine this class data type later in the chapter.

A **primitive data type** is one that is provided as an integral part of the AS3 language and requires no external code. These data types are built into the language. The main primitive data types in AS3 are int, uint, Number, String, and Boolean.

2.3.1 The int Data Type

The int data type is used to store whole numbers, which are known as integers. An int value can be the number zero or any positive or negative value. Examples of valid int values are

    1   2   199   −4   78

Such int values cannot contain decimal points, commas, or special symbols, such as dollar signs.

Examples of invalid int values are

    $23.33   3.0   1,222

The storage allocation for an int is four bytes (32 bits), which provides a range of values from −2147483648 to 2147483647.

2.3.2 The uint Data Type

The uint data type is used for storing and working with positive (unsigned) whole numbers. The uint values are similar to the int values in that they cannot contain decimal points, commas, or special symbols. The storage allocation is also 32 bits for a uint—an important consideration because a uint object can store only a positive number. The maximum value for an unsigned number is twice that of the int data type. The range of integers that can be represented by the uint data type goes from 0 to 4294967295.

The uint data type can be used when storing numeric data that will never be less than 0. It is often used for storing pixel color values that require 32 bits. The color white is represented by the hexadecimal number FFFFFFFF or 4294967295. You can see that this number can be stored in a uint data type but not in an int data type.

2.3.3 The Number Data Type

A floating-point number, which is also called a real number, can be the number zero or any positive or negative number that contains a decimal point. In AS3, the Number data type is used to represent floating-point numbers. To store a floating-point number, you must include a decimal point in the number. If you omit the decimal point, the number will be stored as an integer.

Examples of Number values are

3.0   −3.4567   6.0001   3.5555e-3

The number 3.5555e-3 is exponential notation for 3.5555 multiplied by 10^{-3}, or .0035555.

Like the int and uint values, Number values may contain only a sign, digits 0–9, and a decimal point. Special symbols, such as a currency sign and commas, are not allowed. Examples of invalid Number data values are the following:

2,345.99   €4555,99 $143.94

Exponential Notation and Precision   A Number can also be written in exponential notation, which is similar to scientific notation and is commonly used to express both very large and very small values in compact form. In exponential notation, the letter *e* stands for exponent. The number following the *e* represents a power of 10 and indicates the number of places the decimal point should be moved to obtain the standard decimal value. Examples of valid exponential notation and their decimal value follow:

.000000012	1.2 e-8	1.2×10^{-8}
.0000000012	1.2 e-9	1.2×10^{-9}
12000000000000.0	1.2 e13	1.2×10^{13}
120000000000000.0	1.2 e14	1.2×10^{14}

AS3 allocates 8 bytes for Number data values. This is the IEEE standard double-precision format, which provides a range of values from ±4.94065645841246544e-324 to ±1.7976931486231570e+308. (IEEE is an acronym for the Institute of Electrical and Electronics Engineers.) This standard format uses 64 bits and was one of several sponsored by the Standards Committee of the IEEE Computer Society.

Although this range of numbers is enormous, the cost of this range is precision. Specifically, the fractional part of a number is often approximated when this scheme is used. For example, the fraction 1/3 requires an endless number of bits to be represented precisely. The `Number` data type uses a fixed number of bits, with the result that 1/3 will be stored as an approximation. If your application requires absolute precision with decimal numbers, you need to use software that implements decimal floating-point arithmetic as opposed to binary floating-point arithmetic.

2.3.4 The `String` Data Type

The `String` data type is used to store textual information. Textual information can consist of a single character or a series of individual characters. These characters come from an available character set that differs somewhat from computer to computer, but always includes the letters of the alphabet (both uppercase and lowercase), the ten digits 0, 1, 2, 3, 4, 5, 6, 7, 8, and 9, and special symbols such as @, $, !, ?, *, #, and so on.

`String` values containing more than one character must be enclosed in double quotation marks. Examples of valid `String` values containing more than one character follow:

```
"The sky is blue"    "Apples are tasty!"    "543"
```

`String` values may also contain a single character. `String` values containing a single character may be enclosed in single quotation marks or double quotation marks. Examples of valid `String` values containing one character include these:

```
'a'    '5'    'A'    "A"
```

String Concatenation Operator   Strings can be built using the concatenation operator, +. The same operator performs addition of numbers. When used with `String` data types, it will concatenate two strings.

Character Codes   It is important to note the difference between strings and numeric values. The string value '5' is not the same as the integer value 5. '5' is a character that is stored using a common character set, such as the ASCII or Unicode character set. The ASCII character set is shown in Table 2-3. Most computer languages, including AS3, use ASCII (pronounced "AS-KEY"), which is an acronym for American Standard Code for Information Interchange. ASCII represents each character using a unique integer code.

For the computer to work with character data, the individual characters must be converted to numeric (actually, binary) code. In other words, when you press a character on the keyboard, the computer sees the numeric representation of that character, not the character itself. Using the ASCII character code, the character '5' is represented by the number 53. The character 'A' is represented by the ASCII character code 65.

TABLE 2-3 ASCII Character Code

Character	Code	Character	Code	Character	Code
!	33	A	65	a	97
"	34	B	66	b	98
#	35	C	67	c	99
$	36	D	68	d	100
%	37	E	69	e	101
&	38	F	70	f	102
'	39	G	71	g	103
(	40	H	72	h	104
)	41	I	73	i	105
*	42	J	74	j	106
+	43	K	75	k	107
,	44	L	76	l	108
-	45	M	77	m	109
.	46	N	78	n	110
/	47	O	79	o	111
0	48	P	80	p	112
1	49	Q	81	q	113
2	50	R	82	r	114
3	51	S	83	s	115
4	52	T	84	t	116
5	53	U	85	u	117
6	54	V	86	v	118
7	55	W	87	w	119
8	56	X	88	x	120
9	57	Y	89	y	121
:	58	Z	90	z	122

The Escape Sequence The backslash character, \, is referred to as an **escape character**. It has a special meaning in most programming languages, including AS3.

Escape sequences—the combination of the backslash character followed by a select group of characters—are used to control the placement of text. In particular, the escape sequence \n is used to insert a **newline character** (the character generated by the Return or Enter key) into the string.

Another commonly used escape sequence is \t, which is used to insert a **tab character** (the character generated by the Tab key) into the string. A list of common escape sequences appears in Table 2-4.

TABLE 2-4 Common Escape Sequences

Escape Sequence	Character Inserted
\n	Newline
\t	Horizontal tab
\\	Backslash
\'	Single quotation mark
\"	Double quotation mark

Here is a look at a few examples. Each of these examples uses a trace statement. As demonstrated in Tutorial 4 from Chapter 1, the trace statement is used to display values to Flash's Output window during program development.

Example 1

```
trace("There\ngoes\nthe\ntide.");
```

Evaluation

This trace statement contains a string that utilizes three newline escape sequences.

The output displayed will be

```
There
goes
the
tide.
```

Example 2

```
trace("There\tgoes\tthe\ttide.");
```

Evaluation

The string in this trace statement contains three tab escape sequences. Each word will be separated by a single tab.

The output displayed will be

```
There     goes     the       tide.
```

Example 3

```
trace("There\"goes\" the tide.");
```

Evaluation

This statement contains three double quotation mark escape sequences.
The output displayed will be

There "goes" the tide.

Example 4

```
trace("Hello " + "There");
```

Evaluation

This example illustrates the concatenation of two strings.
The output will be

Hello There

Example 5

```
var  word:String = "earth";
trace("Hello " + "there " + word);
```

Evaluation

The variable word has been defined and initialized to the string "earth". This example illustrates the use of the concatenation operator for building strings with values stored in variables.
The output will be

Hello there earth

2.3.5 The Boolean Data Type

A Boolean data value can hold only one of two values: true or false. AS3 treats the number zero (0) as **false** and any nonzero number value as **true**. This data type will not be discussed further until Chapter 5, when we explore Boolean logic and the selective control structure.

2.3.6 AS3 Data Type Member Functions

One of the major advantages of object-oriented programming is its emphasis on the creation of software models of data objects. In AS3, a data object can be thought of as a storage structure in which the programmer can declare

- The value of the data object
- Operations on the object

These operations are called **member functions**, or **methods**. The concept of functions, particularly methods, will simply be touched on here, as only a limited understanding is required at this point. Methods will be explained in further detail in later chapters.

To understand what a member function is, we will look at a basic data object, a variable. The following instruction creates a variable named `angle`:

```
var    angle:Number = 34.567122234;
```

From this declaration, we know three facts about `angle`:

Fact 1: The variable `angle` is a member of the `Number` data type.

Fact 2: The data value that this object stores is the number 34.567122234.

Fact 3: Because it is a member of the `Number` data type, a set of special operations, called methods, can be performed on the variable's data value.

Here are three useful methods that are defined for the `Number`, `int`, and `uint` data types:

- `toFixed`: This method returns a string representation of the number in fixed-point notation.
- `toPrecision`: This method returns a string representation of the number in exponential notation.
- `toString`: This method returns the string representation of the object.

The general notation for accessing a method is

identifierName.method()

In this expression, the member function named `method()` is associated with the object named `identifierName`. Because a dot (or period) is used to connect an object with its member function, this notation is often referred to as **dot notation**.

Here is an example to illustrate accessing a method.

Example

```
var    angle:Number = 34.567122234;
trace(angle.toPrecision(3));
```

Evaluation

`angle.toPrecision(3)` calls the method `toPrecision` associated with the data object `angle`. As a result, the number value stored in `angle` is displayed with three decimal places, a precision of three.

The output displayed by this code segment is

```
34.567
```

In the case study that appears later in this chapter, a Flash application program is used to compute the wages earned by an employee. The case study illustrates the application design process starting with the algorithm design and ends with the implementation of the program in Flash and AS3. As with the previous case study, this case study shows what a complete application program in Flash will look like.

2.4 AS3 Programming Basics

2.4.1 Variable and Constant Declarations

To allocate memory for a data object, programs require a special statement called a **declaration**. The computer keeps track of the actual memory address that corresponds to the name of each data object the programmer assigns.

Data objects come in two forms: variable and constant. Variables and constants are nothing more than memory locations that are specified by using identifier names. A variable is a dynamic data object, meaning it can take on different values. For example, in the previous case study, the Batting Average Calculator called for three data objects: (1) the number of times at bat, (2) the number of hits, and (3) the computed batting average. All three of these data objects are variables because their values may differ each time the program is executed.

A constant is a static data object—that is, one whose value will not change during the course of program execution. An example of a constant would be the value of a nickel. A nickel will always be 5 cents. It is a static value that will not change.

A declaration statement has a general format that requires the name of the data object and the specification of its data type. Once a declaration statement is performed, the data object can be referred to in the program.

For a variable data object, the declaration format is

```
var      identifierName:DataType ;
```

For a constant data object, the format is

```
const    identifierName: DataType ;
```

The keyword `var` is used to define a variable and the keyword `const` is used to define a constant. `identifierName` is a user-selected name and `DataType` designates a valid AS3 data type. For example, in the Batting Average Calculator, the appropriate AS3 declaration statements for the three data objects would be

```
var atBats:uint;
var hits:uint;
var battingAvg:Number;
```

All three data objects are identified as variables. The first two are members of the uint data type; the third is a Number. Notice that each statement ends with a semicolon.

Although declaration statements may be placed anywhere within a function, most declarations are typically grouped together and placed immediately after the function's opening brace. In all cases, however, the declaration of a data object must be performed before the data object can be used.

Identifiers   Identifiers are the names we assign to the data objects we declare. An identifier is nothing more than a distinctive name that allows us to uniquely represent and identify a data object. All programs require programmer-supplied identifiers, which must adhere to the following rules:

Rule 1. Identifiers must start with a letter of the alphabet or an underscore (_).

Rule 2. Identifiers must consist of only letters, digits, and underscores.

Rule 3. AS3 is case sensitive. This means that identifiers will have different names if the cases are different. For example, *atBat* is not the same as *AtBat*.

Rule 4. Identifiers may not be given the names of AS3 keywords or library identifiers. The latter are reserved words that are restricted in their use; they cannot be used for other purposes. You will learn more about individual keywords in subsequent chapters. There are about 80 keywords in AS3. Table 2-5 shows the most commonly used AS3 keywords.

In addition to the syntax rules for identifiers, certain conventions of style are used in programming and adhered to by the authors in this book.

Style Rule 1. Data objects should always be given meaningful identifiers. They make a program easier to read and, therefore, more understandable. For example, when creating a variable to store the number of hours worked, it is best to use a variable identifier called hoursWorked rather than the more cryptic name of X.

Style Rule 2. To distinguish between visual objects (such as buttons and text fields) displayed on the screen and code variables and functions, use an uppercase letter to begin the name of a given visual object. An exception applies to reserved AS3 words. For example, a button displayed on the screen can be named ComputeBtn while a function will be named computeAvg(). Note that a variable object named x would be an error because lowercase x is an AS3 keyword. Therefore, changing it to X is an exception to this style rule.

Style Rule 3. To distinguish between constant and variable data objects, it is best to follow the simple convention of using all caps for constant identifiers. For example, when creating a constant to store the number of days in a week, it is better to use

```
const DAYSPERWEEK:uint = 7;
```

instead of

```
const daysperweek:uint = 7;
```

Style Rule 4. It is good practice to initialize variable data objects when they are defined. When a variable is not initialized, its initial value will be some arbitrary value from memory.

TABLE 2-5 AS3 Keywords

alpha	false	namespace	switch
AS3	final	native	this
break	finally	null	throw
case	for	override	true
catch	function	package	try
class	get	parameter	use
const	if	private	var
continue	implements	protected	while
default	import	public	with
do	in	return	x
dynamic	include	rotate	xml
each	interface	set	y
else	internal	static	
extends	label	super	

Here is a look at a few declaration statements.

Example 1

```
var tax  Amount:Number;
```

Evaluation

This declaration is invalid. Spaces are not allowed in identifiers.
    The correction is

```
var     taxAmount:Number;
```

Example 2

```
var Test2:Number;
```

Evaluation

This declaration is valid, but the identifier has broken a style rule. Digits are allowed in identifiers as long as the name begins with a letter. Variable identifiers, however, should begin with a lowercase letter.

The correction is

```
var     test2:Number;
```

Example 3

```
var 1stTest:Number;
```

Evaluation

This statement is invalid. Identifiers may not begin with a digit.

A correction is

```
var     test_1st:Number;
```

Example 4

```
var year:Number;
```

Evaluation

This declaration is valid, but it is inefficient. The variable `year` will likely hold only positive whole numbers. The data type `Number` is not a good choice.

A better declaration is

```
var     year:uint;
```

Example 5

```
var alpha:Number;
```

Evaluation

This declaration is invalid because `alpha` is a reserved keyword.

A better declaration is

```
var     Alpha:Number;
```

Example 6

```
var rmdmxxx:uint;
```

Evaluation

This declaration is poorly written. The identifier name rmdmxxx is cryptic and difficult to read. Readability is an important aspect of programming.

Example 7

```
var INCHES_PER_FEET:int = 12;
```

Evaluation

This declaration is technically valid, but it is more appropriate as a constant declaration. The number of inches per feet is a static value—and hence a constant. Remember that constants must always be initialized to a value.

A better declaration is

```
const INCHES_PER_FEET:int = 12;
```

2.4.2 Reading Input from a Text Field

Oftentimes, applications require users to input values, such as in the Batting Average Calculator from the case study earlier in this chapter. For example, in the task description of the calculateAvg() function for this case study, we used the words "Read the text from text fields." This basic input operation can be performed through the use of AS3 code and input text fields. Users use the mouse to select the text field on the Stage and enter information using the keyboard.

All text fields—whether they are specified as *dynamic* or *input*—will store values as text. When a user enters a number into a text field, it is actually text. For example, the value entered in the following text field is the text string "45.50" and not the number 45.50:

Enter the price: | $ 45.50 |

As demonstrated in Tutorial 4 from Chapter 1, when values are placed in a dynamic text field, the .text notation is used. For example, when the string "Hello World!" was placed in the text field Output, the following instruction was used to perform the task:

```
Output.text = "Hello World!";
```

The text from a text field is retrieved using the same .text notation. Numeric input will require conversion to a data type format that is compatible for an assignment to a declared AS3 variable. In the following code segment, input from the text fields Input1 and Input2 is retrieved and stored as numbers in the variables temperature and humidity, respectively.

```
1   //TASK 1: DECLARE VARIABLES
2   var temperature:Number;
3   var humidity:Number;
4
5   //TASK 2: GET DATA FROM THE INPUT TEXT FIELDS
6   temperature = Number(Input1.text);
7   humidity = Number(Input2.text);
```

2.4.3 Statements and Calculations

The individual instructions that you use to write a program in a programming language are called statements. A programming statement can consist of keywords, operators, punctuation, and other programming elements, arranged in a logical order to perform an operation.

The operations for **addition** and **subtraction** are denoted in AS3 by the + and − symbols, respectively. **Multiplication** is denoted by the asterisk symbol, *, and **division** by the forward slash symbol, /.

Thus, to compute the number of hours in a week, the expression

```
7 * 24
```

is evaluated by multiplying the literal value 7, the number of days in a week, by the literal value 24, the number of hours in a day.

In the following code segment, the first statement declares a variable named feetDistance as a Number. The second statement assigns this variable the value of 3.0 multiplied by the current value of the variable yardDistance.

```
var  feetDistance:Number;
feetDistance = 3.0 * yardDistance;
```

2.4.4 Comments and Code Documentation

Because programs are very seldom written, used, and then discarded, it is important that they be well documented. It is the documentation that assists the next person who needs to use, modify, or correct those programs that live on long after the programmer who created them. In visually complex applications, a detailed storyboard serves as useful documentation. However, the storyboard alone fails to show the intent of the programmer or the logic flow of the program.

The use of comments—that is, English sentences embedded in the code—serves as the best means for program documentation. Comments should be used to describe the data and explain the operations being performed so that a reader who is unfamiliar with the program may learn the purpose or intent of the code.

In this book, we have documented our code as we constructed our solutions. It is highly recommended that all programs be thoroughly documented with comments so that anyone using the code will understand the role and structure of component pieces and segments of code. It is frequently necessary to add even more documentation after the testing phase determines that the program correctly provides the solution. AS3 supports two types of comments: single-line comments and multiple-line comments. Single comment lines begin with two forward-leaning slashes (//) anywhere on the line. All content on that line following the // is ignored during processing. Multiple-line comments are enclosed between /* and */.

Often programmers will insert comments at the top of a program to give a brief explanation of the program and information about the programmer. You can also include comments before each important step in the code to provide a brief description explaining the purpose of a segment of instructions.

Example 1

This example illustrates AS3 comments using the two forward-leaning slashes.

```
1   //TASK : DECLARE VARIABLES FOR BIRTHDATE
2   var birthYear:uint;    //YEAR OF BIRTH
3   var birthMonth:uint;   //MONTH OF BIRTH
4   var birthDay:uint;     //DAY OF BIRTH
```

Example 2

As shown in this example, AS3 comments occupying multiple lines can be easily specified. Comment lines 1–5 are enclosed between /* and */.

```
1   /* ----------------------------------------------
2   TASK 1:
3   A.  DECLARE VARIABLES
4   B.  GET DATA FROM INPUT TEXT FIELDS
5   ----------------------------------------------*/
6       var temperature:Number;
7       var humidity:Number;
8       temperature = Number(Input1.text);
9       humidity = Number(Input2.text);
```

2.4.5 Testing

It is well understood that a thorough initial analysis of a problem and a good design will reduce the number of problems during the development of the solution. For beginning programmers, the most common problem is the syntax error, in which a program contains a violation of the language rules. A good design means that the big problems will be avoided, but the process of testing and making refinements is an expected part of software development.

Testing an application should be done early and often, with a focus on the following key characteristics:

1. Program correctness. No matter how nice a program looks, if it does not produce correct and complete results, it is worthless. It is possible that the results produced by the program may be wrong because of logical errors that are not easily detected. The only way to validate and verify the correctness of an application is to run as many tests as possible. An application may be correct for some scenarios, but not for others.

2. Application robustness. Programmed applications must be tested for stability under as many conditions as possible. The best way to ensure that an application will not crash and will remain stable during complex calculations is protracted testing of the developers' assumptions.

3. Users' experience. User testing will demonstrate the effectiveness of the interface. It will also help to identify navigation and human–computer interface design problems.

I FIGURE 2-5 Wages application.

2.5 Case Study 2: Planning the Wages Application

Problem   Don, the owner of Don's Bike Shop, would like a simple Internet application, such as the one shown in Figure 2-5, for his employees to access to compute their wages. All of Don's employees are paid by the hour. Only full hours worked are recorded. In other words, an employee may work for 5 hours, but not 5 hours and 15 minutes. Overtime hours are paid at a rate of one and one-half times the employee's regular rate of pay.

The objectives of this case study are as follows:

1. Declare variable data objects.

2. Explore the use of AS3 data types.

3. Construct strings of text for output to a dynamic text field.

4. Format numbers for output with two decimal places.

Problem Analysis   Similar to the first case study, this application is also data driven. Its primary objective is to compute wages earned by an employee. After considering the problem, it is determined that three input values will be required from the user to compute wages:

- Number of regular hours worked

- Number of overtime hours worked

- Rate of pay

For output, Don feels that it would be helpful if regular wages and overtime wages were displayed in addition to the total wages earned. Therefore, three data values will be computed and then displayed in a coherent way:

- Regular wage earnings

- Overtime wage earnings

- Total wages earned

The complete set of fleshed-out data objects required for this application is described in detail in Table 2-6. The first two data objects on the list are members of the uint (unsigned integer) data type because the hours worked by an employee are restricted to full hours. In addition, negative hours are invalid.

TABLE 2-6 Required Data Objects for Wages Application

Object Identifier	Description	Data Type
regularHours	Variable data object that stores the number of regular hours worked by the employee.	uint
overtimeHours	Variable data object that stores the number of overtime hours worked.	uint
payRate	Variable data object that stores the rate of pay per hour worked.	Number

TABLE 2-6 Required Data Objects for Wages Application (continued)

Object Identifier	Description	Data Type
regularWages	Variable data object that stores the computed regular earnings based rate of pay for regular hours worked. Computation: regularWage = regularHours * payRate	Number
overtimeWages	Variable data object that stores the computed overtime earnings based on overtime hours worked at time-and-a-half pay. Computation: overtimeWage = overtimeHours * 1.5 * payRate	Number
totalWages	Variable data object that stores the total computed wages earned. Computation: totalWages = regularWage + overtimeWage	Number

Visual Design   This application will utilize a single interactive screen containing an interactive button and text fields for inputting hours worked and rate of pay. General titles and labels are added for user navigation. The storyboard and timeline construction of this application are shown in Figure 2-6. All visually interactive objects are listed in Table 2-7.

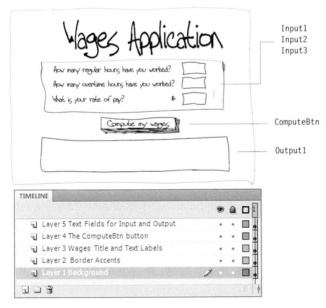

FIGURE 2-6 Storyboard sketch and timeline construction for the Wages application.

TABLE 2-7 Interactive Visual Objects

Object Identifier	Description	Type of Object
Input1	Where the user inputs text that will be converted and stored in the AS3 data object regularHours.	Input text field
Input2	Where the user inputs text that will be converted and stored in the AS3 data object overtimeHours.	Input text field
Input3	Where the user inputs text that will be converted and stored in the AS3 data object payRate.	Input text field
ComputeBtn	Where the user activates the computation process.	Button
Output1	Used to display wage information.	Dynamic text field

Algorithmic Design   The structure for this application will consist of two functions, as shown in Figure 2-7. The main function is wagesApp(), which is also the constructor function. The subfunction computeWages() is responsible for retrieving the input, computing wages, and outputting calculated information to the screen.

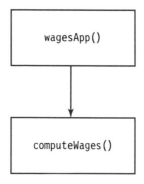

▌ FIGURE 2-7 Functions used in the Wages application.

The document class for this application will also be named wagesApp. This means that the AS3 filename will be wagesApp.as.

The design of these two functions is outlined as follows.

Function wagesApp() Design   This is the main function of the Wages application and the class document constructor. Once the application is loaded, this function will begin. It performs the sole task of activating the button on stage.

> Task. Construct a listener event that waits for the user to click the button instance named ComputeBtn. Once this button is clicked, the function computeWages() is called.

Function computeWages() Design   This function is the workhorse of the application. It collects the required input data and computes the earned wage information. The function performs four tasks:

Task 1. Declare the variables used for input, computation, and output.

Task 2. Gather the input from text fields Input1, Input2, and Input3 located on the Stage. Store these values in the variables regularHours, overtimeHours, and payRate.

Task 3. Compute regularwages, overtimeWages, and totalWages.

Task 4. Display the wages computed in Task 3 in the dynamic text field Output1. Use the toFixed method to display values with two decimal places.

Physical Implementation and Documentation   The complete documented program solution is shown here. The required class package and import library classes have been added at the beginning of the file.

wagesApp.as

```
1      package {
2      import flash.display.*;
3      import flash.events.*;
4
5      public class wagesApp extends MovieClip {
6
7          function wagesApp() {
8              //TASK :  LISTEN FOR A MOUSE CLICK EVENT TO COMPUTE WAGES
9              ComputeBtn.addEventListener(MouseEvent.CLICK,ComputeWages);
10         }
11
12         function ComputeWages(event:MouseEvent) {
13             //TASK 1: VARIABLE DECLARATIONS
14             var regularHours:uint;
15             var overtimeHours:uint;
16             var Rate:Number;
17             var regularWages:Number;
18             var overtimeWages:Number;
19             var totalWages:Number;
20
21             //TASK 2: GATHER INPUT
22             regularHours=uint(Input1.text);
23             overtimeHours=uint(Input2.text);
24             Rate=Number(Input3.text);
25
26             //TASK 3:  COMPUTE THE WAGES
27             regularWages=regularHours*Rate;
28             overtimeWages=overtimeHours*1.5*Rate;
```

```
29          totalWages=regularWages+overtimeWages;
30
31          //TASK 4:  DISPLAY WAGE INFORMATION IN THE OUTPUT TEXT FIELD
32          Output1.text= "Your regular earnings are $" +
33                  regularWages.toFixed(2) + " and your overtime earnings "
34                  "are $" + overtimeWages.toFixed(2) + ".  Your total "
35                  "wages are $" + totalWages.toFixed(2);
36      }
37   }//END OF THE CLASS DEFINITION
38 }//END OF THE PACKAGE
```

■ 2.6 Graphical User Interface and Flash's UI Components

An important aspect of an application is its graphical user interface (GUI). GUIs represent the interaction between the user and the application through a blend of graphical elements and a navigation system. A well-designed GUI system allows the user to focus on the tasks at hand rather than trying to decipher complex interactions via the keyboard and the mouse. As far as the interactive user experience is concerned, simple is usually best. Simple experiences are often the most difficult to design and may require complex programming.

The components that are used to create the GUI systems shown in Figure 2-8 and Figure 2-9 are part of Flash. With the use of Flash and AS3, or just AS3 by itself, developers can add intuitive GUI components to an application and create a distinctive "look" and "feel."

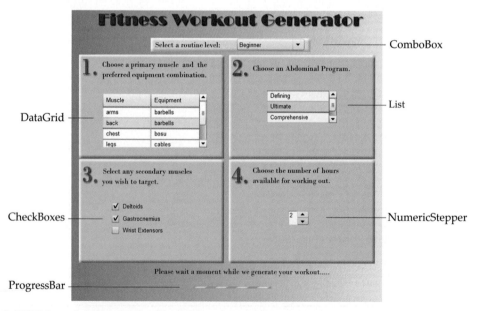

I FIGURE 2-8 Graphical user interface for a fitness generator application.

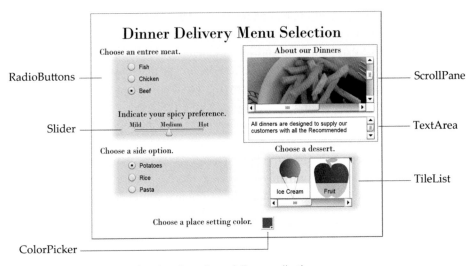

Dinner Delivery Menu Selection

RadioButtons

ScrollPane

Slider

TextArea

TileList

ColorPicker

I FIGURE 2-9 Graphical user interface for a dinner delivery application.

The GUI components provided by Flash are called UI components (user interface components). All of these components are located in the Components panel (choose **Window > Components**), as shown in Figure 2-10. In this section, we briefly describe each of the GUI components found in this panel, several of which will be used in the last case study of this chapter. For an in-depth examination of these components, refer to a Flash reference guide.

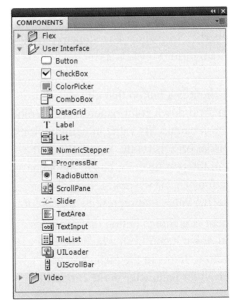

I FIGURE 2-10 Flash's Components panel for user interface elements.

Placing a UI component in an application can be done by dragging a selected UI component from the Components panel to the Stage. Once placed on the Stage, this UI component instance can be named and its parameters set in the Properties Inspector. Parameters can be set to visually alter the component, such as by applying scroll bars to a TileList. In addition, data parameters are used to apply restrictions, such as specifying the minimum and maximum values of a NumericStepper.

All instances of a UI component must be named so that AS3 program files can reference them.

Flash's UI components can provide a rich interface, but their use also increases the size of the final application. As you become more skilled at programming, you will be able to overcome this disadvantage by building a similar set of UI components using AS3 code.

Button	We are already familiar with the Button component. It is simply any area that triggers an action when clicked. As shown in the earlier case studies, buttons are a fundamental UI component for many applications. Buttons can be built from scratch or added to an application using Flash's Components panel or the Button Library, as shown in Tutorial 4 of Chapter 1. Any ready-made buttons provided by Flash can be significantly altered in appearance.
CheckBox	A CheckBox provides users with the ability to select or deselect information. In essence, it is a selection button that has a true or false value. Labels and label placements can be specified in the Properties Inspector. The value returned by the expression `CheckBoxIdentifierName.selected` will be a true or false value.
ColorPicker	The ColorPicker component is a button that allows the user to select a color from a drop-down color panel. Once a color is selected, the application can use its value in computations or apply the color to visual objects on the Stage. When the user selects a color from the pop-up color panel, the value returned using the notation `IdentifierName.selectedColor` will be a numeric (base 10) value that represents that color.
ComboBox	A ComboBox component is a choice button that provides a list of items in a drop-down menu from which the user can make a single selection. Items in the menu can be added using the data Provider parameter in the Properties Inspector. When the user selects an item from the list, the

	data value that corresponds to the label is returned using the notation `IdentifierName.selectedItem.data.`
DataGrid	A DataGrid is a two-dimensional grid of rows and columns. This component is especially valuable because it can be populated with data from external files. A user selects an entire row from a DataGrid.
Label	One way of providing single-line instructions or information through a GUI is with Labels. The Label component is very similar to the static text used in Tutorial 4 in Chapter 1 and in the interface screens from the previous case studies. Text displayed in a Label is "static" because the user cannot alter it.
List	The List component is a scrollable list of items, such as a list of text elements or a collection of photographs from which the user can make a selection. It is possible to design Lists for either a single selection or multiple selections. List items can be added using the data Provider parameter in the Properties Inspector. Figure 2-11 shows four items in the List component. Each item has a label, such as "Rice," and a corresponding data value. When the user selects Pasta from the list, the value returned using the notation `IdentifierName.selectedItem.data` will be 2—its assigned data value.
NumericStepper	The NumericStepper component provides a scrollable list of consecutive numbers from a minimum value to a maximum value. This component allows the user to rapidly move through the list to select a numeric value. The properties that can be set for this component are maximum, minimum, stepSize, and value. When the user selects a numeric value from this interface component, the numeric value returned using the notation `IdentifierName.value` is simply the number value selected.
ProgressBar	The ProgressBar shows the progress of content that takes a long time to load, such as video, photos, and sounds. This component is useful for indicating to the user that the application will execute once these large elements have fully loaded.
RadioButton	A RadioButton is essentially a collection of check boxes grouped together to form a group of buttons where only one

button in the group can be selected (true). Selecting one button forces all other buttons in the group to be unchecked (false). Each RadioButton must be given an instance name in the Properties Inspector. To ensure only one RadioButton in the group is selected at any moment, the same group name must be specified in the Properties Inspector. RadioButtons can be assigned eventListeners to determine which button in the group is selected. The value of a RadioButton is returned using the notation `IdentifierName.value`.

ScrollPane   You can use the ScrollPane component to display content that is too large for the area into which it is loaded. For example, a photograph may be too large for a small space on the Stage. However, by loading it into a ScrollPane, the user can view the entire image by scrolling. The data source, such as the name of the image, along with scrolling specifics, can be assigned in the Properties Inspector.

Slider   The Slider component allows the user to select a continuous range of values by sliding a button between minimum and maximum values. Additional property values, such as scroll size, can also be assigned in the Properties Inspector. The numeric value of the user's selection can be returned using the expression `SliderIdentifierName.value`.

TextArea   The TextArea component is used to display small or large amounts of scrollable text. It can also be modified to perform as an input text field.

TextInput   The TextInput component is a single-line area that receives user input from the keyboard. In the previous case studies, input text fields have been used for this purpose.

TileList   The TileList component consists of a list that is made up of rows and columns of items, including visual objects. As with the List UI component, TileList items can be added using the data Provider parameter in the Properties Inspector.

UILoader   The UILoader component is used to store and display image files, such as JPEG, PNG, GIF, and SWF files. A source parameter, such as the web address of an image, can be assigned in the Properties Inspector.

UIScrollBar
The UIScrollBar component allows developers to add scroll bars to text fields. You can add a scroll bar to a text field during development by dragging this UI component onto a dynamic or input text field and then specifying the scroll-TargetName parameter in the Properties Inspector.

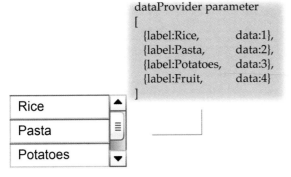

dataProvider parameter
[
  {label:Rice,   data:1},
  {label:Pasta,   data:2},
  {label:Potatoes, data:3},
  {label:Fruit,   data:4}
]

| FIGURE 2-11 Instance of a List component with items added in the dataProvider parameter.

2.7 Case Study 3: Car Loan Calculator with UI Components

Problem   Peter Rogers owns a used car dealership in California and finances all the cars he sells at a simple interest rate of 9%. Customers can choose loan terms that extend from one year to eight years. For all the cars he sells, Peter offers his customers a special warranty costing $1000 that can be added to the car sales price.

Peter would like a calculator application, such as the one shown in Figure 2-12, that computes car loan information and that his customers can utilize online to explore cost and finance options. This online calculator will enable his customers to experiment with costs and make an informed decision before arriving at his car lot to buy the car they want.

The primary objectives of this case study are as follows:

1. Explore the use of selected Flash UI components.

2. Retrieve data values from a UI component.

3. Construct an application that utilizes two interface screens.

4. Format output text.

5. Format numbers for output with two decimal places.

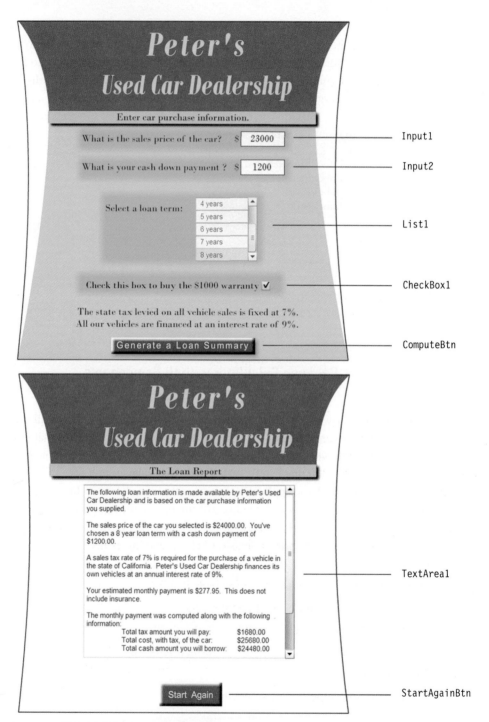

FIGURE 2-12 The input and output screens for Peter's car loan calculator.

Problem Analysis   This car loan calculator will be an invaluable tool for Peter's customers who are considering purchasing a car. They will be able to obtain a fairly accurate idea of the monthly payment they can expect to pay.

Computing the monthly car loan payment will depend on a number of factors, such as the sales tax rate, which in California is fixed at 7%. In addition, we know that Peter charges an interest rate of 9%. Before computing the loan summary, the calculator will also need the following information, which will be input by the buyer:

- What is the sales price of the car?
- What is the cash down payment?
- How long is the loan term in years?
- Will the buyer accept the warranty offer? If yes, its cost of $1000 will be added to the sales price of the car.

The output of this calculator will be a detailed summary of the loan. This summary will supply answers to the following questions:

- What is the price of the car including the warranty?
- How much tax will be paid by the buyer?
- What is the total cost of the car, including tax?
- How much money is to be borrowed?
- How many months is the loan period?
- What is the interest amount that will be paid? Because Peter uses a simple interest rate, the interest amount is computed from the original borrowed amount alone, rather than compounded on earned interest.
- What is the full loan amount?
- What is the monthly payment?

The data objects required for constant values, input, and output, along with the computations, are listed in Table 2-8 and Table 2-9.

TABLE 2-8 Required Constant Objects for Car Loan Calculator Application

Constant Object	Description	Data Type
SALES_TAX_RATE	Sales tax rate is fixed at 7% (0.07).	Number
INTEREST_RATE	Interest rate for all cars financed is 9% (0.09).	Number
MONTHS_PER_YEAR	Number of months in any given year is 12.	uint

TABLE 2-9 Required Variable Objects for Car Loan Calculator Application

Variable Object	Description	Data Type
carPrice	Sales price of the car.	Number
downPayment	Cash down payment to be applied to the car purchase.	Number
years	Number of years for the loan term.	uint
months	Number of months in the loan term: `months = years * MONTHS_PER_YEAR;`	uint
taxAmt	Tax amount computed as the sales price of the car multiplied by the sales tax rate: `taxAmt = carPrice * SALES_TAX_RATE;`	Number
totalCost	The total cost of the car includes the sales price of the car plus the tax amount: `totalCost = carPrice + taxAmt;`	Number
borrowedAmt	The borrowed amount is the total cost of the car minus the cash down payment: `borrowedAmt = totalCost - downPayment;`	Number
interestAmt	The interest amount is the borrowed amount multiplied by the interest rate: `interestAmt = borrowedAmt * INTEREST_RATE;`	Number
loanAmt	The full loan amount is the borrowed amount plus the interest amount: `loanAmt = borrowedAmt + interestAmt;`	Number
monthlyPay	The computed monthly payment is the loan amount divided by the number of months of the loan: `monthlyPay = loanAmt / months;`	Number

Visual Design　The loan calculator's interface must be easy to use, yet must restrict the user's input. For example, Peter does not allow loan terms other than one year to eight years. In addition, selection of the warranty requires a simple yes or no type of response. The input requirements for this application will consist of input text fields, a List UI component (drop-down menu), and a CheckBox UI component for the warranty yes/no answer. For output, a scrolling TextArea will be used to display an easy-to-read loan summary. Table 2-10 lists the visual objects along with descriptions of their specific use.

The loan calculator application will utilize two interface screens. Figure 2-12 shows the completed screens along with identification of the interactive visual objects. The input screen is the first screen the user will see; it is where Peter's potential

TABLE 2-10 Visual Objects Used in the Input/Output Screens

Visual Object Identifier	Location	Type of Object	Description of the Object
Input1	Frame 1	Input text box	Used to input the sales price of the car.
Input2	Frame 1	Input text box	Used to input the cash down payment.
List1	Frame 1	List UI component	Used to input the term years of the loan. **Value Assignments:** This component contains eight sets of labels and data representing loan terms. These labels and data are added to its dataProvider parameter in the Properties Inspector. For example, the first label in the list is **1 year** and the data value that corresponds to it is **1**. **Data Retrieval:** A List numeric value is retrieved by `componentName.selectedItem.data`
CheckBox1	Frame 1	CheckBox UI component	Used to indicate a "yes" or "no" for the warranty offer. **Data Retrieval:** A CheckBox Boolean value is retrieved by `componentName.selected`
ComputeBtn	Frame 1	Button	Used to start the computation process. This interactive button is labeled "Generate a Loan Summary."
TextArea1	Frame 2	TextArea UI component	Used to display the loan summary generated by the application. This UI component has its verticalScrollPolicy parameter set to on and its wordWrap parameter set to true in the Properties Inspector.
StartAgainBtn	Frame 2	Button	Used to start the input process again. This interactive button is labeled "Start Again."

customer will input all relevant loan information. Once this customer clicks the ComputeBtn button, the results that summarize the loan computations will appear in an output screen.

With the use of Flash's Timeline, it is convenient to represent the first screen on frame 1, and the second on frame 2. This setup is illustrated in Figure 2-13. Multiple

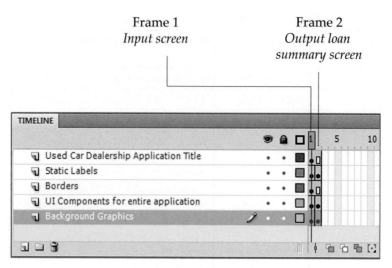

FIGURE 2-13 The Timeline construction for the Car Loan Calculator application.

layers are used in the Timeline to compartmentalize visual objects, such as UI components, graphics, text fields, and buttons.

When creating an interface that utilizes links to various areas of your content, such as with multiple interface screens, an important aspect of storyboarding is charting the flow of the interactive interface from the user's perspective. In the previous case studies, this step was not necessary because a single screen was used for all input and output content. Organizing the flow of content can be done with a navigation map that is connected to the storyboard. As shown in Figure 2-14, the Car Loan Calculator application uses a linear navigation in which the user moves sequentially from the input screen to the output screen and back again. A nonlinear navigation allows users to navigate more freely through the content of an application.

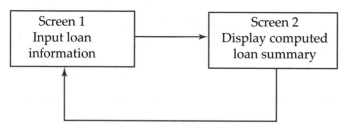

FIGURE 2-14 Navigational map illustrating the interactive flow for the Car Loan Calculator application.

Program Design The document class for this application will be named `carApp`. This means that the AS3 filename will be `carApp.as`. It is assumed that the graphic elements used in the storyboards, along with their objects, have been constructed and correctly named.

The structure for this program consists of three algorithms representing three functions derived from the problem definition and the storyboard. Table 2-11 lists the functions used in the application and Figure 2-15 shows the relationship and flow between these functions.

TABLE 2-11 Car Loan Calculator Application Functions

Function Name	Description
carApp()	This class constructor is for the application. As the class constructor, it will execute immediately once the application is launched.
computeLoan()	Reads the input values and computes the loan summary information. Once computed, this information is displayed in frame 2.
returnToInput()	Returns the user back to the input screen (frame 1).

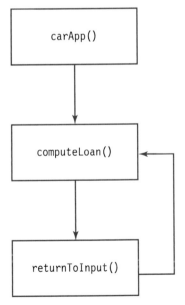

| FIGURE 2-15 Relationship of functions used by the Car Loan Calculator application.

carApp.as   The required class `package` and import library classes are placed at the beginning of the file. The `flash.display` library class is the base class needed for the main function `carApp()` and the `flash.events` library class is necessary for all button interactivity.

```
1  package {
2    //THE LIBRARY CLASSES NEEDED
3    import flash.display.*;
4    import flash.events.*;
5
```

The application requires three constants for calculating the monthly payment. These constants (lines 7 through 9) define the sales tax, the interest rate, and the number of months in a year.

```
6     //THE DOCUMENT CLASS DEFINITION
7     public class carApp extends MovieClip {
8       //CONSTANTS USED BY THE APPLICATION
9       const SALES_TAX_RATE:Number=.07;
10      const INTEREST_RATE:Number=.09;
11      const MONTHS_PER_YEAR:uint=12;
12
```

The last two lines of the AS3 file contain closing curly brackets to close the document class and the package.

```
91    }
92  }
```

The algorithm for each function in the application is designed as follows.

Function carApp() Design   The main algorithm, `carApp()`, is simply the class constructor function that will load immediately once the application is launched. This function creates a listener event that waits for the user to click `ComputeBtn`. Once this button is clicked, the sub-algorithm `computeLoan()` is called. Prior to clicking the `ComputeBtn`, the user should have entered his or her relevant loan information.

The `carApp()` function performs two tasks.

Task 1. By using the AS3 instruction `gotoAndStop(1)`, the layout screen for input, located in frame 1, is activated and held (the Timeline playhead will stop on this frame). Frame 1 contains all of the visual elements that make up the data entry for this calculator application.

Task 2. A listener event is constructed to wait and listen for the user to click the button instance named `ComputeBtn`. Once this button is clicked, the function `computeLoan()` is called.

```
13  //CLASS CONSTRUCTOR FUNCTION:  RUNS IMMEDIATELY UPON LAUNCH
14  function carApp() {
15      //TASK 1:  STOP AT THE INPUT SCREEN
16      gotoAndStop(1);
17      //TASK 2:  LISTEN FOR THE USER TO COMPUTE THE LOAN INFORMATION
18      ComputeBtn.addEventListener(MouseEvent.CLICK,computeLoan);
19  }
20
```

> computeLoan() is called when the
> ComputeBtn button is clicked.

Function computeLoan() Design   The computeLoan() function is called once the user clicks the ComputeBtn. There are 10 tasks within this function, whose objective is to calculate the loan summary and display it in the TextArea UI component located in frame 2.

Task 1. Declare the variable objects required by the input, calculations, and output. These variables were outlined in Table 2-9.

Task 2. Read the values from input text fields Input1, Input2, and Input3, located on the screen, into the data objects carPrice, downPayment, and years, respectively.

Task 3. Test whether the check box for the warranty is true. If it is true, add 1000 to the car price.

Task 4. Convert the number of years for the loan to months. This is done by multiplying years by 12, which is stored in the constant object MONTHS_PER_YEAR.

Task 5. Compute the borrowed amount. This requires computing the tax amount and adding it to the total cost of the car.

```
taxAmt      = priceCar  *  SALES_TAX_RATE
totalCost   = priceCar  +  taxAmt
borrowedAmt = totalCost  -  downPayment
```

Task 6. Compute the interest and loan amount.

```
interestAm  = borrowedAmt  *  INTEREST_RATE
loan amount = borrowedAmt  +  interestAmt
monthlyPay  = loanAmt     /  months
```

Task 7.   Compute the monthly payment.

Task 8.   Activate the output screen in frame 2.

Task 9.   Display all loan information in the TextArea component instance TextArea1.

Task 10. Register a listen event for a mouse click of the StartAgainBtn that reactivates the function returnToInput().

```
21  function computeLoan(event:MouseEvent) {
22      //TASK 1: DECLARE THE VARIABLES USED FOR LOAN COMPUTATIONS
23      var carPrice:Number;
24      var downPayment:Number;
25      var years:uint;
26      var months:uint;
27      var taxAmt:Number;
28      var totalCost:Number;
29      var borrowedAmt:Number;
30      var interestAmt:Number;
31      var loanAmt:Number;
32      var monthlyPay:Number;
33
34      //TASK 2:  ASSIGN VALUES FROM INPUT TEXT BOXES TO THE INPUT VARIABLES
35      carPrice=Number(Input1.text);
36      downPayment=Number(Input2.text);
37      years=List1.selectedItem.data;
38
39      //TASK 3: IF USER SELECTED WARRANTY CHECK BOX, ADD 1000 TO THE CAR PRICE
40      if (CheckBox1.selected) {
41          carPrice=carPrice+1000;
42      }
43
44      //TASK  4:  COMPUTE THE NUMBER OF MONTHS OF THE LOAN TERM
45      months=years*MONTHS_PER_YEAR;
46
47      //TASK 5:  COMPUTE THE BORROWED AMOUNT
48      taxAmt=carPrice*SALES_TAX_RATE;
49      totalCost=carPrice+taxAmt;
50      borrowedAmt=totalCost-downPayment;
51
52      //TASK 6: COMPUTE THE INTEREST AMOUNT AND LOAN AMOUNT
53      interestAmt=borrowedAmt*INTEREST_RATE;
54      loanAmt=borrowedAmt+interestAmt;
55
56      //TASK 7:  COMPUTE THE MONTHLY PAYMENTS
57      monthlyPay=loanAmt/months;
58
```

```
59    //TASK 8: DISPLAY THE OUTPUT SCREEN IN FRAME 2
60    gotoAndStop(2);
61
62    //TASK 9:  DISPLAY CAR PURCHASE INFORMATION IN SCROLLABLE TEXTAREA
63    TextArea1.text = "The following loan information is made" +
64    " available by Peter's Used Car " +
65    "Dealership and is based on the car purchase information you supplied." +
66    "\n\nThe sales price of the car you selected is $" + carPrice.toFixed(2)+
67    ".  You've chosen a " + years + " year loan term with a down payment of $" +
68    downPayment.toFixed(2) + "." +
69    " \n\nA sales tax rate of 7% is required in the" +
70    " state  of California. Peter's Car Dealership finances its own vehicles at" +
71    "an annual interest rate of 9%. \n\nYour estimated monthly payment is $" +
72    monthlyPay.toFixed(2) + "." + "  This does not include insurance." +
73    "\n\nThe monthly payment was computed " +
74    "along with the following information:" +
75    "\n\t\t\t Total tax amount you will pay:         \t$" + taxAmt.toFixed(2)+
76    "\n\t\t\t Total cost, with tax, of the car:    \t$" + totalCost.toFixed(2)+
77    "\n\t\t\t Total cash amount you will borrow:  \t$" + borrowedAmt.toFixed(2)+
78    "\n\t\t\t Total interest amount to be paid:    \t$" + interestAmt.toFixed(2)+
79    "\n\nYour total payments over the life of the loan are $" + loanAmt.toFixed(2);
80
81    //TASK 10:  LISTEN FOR THE USER TO TRY ANOTHER CAR PURCHASE
82    StartAgainBtn.addEventListener(MouseEvent.CLICK,returnToInput);
83  }
84
```

Function returnToInput() Design   The objective of this function is to activate the layout screen so the user may input his or her car loan information.

This function performs two tasks:

Task 1. Activate screen 1, the input screen on frame 1 in the Timeline.

Task 2. Construct a listener event that waits for the user to click the button instance named ComputeBtn. Once this button is clicked, the function computeLoan() is called to compute the specific loan information.

```
85  function returnToInput(event:MouseEvent) {
86     //TASK 1:  RETURN TO THE INPUT SCREEN ON FRAME 1
87     gotoAndStop(1);
88     //TASK 2:  LISTEN FOR THE USER TO COMPUTE THE LOAN INFORMATION
89     ComputeBtn.addEventListener(MouseEvent.CLICK,computeLoan);
90  }
```

Review Questions

1. For the following numbers, identify valid data types that can represent them.

   a. 200

   b. −250.00

   c. −3.5e-4

2. Determine the data types appropriate for the following data.

   a. The number of months in a year

   b. The age of a student

   c. The width of a room

3. How are comments inserted into code?

4. What is a library? Give two examples.

5. Name four keywords that are reserved words in AS3.

6. Of the following, which are illegal identifiers?

   a. `Temp_X`

   b. `Site-Num`

   c. `Tax%`

   d. `T1`

   e. `1T`

   f. `int`

7. Explain the difference between a constant and a variable. Give an example of each.

8. Identify the escape sequence that begins a new line of text.

9. What output is produced by the following code segment?

```
var X:int  = 7;
var Y:int  = 6;
X = Y;
trace(X);
trace(Y);
```

10. The following segment of code contains syntax errors. Locate the syntax errors and correct them. How might you make this code more efficient?

```
var Num1: Number = 24;
var Num  2: Number = 25;
var Num3 = 26;
```

```
var Average:Number = Num1;
Average = Average + Num    2;
Average = Average + num3;
Average / 3.0 = Average;

trace ( "The resulting average is "  + Average);
```

Programming Exercises

1. Create the design for an application that allows the user to enter two names, each in a separate text field. After clicking a Swap button, the names in the two text fields should be swapped.

2. Write a temperature conversion program that converts a temperature in degrees Fahrenheit to degrees Celsius.

$$Celsius = (Fahrenheit - 32.0) / 1.8$$

3. Sally's Burger Emporium would like an application that allows customers to select a choice of meal items and then calculates the total price. Tax should be computed as 7%. Create this application using UI components.

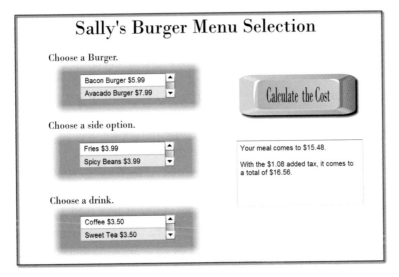

I FIGURE 2-16 Design for Sally's Burger Emporium application.

Possible Lunch Items

Burgers:
  Bacon Burger $5.99
  Avocado Burger $7.99
  Western Burger $7.25
  Veggie Burger $3.99
Sides:
  Fries $3.99
  Spicy Beans $3.99
  Chili Fries $3.25
  Cole Slaw $1.99
  Macaroni Salad $1.00
Drinks:
  Coffee $3.50
  Sweet Tea $3.50
  Soda $2.99
  Water $1.99

4. Write a program that computes the area of a rectangle, as well as its perimeter, given its width and height. Use UI components, such as Sliders and Steppers, to restrict the width and height to a range between 20 and 30 using only integer values.

5. Darwin, Minnesota, is known, among other things, for being the residence of one of the world's largest balls of twine. This ball of twine is a source of great pride to the community and headlines a yearly festival. The creator of the ball was Francis A. Johns, who worked on it for 39 years beginning in 1950. He died in 1989 after building it into a 12-foot-high sphere. But how much does the ball of twine weigh? Develop an interactive application that allows the user to enter the height of the ball along with the density of the twine. Use this input to compute and display the weight of the ball.

   Tip: weight = density * volume, where the volume of a sphere is $\frac{4}{3}$ PI * radius^3.

6. Interest on credit card accounts can be quite high. Most credit card companies compute interest on an average daily balance. Create an application that computes the average daily balance and the monthly interest charge on a credit card account. Your program should ask the user for a previous balance, payment amount, the number of days in the billing cycle, the day of the billing cycle the payment was made, and the monthly interest rate. Here is an algorithm for computing the average daily balance and the monthly interest charge on a credit card:

Step 1: Read as input the net balance shown on the statement and the number of days in the billing cycle. Multiply this net balance by the number of days in the billing cycle.

Step 2: Read as input the number of days the payment was received before the statement date. Also read as input the net payment received. Multiply these values together.

Step 3: Subtract the result of the calculation in Step 2 from the result of the calculation in Step 1.

Step 4: Divide the result of Step 3 by the number of days in the billing cycle. This value is the average daily balance.

Step 5: Read as input the monthly interest rate. Compute the interest charge for the billing period by multiplying the average daily balance by the monthly interest rate.

7. If you are like most people, you collect a fair amount of change in your pocket. A painless savings plan is to dump all of the loose change into a jar at the end of the week. Of course, you might like some idea of the amount of money you will save in a year so that you can start thinking about what you want to buy. In this exercise you will write an interactive program to estimate the yearly savings based on the amount of change saved at the end of four weeks. The amount of change saved at the end of each week will be recorded as four numbers: the number of pennies, nickels, dimes, and quarters.

8. Create an application containing a single text field and a button. The user can enter a number in the text field and double its value by clicking the button. The input value and the computed result should be placed in the same text field.

3

Operations, Basic Functions, and Game Math

Introduction

Application programs, whether they are written in AS3, C++, Java, or some other language, feature standard operations and functions. An important step in learning to program is understanding how these simple operations work. This chapter begins with an examination of mathematical expressions containing operators for computing and manipulating numeric values.

The ability to write functions is a natural part of problem solving in a programming environment. In addition to allowing programmers to construct functions, the AS3 language comes equipped with a set of built-in mathematical functions that are enormously useful in many programming projects, especially in game programming. This chapter examines these functions, along with the programming strategy of splitting a problem into smaller, easy-to-manage pieces and solving them in simpler functions.

The subject of functions is somewhat advanced and will be explored in depth in Chapter 8. However, because AS3 applications require the use of functions early on, this chapter introduces them using an uncomplicated and limited approach.

3.1 Numeric Expressions

In AS3, an expression is a sequence of one or more data objects, called operands, and zero or more operators that combine to produce a value. When the following statement executes

```
var num1:int = 10  -  5  +  6 ;
```

Numeric expression: three operands and two operators

the value of the expression 10 - 5 + 6 will be stored in the variable num1. The 10 - 5 + 6 numeric expression consists of three data objects (10, 5, and 6) and two operators

101

(- and +) and has the value 11. The data objects in this example are literal values as opposed to variables. The expression is evaluated from left to right.

Numeric expressions do not have to be in the form of mathematical operations. In the following statement, 20 is an expression that contains a single data object and zero operators.

```
var num1:int  =  20 ;
```

Numeric expression: one operand and zero operators

3.1.1 Mathematical Operators

AS3 provides five commonly used operators, listed in Table 3-1, for building mathematical expressions and, in turn, manipulating data. Arithmetic operations in AS3 include the add, subtract, multiply, modulus, and divide operations, as well as increment and decrement operations, which are discussed later in this chapter.

TABLE 3-1 Basic Mathematical Operators

Operator	Operation
*	Multiplication
/	Division
%	Modulus, computes the remainder of division
+	Addition, unary positive sign
-	Subtraction, unary negative sign

The addition (+), subtraction (-), multiplication (*), and division (/) operators are straightforward and do not need any further explanation. The modulus operator (%), also called the remainder operator, is used to generate the remainder that occurs when you divide two numbers. For example, in the expression 8 % 5, 5 does not divide evenly into 8, so the remainder is 3.

In some languages, such as C++, the modulus operator is defined for integers only. AS3 is versatile and allows expressions to be built using any type of operand as long as the result of the expression can be stored as a numeric value. Such operations can be performed on any numeric data type. Hence, it is useful to the programmer to make sure the data type is appropriate for the intended operation.

Example 1

```
3 * -5
```

Evaluation

This expression multiplies 3 by -5 and yields the value -15.

Example 2

    5 / 2

Evaluation

In some programming languages, such as C++, this operation is called integer division because both the numerator and the denominator are whole numbers (integers). As a result, these languages will produce an integer for the division, 2, with the fraction .5 truncated.

In AS3, division results in a Number value. This expression computes to 2.5.

Example 3

    2 % 3

Evaluation

The numerator is less than the denominator, so the quotient is zero and the remainder is 2. The following shows the long division to illustrate this calculation.

$$
\begin{array}{r}
0 \\
3\overline{)\,2} \\
\underline{0} \\
2
\end{array}
$$

Example 4

    21 % -2

Evaluation

This expression shows the behavior of the modulus operator on negative numbers. The numerator is positive; thus, regardless of what the denominator is, the result will always be a positive number. Obviously, −2 can be divided into 21 −10 times with a remainder of 1. Examine the long division below.

$$
\begin{array}{r}
-10 \\
-2\overline{)\,21} \\
\underline{20} \\
1
\end{array}
$$

Example 5

```
-21 % -2
```

Evaluation

Unlike in the previous expression, a negative numerator will always result in a negative remainder. The following long division is used to illustrate the process of computing the remainder.

$$
\begin{array}{r}
10 \\
-2\,\overline{)\,-21} \\
-20 \\
\hline
-1
\end{array}
$$

Example 6

```
10.5 % 3.0
```

Evaluation

Real numbers can be used with the modulus operator in AS3, unlike in languages such as C++. The result is 1.5.

3.1.2 Mixed-Type Expressions and Type Conversions

AS3 allows mixed-type operands for many expressions. A mixed-type expression contains operands of different data types as illustrated in the following expression. In this example, the first operand is a Number data type while the second operand is an int data type. These two operands happen to be compatible in AS3.

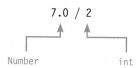

Although the extent to which mixed-type expressions are allowed is implementation dependent, some evaluations require matching data types in AS3. The following discussion is useful on those occasions when mixed-type expressions are the cause of erroneous computations. In the following expression, the mixed-type operands are not compatible. The resulting value produces a logic error depending on how it is assigned.

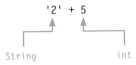

The process of explicitly converting the type of an operand, and thereby making it compatible, is called type conversion. Consider the following expression. Because the data type String is used, the operand 5 is converted to the same data type as '2', a String. This expression produces a value equivalent to "25", but as a string instead of a number.

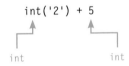

In the next type conversion, the first operand of the expression is converted to an integer. The final result of this expression is 7.

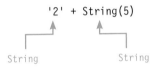

The type conversions int() and uint() will truncate the fractional part of any number. In the following expression, the fixed floating-point number is not rounded up. The final result is 7.

Because of type conversions, the following three expressions contain operands of the same data type:

    String(5.2) + "5.2"   7.0 / Number(2)   int(7.77) % 2

The type of an expression can be explicitly converted to a different type as follows:

Form: Type (Expression)

Where: **Type** is a valid AS3 type.

   Expression is any AS3 expression.

Purpose: The type of the value produced by **Expression** is converted to **Type**.

The next five examples demonstrate type conversions, including some type conversion errors.

Example 1

```
int (5.8) % 2
```

Evaluation

This type expression coerces the numeric value 5.8 into the integer 5. An `int` type conversion requires the truncation of the fraction of a real number. In addition, rounding up does not occur with `int()`. The result in this example is 1.

Example 2

```
int (.9999999)
```

Evaluation

This type expression produces 0. Remember that no rounding up occurs, but rather the truncation of the fractional part of the number.

Example 3

```
uint (-5.666)
```

Evaluation

This expression will result in a type conversion logical error. As a negative number, −5.666 cannot be correctly converted to an unsigned integer.

It is impossible to convert a negative integer into a positive integer without using the absolute value function found in the Math library, discussed later in this chapter. The more appropriate conversion is `uint(Math.abs(-5.666))`, which produces a value of 5.

Example 4

```
String.fromCharCode(65)
```

Evaluation

This type conversion converts the numeric ASCII code 65 to its `String` value, A.

Example 5

```
Number('A')
```

Evaluation

This type conversion incorrectly attempts to convert the character 'A' to its ASCII code of 65. In AS3, this is an incompatible conversion and will result in a value that cannot be identified as a number.

The correct way to convert a character to its corresponding numeric ASCII code is to use the method function charCodeAt:

```
var Letter:String = 'A'
var LetterASCII:Number = Letter.charCodeAt();
```

3.1.3 Operator Precedence

When more than one operation is performed in an expression, the priority of the operations must be determined. The arithmetic operators can be subdivided into two groups: the additive operators (+ and -) and the multiplicative operators (*, /, and %). These categories are important because they are used to determine the order in which operators in an expression are applied. The order of evaluation in an expression is determined by operator precedence.

Programming languages follow operator precedence, as shown in Table 3-2, in concert with the following rules:

1. Operations within parentheses are performed first.

2. If there are nested parentheses (parentheses within parentheses), the innermost operators are performed first.

3. The *, /, and % operators have the highest priority among the five arithmetic operators. As with all the arithmetic operators, they are evaluated from left to right within the expression.

4. The + and – operators have the lowest priority and are performed last, from left to right within the expression.

TABLE 3-2 Operator Priority

Operator	Priority
( )	Level 1 priority (highest)
* / %	Level 2 priority
+ –	Level 3 priority (lowest)

Example 1

```
2 + 3 * 5
```

Evaluation

The * operator has higher precedence than +, so the multiplication is performed before the addition. This expression is evaluated in a series of operations governed by rules of priority.

Step 1:

$$2 + 3 * 5$$

Step 2:

$$2 + 15$$

Final value: 17

Example 2

$$12 + 3 + 5$$

Evaluation

In most programming languages, the operators +, -, *, /, and % are all left-associative. This means that in an expression having multiple operators with the same priority, the expression is evaluated from left to right. The first operation produces 15 + 5. The final result is 20.

Example 3

$$2 * (3 + 5)$$

Evaluation

This example illustrates the use of parentheses to change existing priorities. Without the parentheses, multiplication would have been performed first. With parentheses, the addition (3 + 5) has a higher priority. The final value is 16.

Example 4

```
int (7 + .88)  % 2
```

Evaluation

The parentheses around the addition operation occur before the type conversion. The operation int (7.88) occurs next, which produces a final operation of 7 % 2. The result is 1.

Example 5

$$7 * 10 - 5 \% 3 * 4 + 9$$

Evaluation

In this example, multiplication is performed first, followed by %, then by multiplication again, as shown in the following steps.

Step 1:

$$7 * 10 - 5 \% 3 * 4 + 9$$

Step 2:

$$70 - 5 \% 3 * 4 + 9$$

Step 3:

$$70 - 2 * 4 + 9$$

Step 4:

$$70 - 8 + 9$$

Step 5:

$$62 + 9$$

Final value:

$$71$$

3.2 Assignment Statements

The role of an assignment statement is to assign a value to a variable. Many assignments can be made to the same variable, which means that an assignment statement is also a replacement statement—a variable's value can be replaced with another value. Once an assignment is made to a variable, its original value will be overwritten.

In general, an assignment statement is expressed as follows:

Form: **Variable = Expression**

Where: **Variable** represents a valid AS3 declared variable.

   Expression may be a constant, another variable to which a value has previously been assigned, or a formula to be evaluated, whose type is the same as that of **Variable**.

Behavior:

   1. **Expression** is evaluated, producing a value.
   2. The value is then assigned to **Variable**.

3.2.1 The Basic Assignment Operator and Errors

The basic assignment operator in AS3 is =. In the four assignment statements that follow, the operator = is used to assign the value of an expression to the variables num1, num2, num3, and num4.

```
1   num1 = Y;
2   num2 = Y + 3;
3   num3 = 7 / 2;
4   num4 = X + 3 ;
```

The rules governing this fundamental assignment operator are as follows:

1. The assignment is always made from right to left. An error often committed by new programmers is reading the assignment from left to right.

2. Only one variable can be on the left of the assignment operator.

3. It is considered good programming style to match data types when using assignments: integers to int variables, unsigned integers to uint variables, and so on.

Here are several examples of valid and invalid assignment statements.

Example 1

```
1   var num1:uint = 2.3;
2   trace (num1);
```

Evaluation

The variable num1 is declared as an unsigned integer on line 1. Because the value 2.3 can be coerced into an integer by simply truncating the fraction, this assignment statement is considered valid, but with data loss. The output produced by this segment of code is 2.

Example 2

```
1   var num1:Number = 3.5555e-3;
2   trace (num1);
```

Evaluation

The statement on line 1 is valid. The expression in this example is a real number written in scientific notation. The output produced by this segment of code is .0035555.

Example 3

```
1    var num1:Number = 9.1234e-3 + 2;
2    trace (num1);
```

Evaluation

This segment of code illustrates the usage of mixed data types in an expression. The expression on line 1 is an integer added to a real number. No data is lost in this assignment. The output produced by this segment of code is 2.0091234.

Example 4 Invalid Assignment

```
1    var num1:int;
2    13 + 2 = num1;
```

Evaluation

This assignment is invalid because the expression on line 2 sits on the left side of the assignment operator. The variable to be assigned, num1, must be located on the left, followed by the assignment operator, =, and the expression on the right.

Example 5 Invalid Assignment

```
1    const MAX:int = 100;
2    MAX = 200;
```

Evaluation

This assignment is invalid because MAX is defined as a constant on line 1 and cannot be reassigned a new value on line 2.

Example 6 Invalid Assignment

```
1    var num1:uint = -100;
```

Evaluation

This assignment is invalid because the data types do not match. num1 is declared as an unsigned integer and -100 is a signed integer.

Example 7 Invalid Assignment

```
1    var num1:uint = "A";
```

Evaluation

This assignment is invalid in AS3 because the data types are incompatible.

Example 8 Invalid Assignment

```
1    var fruit:String = 'apple';
2    trace( fruit);
```

Evaluation

The assignment statement in line 1 is invalid because the expression is incorrectly written. A string of multiple characters requires double quotes. With AS3, fruit will be assigned only the first letter. The output produced by this segment of code is a.

3.2.2 Increment and Decrement Operators

AS3 has a pair of operators that increment or decrement numeric variables by one. The increment operator, ++, precedes or follows a variable in a complete AS3 statement. For example, the statements in the following code segment perform the exact same operation. Both add 1 to the variable num1.

```
1    ++num1;
2    num1 = num1 + 1;
```

Like the increment operator, the decrement operator, --, precedes or follows a variable. The decrement operation has the effect of subtracting one from the variable. When these operators precede a variable, they are called **prefix** operators; when they follow a variable, they are called **postfix** operators. Table 3-3 lists the increment and decrement operators.

For more complex operators, the increment and decrement operators can be used as operators within an expression.

TABLE 3-3 Increment and Decrement Operators

Operator	Terminology	Result
Object++	Post-increment	Returns the current value of the data object and then adds 1 to the data object.
++Object	Pre-increment	Adds 1 to the data object and then returns the value.
Object--	Post-decrement	Returns the current value of the data object and then subtracts 1 from the data object.
--Object	Pre-decrement	Subtracts 1 from the data object and then returns the value.

Take a look at the following examples.

Example 1

```
1   var num1:Number = 3.5;
2   num1--;
3   trace (num1);
4    --num1;
5   trace (num1);
```

Evaluation

This example illustrates the simplest usage of a decrement operator. The variable called num1 is declared and initialized to 3.5 on line 1. The num1--; on line 2 is a post-increment, and --num1; on line 4 is a pre-increment. The first num1-- is decremented *after* being used; in the second --num1 is decremented *before* being used. The results are exactly the same because a decrement by 1 is the only operation performed in these instructions. The output produced by this segment of code is

```
2.5
1.5
```

Example 2

```
1   var num1:int = 3;
2   var num2:int = 7;
3   num1 = num2++;
4   trace (num1);
5   trace (num2);
```

Evaluation

This example illustrates the subtle difference between the postfix and prefix use of the increment/decrement operator. The statement on line 3 is actually two assignment statements combined into one. Both num1 and num2 will be reassigned new values. The instruction on line 3 can be deconstructed into the following two statements executed in precise sequence:

1. num1= num2;

2. num2++;

The statement num1= num2 is executed first and the value 7 is assigned to num1. The operation num2++ is executed last because it contains a postfix ++

operator. The value 8 is assigned to num2. The output produced by this segment of code is

> 7
> 8

Example 3

```
1   var num1:int = 3;
2   var num2:int = 7;
3   var num3:int = 9;
4   num1 = ++num2  + num3--;
5   trace (num1);
6   trace (num2);
7   trace (num3);
```

Evaluation

The expression on line 4 reassigns new values to both num2 and num3. Because line 4 is an assignment statement, num1 will be assigned a new value. In the end, the statement on line 4 is actually three assignment statements combined into one. It can be deconstructed as follows:

1. ++num2;   Performed first because of the prefix ++.

2. num1=num2+num3;   Main assignment is performed after the prefix operations.

3. num3--;   Once all prefix and main assignments are performed, the remaining postfix operations are performed.

The output produced by this segment of code is

> 17
> 8
> 8

3.2.3 Compound Assignment Operators

All of the arithmetic operators have corresponding assignment operators called compound assignment operators, shown in Table 3-4.

TABLE 3-4 Compound Assignment Operators

Operator	Operation
=	Simple assignment
+=	Compound addition assignment
-=	Compound subtraction assignment
*=	Compound multiplication assignment
/=	Compound division assignment
%=	Compound modulus assignment

Compound operators combine the assignment operator, =, with an arithmetic operator and provide shorthand notation for assignments statements. For example, the statements in the following segment of code are equivalent. Both perform the same operation of adding 5 to the variable num1.

```
1   num1 = num1 + 5;
2   num1 += 5;
```

Table 3-5 shows a selection of equivalent assignment statements.

TABLE 3-5 Equivalent Assignments

Assignment Statement	Equivalent to
num1 += num2 + num3;	num1 = num1 + num2 + num3;
num1 /= num2;	num1 = num1 / num2;
num1 *= 2;	num1 = num1 * 2;
num1 %= num2 + num3;	num1 = num1 % (num2 + num3);
num1 -= num3;	num1 = num1 - num3;

Consider the following example.

Example

```
1   var sum:Number = 3;
2   var num1:Number = 4;
3   sum += 1.0 / num1++;
4   trace (sum);
5   trace (num1);
```

Evaluation

The expression on line 3 reassigns new values to both `sum` and `num1`. The value in `num1` is incremented last because it is a post-increment. It can be deconstructed as follows:

1. `sum = sum + 1.0 / num1;`

2. `num1++;`

The output produced by this segment of code is

```
3.25
5
```

■ 3.3 The Basics of Writing AS3 Functions

AS3 programs are a collection of functions—that is, small subprograms within a program. The main function within the programs used in this chapter is the constructor. The constructor function runs immediately when the program is launched.

Using functions in a program not only is required by AS3, but also reduces the complexity of a program, thereby greatly improving the program's readability. A primary goal when using functions is to take a complex problem and subdivide it into smaller pieces. In the end, the complete program is constructed from multiple smaller and easier to solve functions.

3.3.1 Function Design

Functions facilitate problem solving by dividing the program's multiple tasks into single tasks and then executing each task in a function. This process is sometimes referred to as "divide and conquer." A good example is the Car Loan Calculator application from the previous chapter. This problem required accomplishing three primary goals, which were assigned to three smaller functions, `carApp()`, `getInput()`, and `computeLoan()`:

1. The main function, `carApp()`, was the constructor and initialized the environment. It displayed the welcome screen and began the process of waiting for the user to click a button to get started. Once the button was clicked, the function `getInput()` was called.

2. The `getInput()` function had the main objective of getting information from the user. It began by displaying the input screen for the user to input the car loan information. Once the necessary input was entered, the function `computeLoan()` was called.

3. The `computeLoan()` function was responsible for performing the computations and communicating the relevant car loan information to the user.

These functions performed a single specific job by executing tasks in a precise order. Once merged together, these functions accomplished the larger overall task.

In addition to subdividing code in manageable pieces, functions offer another benefit. When a task must be performed many times in an application, this task can simply be written as a function that can be called many times.

3.3.2 Defining a Function

The first line of a basic function consists of a function heading, which specifies the name of the function. Following the function name is a pair of parentheses that will hold a listing of data called parameters. Parameters will be discussed in a later chapter. For now, recognize that these parentheses are left empty to indicate a simple function.

Determining the set of instructions to be included in a function is much like designing an algorithm for a program, albeit on a much smaller scale. The block of instructions within a function must be enclosed in curly brackets.

AS3 allows functions to be declared inside or outside other functions. In this text, we have chosen to declare functions independently of other functions. This approach leads naturally to the study of object-oriented programming and keeps the code uncluttered and improves readability.

The syntax of a simplified AS3 function definition follows.

```
function name_of_function () {
    statement 1;

    statement 2;
    statement 3;
    .
    .
    .
    statement n;
}
```

Function Heading

A function heading must contain the reserved word `function`. The function name can be any valid identifier that uniquely recognizes the function. The opening and closing parentheses, (), can be left empty or used to provide information. They are necessary for function definitions. An open curly bracket, {, precedes the function body.

Function Body

The body of the function must follow the open curly bracket. This section contains a collection of AS3 statements that will solve the task at hand.

Function Ending

All functions must end with a closed curly bracket, }.

Take a look at the following example.

Example

```
1   function displayQuote() {
2      trace("The parts of the universe . . . all are connected ");
3      trace("with each other in such a way that I think it to be ");
4      trace("impossible to understand any one without the whole.");
5   }
```

Evaluation

This example shows a complete function definition. This function, which is named displayQuote(), contains and controls the execution of three trace statements. These statements are shown on lines 2–4 and are enclosed in {}. Furthermore, statements within the function body are indented for readability.

The output produced by this function is a famous quote made by the well-known seventeenth-century French mathematician and physicist Blaise Pascal.

3.3.3 Calling a Function and Managing the Flow of Control

Understanding how functions work requires an understanding of the flow of control when a function is called. A function call can be made as a statement or within an expression. In either case, a function is called using its unique identifier name. To keep things simple, we will explore function calls as statements in this chapter and then as expressions in a later chapter, when we examine functions in more depth.

Once a function is called, program control is passed to the function in question. Each instruction within this function is then executed. Once the instruction set has completed execution, control is returned to the calling function, at the precise point where it left off.

The next two examples demonstrate function calls.

Example 1

The code example shown in Figure 3-1 illustrates the flow of control when the function greet() is called.

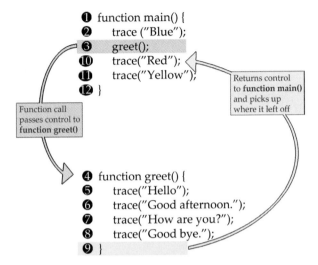

❶ function main() {
❷   trace ("Blue");
❸   greet();
❿   trace("Red");
⓫   trace("Yellow");
⓬ }

Returns control to **function main()** and picks up where it left off

Function call passes control to **function greet()**

❹ function greet() {
❺   trace("Hello");
❻   trace("Good afternoon.");
❼   trace("How are you?");
❽   trace("Good bye.");
❾ }

| FIGURE 3-1 Code segment illustrating a function call and flow of control.

Evaluation

The first function declared is main(), which contains four statements, including a function call to greet(). The flow of operations for this entire segment is executed in a strict sequence:

Operations 1–2: The first line is the function definition of main(), followed by the display of "Blue."

Operation 3: greet() is called. The set of parentheses, (), is used by AS3 to specify greet() as a function call. Program control is passed to greet().

Operations 4–8: The four trace statements in the function greet() are executed.

Operation 9: greet() exits with a closed curly bracket, }. Control is returned to main() where it left off.

Operations 10–11: The two trace statements execute.

Operation 12: main() ends with a curly bracket, which ends the program.

The output produced by the code segment is

```
Blue
Hello.
Good afternoon.
How are you?
Good bye.
Red
Yellow
```

Example 2

```
1   function funcA() {
2       trace("Inside funcA");
3       trace("funcA calling funcB");
4       funcB();
5       trace("funcA calling funcC");
6       funcC();
7       trace("Ending funcA");
8   }
9   function funcC() {
10      trace("Inside funcC");
11      trace("Ending funcC");
12  }
13  function funcB() {
14      trace("Inside funcB");
15      trace("funcB calling funcC");
16      funcC();
17      trace("Ending funcB");
18  }
```

Evaluation

This example defines three complete functions: funcA(), funcC(), and funcB(). Upon examination, the following should be noted:

- funcB is called only by funcA(). [Line 4]

- funcC() is called by both funcA and funcB. [Lines 6 and 16]

The ability to call functions and pass control elsewhere is a powerful concept in programming. With this technique, functions can appear in any order within the program. This example also demonstrates that a task, such as the trace statements found in funcC(), can be performed repeatedly by calling the function many times. Placing the code for a task that will occur over and over again in a function will eliminate the need for duplicate code.

The output produced by this code segment is

```
Inside funcA
funcA calling funcB
Inside funcB
funcB calling funcC
Inside funcC
Ending funcC
Ending funcB
funcA calling funcC
Inside funcC
Ending funcC
Ending funcA
```

Example 3

```
1   package {
2       import flash.display.*;
3       public class playApp extends MovieClip {
4           function playApp() {
5               red();
6               greet();
7           }
8           function red() {
9               trace("RED APPLES.");
10          }
11          function greet() {
12              trace("GOOD AFTERNOON.");
13          }
14      }
15  }
```

Evaluation

This example shows a complete packaged AS3 program. The first statement following the keyword `package` is used to import the required library class `flash.display.*`. Line 3 of the program begins the class definition for `playApp()`.

Within the class definition are the three functions used by this program: `playApp()`, `red()`, and `greet()`. All three functions have the requisite heading, body, and closing curly bracket, }. The first function, `playApp()`, is the class constructor and, therefore, the main function. `playApp()` will automatically run when the program is launched; in this example, it also controls the flow of the program. A function call to `red()` appears on line 5, which displays the string "RED APPLES." and then returns control back to `playApp()`. Execution will continue on line 6, with a function call to `greet()`.

The output produced by this segment of code is

RED APPLES.
GOOD AFTERNOON.

Example 4

```
1  package {
2     import flash.display.*;
3     public class playApp extends MovieClip {
4        function playApp() {
5           green();
6           hello();
7        }
8        function green() {
9           trace("GREEN APPLES");
10          green();
11       }
12       function hello() {
13          trace("HELLO.");
14          green();
15       }
16    }
17 }
```

Evaluation

This example illustrates code reuse as a complete AS3 file. It also contains an error—the function green() calls itself. This by itself is not the error, but rather the fact that the recursive calling of itself, in this case, has no means of returning control to the function that initiated the call.

3.3.4 Event Parameters

The functions in the previous examples used a set of parentheses with nothing in them. In some situations, however, information is placed in the parentheses as a way to pass along data that is needed by a function to perform its required tasks. This data is referred to as a **parameter** or a **list of parameters**. The concept of parameters will barely be touched on here except to provide a brief but necessary look into coding with buttons. Parameters and functions will be covered in more depth in Chapter 8.

Event parameters are important to AS3 because Flash applications are often designed with interface systems that contain buttons or triggers that require the user to interact with the program using the mouse. The following example demonstrates an application featuring a button and an AS3 function with an event parameter.

Example 1

Consider an application that features a button on the Stage named SimpleBtn. This button will be activated by the user with a click of the mouse.

AS3 provides mouse events that listen for mouse interactions on display objects, such as the SimpleBtn button. To listen for an event in which a button on the Stage is clicked, the addEventListener() function is used, as shown in line 2.

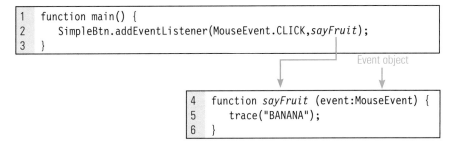

```
1    function main() {
2        SimpleBtn.addEventListener(MouseEvent.CLICK,sayFruit);
3    }
```

Event object

```
4    function sayFruit (event:MouseEvent) {
5        trace("BANANA");
6    }
```

The click event, specified with MouseEvent.CLICK on line 2, is handled by a function call along with an event parameter. In other words, when the user clicks the SimpleBtn on the Stage, the function sayFruit() on line 4 is called and an event parameter is passed. The parameter in this case is the **event object** event:MouseEvent. The single task of function sayFruit() is to display "BANANA"; event:MouseEvent is used to tell the function that it is responding to a mouse event.

Example 2

```
1    package {
2        import flash.display.*;
3        class main extends MovieClip {
4            function main() {
5                apples();
6                HelloBtn.addEventListener(MouseEvent.CLICK,sayHello);
7            }
8            function sayHello (event:MouseEvent) {
9                trace("HELLO.");
10               apples();
11           }
12           function apples() {
13               trace("RED GREEN.");
14           }
15       }
16   }
```

Evaluation

This complete program example illustrates two types of functions. The function `apples()` is a simple function called by the main function and requires no parameters. The `sayHello()` function is called only after the user has clicked the button on the Stage named `HelloBtn`. Because an `addEventListener` initiates this function, it requires an event parameter. The output produced by this segment of code, once the `HelloBtn` has been clicked, is

```
RED GREEN
HELLO.
RED GREEN
```

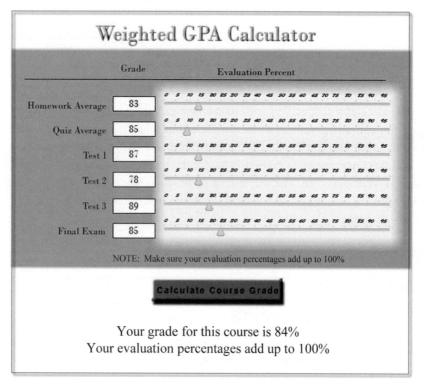

▌ FIGURE 3-2 GPA application.

■ **3.4 Case Study 1: GPA Calculator with Weighted Averages**

Problem   The objective of this case study is to create an interactive application, shown in Figure 3-2, to calculate the grade-point average (GPA) for a course that grades students on homework, quizzes, three tests, and a final exam. This application computes the course grade using a weighted average based on the percentage weights each area of evaluation is assigned—that is, the homework average, quiz average, test 1 score, test 2 score, test 3 score, and final exam. This application will primarily be used to compute the course grade, but a student will find further use for this application as a "what if" analysis tool. Students can specify hypothetical scores and averages, as well as the weights (percentages) identified in the course syllabus.

Problem Analysis   A weighted average involves multiplying the grade of each area of evaluation by its percentage and summing the products. For example, if a student scores a 90 on test 1, which is valued at 25% of the final course grade, and an 80 on the final exam, which is valued at 75% of the grade, the weighted average formula would be

GPA = 90 * .25 + 80 * .75

This application must perform the following general tasks:

1. Provide input text fields for the user to enter the homework average, quiz average, test 1 score, test 2 score, test 3 score, and final exam score.
2. Provide the user with a button to start the GPA calculation process.
3. Get the input values from the text fields and store them in the appropriate variables.
4. Compute the GPA.
5. Display the GPA.

Visual Design   This application will require the input of evaluation scores and weights (percentages) and will produce an output of the calculated GPA results. A single interface screen will be used that requires only one frame in the Timeline.

This interactive application will provide input text fields for the user to enter his or her homework average, quiz average, test scores, and final exam score, and sliders for the input of percentage weights. In addition to the input demands, there will be a button to activate the calculations and a single output text field to display the results. Table 3-6 lists the complete set of visual objects required by this application. Figure 3-3 identifies each object on the interface screen.

TABLE 3-6 Visual Objects Used in the Input/Output Screen

Visual Object Name	Type of Object	Description of the Object
Input1	Input text field	Input of average homework score
Input2	Input text field	Input of average quiz score
Input3	Input text field	Input of score on test 1
Input4	Input text field	Input of score on test 2
Input5	Input text field	Input of score on test 3
Input6	Input text field	Input of final exam score
Output1	Dynamic text field	Used to display the computed GPA
GPAbutton	Button	The interactive button, labeled "Calculate Course Grade," to start the computation process
Slider1	Slider UI component	Input of homework weight percentage
Slider2	Slider UI component	Input of quiz weight percentage
Slider3	Slider UI component	Input of test 1 weight percentage
Slider4	Slider UI component	Input of test 2 weight percentage
Slider5	Slider UI component	Input of test 3 weight percentage
Slider6	Slider UI component	Input of final exam weight percentage

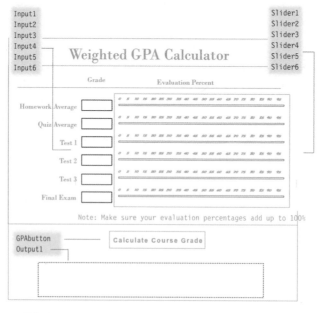

I   FIGURE 3-3 Screen objects for the GPA application.

Algorithmic Design   The AS3 code for this application will consist of two functions, gpaApp() and calculateGrade(), as described in Table 3-7. Figure 3-4 shows the relationship between the two functions. Notice that gpaApp() calls the function calculateGrade().

TABLE 3-7 GPA Program Functions

Function Name	Description
gpaApp()	This function is the main function as well as the class constructor. As a class constructor, it launches when the application begins. gpaApp() calls the next function.
calculateGrade()	This function reads the values input by the user and computes the GPA. It also displays the results.

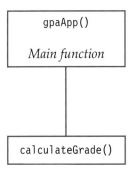

I FIGURE 3-4 Relationship structure of functions for the GPA application.

The first lines of the AS3 file are used to construct the required class package and import the necessary library classes. On line 3, the flash.display library class is a base class of the main function gpaApp(). This will be discussed in detail in later chapters. On line 4, the flash.events library class is necessary for the button interactivity. The last two lines of the AS3 file contain closing curly brackets to close the gpaApp() class and the package.

```
1   package {
2
3      import  flash.display.*;
4      import  flash.events.*;
5
6
7      public class gpaApp extends MovieClip {
8
```
⋮
```
64      }  //END OF THE CLASS -  gpaApp
65  }      //END OF THE PACKAGE
```

These two functions are designed as follows:

Function GPAapp() Design   The main algorithm, GPAapp(), is simply the class constructor function that loads immediately once the application is launched. The objective of this function is to construct a listener event that waits for the user to click GPAbutton. Once this button is clicked, the algorithm calculateGrade() is called.

```
9   function GPAapp() {
10      //TASK: LISTEN FOR THE USER TO CLICK THE BUTTON GPAbutton
11      GPAbutton.addEventListener(MouseEvent.CLICK,calculateGrade);
12  }
13
```

Function calculateGrade() Design   The calculateGrade() function is subdivided into four tasks.

    Task 1. Declare the variables that will store the grades along with the weighted percentages for each area of evaluation. These values will be input by the user using input text fields and sliders. In addition, the gpa variable is defined to hold the value of the main computation of the application.

    Task 2. All of the average scores and the test scores are entered by the user in input text fields. These values must be read into the variables declared in Task 1.

    Task 3. The weights (percentages) are input by the user. Once read from the slider values, the weight variables are initialized to percent values. For example, if homework is weighted as 15%, the variable hwWeight should be initialized to .15. The application requires six weights.

    Task 4. Compute the weights of each evaluation.

    Task 5. Use the computed weights to compute the gpa and convert its type to an integer.

    Task 6. Display the computed gpa in the dynamic text field named output1. The type conversion String is used to turn the numeric value of gpa into a string.

```
14   function calculate(event:MouseEvent) {
15   //TASK 1: DECLARE VARIABLES FOR STORING INPUT VALUES
16
17      //GRADES FOR INDIVIDUAL EVALUATIONS
18      var hw:Number;          // HOMEWORK GRADE
19      var quiz:Number;        // QUIZ GRADE
20      var test1:Number;       // TEST1 GRADE
21      var test2:Number;       // TEST2 GRADE
```

```
22   var test3:Number;        // TEST 3 GRADE
23   var finalExam:Number;     // FINAL EXAM GRADE
24
25   //PERCENT WEIGHTS USED IN THE CALCULATIONS
26   var hwWeight:Number;          // HOMEWORK WEIGHT
27   var quizWeight:Number;        // QUIZZES WEIGHT
28   var t1Weight:Number;          // TEST 1 WEIGHT
29   var t2Weight:Number;          // TEST 2 WEIGHT
30   var t3Weight:Number;          // TEST 3 WEIGHT
31   var finalExamWeight:Number; // FINAL EXAM WEIGHT
32
33   //VARIABLE FOR FINAL GPA CALCULATION
34
35   var gpa:int;
36
37   //TASK 2:  READ GRADES FROM THE INPUT TEXT FIELDS
38   hw = Number(Input1.text);
39   quiz = Number(Input2.text);
40   test1 = Number(Input3.text);
41   test2 = Number(Input4.text);
42   test3 = Number(Input5.text);
43   finalExam = Number(Input6.text);
44
45   //TASK 3: STORE EVALUATION WEIGHTS FROM SLIDERS
46   hwWeight = int(Slider1.value) / 100;
47   quizWeight = int(Slider2.value) / 100;
48   t1Weight = int(Slider3.value) / 100;
49      t2Weight = int(Slider4.value) / 100;
50   t3Weight = int(Slider5.value) / 100;
51   finalExamWeight = int(Slider6.value) / 100;
52   //TASK 4:  COMPUTE THE VALUE OF EACH GRADE EVALUATION
53   hw *= hwWeight;
54   quiz *= quizWeight;
55   test1 *= t1Weight;
56   test2 *= t2Weight;
57   test3 *= t3Weight;
58   finalExam *= finalExamWeight;
59   //TASK 5: COMPUTE THE GPA
60   gpa = int(hw + quiz + test1 + test2 + test3 + finalExam);
61   //TASK 6  DISPLAY THE GPA
62   Output1.text="Your grade for this course is\n" + String(gpa) + "%";
63 }
```

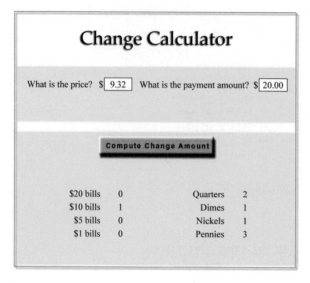

I FIGURE 3-5 Application for calculating change.

■ 3.5 Case Study 2: Make Change Calculator

Problem   This application, shown in Figure 3-5, allows the user to enter the price of an item he or she wishes to purchase, along with the payment amount. After the user clicks a button, the application computes the correct change and displays it in pennies, nickels, dimes, quarters, $1 bills, $5 bills, $10 bills, and $20 bills.

Problem Analysis   Computing the correct change after a transaction involves remainder division. For example, to compute the number of quarters to be returned, the change that is less than 1 dollar must be divided by 25 cents. The remainder of the change is then divided by 10 cents. This can be done simply by using the modulus on integer values.

This application must perform the following general tasks:

1. Provide input text fields for the user to enter the transaction information: price to be paid and the payment amount.

2. Provide the user with a button to start the correct change calculation process.

3. Once the calculation process has begun, get the input values from the text fields and store them in the appropriate variables.

4. Compute the individual number of coins and bills to be returned.

5. Display the results in multiple dynamic text fields.

Visual Design   This application will use one screen for the combined input and output. Two input text fields are required for the user to enter the price and payment amounts. The majority of the screen will consist of output text fields for the exact change amount returned. Table 3-8 and Figure 3-6 outline the required text fields used in this application as well as the button used to activate the calculations and display.

TABLE 3-8 Visual Objects Used in the Input/Output Screen

Visual Object Name	Type of Object	Description of the Object
Input1	Input text field	Used to input the price of an item
Input2	Input text field	Used to input the payment amount
Output1	Dynamic text field	Displays the number of $20 bills
Output2	Dynamic text field	Displays the number of $10 bills
Output3	Dynamic text field	Displays the number of $5 bills
Output4	Dynamic text field	Displays the number of $1 bills
Output5	Dynamic text field	Displays the number of quarters
Output6	Dynamic text field	Displays the number of dimes
Output7	Dynamic text field	Displays the number of nickels
Output8	Dynamic text field	Displays the number of pennies
ChangeBtn	Button	Starts the computation process

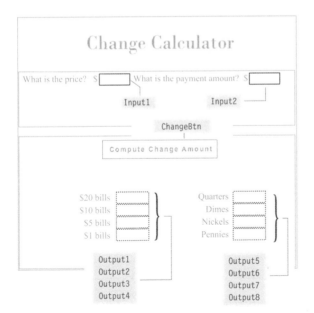

┃ FIGURE 3-6 Visual objects for the change calculator application.

Algorithmic Design   The AS3 code for this application will consist of two functions, shown in Table 3-9. Figure 3-7 shows the relationship between these two functions.

TABLE 3-9 Change Application Program Functions

Function Name	Description
changeApp()	This function is the main function as well as the class constructor. As a class constructor, it launches when the application begins. changeApp() calls the next function.
makeChange()	This function reads the values input by the user and computes the correct change. It also displays the results.

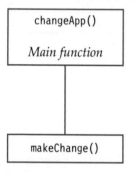

| **FIGURE 3-7** Relationship structure of functions for the change application.

As with all AS3 programs, the required class package and import library classes are placed at the start of the file. The flash.display library class is the base class needed for the main function changeApp(), and the flash.events library class is necessary for all button interactivity. The last two lines of the AS3 file contain closing curly brackets to close the document class and the package.

```
1  package {
2
3      import  flash.display.*;
4      import  flash.events.*;
5
6      public class changeApp extends MovieClip {
7
```

⋮

```
71      }   //END OF THE CLASS changeApp
72  }       //END OF THE PACKAGE
```

The constants needed for this application hold the values for individual coins and bills.

```
8   //CONSTANTS USED IN THE APPLICATION
9   const TWENTYBILL:int = 20;
10  const TENBILL:int = 10;
11  const FIVEBILL:int = 5;
12  const QUARTER:int = 25;
13  const DIME:int = 10;
14  const NICKEL:int = 5;
15
```

The two functions used in the application are designed and coded as follows.

Function changeApp() Design   The main algorithm, changeApp(), is the class constructor function. This function is initiated once the application is executed.

The sole task of this function is to construct a listener event that waits for the user to click the button instance named ChangeBtn. Once this button is clicked, the algorithm makeChange() is called.

```
16  //function changeApp: main function of the application
17     function changeApp() {
18        //TASK: LISTEN FOR THE USER TO CLICK THE BUTTON ON THE STAGE
19        ChangeBtn.addEventListener(MouseEvent.CLICK, makeChange);
20  }
21
```

Function makeChange() Design   The makeChange() function is subdivided into six tasks.

Task 1. Declare the variables that will store calculations and input values.

Variable Name	Data Type	Description
price	Number	The price of the item in the transaction
payment	Number	The payment in the transaction
returnAmt	Number	The amount of money to be returned
bills	int	The number of bills to be returned
coinage	int	The amount of coins to be returned
twenties	int	Number of $20 bills
tenners	int	Number of $10 bills
fivers	int	Number of $5 bills
ones	int	Number of $1 bills
quarters	int	Number of quarters
nickels	int	Number of nickels
dimes	int	Number of dimes
pennies	int	Number of pennies

Task 2. Read the values stored in the text fields and store them in the variables `price` and `payment`.

Task 3. Compute the amount of money to be returned to the user.

Task 4. Split the amount of money to be returned into two amounts, `bills` and `coinage`. The conversion type `int` is used to coerce the values into integers. For example, if the `returnAmt` is 12.76, then `bills` will be assigned 12 and `coinage` will be assigned 76.

An error can result in the computation of `coinage`. This variable represents the fractional part of `returnAmt`, a real value. Real values, unless they have no fractional part, are not stored exactly. This can pose a problem for some calculations but can easily be solved by the following approach: adding .005 to `returnAmt` before multiplying by 100 and performing modulus of 100. At that point, the value can be converted to an integer, resulting in a correct value for `coinage`.

Task 5. Compute the exact change using the modulus operator and division. To determine which sequence of operations is needed to make change, consider a simple part of the solution. Suppose the amount of coinage to be returned is 67 cents and we want to compute the number of dimes to return. First the quarters must be removed and the remaining value divided by 10. The single expression used to obtain this result is

`67 % 25 / 10`

`67 % 25` results in 17. 17 `/` 10 is 1, as in 1 dime.

Task 6. Display the exact change in bills and coins in the output text fields.

```
22  //function makeChange: Collects the payment information input by the user,
23  //computes and displays the owed change amounts to be returned.
24  function makeChange(event:MouseEvent) {
25      //TASK 1:  ALLOCATE MEMORY FOR VARIABLES USED FOR CALCULATIONS
26      var price:Number;       //Price of the item purchased
27      var payment:Number;     //Payment amount
28      var returnAmt:Number;   //Amount of money to be returned
29      var bills:int;          //The amount of money larger than 99¢
30      var coinage:int;        //The amount of money less than $1
31      var twenties:int;       //Number of $20 bills
32      var tenners:int;        //Number of $10 bills
33      var fivers:int;         //Number of $5 bills
34      var ones:int;           //Number of $1 bills
35      var quarters:int;       //Number of quarters
36      var dimes:int;          //Number of dimes
37      var nickels:int;        //Number of nickels
38      var pennies:int;        //Number of pennies
39
```

```
40    //TASK 2: RETRIEVE INPUT FROM THE INPUT TEXT BOXES
41    price =Number(Input1.text);
42    payment=Number(Input2.text);
43
44    //TASK 3:  COMPUTE THE AMOUNT TO BE RETURNED
45    returnAmt = payment - price;
46
47    //TASK 4:  COMPUTE THE DOLLAR AND COIN AMOUNTS SEPARATELY
48    bills = int (returnAmt);
49    coinage = int((returnAmt + .005) * 100) % 100;
50
51    //TASK 5: COMPUTE THE EXACT CHANGE
52    twenties =bills/TWENTYBILL;
53    tenners =bills%TWENTYBILL/TENBILL;
54    fivers =bills%TWENTYBILL%TENBILL/FIVEBILL;
55    ones =bills%TWENTYBILL%TENBILL%FIVEBILL;
56    quarters =coinage/QUARTER;
57    dimes =coinage%QUARTER/DIME;
58    nickels =coinage%QUARTER%DIME/NICKEL;
59    pennies =coinage%QUARTER%DIME%NICKEL;
60
61    //TASK 6: DISPLAY THE COMPUTED CHANGE IN TEXT BOXES ON STAGE
62    Output1.text=String(twenties);
63    Output2.text=String(tenners);
64    Output3.text=String(fivers);
65    Output4.text=String(ones);
66    Output5.text=String(quarters);
67    Output6.text=String(dimes);
68    Output7.text=String(nickels);
69    Output8.text=String(pennies);
70    }
```

■ 3.6 Built-in Math Functions and Constants

In the expressions we have considered so far, the operands have been simple objects like variables and number values. But an operand may also be a value returned by a function. Many languages provide predefined functions, such as square root, logarithm, and absolute value, as part of a library. This is convenient, because a program can simply call such functions when they are needed.

AS3 provides many predefined functions and stores the most commonly used math functions and constant values in a class called Math, which is essentially a mathematical library. Tables 3-10 and 3-11 list the functions and constants provided by AS3's Math library.

To call any of the functions from the Math class, a programmer uses the class name, Math, followed by the dot notation and the function name followed by its argument or list of arguments. An argument is the value operated on by the function. For example, when computing the square root of a number, such as 100, the number 100 is the argument that is passed to the square root function. When arguments are required, they are enclosed within parentheses. The syntax for a Math function call follows:

Math.*functionName* (argument1, argument2, . . . argumentn)

To access special constant values from the Math class, the constant name follows Math and the dot notation. No parentheses are needed, because constant values do not require arguments. The syntax is as follows:

Math.*constantName*

TABLE 3-10 AS3 Math Functions

Math Function Name	Description
abs(n)	Computes the absolute value of a number n.
acos(n)	Computes the arccosine (inverse cosine) of a number n and returns the value in radians.
asin(n)	Computes the arcsine (inverse sine) of a number n and returns the value in radians.
atan(n)	Computes the arctangent (inverse tangent) of a number n and returns the value in radians. This function is used to compute the angles of a right triangle.
atan2(dy, dx)	Computes the angle between two points. The value dy is the measured distance between these two points along the y-axis and dx is the measured distance along the x-axis. The angle returned is in radians.
ceil(n)	Returns the ceiling of the number n. This is the smallest integer not less than n.
cos(angle)	Computes the cosine of an angle, where angle is in radians.
exp(n)	Computes the exponential function e^n.
floor(n)	Returns the floor of a number n. This is the largest integer not greater than n.
log(n)	Computes the natural logarithm of a number n.
max(n_1, n_2, n_3, . . . n_k)	Returns the largest value of a set of numbers n_1, n_2, n_3, . . . , n_k.

TABLE 3-10 AS3 Math Functions (continued)

Math Function Name	Description
min(n₁, n₂, n₃, ... nₖ)	Returns the smallest value of a set of numbers $n_1, n_2, n_3, \ldots, n_k$.
pow(n, m)	Computes and returns n^m.
random()	Returns a random number from 0 up to 1. Arguments are not used when calling this function.
round(n)	Rounds the number n up or down to the nearest integer.
sin(angle)	Computes the sine of an angle, where angle is in radians.
sqrt(n)	Computes the square root of a number n.
tan(angle)	Computes the tangent of an angle, where angle is in radians.

TABLE 3-11 AS3 Math Constants

Constant Name	Description
E	Constant representing the base of natural logarithms, expressed as e. The approximate value is 2.71828182845905.
LN10	Natural logarithm of 10. The approximate value is 2.302585092994046.
LN2	Natural logarithm of 2. The approximate value is 0.6931471805599453.
LOG10E	Base 10 logarithm of E. The approximate value is 0.4342944819032518.
LOG2E	Base 2 of logarithm of E. The approximate value is 0.442695040888963387.
PI	The value of pi. The approximate value is 3.141592653589793.
SQRT1_2	Square root of ¹/₂. The approximate value is 0.7071067811865476.
SQRT2	Square root of 2. The approximate value is 1.4142135623730951.

The following examples illustrate several of these Math functions.

Example 1

```
Math.abs(-37.4)
```

Evaluation

This expression produces the absolute value of -37.4. The result is 37.4.

Example 2

```
trace(Math.floor(9.9456));
```

Evaluation

This trace statement displays the result of the math function floor. In this case, floor yields the integer value not greater than 9.9456. The fraction is truncated, so the integer produced by this expression is 9.

Example 3

```
trace(Math.max(5,6,7,8,9,22));
```

Evaluation

In this example, max will return the largest number in the list of supplied arguments. The output is 22.

Example 4

```
trace(Math.sqrt(100.0));
```

Evaluation

Square root is a commonly used math function. This expression calculates the square root of 100.0. The output is 10.0.

Example 5

```
trace(Math.pow(5,3));
```

Evaluation

This expression computes 5^3. The function pow requires two parameters, the base and the exponent. The output is 125.

Example 6

Task

Display a random number between 0 and 1.

Solution

Generating a random number is often a required task, particularly for game programming. In AS3, we can use the function random(), which is located in the Math library. This function requires no parameters.

```
trace(Math.random());
```

Example 7

Task

Generate a random flip of a coin while using one for heads and zero for tails.

Solution

In this example, a random number is computed and then multiplied by 2. The number is now in the range from zero up to two, $0 \leq number < 2$. By coercing it into an integer type, the number becomes either a 0 (tails) or a 1 (heads). Finally, this random flip is assigned to a variable named `coinFlip`.

```
1   var coinFlip:int = int (Math.random() * 2);
```

Example 8

Task

Generate a random toss of dice.

Solution

In this example, a random number is computed and then multiplied by 6. The number is now in the range from zero to six, $0 \leq number < 6$. By coercing it into an integer type, the number becomes 0, 1, 2, 3, 4, or 5. Adding 1 makes it a possible die toss. Tossing dice requires the sum of two die tosses. The variables `die1`, `die2`, and `dice` are used in this example.

```
1   var die1:int = int (Math.random() * 6) + 1;
2   var die2:int = int (Math.random() * 6) + 1;
3   var dice:int = die1 + die2;
```

Example 9

Task

Compute and display the volume of a sphere.

Solution

The formula to compute the volume of a sphere is $4/3\pi$ radius^3. To perform this computation, the AS3 expression will require the constant `PI`, which is also included in the `Math` class.

Note that `PI` can be implemented as a function call rather than as a constant.

```
1   var volume:Number = 4.0 / 3.0 * Math.PI() *Math.pow(radius, 3);
2   trace (volume);
```

3.7 Game Math and Trigonometry

For programmers who wish to create games, whether they are 2D or 3D, a working knowledge of trigonometry, vectors, matrices, and linear algebra is required. Trigonometric functions are particularly valuable when programming applications that utilize dynamic visual effects due to the basic necessity of calculating angles in which to change the direction of an object in motion. The conversion of radians to degrees and the computation of distances between objects and points on the Stage are also standard tasks requiring a familiarity with trigonometry.

The next two examples demonstrate useful trigonometric functions and strategies for game programming.

Example 1

In this example, we consider the two objects Bullseye and Arrow shown in Figure 3-8. The goal is to compute the angle in which to rotate Arrow so that it points directly at Bullseye and compute the distance it must travel to hit Bullseye square in the center.

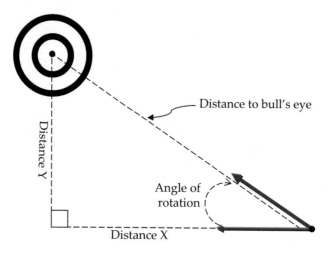

Distance to bull's eye

Distance Y

Angle of rotation

Distance X

I FIGURE 3-8 An arrow points to a bull's eye.

Solution

The first task in solving this problem is to compute the distance the Arrow must travel to hit the Bullseye. The solution to computing the angle in which to rotate Arrow relies on the fact that the distance between Bullseye and Arrow is the hypotenuse of a right triangle. A right triangle is formed by the vertical distance along the y-axis and the horizontal distance along the x-axis.

Given that we are now dealing with the properties of a right triangle, as shown in Figure 3-9, we can use basic trigonometry and the functions found in the Math library to solve this problem. The basic trigonometric expressions used to compute angles and sides of a right triangle are as follows:

- $hypotenuse^2 = opposite^2 + adjacent^2$

- $\theta = \text{Math.atan2(opposite, adjacent)};$
- opposite = sin(θ) * hypotenuse
- adjacent = cos(θ) * hypotenuse

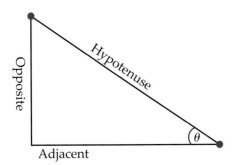

FIGURE 3-9 Right triangle with angle and hypotenuse.

The inverse trigonometric function Math.atan2() is a useful programming variation of the arctangent function because it indicates the slope or direction between two points.

Radians and Degrees It is important to point out that all inverse trigonometric functions in AS3 return angles in radians rather than degrees. In addition, trigonometric functions requiring angles, such as Math.sin() and Math.cos(), will use radian values as arguments.

Converting between radians and degrees is done as follows:

1. angleDegrees = angleRadians * 180 / Math.PI
2. angleRadians = angleDegrees * Math.PI / 180

The following code segment computes the distance and angle between Arrow and Bullseye:

```
1   //TASK 1:  COMPUTE THE DISTANCE BETWEEN THE TWO POINTS
2   var distanceX:Number = Arrow.x  --- Bullseye.x;
3   var distanceY:Number = Arrow.y  --- Bullseye.y;
4   var distance:Number = Math.sqrt(Math.pow(distanceX, 2) + Math.pow(distanceY, 2));
5
6   //TASK 2: COMPUTE THE ANGLE BETWEEN THE TWO POINTS
7   var angleRadians:Number = Math.atan2(distanceY, distanceX);
8
9   //TASK 3:  CONVERT RADIANS TO DEGREES
10  var rotationDegrees:Number = angleRadians * 180 / Math.PI;
```

Example 2

Task

Compute the *x*- and *y*-coordinates of pointA, located at the tip of Arrow. Consider that this point sits on the circumference of a circle with a given radius and an angle of rotation in degrees. We will assume the center of the circle, also the base of Arrow, resides at coordinates 100, 200.

Solution

As shown in Figure 3-10, the computations for this task can be based on the properties of a right triangle, with the length of Arrow being the hypotenuse, as well as the radius of the circle.

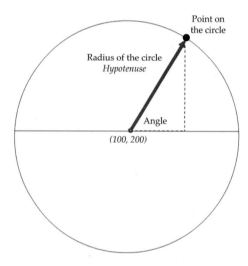

┃ FIGURE 3-10 pointA at the tip of Arrow is computed using right triangle properties.

In the following code segment, the angle of rotation is first converted to radians so that it can be used with the functions sin() and cos():

```
1  //TASK 1: CONVERT THE ANGLE TO RADIANS
2  var angleRadians:Number = angle * Math.PI / 180;
3
4  //TASK 2:  IDENTIFY THE CENTER OF THE CIRCLE
5  var centerX:Number = 100;
6  var centerY:Number = 200;
7
8  //TASK 3: COMPUTE POINT
9  pointAx:Number  = centerX  + Math.cos(angleRadians) * radius;
10 pointAy:Number  = centerY  - Math.sin(angleRadians) * radius;
```

■ 3.8 Case Study 3: Shipping Cost Calculator

Problem   Yellow Pants Delivery, whose shipping cost calculator is shown in Figure 3-11, ships packages across Canada and charges by weight for delivery. Its application allows customers to compute their shipping costs. The delivery charge for the first pound is $2.00, and $0.50 is added onto the charge for each additional 4 ounces. For example:

- A package weighing more than 16 ounces but at most 20 ounces costs $2.50 to deliver.
- A package weighing more than 20 ounces but at most 24 ounces costs $3.00 to deliver.

Problem Analysis   Computing the shipping costs can be easily done using the pre-defined `ceil` function provided by the `Math` class. For example, if the weight of the package to be shipped is 17, 18, 19, or 20 ounces, the cost is the base price of $2.00 plus the additional cost of $0.50. The extra weight is computed by subtracting 16 ounces. For every additional 4 ounces we must tack on 50 cents; therefore we can

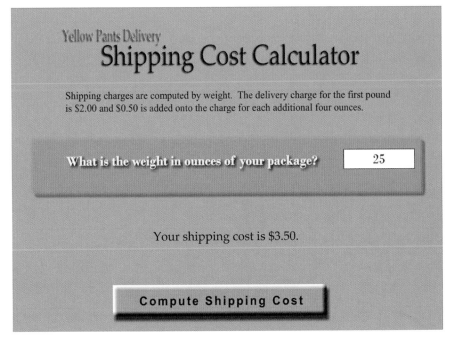

I FIGURE 3-11 Application for computing shipping costs.

divide the extra weight by 4. This results in a fraction, but we can use `ceil` to return an integer, or rather the extra amount to be multiplied by 50 cents.

Ounces	Extra Weight	Divide Extra Weight by 4	`Math.ceil(extra weight)`
17	1	1 / 4 = 0.25	`Math.ceil(0.25) = 1`
18	2	2 / 4 = 0.50	`Math.ceil(0.50) = 1`
19	3	3 / 4 = 0.75	`Math.ceil(0.75) = 1`
20	4	4 / 4 = 1.00	`Math.ceil(1.00) = 1`

Ounces	Extra Weight	Divide Extra Weight by 4	`Math.ceil(extra weight)`
21	5	5 / 4 = 1.25	`Math.ceil(1.25) = 2`
22	6	6 / 4 = 1.50	`Math.ceil(1.50) = 2`
23	7	7 / 4 = 1.75	`Math.ceil(1.75) = 2`
24	8	8 / 4 = 2.00	`Math.ceil(2.00) = 2`

This application must perform the following general tasks:

1. Provide one input text field for the user to enter the shipping weight in ounces.
2. Provide the user with a button to compute the shipping cost.
3. Once the calculation process has begun, get the input value from the input text field and store it in the `ounce` variable.
4. Compute `shippingCost`.
5. Display the results in the dynamic text field.

Visual Design   This application will use a single layout screen for the combined input and output.

Only one piece of information is required by the user—the weight in ounces of the package to be shipped. The output requires a single piece of information—the shipping cost. Table 3-12 and Figure 3-12 outline the required text fields used in this application as well as the button used to activate the calculations and display.

TABLE 3-12 Visual Objects Used in the Input/Output Screen

Visual Object Name	Type of Object	Description of the Object
`Input1`	Input text field	Used to input the weight of the package in ounces
`Output1`	Dynamic text field	Displays the shipping cost for the package
`ComputeBtn`	Button	This interactive button, labeled "Compute Shipping Cost," starts the computation process

Yellow Pants Delivery

Shipping Cost Calculator

Shipping charges are computed by weight. The delivery charge for the first pound is $2.00 and $0.50 is added onto the charge for each additional four ounces.

What is the weight in ounces of your package?   ⬚ ———— Input1

⬚ ———— Output1

Compute Shipping Cost ———— ComputeBtn

| FIGURE 3-12 Visual objects used by the shipping cost calculator.

Algorithmic Design   The AS3 code for this application will consist of two functions, shown in Table 3-13. Figure 3-13 shows the relationship between these two functions.

TABLE 3-13 Shipping Cost Program Functions

Function Name	Description
shippingApp()	This function is the main function as well as the class constructor. As a class constructor, it launches when the application begins. shippingApp() calls the function computeShipping().
computeShipping()	This function reads the values input by the user and computes the correct change. It also displays the results.

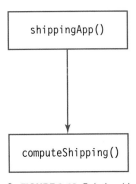

| FIGURE 3-13 Relationship of functions for the shipping cost application.

As with all AS3 programs, the required class package and import library classes are placed at the beginning of the file. The flash.display library class is the base class needed for the main function shippingApp(), and the flash.events library class is necessary for all button interactivity. The last two lines of the AS3 file contain closing curly brackets to close the document class and the package.

```
1   package {
2
3       import  flash.display.*;
4       import  flash.events.*;
5
6       public class shippingApp extends MovieClip {
7
```
⋮
```
35      }//end of the class shippingApp
36  }//end of package
```

The constants needed for this application will hold the values for shipping costs.

Constant Name	Description
BASE_COST	Base price for shipping any package. This cost is paid no matter what the weight of the package is.
ADDED_CHARGE	Added charge for each increment in weight.
ADDITIONAL	Specifies the additional increment of weight that will be charged.
POUND	One pound is equivalent to 16 ounces. This constant represents the ounces in a pound.

```
8   //CONSTANTS USED IN THE SHIPPING COST APPLICATION
9   const BASE_COST:Number = 2.0;
10  const ADDED_CHARGE:Number = .50;
11  const ADDITIONAL:Number = 4;
12  const POUND:Number = 16;
13
```

The two functions used in the application are designed and coded as described next.

Function shippingApp() Design   The main algorithm, shippingApp(), is the class constructor function. This function is initiated once the application is executed.

The sole task of this function is to construct a listener event that waits for the user to click the button instance named ComputeBtn. Once this button is clicked, the function computeShipping() is called.

```
14  function shippingApp () {
15      //TASK: LISTEN FOR THE USER TO CLOCK THE BUTTON ON STAGE
16      ComputeBtn.addEventListener(MouseEvent.CLICK, computeShipping);
17  }
18
```

Function `computeShipping()` Design　The `computeShipping()` function is subdivided into four tasks.

Task 1. Declare the variables that will store calculations and input values.

Variable Name	Data Type	Description
ounces	int	The weight in ounces of the package to be shipped
shippingCost	Number	The computed shipping cost

Task 2. The weight in ounces is stored in the `input1` text field and is read into the variable `ounces`.

Task 3. Compute `shippingCost`. This calculation uses the `Math` function `ceil` to produce the additional cost added onto the base cost.

Task 4. Display the shipping cost with two decimal places.

```
19  function computeShipping (event:MouseEvent) {
20      //TASK 1: DECLARE THE VARIABLES TO BE USED FOR COMPUTATIONS
21      var ounces: int;
22      var shippingCost:Number;
23
24      //TASK 2: CONVERT USER INPUT INTO A NUMBER AND STORE IN VARIABLE
25      ounces =Number(input1.text);
26
27      //TASK 3: COMPUTE THE BASE COST AND SHIPPING COST
28      shippingCost = BASE_COST;
29      shippingCost += Math.ceil((ounces-POUND)/ADDITIONAL)*ADDED_CHARGE;
30
31
32      //TASK 4: DISPLAY THE SHIPPING COST TO THE USER
33      output1.text="The shipping cost is $" + shippingCost.toFixed(2);
34  }
```

■ Review Questions

1. List the mathematical operators used by AS3 and identify their precedence.

2. What is the purpose of the % operator?

3. What is a mixed-type expression? Identify a mixed-type expression that is accepted in AS3. Identify a mixed-type expression that will result in a computation error.

4. What is the basic assignment operator in AS3?

5. Write a statement using the compound addition assignment operator that is equivalent to the following statement: num1 = num1 + 3;

6. Write a statement using the compound division assignment operator that is equivalent to the following statement: num1 = num1 / num2;

7. Describe the advantages of using functions in a program design.

8. Given the following declarations:

```
// CONSTANTS
const   MIN: Number = 2;
const   MAX: int   = 5;
const   REAL: Number  = 1;
// VARIABLES
var Y: int = 7;
 var  Num: int = 2;
var X: Number = 20.0;
 var Fl_Num: Number = 100.0;
 var  t: Number = 4;
```

What value is stored as a result of the following instructions? Indicate whether an error occurs in each case.

a. X = Y/Num + 4;

b. Num = 9.999;

c. X *= 3;

d. X = 2 / t;

e. Y = 2 / t;

f. X = int(5)/2;

g. X = int(5/2);

h. X = Y % 3 + MIN / t + MAX;

i. X = 3 - 4 * X;

j. Fl_Num = MAX / MIN;

k. Fl_Num = 7.0 % 2;

l. Fl_Num = 2 / 4 * Fl_Num;

m. Num = 66 * 2 + 4 % 100;

n. 65= Y;

o. Y = 17 % MAX;

p. Num += Y;

q. MIN = MAX + Fl_Num /3;

r. Y = - 10 / 2 % 4;

s. X++;

t. --Y;

u. X = --Num + Y++;

v. X += Y;

w. X = (MAX - MIN) / ++Num;

x. MAX++;

9. Evaluate the following expressions.

a. 6 - 3 - 3

b. 6 - (3 - 3)

c. 3 + 5 / 2

d. 5 / 2.0

e. 5.0 / (6 - 4 % 6)

f. 2 - 10 % 4

g. 100 / 5 / 2 % 7

h. (1 + 5) % 3 * 2 – 2

i. 4.6 - 2.0 + 3.2

j. 4.6 - 2.0 * 3.2

k. 4.6 - 2.0 / 2 * 3.2

l. -3.0 * ((4.3 + 2.5) * 2.0) - 1.0

m. ((4 * 12) / (4 + 12))

n. 4 * 12 / 4 + 12

o. 1 + 25 % 5

p. 12 % 8 % 20 % 15

10. Show the output produced by the following segments of code.

```
a. var n1:int = -22;
   n1= - n1;
   trace (n1);
```

```
b. var n1:Number = 12;
   n1 += 15.4;
   trace (n1);
```

```
c. const MAX:int = 5;
   var  n1:int = 12;
   n1 -= MAX;
   trace (n1);
```

11. What output is produced by this segment of code?

```
var fx:Number = 3.999999;
var n1:int = fx;
trace (n1);
```

12. The following segment of code is invalid. Explain.

```
var n1:int += 22;
trace (n1);
```

13. What output is produced by this segment of code?

```
var n1:int = 0;
n1 /= 0;
trace (n1);
```

14. What output is produced by this segment of code?

```
var  a:Number = 2;
var  b:Number = 4;
var  n1:Number = 27 / (a / b);
trace (n1);
```

15. The following segment of code is logically invalid. Identify the problem.

```
var  a:int = 2;
var  b:int = 4;
var  c:int = 5;
var average:int = a + b + c / 3;
trace (average);
```

16. What output is produced by this segment of code?

```
var n1:Number = Math.sqrt(-1.01);
trace (n1);
```

17. Define a function that displays what you ate for breakfast.

18. Show the flow of control in the program segment that follows. What output is displayed?

```
1   function fT() {
2       trace("Inside funcA");
3       trace("BLACK");
4       fW ();
5       trace("BLUE");
6       fG();
7       trace("VIOLET");
8   }
9   function fW() {
10      trace("ORANGE");
11      fG();
12  }
13  function fG() {
14      trace("CAR");
15      }
```

19. Which `Math` function can be used to compute 4^7?

■ **Programming Exercises**

1. Write a simple application that displays the squares and cubes of an input number. Test the application with input values whose square roots are whole numbers and whose square roots are not whole numbers.

2. Create an application that displays the square root of an input number. Test the application with a variety of input, including a negative input value. How does the computer respond to the negative input?

3. Sue and Joe operate a business in which they install carpets in local homes. Create an application for computing the cost for carpeting a room. The price for the carpet requires three input values: room length, room width, and carpet price per square yard. In addition to the price of the carpet, each job has two other charges:

    a. All carpets require padding, whose price is fixed at $3.25 per square yard.

    b. The labor for installing the carpet is $1.25 per square yard of carpet.

4. The owner of Redlands Handcrafted Bike Shop ships bikes to locations around the country. These bikes must be shipped in special containers that are available in three sizes: large, medium, and small. The large container can hold 10 bikes, the medium container holds 4 bikes, and the small container can hold exactly 2 bikes.

    Create an interactive program that reads the number of handcrafted bikes to be shipped and prints the number of large, medium, and small containers needed to send the shipment in the minimum number of containers and with the minimum amount of wasted space.

    Use constants for the number of bikes each size of container can hold. Execute this program three times and use the following numbers for input: 3, 48, and 10,598.

5. Mark installs coaxial cable for the Redlands Cable Company. For each installation, there is a basic service charge of $25.00, plus an additional charge of $2.00 for each foot of cable. Mark's boss would like an application to compute the revenue generated by Mark in any given month. For example, if Mark installs a total of 263 yards of cable at 27 different locations during the month of January, he generates $2253.00 in revenue.

4

Display Objects and Programmatic Animation

Introduction

Programming with AS3 is a highly visual endeavor and, therefore, can be subdivided into two parts. The first part is core programming, which consists of the principal elements of the programming language, such as data types, statements and expressions, and control and data structures. The second part of programming with AS3 centers on multimedia; it consists of the event system, along with the construction, manipulation, and interaction of rich multimedia elements, such as graphics, visual effects, animation, sound, and video.

Multimedia programming is the topic of this chapter. Four areas are covered:

- The `DisplayObject` class and a first look at the concepts behind the creation of programmatic animation using AS3
- Event-driven applications and the Flash event system that supports interactivity and animation
- Real-time creation and display of multimedia elements
- The looping nature of the Timeline

■ 4.1 Display Objects and the `DisplayObject` Class

Flash is a tool for creating rich media objects such as graphics, text fields, interactive buttons, animation and visual effects, and sound and video. One of the most compelling characteristics of AS3 is its ability to allow users to construct, control, and interact with media objects. Throughout the remainder of this book, media objects will be referred to as **display objects**.

The first three tutorials from Chapter 1 explored the bare basics of building simple display objects that populate a Flash movie. In terms of writing AS3 programs, it is important to understand that these display objects are members of a class called `DisplayObject`.

The `DisplayObject` class is a built-in AS3 class that describes the general underlying functionality of the display objects that occupy a Flash movie. Specifically, all display objects sitting on the Stage will inherit the characteristics and functionality passed on from the `DisplayObject` class.

153

4.1.1 DisplayObject Subclasses

The DisplayObject class encompasses a subset of display classes, which are listed in Table 4-1. These subclasses represent a specific type of display object within a Flash movie, such as the **Text field** and **MovieClip** classes we have used thus far. Each of these subclasses provides extra functionality and information beyond what the DisplayObject class provides. Thus a MovieClip display object will inherit attributes and functionality not only from the DisplayObject class, but also from the MovieClip class.

TABLE 4-1 Subclasses of the DisplayObject Class

Subclass Name	Description
SimpleButton	Interactive buttons.
Text field	Dynamic and input text fields.
MovieClip	A flexible display object that can represent a simple vector drawing or something more complex with a Timeline.
Sprite	A fundamental display object for displaying graphics. In general, a Sprite can be thought of as a MovieClip without a Timeline, or rather a vector drawing that resides in a single frame in the Timeline. This display object is created in real time.
Shape	A simple vector drawing in a geometric shape such as a circle, rectangle, triangle, or line. These display objects are drawn on the Stage in real time.
Bitmap	A display object for images such as photographs. This class allows for the creation and manipulation of nonvector images.
Video	A subclass of DisplayObject used for video. This subclass resides in the flash.media package and is used to control video elements.

The import instruction

```
import flash.display.*;
```

ensures that the entire collection of DisplayObject subclasses, as well as the subclasses that support them, will be imported in a package. For example, the **Graphics** class provides necessary drawing functionality to the **Shape** class. The asterisk in flash.display.* implies that *all* subclasses and supportive classes are imported.

It is also possible to import specific DisplayObject subclasses individually. For example, if an application requires dynamically drawing a rectangle during the execution of Flash movie, then the import statements can be

```
import flash.display.Graphics;
import flash.display.Shape;
```

We have not yet used the `Graphics` class, but it is required to support the drawing of dynamic shapes. The `Shape` class is used to represent a dynamic drawing. Although you can certainly write separate import statements for each display object subclass and their support classes, it is more common to use the all-inclusive `flash.display.*`.

Before delving into the ideas behind the display objects, we need to better understand subclass membership.

The following examples illustrate class membership for given display objects seen on the Stage. The `is` operator is used to identify whether a display object is a member of a specific class. A value of "true" is returned if the display object is a member of a class and a value of "false" is returned otherwise. Later, we will see the inheritance indicated by this membership.

Consider Figure 4-1, in which instances of a button symbol and a `MovieClip` symbol have been placed on Stage. They are named GoBtn and Ball, respectively.

GoBtn
Button

Ball
MovieClip

| FIGURE 4-1 Flash stage containing two display objects.

Example 1

What output is produced by the following three `trace` statements?

```
1   trace(GoBtn is SimpleButton);
2   trace(GoBtn is DisplayObject);
3   trace(GoBtn is MovieClip);
```

Evaluation

Line 1: The instance GoBtn seen on the Stage and in Figure 4-1 is an instance of a button symbol. Buttons are members of the `SimpleButton` class.

Line 2: Buttons are display objects and, therefore, members of the `DisplayObject` class.

Line 3: Buttons and `MovieClip`s are both interactive elements in Flash, but they are not identical. Each inherits characteristics from the `DisplayObject` class, but as members of independent subclasses, each has its own additional set of characteristics and functionality.

The output produced is

```
true
true
false
```

Example 2

What output is produced by the following three `trace` statements?

```
1    trace(Ball is DisplayObject);
2    trace(Ball is MovieClip);
3    trace(Ball is Shape);
```

Evaluation

Line 1: The instance `Ball`, shown in Figure 4-1, is a display object and, therefore, a member of the `DisplayObject` class.

Line 2: `Ball` is also an instance of a `MovieClip` symbol stored in the library, which makes it a member of the `MovieClip` subclass.

Line 3: `Ball` appears to be a simple shape—it is easily recognized as a circle. Nevertheless, it is not a member of the `Shape` class. Members of the `Shape` class must be created programmatically using AS3's graphics package. This display object was instead placed on the Stage as an instance of an existing `MovieClip` symbol stored in the library. We will explore `Shape` display objects later in the chapter.

The output produced is

```
true
true
false
```

4.1.2 `DisplayObject` Properties

An important feature of the `DisplayObject` class is the properties it supplies to all inherited display objects. A property is nothing more than a characteristic such as an object's width or *xy*-location on the Stage. Recall that the Property window of Flash reveals a collection of properties for any given display object selected on stage. When a blank part of the Stage is selected, the Property window shows the attributes of the Flash movie document, which tells us that even the Stage itself is a display object.

As members of the `DisplayObject` class, all display objects inherit a basic set of properties. Table 4-2 lists an important set of `DisplayObject` properties that can be used by AS3 programmers. As you will see, these properties behave like variables that can be assigned new values. The dot notation (`.`) is used in AS3 to access an individual property. For example, to change the location of a display object named `Ball`, we could use the following instruction:

```
Ball.x = 32;
```

Additional properties are listed in Table 4-3.

TABLE 4-2 Some Useful Properties of the DisplayObject Class

DisplayObject Property Name	Property Description
alpha	Transparency value of the display object. The value 1 represents the maximum opacity level; the value 0 represents a completely transparent, or invisible state.
Height	Height of the display object, in pixels.
mouseX	The x-coordinate of the mouse position, in pixels.
mouseY	The y-coordinate of the mouse position, in pixels.
rotation	Rotation of the object, in degrees.
rotationX	Rotation, in degrees, along the horizontal axis in 3D. (See Figure 4-2.)
rotationY	Rotation, in degrees, along the vertical axis in 3D. (See Figure 4-2.)
rotationZ	3D rotation of the object along the z-axis, in degrees. (See Figure 4-2.)
scaleX	The horizontal scale (percentage) of the object as applied from the registration point.
scaleY	The vertical scale (percentage) of an object as applied from the registration point of the object.
Visible	The visibility of the object on the Stage. This property can be set to "true" or "false."
Width	The width of the display object, in pixels.
x	The x-coordinate of the `DisplayObject` instance relative to the local coordinates of the parent `DisplayObjectContainer`.
y	The y-coordinate of the `DisplayObject` instance relative to the local coordinates of the parent `DisplayObjectContainer`.

TABLE 4-3 `MovieClip` Methods

Method	Behavior
`gotoAndPlay(frame)`	Moves the playhead to the specified frame and continues to play.
`gotoAndStop(frame)`	Moves the playhead to the specified frame and stops.
`nextFrame()`	Moves the playhead to the next frame and stops.
`prevFrame()`	Moves the playhead to the previous frame and stops.
`play()`	If the playhead has stopped on a frame, begins playing the MoveClip again.
`stop()`	The playhead will be forced to stop on the frame.

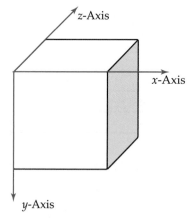

FIGURE 4-2 The Flash stage has three dimensions: x, y, and z.

The next three examples illustrate the usage of the inherited `DisplayObject` properties.

Example 1

Figure 4-3 shows four `MovieClips` on stage: `Ball`, `RightIris`, `LeftIris`, and `Mouth`. These display objects can be easily altered by reassigning the inherited display object properties. Which changes will result after the execution of the following code?

```
1    Mouth.width = 100;
2    Mouth.height = 100;
3    RightIris.visible = false;
4    LeftIris.visible = false;
5    Ball.x = 207;
6    Ball.y = 130;
7    Ball.width = 25;
8    Ball.height = 25;
```

Evaluation

This example illustrates how inherited properties for given instances can be reassigned new values so as to create a completely different visual. The reassignment of property values is often used when programming animations. This segment of code will result in the alterations that appear in the last graphic in Figure 4-3.

Display objects placed on the Stage before the AS3 code executes

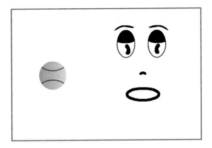

Display objects after AS3 code executes

❙ FIGURE 4-3 Programmable `MovieClips`.

Example 2

The first graphic in Figure 4-4 shows a `MovieClip` instance named `Airplane`, which sits on the Stage in a layer above the graphic of a cloud. What does the image look like after the execution of the following code?

```
1   Airplane.scaleY *=2;
2   Airplane.scaleX *=2;
3   Airplane.alpha=.75;
```

Evaluation

Both the `scaleY` and `scaleX` values of `Airplane` have been doubled, producing an `Airplane` twice the original size. The `alpha` property, representing the

MovieClip instance
of Airplane placed
on the Stage

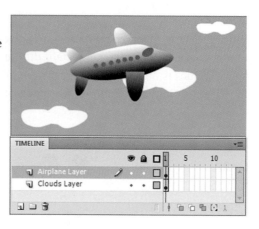

The display object
after the AS3 code
executes

I FIGURE 4-4 Programmable MovieClips placed in separate layers.

transparency of the MovieClip, is assigned a value of .75, which reduces its
original opacity by 25%. The second image in Figure 4-4 shows the alterations
resulting from this segment of code.

Example 3

In this example we consider a dynamic text field placed on the Stage containing
a binary string, as shown in Figure 4-5. This text field is named Messg, and its
default registration point is anchored in the upper-left corner of the text field.

For the DisplayObject properties of a text field to be used in AS3, its font
must be embedded in the Flash movie. Users of Flash know that embedding a
font means that its vector information is stored in the movie, making the font
appear flawlessly, even if it is not installed on the user's computer.

```
01000001
01010011
00110011
```

▌ FIGURE 4-5 A dynamic text field, Messg, containing a series of 1's and 0's placed on the Stage.

The following code examines instructions that rotate the text in three dimensions. The results of each rotation, as well as the final output of the code, are shown in Figure 4-6.

```
1   Messg.rotationZ = 60;
2   Messg.rotationX = 60;
3   Messg.rotationY = 60;
```

Line 1 rotates the dynamic text field Messg along the *z*-axis. The *z*-axis is perpendicular to the page and, as shown in Figure 4-6, is a simple clockwise rotation. The second graphic in Figure 4-6 shows the rotation of the text along the *x*-axis. The third graphic in Figure 4-6 is the rotation along the *y*-axis. Note that distortions in display objects will occur when they are rotated in 3D along the *x*- and *y*-axes. The final graphic in Figure 4-6 shows the result when all three rotations occur simultaneously.

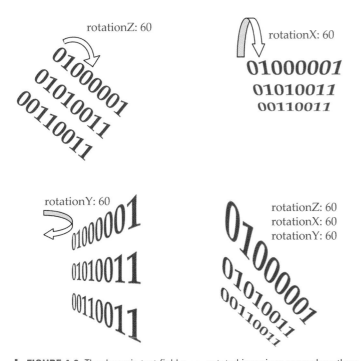

▌ FIGURE 4-6 The dynamic text field Messg rotated in various ways along three dimensions.

■ 4.2 MovieClips and the MovieClip Class

The various display objects available in Flash are compelling for different reasons. MovieClips, however, are the most important display objects when it comes to creating games and dynamic animations. These objects are programmable and can be made to do things and react in ways that are not predetermined. As a consequence, games such as billiards applications rely heavily on MovieClips.

In addition, MovieClip instances can be easily created and placed in a movie during runtime. For example, the game known as Tetris requires that falling blocks be deployed during runtime. These Tetris blocks must be created on the fly and manipulated to behave algorithmically.

This section examines the potential of MovieClips for programming animation. We begin by discussing two specific ways to construct these MovieClips (mini-movies and composite display objects).

4.2.1 MovieClips Constructed as Mini-movies

Since the tutorials in Chapter 1, we have used MovieClips primarily for decoration and fixed animation. As programmable display objects, MovieClips can take several general forms. A single-frame MovieClip represents a vector drawing, a simple graphic located on frame 1. This is also referred to as a *sprite*, which we will explore in a later section in this chapter.

At their essence, MovieClips employ one or more frames with playback functionality provided by the MovieClip class. When a MovieClip symbol is built using multiple frames, it can then be deployed as a mini-movie that will loop over and over again once it is placed on the Stage.

Example

Task

Construct a MovieClip containing a frame-by-frame animation of a man walking in place. The animation of this type of MovieClip, featuring playback behavior, will be illustrated later in this chapter.

Solution

As shown in Figure 4-7, this MovieClip symbol is an independent movie containing five frames in its Timeline. Once placed on the Stage, these frames will loop over and over again.

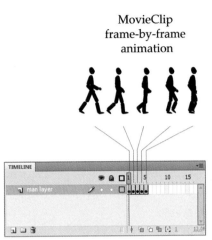

MovieClip
frame-by-frame
animation

| FIGURE 4-7 MovieClip constructed as a mini-movie of a figure walking.

4.2.2 MovieClips Constructed as Composite Objects

A MovieClip can be built as a composite object that embodies a complex real-world entity. In this way, the MovieClip serves as a container that holds other MovieClips or display objects. Consider a display object that represents a car. A car MovieClip is composed of other objects such as tires, an engine, a steering wheel, and windows, each of which may be programmed separately.

AS3 programmers can manipulate these MovieClip instances in exactly the same way as they work with simple MovieClips. The benefit of composite MovieClips is the ease with which a complex object can be modeled, maintained, and extended.

Each display object instance within a composite MovieClip must be given a unique identifier name. By doing so, it becomes possible to access the main MovieClip, as well as its composite elements, and imbue them with functionality. The next two examples illustrate the construction of a composite MovieClip and the AS3 code that manipulates it. Dot notation is used to identify composite display objects in AS3.

Example 1

Task

In this example we will build a MovieClip symbol of a man's visage composed of programmable features. This MovieClip symbol will be named ManFaceMC. An instance of ManFaceMC will be placed on the Stage and named Man.

Solution

The individual `MovieClip` symbols that will make up the final composite `ManFaceMC` must be constructed first. For this example, the eyes, brows, hair, and mouth can all be programmed to provide a change in expression. Specifically, the eyes can become large or small to reveal surprise or anger, the lips can take on a grim line, the brows can furrow, and the hair can tilt up or down to indicate a more severe or pleasant appearance.

The complete `MovieClip` symbol for `ManFaceMC` to be used for the instance of `Man` is shown in the first graphic of Figure 4-8. `ManFaceMC` contains instances of the required `MovieClip` symbols:

- `EyebrowMC` (Note: Two instances of this symbol are placed on stage representing the left and right brow.)
- `EyesMC`
- `HairMC`
- `LipsMC`

It is important that each of the `MovieClip` instances within `ManFaceMC` be named in the Properties Inspector. The names of the instances within `ManFaceMC` are as follows:

- `Eyes`
- `LeftBrow`
- `RightBrow`
- `Hair`
- `Lips`

The second graphic in Figure 4-8 shows a `MovieClip` instance placed on the Stage and named `Man`. `Man` embodies the programmable features of a character's face.

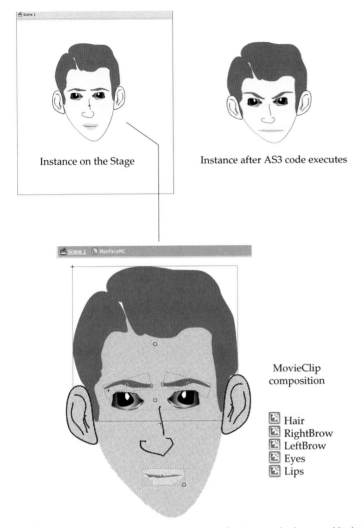

Instance on the Stage

Instance after AS3 code executes

MovieClip
composition

Hair
RightBrow
LeftBrow
Eyes
Lips

I FIGURE 4-8 A composite MovieClip symbol of a character's visage and its instance placed on the Stage.

Example 2

Task

In this example, we will write the AS3 code that utilizes the composite MovieClip elements of Man, constructed in Example 1, to alter the character's expression to exhibit anger. The expression can be accomplished by programming five alterations to Man's features:

1. Furrow the brow.

2. Enlarge the eyes.

3. Narrow the lips to appear grim.

4. Move the hair farther down on the forehead.

5. Tilt the entire head forward along the *x*-axis in three dimensions.

The final expression formed by these alterations is shown in the last graphic of Figure 4-8.

Solution

Dot notation is used to access each of the composite display objects in Man.

```
1   //TASK 1: FURROW BROW
2   Man.RightBrow.rotation -= 20;
3   Man.LeftBrow.rotation += 20;
4
5   //TASK 2: ENLARGE EYES
6   Man.Eyes.scaleY *= 1.09;
7
8   //TASK 3: MAKE MOUTH GRIM
9   Man.Lips.width += 30;
10  Man. Lips.height -=10;
11
12  //TASK 4: BRING HAIR DOWN
13  Man.Hair.y+= 20;
14
15  //TASK 5: ROTATE FACE IN 3D ALONG THE HORIZONTAL AXIS.
16  Man.rotationX += 20;
```

4.2.3 MovieClip Timeline Methods

MovieClips can play, stop, or be instructed to move the playhead to a particular frame. For MovieClip instances that employ more than one frame, the MovieClip class provides added functionality through a collection of methods for controlling the Timeline in this fashion. Table 4-3 lists some of the most commonly used MovieClip methods dealing with the Timeline, though it is not an exhaustive list.

Example 1

This example illustrates use of the MovieClip method nextFrame() for creating a simple slideshow of photographs, like that shown in Figure 4-9. A MovieClip instance appears on the Stage that is named Photos and that consists of five frames, with each frame containing a different photograph. Photos is essentially a frame-by-frame animation that will be used to present a series of images. On the lower-middle portion of the Stage is a button named NextBtn that allows the user to move to the next photo in the MovieClip.

Photos   NextBtn

FIGURE 4-9 A slideshow application consisting of a button and a collection of photos loaded into a MovieClip.

Solution

The method nextFrame(), as shown on line 15, forces the playhead to move to the next frame within the MovieClip. This method also holds the playhead in place once it moves to the next frame.

```
1   package {
2       import flash.display.*;
3       import flash.events.*;
4
```

```
5    public class SlideShowApp extends MovieClip {
6        function SlideShowApp() {
7            //TASK 1:  BEGIN THE SLIDESHOW ON THE PHOTOGRAPH IN FRAME 1
8            Photos.gotoAndStop(1);
9            //TASK 2:  REGISTER AN EVENT LISTENER FOR THE BUTTON
10           NextBtn.addEventListener(MouseEvent.CLICK,nextPhoto);
11       }
12
13       function nextPhoto(event:MouseEvent) {
14           //TASK :  ACTIVATE THE NEXT PHOTOGRAPH
15           Photos.nextFrame();
16       }
17   }
18 }
```

Example 2

Composite MovieClips containing looping elements, along with timeline functionality, provide a mechanism for building controlled programmatic animations. In this example, the user will interactively animate a character on stage by clicking a desired button. The application for this example is shown in the first graphic of Figure 4-10.

To understand this application, consider three individual MovieClip symbols representing animated loops of the character relaxing, dancing, and jumping. Relaxing is a brief animation of the character simply breathing in and out. Dancing and Jumping contain a handful of frames of choreographed movement. Figure 4-10 shows each MovieClip symbol and the frames they utilize for their animation.

Also consider a MovieClip named Man that serves as a container for these activities; this composite object stores the activities on individual frames. For example, Relaxing is placed in frame 1, Dancing in frame 2, and Jumping in frame 3.

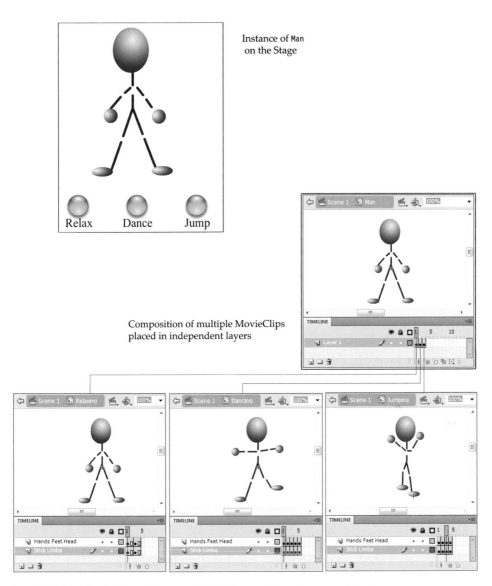

FIGURE 4-10 Application and components of a figure relaxing, dancing, and jumping.

Solution

By using the MovieClip method gotoAndStop(), the three animated MovieClips can be accessed, allowing the user to control the animation of the character on stage.

This complete example can be downloaded from the companion website and examined further.

```
1   package {
2      import flash.display.*;
3      import flash.events.*;
4
5      public class PerformApp extends MovieClip {
6         function PerformApp() {
7            //TASK 1:  HOLD PLAYHEAD AT FRAME 1 FOR MAN MOVIECLIP
8
9            Man.gotoAndStop(1);
10           //TASK 2:  ACTIVATE RELAX, DANCE, AND JUMP BUTTONS
11           RelaxBtn.addEventListener(MouseEvent.CLICK,makeRelax);
12    DanceBtn.addEventListener(MouseEvent.CLICK,makeDance);
13           JumpBtn.addEventListener(MouseEvent.CLICK,makeJump);
14        }
15     //EVENT HANDLER TO HOLD ON FRAME 1 OF MAN MOVIECLIP
16        function makeRelax(event:MouseEvent) {
17           Man.gotoAndStop(1);
18        }
19     //EVENT HANDLER TO HOLD ON FRAME 2 OF MAN MOVIECLIP
20        function makeDance(event:MouseEvent) {
21           Man.gotoAndStop(2);
22        }
23     //EVENT HANDLER TO HOLD ON FRAME 3 OF MAN MOVIECLIP
24        function makeJump(event:MouseEvent) {
25           Man.gotoAndStop(3);
26        }
27     }
28  }
```

4.2.4 Adding Custom Properties to `MovieClip` Instances

`MovieClip` instances inherit properties from the `DisplayObject` base class that are commonly associated with appearance and location. In addition to these inherited properties provided by the `DisplayObject` class, programmers routinely ascribe custom properties to individual `MovieClip` instances, particularly in cases where an application performs advanced and programmable animations.

The following example demonstrates the idea of adding programmable properties to a given `MovieClip` instance.

Example

Consider two `MovieClip` instances on the Stage with the names `Airplane1` and `Airplane2`. As both airplanes fly across the stage, each travels at a specified velocity, burns fuel, and fluctuates in altitude. Properties will be used to hold these values specific to an individual airplane. These custom properties can easily be defined as part of a MovieClip instance by simply using them in the constructor function of the document class.

Solution

The following code creates and initializes three custom properties for Airplane1 and Airplane2. Notice that Airplane1 flies at a faster velocity and higher altitude than Airplane2. Both airplanes may share the same property, but each property value is customized for the respective symbols.

```
1   package {
2       import flash.display.*;
3       import flash.events.*;
4
5       public class PlaneApp extends MovieClip {
6           function PlaneApp () {
7               //TASK 1: CREATE AND INITIALIZE VELOCITY
8               Airplane1.velocity=345;
9               Airplane2. velocity =125;
10
11              //TASK 2: CREATE AND INITIALIZE ALTITUDE
12              Airplane1.altitude=500;
13              Airplane2.altitude=270;
14
15              //TASK 3: CREATE AND INITIALIZE FUEL
16              Airplane1.fuel=70;
17              Airplane2. fuel =70;
18          }
19      }
20  }
```

■ 4.3 The Event System and Interactivity

An **event** is a mouse click, a mouse movement, the user hitting a key on the keyboard, or anything else that triggers a response. An **event-driven application** is one in which the user can interact with elements on the screen by generating an event. In the case studies we have seen so far, the button display object has been the primary event object—that is, the object from which the event is activated.

Events are an integral part of building graphical user interfaces and interactive multimedia-rich applications. An **event system** monitors the environment for routine events, such as when the user clicks a button on the Stage. An event such as this requires a mechanism not only for detecting the event, but also for delegating a response.

4.3.1 An Event Listener and Event Types

In AS3, events represent all activity that goes on between the user and the application. The first step in working with events is to register an **event listener** that simply listens and waits for a specific event to take place. We have already seen many examples of this behavior, such as when we registered an event listener for the buttons in previous case studies.

Registering an event is done using the `addListenerEvent()` method. Once an event is detected, it is communicated to an **event handler** function, which determines how to handle the event so the user receives an appropriate response.

The general format for registering listener events is the following:

EventObject.addEventListener(*EventType.EVENT*, *eventHandler*);

`EventType` is the category of the event and `EVENT` is the specific event within that category. The event types covered in this chapter are mouse events, keyboard events, and a frame event called `ENTER_FRAME`. `EventObject` identifies the active display object that is used to trigger the registered event. For example, a button is often the `EventObject` for a registered mouse click event. Listener events can be especially useful when used with display objects other than buttons.

An `eventHandler` is simply a function that responds to a triggered event. The general format for declaring an event handler is shown next. This type of function requires a single `Event` parameter that describes the event type:

function *eventHandler* (Event:*EventType*){

    }

For any given Flash application, many types of events can be triggered. The fundamental categories of events deal with the mouse, keyboard, timers, and the looping nature of frames in a timeline. All of these possibilities except timer events are discussed in the following subsections. Timer events will be explored in the final section of this chapter.

4.3.2 Mouse Events

A mouse event is typically generated by using an input device, such as a mouse, a pen, or a trackball. In AS3, `MouseEvent` is the keyword that identifies the mouse general event category. Within this category are a variety of specific mouse events, such as clicking and double-clicking. Table 4-4 shows a partial list of mouse events.

TABLE 4-4 Mouse Events

Event Name	Description
CLICK	Indicates the primary button on the pointing device has been clicked.
DOUBLE_CLICK	Indicates the primary button on the pointing device has been double-clicked.
MOUSE_WHEEL	Indicates the mouse wheel is activated.
MOUSE_DOWN	Indicates the primary button on the pointing device is being depressed.
MOUSE_MOVE	Indicates the position of the pointing device has moved vertically or horizontally.
MOUSE_OUT	Indicates the position of the pointing device has moved vertically or horizontally outside the boundary of the referenced display object.
MOUSE_OVER	Indicates the position of the pointing device is within the boundary of the referenced display object.
MOUSE_UP	Indicates the primary button on the pointing device has been released.
ROLL_OVER	Indicates the position of the pointing device has just moved within the boundary of the referenced display object. Unlike MOUSE_OVER, this event is read once.
ROLL_OUT	Indicates the position of the pointing device has just moved outside the boundary of the referenced display object. Unlike MOUSE_OUT, this event is read once.

The next three examples illustrate registered mouse events. For each of these examples, assume that we have a Flash movie containing three MovieClips—Cup, Bottle, and Hamburger—as shown in Figure 4-11.

I **FIGURE 4-11** Flash's Stage containing the MovieClip instances Cup, Bottle, and Hamburger.

Example 1

In this example, we will register an event that will be triggered if the user moves the mouse pointer off Bottle. The response to this event will be the output of the text string "Exit Bottle" in the Output window.

Registered Event

```
1    Bottle.addEventListener(MouseEvent.MOUSE_OUT, sayMyName);
```

The registered event in line 1 has three important elements:

- An event listener is registered referencing the display object named `Bottle`, which is the event object.

- `MouseEvent` is the type of event that will be triggered; the specific event is `MOUSE_OUT`. This event will be triggered when the mouse exits the blue bottle.

- The event handler (lines 2–4) is the function that will respond to the event. This function is named `sayMyName()`.

Event Handler

```
2    function sayMyName (event:MouseEvent) {
3        trace("Exit bottle");
4    }
```

Example 2

This example illustrates an event listener with no display object reference. This event will be triggered once the mouse rolls over any interactive display object sitting on the Stage: `Bottle`, `Cup`, or `Hamburger`. This event is handled by the function `whoAmI()`.

Registered Event

```
1    addEventListener(MouseEvent.ROLL_OVER, whoAmI);
```

Event Handler

The mechanism used to identify the object that triggered the event is `event.currentTarget`, as shown on line 3. The complete event handler `whoAmI()` might be coded as follows:

```
2    function whoAmI (event:MouseEvent) {
3        var whichDisplayObj = (event.currentTarget);
4        trace("whichDisplayObj");
5    }
```

Example 3

This example illustrates a registered event listener referenced by the display object `stage`. Clicking anywhere on the Stage, including a display object or a blank area on the Stage, will trigger the listener, which will respond by calling the function `anyWhere()`.

Registered Event

```
1   stage.addEventListener(MouseEvent.CLICK, anyWhere);
```

Event Handler

The event handler anyWhere might be coded as follows:

```
2   function anyWhere (event:MouseEvent) {
3       trace("You just clicked anywhere on the stage.");
4   }
```

4.3.3 Keyboard Events

The general event type called keyboardEvent is used to implement keystroke handling. This feature is especially valuable when you are creating games that require direction handling with the arrow keys. Other applications that might rely on this type of event are those that use multiple text fields for data entry. The keyboardEvent has the potential to trap the Tab or Enter keystroke and move the cursor to the next text field.

Two specific events are included in this category, as listed in Table 4-5. The KEY_DOWN event occurs when the key is pressed. The KEY_UP event is generated when the key is released. When working with text fields, the KEY_DOWN event recognizes when text is being input.

A collection of properties within keyboardEvent are available for identifying keys that have been triggered. Two of these properties are keyCode and charCode. It is useful to distinguish between these properties because they do not always return the same value.

A keyCode is the value of the physical button on the keyboard, whereas a charCode is the ASCII value of the resulting character. It is often the case that the user will press a key on the keyboard that produces different results for charCode and keyCode. For example, the A key on the keyboard has a keyCode of 65, which represents the physical button on a U.S. keyboard. However, pressing the A key will produce the lowercase character 'a', which has an ASCII value of 97. The keyCode and charCode will be the same when the user hits the A key while simultaneously holding the Shift key. The resulting character is an uppercase 'A,' which is the ASCII value 65. The keyboardEvent properties are listed in Table 4-6.

TABLE 4-5 Keyboard Events

Event Type	Description
KEY_DOWN	Keyboard events are triggered when the user interacts using the keyboard.
KEY_UP	The Event class can also be used in event listener functions.

TABLE 4-6 Keyboard Event Properties

keyEvent Property	Description
charCode	Returns the ASCII character code value of the key pressed or released.
ctrlKey	Returns true if the Ctrl key is held down. On a Macintosh, a value of true will also be returned if the Command key is held. false is returned if the Ctrl or Command key is not pressed.
currentTarget	Returns the display object that is the target of the listener event.
keyCode	Returns the key code value of the key pressed or released.
shiftKey	Returns true if the Shift key is held and false if it is not.

The next two examples illustrate registered keyboard events.

Example 1

For this example, we will assume that InputBox is the name of an input text field on the Stage. In the registered event instruction, shown on line 1, it should be clear that the event listener is referenced to InputBox. The event KEY_DOWN will be triggered during keyboard input to this text field.

The function checkKey() will respond once the user begins typing into this input text field.

Registered Event

```
1    InputBox.addEventListener(KeyboardEvent.KEY_DOWN, checkKey);
```

Event Handler

The event handler checkKey might be coded as follows:

```
2    function checkKey (event:KeyboardEvent) {
3        trace("Data is being entered into Input text field. ");
4    }
```

Example 2

This example demonstrates a registered global key event. It is created by referencing the event listener to stage.

Registered Event

```
1    stage.addEventListener(KeyboardEvent.KEY_DOWN, whatKey);
```

Note that only a narrowly defined set of keys will trigger this type of registered event. Specifically, these keys are the up arrow, the down arrow, the left arrow, the right arrow, and the spacebar. The key codes for directional keys on a U.S. keyboard are the same as the ASCII character codes.

Up arrow key: 38

Down arrow key: 40

Left arrow key: 37

Right arrow key: 39

Spacebar key: 32

Event Handler

The event handler whatKey might be coded as follows:

```
2   function whatKey (event:KeyboardEvent) {
3       trace("The key is ", event.keyCode);
4   }
```

4.3.4 Animation and the ENTER_FRAME Event

In the tutorials in Chapter 1, we saw that fixed animations can be achieved in Flash using a collection of frames containing graphics and forcing the playhead to move from frame to frame. Once the last frame in the movie is encountered, the playhead loops back to the beginning and the process repeats itself. These linear animations required no programming and, therefore, were predictable. In contrast, the creation of unpredictable or user-controlled animations can be achieved only by writing a program.

To understand programmed animations created in AS3, we need to explore the ENTER_FRAME event. This ENTER_FRAME event occurs when the playhead enters a frame. For example, if a Flash movie contains a single frame, the playhead essentially loops again and again within this single frame, and the ENTER_FRAME event is triggered each time. This ENTER_FRAME looping mechanism can also be employed with frames forced to stop with a stop() action. The importance of ENTER_FRAME as a looping mechanism derives from its use in monitoring and altering a display object within a frame loop.

Example

Consider a MovieClip instance named Ball that occupies a single frame in the Timeline, as shown in Figure 4-12. The objective of this example is to use the ENTER_FRAME event to force the Ball to roll to the right side of the Stage, as the arrow in the figure indicates.

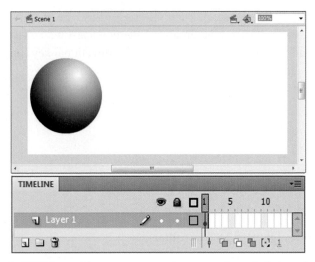

FIGURE 4-12 The MovieClip named Ball occupies a single frame in the Timeline.

By using the ENTER_FRAME looping mechanism, the position of the ball can be modified each time the playhead enters frame 1 as it endlessly loops within this single frame. At a frame rate of 20.0 fps, the position of the ball will be updated 20 times per second.

Solution

```
1   package {
2       import  flash.display.*;
3       import  flash.events.*;
4
5       public class RollBallApp extends MovieClip {
6
7           function RollBallApp () {
8               //TASK 1: INITIALIZE THE PROPERTIES FOR BALL
9               Ball.x = 20;
10              Ball.xVelocity = 3;
11
12              //TASK 2: REGISTER AN EVENT LISTENER TO LOOP IN A FRAME
13              addEventListener(Event.ENTER_FRAME,moveBall);
14          }
15
16          function moveBall (event:Event) {
17              //TASK 1: ADD BALL'S VELOCITY TO ITS X LOCATION
18              Ball.x += Ball.xVelocity;
19              //TASK 2: ROTATE BALL AS IT ROLLS
20              Ball.rotation += Ball.xVelocity;
21          }
22      }
23  }
```

Line 7: This line is the constructor for the application.

Lines 9–10: Set Ball's initial *x*-position. Create the custom property xVelocity for Ball. This property will be used to move Ball in a fixed velocity along the *x*-axis.

Line 13: The event ENTER_FRAME is registered but not referenced to any specific object. This will create a generic loop.

Line 16: This line is the declaration of function moveBall(), the event handler. The event parameter for moveBall() is simply a generic Event.

Lines 18–20: The value stored in the *x*-property of Ball is updated. Ball is also rotated by 3 degrees. These two statements will occur every time the playhead enters frame 1, creating a loop in which Ball will roll across the stage.

4.3.5 Removing an Event Listener

You may have noticed in the previous example that Ball eventually rolled off the stage. Even though we could no longer see the ball display object, the ENTER_FRAME looping mechanism continued to loop no matter what. The ball resumed rolling farther and farther away from the viewable Stage.

Once an event listener is registered, it can and will consume a small portion of the application's runtime resources. Thus, even though the ball no longer appeared on the Stage, it continued to take up resources. Not surprisingly, an over-abundance of registered listener events can make an application sluggish. Once an event listener is no longer needed, it should be removed, thereby freeing up its resources. A worst-case scenario is a Flash application overwhelmed with superfluous event listeners causing it to slow down or maybe even crash.

To remove, or unregister, an event listener, we use the method removeEventListener(). Note that removing an event listener often requires precise timing, such as when a ball rolls off the stage. The topic of making decisions based on a specific condition will be explored in a later chapter.

The general format for unregistering listener events is the following:

```
eventObject.removeEventListener(EventType.EVENT_NAME, eventHandler);
```

The following example illustrates how to remove an event listener once it is no longer needed.

Example

For this example, consider a button instance named OneTimeButton. This aptly named button reveals how it will be designed. During the execution of the application, the button can be clicked only once. Upon this event happening, a message will appear and the button will no longer respond to clicks.

Solution

This code solution shows how an event listener can be created and removed once it has accomplished its task. OneTimeButton allows the user to click and display a greeting in the Output window. Once the greeting is displayed, the listener event is removed.

Line 7: The mouse event named CLICK is registered and referenced to the button named OneTimeButton. The function that will handle the CLICK event is identified as doIt().

Line 11: The CLICK listener event is removed.

```
1   package {
2       import  flash.display.*;
3       import  flash.events.*;
4
5       public class example extends MovieClip {
6           function example () {
7               OneTimeButtton.addEventListener(MouseEvent.CLICK, doIt);
8           }
9           function doIt (event:MouseEvent) {
10              trace("You can click me only once!");
11              OneTimeButtton.removeEventListener(MouseEvent.CLICK, greet);
12          }
13      }
14  }
```

■ 4.4 Case Study 1: Animated City Scene

Problem and Analysis   In this application, a city scene becomes animated. Specifically, a car drives at a fixed velocity along a road with its wheels rotating as it moves. A small ball rolls down a sidewalk, and the sun gradually sets as time passes. In addition to the action in the animation, the car's fuel is depleted as it drives across the Stage; however, the animation will not reveal this fact. Three scenes from this animation are illustrated in Figure 4-13.

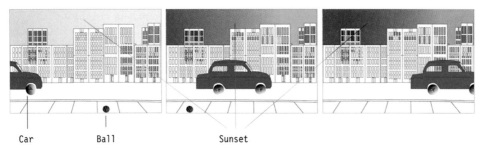

Car   Ball   Sunset

❚ FIGURE 4-13 Three snapshots of a programmed animation for the application `cityLifeApp`.

The objectives of this case study are as follows:

- Work with `MovieClip` properties.
- Explore the potential of programmed animation.
- Work with the concept of looping using the `ENTER_FRAME` event.

Visual Design   This programmed animation will require three display objects on the Stage: `Car`, `Ball`, and `Sunset`. `Car` is a composite `MovieClip` containing two nested `MovieClips` for each wheel. The `MovieClip` instance named `Sunset` is a basic rectangle containing a gradient color blend. These three `MovieClips` are identified in Table 4-7. An additional `MovieClip` is the city image, which is not included in the required display objects because it will not be programmed.

TABLE 4-7 Display Objects Used by the City Scene Animation Application

Display Object	Details
Car	`MovieClip` instance: This symbol is composed of two additional elements representing front and back wheels. These wheels are separate `MovieClip` instances with the names `Wheel1` and `Wheel2`.
Ball	`MovieClip` instance: `Ball` utilizes the Filter property, found in the Properties Inspector, to create a shadow on the sidewalk as it rolls toward the opposite end of the Stage.
Sunset	`MovieClip` instance: This symbol is created as a simple rectangular shape consisting of colors depicting a sunset. A sunset can be created by using this instance and then modifying its `alpha` property.

The main timeline is organized with five layers in a single frame. Figure 4-14 depicts this timeline. `Sunset` is placed on the bottom of all the layers so that it appears behind the city buildings so as not to obscure other display objects as it emerges into full view. The frame rate for this animation is set to 12 frames per second.

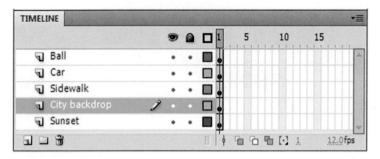

FIGURE 4-14 Timeline for `cityLifeApp`.

Program Design   The code for this application will consist of two functions, `cityLifeApp()` and `cityMoves()`, as described in Table 4-8. The relationship between these two functions is very basic. `cityLifeApp()` registers an `ENTER_FRAME` listener event, which in turn calls the function `cityMoves()`. The name of the document class for this application is `cityLifeApp`.

TABLE 4-8 Program Functions for `cityApp`

Function Name	Description
`cityLifeApp()`	The main function as well as the class constructor. This function is responsible for triggering the initial `ENTER_FRAME` event.
`cityMoves()`	The event handler for an `ENTER_FRAME` event. This function is the engine behind the animation for this application; it is responsible for all animations.

The first lines of the program construct the required class package and import the necessary library classes. On line 3, the `flash.events` library class is imported; it is necessary when working with the event system. The last two lines of the AS3 file contain closing curly brackets to close the class and the package.

```
1   package {
2       import flash.display.*;
3       import flash.events.*;
4
5       public class cityLifeApp extends MovieClip {
```

```
36      }//end of the class cityLifeApp
37   }//end of package
```

The two functions `cityApp()` and `cityMoves()` are designed as follows.

Function `cityLifeApp()` Design   Both custom properties and the built-in properties of the `MovieClip` instances are essential to this application. In this main function, custom properties must be defined. In addition, all properties used by the application will be initialized to create a starting city scene. Table 4-9 lists all properties used in this application.

TABLE 4-9 Custom Properties Assigned to `cityApp` MovieClips

MovieClip Instance	Property
Ball	x: the current location of Ball on the x-axis.
	xVelocity: the fixed velocity of the ball along the x-axis.
Car	x: current location of Car on the x-axis.
	xVelocity: the fixed velocity the car will travel along the x-axis.
	fuelAmt: amount of fuel in the car's gas tank.
Sunset	alpha: current visibility of the sunset as it gradually fades into view.
	fadeInAmt: the fixed value for the amount that the sunset will emerge or fade in.

As the main algorithm, `cityLifeApp()` has two primary tasks.

Task 1: Initialize the MovieClip instances that will become animated during the execution of the movie. The Ball and Car positions are set to the opposite ends of the Stage. Sunset begins in a completely transparent state. This task also entails creating and initializing custom properties associated with each MovieClip instance.

Task 2: Register the listener event for performing an animation within the frame loop, ENTER_FRAME.

```
6    function cityLifeApp () {
7        //TASK 1 : INITIALIZE THE MOVIECLIP INSTANCES ON STAGE
8        Ball.x = 500;
9        Ball.xVelocity = -2;
10
11       Car.x = 10;
12       Car.xVelocity = 2;
13       Car.fuelAmt = 20;
14
15       Sunset.alpha = 0;
16       Sunset.fadeInAmt = .007;
17
18       //TASK 2: ADD A LISTENER TO LOOP WITHIN THE FRAME
19       addEventListener(Event.ENTER_FRAME,cityMoves);
20   }
21
```

Function cityMoves() Design   The function cityMoves() drives the animation. As the event handler for the ENTER_FRAME event, it will perform the following three tasks at a frame rate of 12 fps:

Task 1: Drive the car across the Stage by adding its xVelocity to its x position. To enhance the animation, the embedded wheels of the car are rotated. As the car is driven, its fuel will be burned, or decremented by 0.25 gallon with each frame loop.

Task 2: Roll the ball down the sidewalk in the opposite direction of the car by subtracting its xVelocity from its x position. As the ball moves, its rotation is adjusted.

Task 3: The sunset gradually becomes visible as its alpha property value is incremented by the fadeIn value.

```
22  function cityMoves(event:Event) {
23      //TASK 1:  DRIVE THE CAR ACROSS THE STAGE
24      Car.x += Car.xVelocity;
25      Car.Wheel1.rotation += 3;
26      Car.Wheel2.rotation += 3;
27      Car.fuelAmt -= .25;
28
29      //TASK 2: ROLL BALL IN THE OPPOSITE POSITION OF THE CAR
30      Ball.x -= Ball.xVelocity;
31      Ball.rotation -= 5;
32
33      //TASK 3:  SUNSET GRADUALLY APPEARS
34      Sunset.alpha += Sunset.fadeIn;
35  }
```

The frames per second rate is effective within a range of 6 to 120 fps. However, 15 fps is considered by many in the industry to be the minimum rate to achieve the illusion of a moving image. When creating games, a higher frame rate is often desirable. A slower frame rate of 10 fps and a higher frame rate of 60 fps may cause imperfections in an otherwise smooth animation.

4.5 Case Study 2: Garden Arrangement and the Buzzing Bee

Problem and Analysis   In this application, as shown in Figure 4-15, a garden contains six flowers and a bee. Each flower is draggable and can be plucked from the garden and arranged in the flower pot sitting on stage. The bee is attracted to the cursor, constantly following the user as he or she tries to arrange the flowers in the flower pot.

Bee   Flower1   Flower2   Flower3   Flower4   Flower5   Flower6

Display objects
placed on the Stage

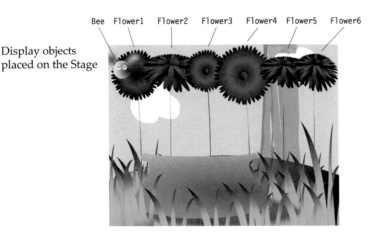

Final flower
arrangement

❙ FIGURE 4-15 Interactive application containing flowers and a bee.

The objectives of this case study are as follows:

- Work with the MOUSE_UP and MOUSE_DOWN events.
- Use the methods startDrag() and stopDrag().
- Explore the potential of event.currentTarget for recognizing the display object being dragged.
- Compute distances between objects so as to program realistic motion.

Visual Design   This application requires seven interactive display objects, as shown in Figure 4-15. Each of these display objects is a MovieClip instance. They are named as follows: Flower1, Flower2, Flower3, Flower4, Flower5, Flower6, and Bee.

The arrangement of the graphics in the Timeline will take into consideration that Bee must not be obscured from view at any time and, therefore, will occupy the top layer. Figure 4-16 shows the visual for this Timeline. The frame rate for this animation is set to 20 fps.

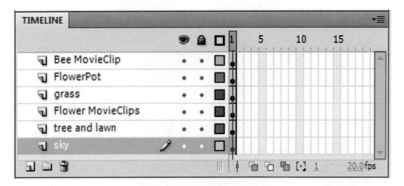

❘ FIGURE 4-16 Timeline for the garden application.

Program Design   The AS3 code for this application consists of four functions, as described in Table 4-10. The document class for the application is named gardenApp and the AS3 file is named gardenApp.as.

TABLE 4-10 gardenApp Program Functions

Function Name	Description
gardenApp()	The main function as well as the class constructor. Its primary tasks involve initialization and registering the events for the application.
flowerStartDrag()	The event handler that responds to the user dragging a flower to a new location on the stage. MOUSE_DOWN is the event that triggers this function.
flowerEndDrag()	The event handler that responds to a MOUSE_UP event. This function is called to signify the end of a flower being dragged.
beeFollowsMe()	The event handler that responds to an ENTER_FRAME event. This function provides the mechanism that allows Bee to follow the mouse cursor.

The first lines of the AS3 file are used to construct the required class package and import the necessary library classes. The flash.display library class is a base class of the main function gardenApp(). It is also the base class for the display objects on stage. The flash.events library class handles the registered events needed for this application.

```
1   package {
2      import flash.display.*;
3      import flash.events.*;
4
5      public class gardenApp extends MovieClip {
6
```

⋮

```
52     }//end of the class gardenApp
53  }//end of package
```

The four functions of the application are designed as follows.

Function gardenApp() Design   The main algorithm, gardenApp(), which is also the class constructor function, will load once the application is launched. The most important task performed by this function is the registration of the listener events.

Task 1: The MovieClip instance Bee will follow the cursor at a fixed velocity. To imbue Bee with its own individual velocity, this property is created and initialized.

Task 2: Construct exactly two listener events for every flower instance located on stage. The first event is a MOUSE_DOWN: Once the user begins to drag a flower, the mouse will be down. The second event is a MOUSE_UP: When the user finishes dragging a flower and releases the mouse, the mouse will be up.

Task 3: An ENTER_FRAME listener event is registered. This event will be used to compute the new location of Bee at every frame loop interval. The handler for this event is the function beeFollowsMe().

```
7   function gardenApp() {
8      //TASK 1: CREATE VELOCITY PROPERTY FOR BEE
9      Bee.velocity = 20;
10
11     //TASK 2:  ADD LISTENER EVENTS TO EACH FLOWER
12     Flower1.addEventListener(MouseEvent.MOUSE_DOWN, flowerStartDrag);
13     Flower1.addEventListener(MouseEvent.MOUSE_UP, flowerEndDrag);
14     Flower2.addEventListener(MouseEvent.MOUSE_DOWN, flowerStartDrag);
15     Flower2.addEventListener(MouseEvent.MOUSE_UP, flowerEndDrag);
16     Flower3.addEventListener(MouseEvent.MOUSE_DOWN, flowerStartDrag);
17     Flower3.addEventListener(MouseEvent.MOUSE_UP, flowerEndDrag);
18     Flower4.addEventListener(MouseEvent.MOUSE_DOWN, flowerStartDrag);
19     Flower4.addEventListener(MouseEvent.MOUSE_UP, flowerEndDrag);
20     Flower5.addEventListener(MouseEvent.MOUSE_DOWN, flowerStartDrag);
21     Flower5.addEventListener(MouseEvent.MOUSE_UP, flowerEndDrag);
22     Flower6.addEventListener(MouseEvent.MOUSE_DOWN, flowerStartDrag);
23     Flower6.addEventListener(MouseEvent.MOUSE_UP, flowerEndDrag);
24
25     //TASK 3: ADD LISTENER FOR A FRAME EVENT
26     addEventListener(Event.ENTER_FRAME,beeFollowsMe);
27  }
28
```

Function flowerStartDrag() Design   There are six flowers to arrange, each of which will be dragged in exactly the same manner. The generic event handler flowerStartDrag() is designed to be used with all of the flowers. The specific flower being dragged can be easily recognized using event.currentTarget, as shown in line 30.

Once the flower is identified, its method `startDrag()` can be called (line 31). The `startDrag()` method is native to AS3.

```
29  function flowerStartDrag(event:MouseEvent) {
30       //TASK 1:  IDENTIFY WHICH OBJECT IS BEING DRAGGED
31       var gardenObject = (event.currentTarget);
32       //TASK 2:  TRIGGER A METHOD THAT STARTS THE DRAGGING PROCESS
33       gardenObject.startDrag();
34  }
35
```

Function flowerEndDrag() Design   The `flowerEndDrag()` event handler uses `event. currentTarget` to identify which flower triggered the `MOUSE_UP` event. Once identified, the flower is released by calling the method `stopDrag()`. Like the previously used `startDrag()`, the `stopDrag()` method is native to AS3.

```
36  function flowerEndDrag(event:MouseEvent) {
37       //TASK 1:  IDENTIFY WHICH OBJECT IS BEING DRAGGED
38       var gardenObject = (event.currentTarget);
39       //TASK 2:  TRIGGER A METHOD THAT STOPS THE DRAGGING PROCESS
40       gardenObject.stopDrag();
41  }
42
```

Function beeFollowsMe() Design   Bees can be rather annoying in a garden, buzzing around while the intrepid gardener tries to tend to the plants. The virtual bee in this application is no different. You can drive bees away or move to a different location, but they will eventually find you again. The `beeFollowsMe()` function mimics this behavior. This function performs two tasks:

Task 1: For `Bee` to follow the mouse cursor, its x and y positions will be updated based on the computed distance between Bee and the mouse cursor. The position of the mouse cursor is stored in the properties `mouseX` and `mouseY`, both of which are reserved keywords.

Task 2: To create both ease of movement and the impression of evading the bee, the computed distance is divided by its velocity and then added to its location. Figure 4-17 shows this distance divided by two. In this way, Bee's position will gradually get closer to the cursor if the mouse remains in the same position.

```
43  function beeFollowsMe(event:Event) {
44     //TASK 1: COMPUTE DISTANCE FROM BEE TO CURSOR
45     var distanceX = mouseX -  Bee.x;
46     var distanceY = mouseY -  Bee.y;
47
```

```
48    //TASK 2: MOVE BEE CLOSER TO CURSOR
49    Bee.x += distanceX / Bee.velocity;
50    Bee.y += distanceY/ Bee.velocity;
51  }
```

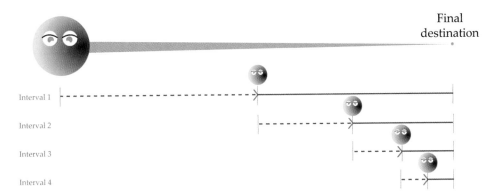

Interval 1
Interval 2
Interval 3
Interval 4

❙ FIGURE 4-17 The distance between Bee and its destination is halved at each interval.

■ 4.6 Adding and Removing Display Objects During Execution

4.6.1 The new Operator and the addChild Mechanism

In AS3, display objects can easily be added to the Stage during program execution using the new operator and the method addChild. Objects added during runtime, versus those created on the Stage or in the library beforehand, are called dynamic objects. The new operator is used to allocate the necessary memory for the dynamic object, while addChild visually places the object on the Stage.

Before discussing the addition of MovieClip instances to the Stage during runtime, which requires the introduction of an additional concept, we will look at two examples of adding text fields.

Example 1

This code example adds a text field display object to the stage during runtime.

```
1   var Fruit:Text field = new Text field();
2   Fruit.text = "Red Apples";
3   Fruit.border = true;
4   Fruit.x = 20;
5   Fruit.y = 20;
6   addChild(Fruit);
```

Evaluation

Line 1: Declares the display object instance named Fruit by allocating new memory of type Text field. Text field, along with its methods and properties, is located in the text class.

Lines 2–5: Assigns initial values to the text field display properties. This includes identifying the text that will appear within the text field, specifying a border, and initializing its location on the Stage.

Line 6: Places the Fruit text field on the Stage.

Example 2

This example illustrates how a newly defined text field can be formatted during creation. Formatting text requires a TextFormat object that is used specifically for this purpose.

```
1   var Fruit:Text field = new Text field();
2   Fruit.text="Sour Green Apples\nRed Apples";
3   Fruit.x=20;
4   Fruit.y=20;
5   Fruit.width = 250;
6
7   var FruitFormat:TextFormat = new TextFormat();
8   FruitFormat.color=0x00FF00;
9   FruitFormat.font="Impact";
10  FruitFormat.size = 25;
11  FruitFormat.align = TextFormatAlign.RIGHT;
12  Fruit.setTextFormat(FruitFormat);
13
14  addChild(Fruit);
```

Evaluation

Lines 1–5: Declares and initializes the text field display object named Fruit.

Line 7: Declares the text format object named FruitFormat by allocating new memory of type TextFormat.

Lines 8–11: Assigns formatting values to a selection of TextFormat properties such as those specifying the color, font, size, and alignment of the text. Line 8 assigns a value using a hexadecimal representation (0xRRG-GBB).

Line 12: Applies this format object to the Fruit text field using the method setTextFormat.

4.6.2 The removeChild Mechanism and the Value null

When an application no longer needs an object that has been added during runtime, the method removeChild is used to remove the visual object from the stage. Even though the visual image may be gone, however, its associated memory continues to exist.

It is strongly advised that the associated memory of a removed display object also be eliminated. This can be done by setting the display object's value to null, which will effectively free the object's associated memory. Specifically, null means that the object has no value.

In AS3, both null and removeChild are reserved words.

Example

In the previous example, a text field named Fruit was created during runtime. To delete this display object, we first remove its visual image from the Stage and then assign the display object the value null.

```
1   removeChild(Fruit);
2   Fruit = null;
```

4.6.3 Exporting Library Symbols for the Creation of MovieClips and Sounds

Unlike text fields, instances of MovieClip and embedded sound symbols must be exported for them to be created dynamically in AS3. The reason for this requirement is a simple issue of performance: Specifying only those MovieClip and sound symbols that will be exported means that the size of the application is reduced. Symbols that are not made available for export do not require extra memory.

External sounds can also be generated dynamically and streamed into the application. These sounds are not stored as symbols in the Library, but rather exist as separate files.

During the process of exporting a MovieClip symbol or embedded sound, Class and Base Class attributes are activated that can then be linked to the specific sound or MovieClip symbol within the Library. The newly created class is then available to be used with the new operator and the addChild method to construct a dynamic MovieClip or sound instance. Figure 4-18 shows a library containing two symbols with export class linkages.

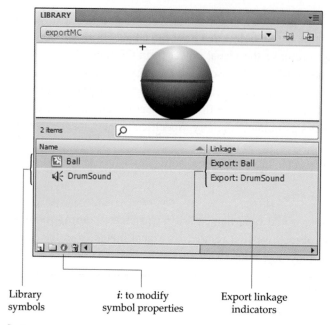

| FIGURE 4-18 The library containing MovieClips and sound symbols for export.

Exporting a library symbol is a straightforward procedure. The basic steps to export a symbol for AS3 are as follows:

Step 1:   Select the MovieClip or sound symbol in the Library panel and click the *i* icon to access and modify its properties and activate the linkage class. Figure 4-18 shows the location of the *i* icon on the Library window.

Step 2:   Once the dialog box representing the symbol's properties appears, you must use the advanced settings to access its linkage options. Click the **Export for AS3** check box to activate the **Class** and **Base class** fields. A class that is used to build another class is called the Base class.

Figure 4-19 shows the dialog box used to create an export linkage for a MovieClip symbol named Ball. The Base class for an exported MovieClip symbol is flash. display.MovieClip. In this case, the newly created exported class is called Ball. By default, the Class field is assigned the symbol name, with spaces removed. A "Class Warning" dialog box appears when this new class symbol is created.

Sound symbols will automatically be given the Base class flash.media.Sound. This class allows you to create sound objects, play and stop a sound, and load and play external sound files. More detailed control of sound can be achieved but will not be discussed in this textbook.

The following examples illustrate more fully the process of creating display objects in real time. For these examples, consider the MovieClip symbol Ball created and used in the Flash library from Figure 4-18.

| FIGURE 4-19 Export linkage dialog box for symbols in the Library.

Example 1 Adding MovieClips

The following segment of code uses the new operator to place three instances of
Ball on the Stage. This is similar to the method used to place a new text field
on the Stage.

```
1   var ball1 = new Ball();
2   ball1.x = 50;
3   ball1.y = 20;
4   addChild(ball1);
5
6   var ball2 = new Ball();
7   ball2.x = 250;
8   ball2.y = 70;
9   ball2.width = ball2.height = 50;
10  addChild(ball2);
11
12  var ball3 = new Ball();
13  ball3.x = 370;
14  ball3.y = 20;
15  ball3.alpha = .70;
16  addChild(ball3);
```

Evaluation

This example illustrates the construction of three variables, all members of the Ball class. Each variable is a runtime display object instance of the exported Ball MovieClip symbol in the library shown in Figure 4-18. The resulting instances are shown in Figure 4-20.

ball1   ball2   ball3

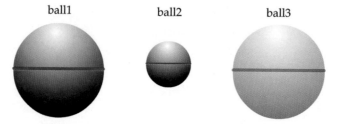

I **FIGURE 4-20** Three ball instances of the same Ball symbol added to the stage during runtime.

Example 2 Changing the Color of a Newly Created Display Object

When a MovieClip instance is created during runtime, its color can be altered. However, programmers cannot directly change the color property of a MovieClip instance. This example illustrates how a ColorTransform object must be constructed specifically for this purpose.

Every display object has a property called transform.colorTransform. Once a ColorTransform object has been constructed, we can access and alter this property.

```
1    package {
2        import flash.display.*;
3        import flash.geom.ColorTransform;
4
5        public class ballApp extends MovieClip {
6
7            function ballApp () {
8                var ball1 = new Ball();
9                var ballColor:ColorTransform = new ColorTransform();
10               ballColor.redOffset = 0;
11               ballColor.greenOffset = 255;
12               ballColor.blueOffset = 255;
13               ball1.transform.colorTransform = ballColor;
14               addChild(ball1);
15           }
16       }
17   }
```

Evaluation

This code example begins by creating a `Ball` display object variable named `ball1` during runtime. Before it places the display object on the Stage, the color of `ball1` is transformed to red.

Line 3: To utilize the `transform.colorTransform` property, the library `flash.geom.ColorTransform` must be imported into the package.

Line 8: A variable `ball1` is declared by allocating `new` memory of type `Ball`.

Line 9: The `ballColor` object is created. It is a member of the `colorTransform` that will hold the new color settings for `ball1`. Notice that the `new` operator can be used to allocate memory for many types of objects.

Lines 10–12: Assigns the offset color values for red, green, and blue, which provides the potential of mixing colors. The color offset properties as seen in these instructions are native to AS3 and are reserved words. Each color offset property expects an unsigned integer value in the range of −255 to 255. For example, in lines 11 and 12, the offsets for green and blue are assigned the highest possible values.

Offset Property	255 ⟷	−255
`redOffset`	Red ⟷	Cyan
`greenOffset`	Green ⟷	Magenta
`blueOffset`	Blue ⟷	Yellow

Line 13: Assigns the `ballColor` object containing the color settings to `ball1`.

Line 14: Adds `ball1` to the stage. The transformed ball is shown in Figure 4-21.

▌ FIGURE 4-21 The color transformation in the display object (instance) named `ball1`.

Example 3 Creating a Sound

This example shows the construction of a sound created and then played many times during the execution of the movie. The application in this example uses the DrumSound export symbol found in the library shown in Figure 4-18.

```
1   package {
2       import flash.display.*;
3       import flash.events.*;
4
5       public class playDrumApp extends MovieClip {
6           var drum:DrumSound = new DrumSound();
7
8           function playDrumApp () {
9               stage.addEventListener(MouseEvent.CLICK, playIt);
10          }
11          function playIt(event:MouseEvent) {
12              drum.play();
13          }
14      }
15  }
```

Evaluation

Line 6: Declares the variable drum and assigns it DrumSound by using the new operator.

Line 9: Registers an event listener referenced by the Stage. Thus clicking anywhere on the Stage will trigger the event handler playIt.

Line 12: Plays the drum sound by calling the play() method.

◼ 4.7 Case Study 3: Menu-Driven Random Artwork

Problem and Analysis   This case study examines an application that will produce an interactive art piece consisting of randomly placed splashes of paint, as illustrated in Figure 4-22.

Constructing menu systems is often desirable when creating graphical user interfaces and media-rich applications. This case study utilizes a basic menu system created with buttons. By clicking these buttons, the user can select one of four colors of paint, which is then splashed on the canvas at a random spot. An appropriate paint splatter sound is played when a splash of paint occurs.

FIGURE 4-22 An artwork application in which paint is interactively splattered onto the canvas.

Objectives of this case study are as follows:

- Work with export linkage and the creation of display objects in real time.
- Transform the color of a display object using AS3 code and the transform object.
- Explore the potential of creating sounds in real time.

This application must perform the following general tasks:

- Provide interactive buttons that change the color of the paint.
- Compute a random spot on the canvas away from the menu system. It is important that paint not be splattered on the menu; otherwise, buttons obscured from view cannot be activated.
- Create a splash of paint (a MovieClip instance) and place it on the computed spot on the Stage.
- To enhance this interactive artwork, generate a splashing sound when the paint hits the canvas.

Visual Design   The menu is a vital feature of this art application, in that it gives the user control over the use of color in the artwork. Animation is often a practical means for drawing users' attention to an important element, such as a menu system or other interactive elements in an application. As this art application loads, it will create a very brief introductory animation to emphasize the menu system. Selected frames of this introductory animation are shown in Figure 4-23.

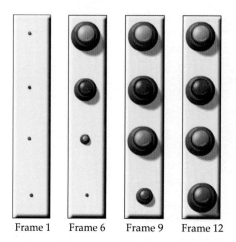

Frame 1   Frame 6   Frame 9   Frame 12

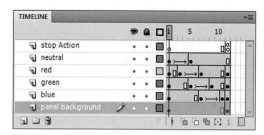

I FIGURE 4-23 Composition of the Menu MovieClip.

As seen in Figure 4-23, the menu system in this application is a composite MovieClip named Menu that consists of four color buttons. The animation for Menu occurs in the first 11 frames, which feature staggered motion tweens. The animation ends with the final appearance of all four color buttons on frame 12. The twelfth frame of Menu contains a stop() action that forces the playhead to stop on that frame. The second graphic in Figure 4-23 shows the timeline used by Menu. Table 4-11 lists the objects used by the application.

TABLE 4-11 Objects Used by the Artwork Application

Object	Details
Menu	A MovieClip instance sitting directly on the Stage, which is composed of multiple display objects, as shown in Figure 4-23.
	Composition of the Menu MovieClip symbol:
	NeutralPaintBtn: Button
	RedPaintBtn: Button
	GreenPaintBtn: Button
	BluePaintBtn: Button

TABLE 4-11 Objects Used by the Artwork Application (continued)

Object	Details
Paint	A MovieClip class exported for AS3. This element exists as a MovieClip Library symbol with an export link. The name of this export MovieClip class is the same as the Library symbol, Paint. Paint uses frame-by-frame animation depicting the different stages of paint, as vector drawings, being thrown onto the canvas. The final frame contains a stop() action.
PaintSound	A sound class exported for AS3. This element exists in the Library as a symbol with an export link. The name of the export sound class is the same as the Library symbol, PaintSound. This sound is a liquid substance hitting a hard surface.

Program Design   The AS3 code for this application will consist of six functions, as described in Table 4-12. If you like, you can experiment further with the color blends for red, green, and blue. The relationship between these functions is illustrated in Figure 4-24.

TABLE 4-12 Artwork Program Functions

Function Name	Description
artworkApp()	This function is the main function as well as the class constructor. As a constructor, it launches when the application begins.
mixNeutral()	The CLICK event handler for NeutralPaintBtn. It sets the color to a neutral value, the original color of the Paint MovieClip.
	Color settings: Red amount: 0; Green amount: 0; Blue amount: 0
mixReddish ()	The CLICK event handler for RedPaintBtn. It sets the color to a red tint.
	Color settings: Red amount: 86; Green amount: −172; Blue amount: −2
mixGreenish()	The CLICK event handler for GreenPaintBtn. It sets the color to a greenish hue.
	Color settings: Red amount: 0; Green amount: 37; Blue amount: −135
mixBluish()	The CLICK event handler for BluePaintBtn. It sets the color to a blue tint.
	Color settings: Red amount: −5; Green amount: −44; Blue amount: 94
splashPaint()	Called by all of the event handlers—mixReddish(), mixBluish(), mixGreenish(), and mixNeutral()—to generate a splash of paint.

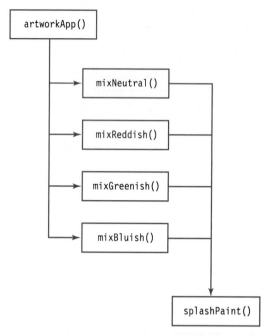

| FIGURE 4-24 Relationship of functions for the artwork application.

The document class for this application is named artworkApp and the AS3 file is named artworkApp.as.

As with all AS3 programs, the required class package and import library classes are placed at the start of the file. The flash.display library class is required for working with the display objects, and the flash.events library class is necessary for all button interactivity. As seen on line 5, flash.geom.ColorTransform is required for altering the color of the splashes of paint that will hit the canvas. The final two lines of the AS3 file contain closing curly brackets to close the document class and the package.

```
1   package {
2
3     import  flash.display.*;
4     import  flash.events.*;
5     import flash.geom.ColorTransform;
6
7     public class artworkApp extends MovieClip {
8
```

⋮

```
78     }//end of the document class artworkApp
79 }//end of package
```

The constants needed for this application deal with the size of the canvas on which the paint will be thrown. The height of the canvas, CANVAS_HEIGHT, is simply the Stage height. The width is set at a fixed value of 250. Because throwing paint on top of a button will interfere with its access, an offset will be used to shift the paint away from the menu. OFFSET is set to 125, which is roughly the width of the menu.

```
9   //CONSTANTS USED IN THE APPLICATION
10  const CANVAS_HEIGHT:Number=stage.stageHeight;
11  const CANVAS_WIDTH:Number=250;
12  const OFFSET:Number=125;
13
```

In this application, a collection of variables is declared outside the definition of a specific function. These variables, which are referred to as global variables, are accessible to all functions in the package. In this application, the global variables redAmount, blueAmount, and greenAmount are used to set the color amount that will be applied to a color transformation object. These variables are initialized to zero (lines 15–17) at the start of the application. The variable object that holds the exported library sound PaintSound is defined globally on line 18.

```
14  //VARIABLES USED IN THE APPLICATION
15  var redAmount:int = 0;
16  var blueAmount:int = 0;
17  var greenAmount:int = 0;
18  var splashSound:PaintSound = new PaintSound();
19
```

The functions used in the application are designed and coded as follows.

Function artworkApp() Design   The sole task of the main algorithm, artworkApp(), is to construct listener events that wait for the user to click any one of the color buttons embedded in Menu.

```
20  function artworkApp () {
21      Menu.NeutralPaintBtn.addEventListener(MouseEvent.CLICK,mixNeutral);
22      Menu.RedPaintBtn.addEventListener(MouseEvent.CLICK,mixReddish);
23      Menu.GreenPaintBtn.addEventListener(MouseEvent.CLICK,mixGreenish);
24      Menu.BluePaintBtn.addEventListener(MouseEvent.CLICK, mixBluish);
25  }
26
```

Function mixNeutral() Design   The event handler, mixNeutral(), sets the global variables related to color to neutral values by removing the red, blue, and green amounts.

Once the color amounts have been set on lines 28–30, the function `splashPaint()` is called to perform the actual tossing of paint onto the canvas.

```
27  function mixNeutral(event:MouseEvent) {
28      redAmount = 0;
29      blueAmount = 0;
30      greenAmount = 0;
31      splashPaint();
32  }
33
```

Function `mixReddish()` Design   The event handler, `mixReddish()`, sets the global variables related to color to reddish values by increasing the red amount and decreasing the blue and green amounts. The function `splashPaint()` is called to create and display a splash of paint at a random location on the canvas.

```
34  function mixReddish(event:MouseEvent) {
35      redAmount = 86;
36      blueAmount = -2;
37      greenAmount = -172;
38      splashPaint();
39  }
40
```

Function `mixGreenish()` Design   This event handler sets the global color variables to greenish tint values and calls the function `splashPaint()`.

```
41  function mixGreenish(event:MouseEvent) {
42      redAmount = 0;
43      blueAmount = -135;
44      greenAmount = 37;
45      splashPaint();
46  }
47
```

Function `mixBluish()` Design   The function `mixBluish()` is the final event handler for mixing the paint. The global color variables are set to bluish values. As with the previous event handlers, the function `splashPaint()` is called to toss paint onto the canvas.

```
48  function mixBluish (event:MouseEvent) {
49      redAmount = -5;
50      blueAmount = 94;
51      greenAmount = -44;
52      splashPaint();
53  }
54
```

Function `splashPaint()` Design The function `splashPaint()` generates the paint display object, places it on the canvas (i.e., the Stage), and plays the sound that corresponds to paint splashing on a canvas. The set of tasks are as follows:

Task 1: Create a `Paint MovieClip` instance named `bitOfPaint`.

- `Paint` is the export linkage name of the symbol in the library.
- `bitOfPaint` is the display object that will be constructed.

Task 2: Set the properties of the newly created `bitOfPaint`. Set the `alpha` property to .5 so that the paint appears textured.

Task 3: Apply color using the `ColorTransform` object.

Task 4: Add the child object to the stage.

Task 5: Play the global sound `splashSound`. (`PaintSound` is the name of the export sound symbol in the library, and `splashSound` is the sound object that will be played.)

```
55  function splashPaint() {
56     //TASK 1: CREATE A NEW VARIABLE TO HOLD THE PAINT
57     var bitOfPaint:Paint=new Paint;
58
59     //TASK 2: COMPUTE A SIZE AND RANDOM SPOT TO THROW PAINT
60     bitOfPaint.scaleX=bitOfPaint.scaleY=Math.random() + .7;
61     bitOfPaint.x=Math.random()*CANVAS_WIDTH + OFFSET;
62     bitOfPaint.y=Math.random()*CANVAS_HEIGHT;
63     bitOfPaint.alpha=.5;
64
65     //TASK 3: USE A COLOR TRANSFORM OBJECT TO ALTER PAINT COLOR
66     var paintColor:ColorTransform=new ColorTransform();
67     paintColor.redOffset=redAmount;
68     paintColor.greenOffset=greenAmount;
69     paintColor.blueOffset=blueAmount;
70     bitOfPaint.transform.colorTransform=paintColor;
71
72     //TASK 4: ADD THE PAINT TO THE STAGE
73     addChild(bitOfPaint);
74
75     //TASK 5: PLAY THE SPLASH SOUND
76     splashSound.play();
77  }
```

4.8 Sprites and Vector Drawing

Every programming language that supports graphics has a set of graphics operations. These operations typically assume the existence of a virtual pen. In AS3, the three most commonly used operations are `lineStyle()`, `moveTo()`, and `lineTo()`. In addition to drawing lines, AS3 uses the operations `beginFill()` and `endFill()` to apply color to a geometric area between three or more points.

All of these operations are member functions of the graphics class, which also includes the shape drawing operations `drawCircle()`, `drawEllipse()`, and `drawRect()`. Table 4-13 shows commonly used graphic operations.

TABLE 4-13 Common Graphic Methods

`lineStyle(thickness, color, alpha)`	Used to set the style of line. Setting the line's `thickness`, `color`, and `alpha` values should be done prior to drawing lines and geometric shapes.
`moveTo(x, y)`	Used to position the pen at a starting x, y location on the Stage.
`lineTo(x, y)`	Used to draw a line from the pen's current position to a new position, identified by the x, y coordinates. The line drawn uses the existing line style. The current drawing position is set to (x, y) once the line is completed.
`curveTo(ctrlX, ctrlY, destX, destY)`	Used to draw curved lines. This function approximates a Bezier curve. The start of the curve will begin at the pen's current x, y position and will end at the destination point (destX, destY). The curve will bend at a control point, identified by ctrlX and ctrlY.
`beginFill(color, alpha)`	Used to select a solid color for filling geometric shapes.
`endFill()`	Serves two purposes: 1. Closes a geometric shape with a line and then fills the interior with color. 2. Terminates the color choice for filling a geometric shape. The fill color will be nonexistent.
`drawCircle(x, y, radius)`	Used to draw a circular shape with a given radius. The center of the circle is specified by the x, y coordinates.
`drawEllipse(x, y, width, height)`	Used to draw an ellipse of a given width and height. Unlike with the `drawCircle()` function, the x, y coordinate values specify the upper-left corner of the ellipse.
`drawRect(x, y, width, height)`	Used to draw a rectangle with a given width and height. The x, y coordinates specify the upper-left location of the rectangle.

In AS3, a **sprite** is a two-dimensional graphic object that can be easily animated and made interactive. Sprites are much less elaborate than `MovieClip` objects, so they require a minimal amount of memory. A sprite display object does not utilize a timeline and is often used with graphic drawing operations. These objects are especially useful for generating simple display objects in real time. For example, they would be helpful in a rocket game that requires a mass of similar shapes be generated representing sparks from take-off.

Example 1

This example illustrates how to draw a diagonal line beginning at the origin (0, 0) and ending at the point (50, 50).

```
1   graphics.lineStyle(1, 0x000000);
2   graphics.moveTo(0,0);
3   graphics.lineTo(50, 50);
```

Evaluation

The style of the line is set to a thickness of 1 and the color is set to black (0x000000). On line 2, the pen is moved to an original position (0, 0). A diagonal line is then drawn from the origin to point (50, 50) on the stage. The resulting graphic is shown in Figure 4-25.

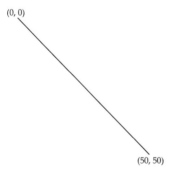

I FIGURE 4-25 Diagonal line drawn from (0, 0) to (50, 50).

Example 2

This example shows how to draw a curved line.

```
1   graphics.lineStyle(1, 0x000000);
2   graphics.moveTo(0,10);
3   graphics.curveTo(50, 50,100,10);
```

Evaluation

The pen is placed at the origin of (0, 10). The ending point of the curved line is (100, 10). The control point (50, 50), will shape the curve. The resulting graphic is shown in Figure 4-26.

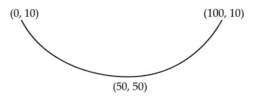

(0, 10)   (100, 10)

(50, 50)

❙ FIGURE 4-26 Curved line drawn from (0, 10) to (100, 10), with a dip at (50, 50).

Example 3

In the first example, we examined a segment of code that created a diagonal line. On some occasions, we need to lift the pen to draw multiple lines that may, or may not, be continuous. This example looks at the process of drawing such lines.

```
1    graphics.lineStyle(1);
2    graphics.lineTo(100, 150);
3    graphics.moveTo(150,100);
4    graphics.lineTo(125, 100);
5    graphics.moveTo(125,125);
```

Evaluation

This segment of code draws two lines. The first line is a diagonal line beginning at (100, 150) and ending at (150, 100). The second line begins at (125, 100) and ends at (125, 125). When this operation is completed, the designated point becomes the new position of the pen. The resulting graphic is shown in Figure 4-27.

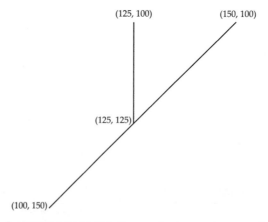

(125, 100)   (150, 100)

(125, 125)

(100, 150)

❙ FIGURE 4-27 Multiple lines can be drawn using `moveTo()`.

Example 4

In addition to drawing lines, applications often need to fill shapes with a flat color. In this example, a triangle is created with a four-pixel border in green. The color red is used for the fill. The resulting graphic is shown in Figure 4-28.

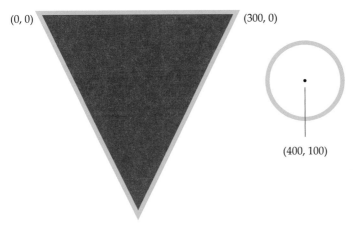

I FIGURE 4-28 A triangle drawn with color and a circle drawn without color.

```
1   graphics.lineStyle(4, 0x00FF00);
2   graphics.beginFill(0xFF0000);
3
4   graphics.moveTo(0,0);
5   graphics.lineTo(300,0);
6   graphics.lineTo(150,300);
7   graphics.endFill();
8
9   graphics.drawCircle(400, 100, 50);
```

Evaluation

Line 1: The line thickness is set to 4 and the color is set to green.

Line 2: The function beginFill() is used to set the fill color—in this case, to red.

Lines 4–7: These instructions create the geometric shape of the triangle. The pen is positioned and the first line is drawn connecting the point of origin with the point (0, 0). The second line is drawn connecting where the pen left off with the point (300, 0). The geometric shape of a triangle is formed once the endFill() operation closes the last line connecting the point (150, 300) with the point of origin, (0, 0).

Line 9: The endFill() operation (from line 7) terminates the selection of color. Thus the circle created on this line will have no color applied to its interior.

Example 5

The sprite display object is a variable object with an identifier name. Sprites are programmable, which makes them simple to animate and interact with. Because sprites do not use a timeline, they require very little memory.

In this example, the sprite named RightTriangle is drawn in real time. RightTriangle is a display object and inherits all the properties of this base class; it is also an instantiation of the Sprite class. The resulting graphic for this example is shown in Figure 4-29.

```
1   var RightTriangle:Sprite = new Sprite();
2   RightTriangle.graphics.moveTo(10,10);
3   RightTriangle.graphics.beginFill(0xFF0000);
4   RightTriangle.graphics.lineStyle(4, 0x000000);
5   RightTriangle.graphics.lineTo(130,10);
6   RightTriangle.graphics.lineTo(10,200);
7   RightTriangle.graphics.endFill();
8   addChild(RightTriangle);
9
10  trace(RightTriangle is DisplayObject);
11  trace(RightTriangle is Sprite);
12  trace(RightTriangle is MovieClip);
```

Evaluation

Line 1: The variable RightTriangle is defined as a Sprite.

Lines 2–8: The shape representing RightTriangle is constructed on the Stage.

Lines 10–12: The trace statements illustrate that RightTriangle is a member of both the DisplayObject base class and the Sprite class, but is not a member of the MovieClip class. The output for these three trace statements is true   true   false.

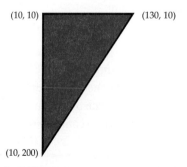

FIGURE 4-29 RightTriangle sprite drawn on the Stage.

Example 6

This example illustrates how to create an interactive geometric shape in real time and programmatically animate it. In this case, the shape will be a simple ball that rolls from the left side of the Stage to the right side.

```
1   var ball:Sprite;
2   function createBall() {
3       var xOrigin:int=0;
4       var yOrigin:int=0;
5       var Radius:int= 50;
6
7       ball=new Sprite();
8       ball.graphics.beginFill(0xFF0000);
9       ball.graphics.drawCircle(xOrigin, yOrigin, Radius);
10      ball.x=10;
11      ball.y=50;
12      addChild(ball);
13
14      ball.addEventListener(Event.ENTER_FRAME,rollBall);
15      ball.addEventListener(MouseEvent.CLICK,sayName);
16  }
17  function rollBall(event:Event) {
18      ball.x++;
19  }
20
21  function sayName(event:MouseEvent) {
22      trace("My name is ball");
23  }
24
```

Evaluation

Line 1: The variable that will eventually store the geometric shape is declared as a Sprite and given the name ball.

Lines 3–5: These lines declare variables to hold the origin point and radius of the ball to be created.

Lines 7–12: These lines create ball with its center anchored at (0, 0) and a radius of 50 pixels. The shape is placed on the stage at the point (10, 50).

Lines 14–15: ball is referenced by two registered event listeners. The first event listener is used to create an animation of the ball rolling across the stage. The second event is used for interactivity.

Lines 17–19: The event handler for ENTER_FRAME event is defined. This function is used to roll ball along the x-axis in increments of 1 with each frame entry loop.

Lines 21–23: The event listener for `MouseEvent.CLICK` is defined. This function is used to make `ball` interactive, allowing the user to click and display its name.

4.9 Case Study 4: The Parthenon in AS3

Problem and Analysis   The city of Athens is situated on the mainland of Greece. The first settlement of Athens was located on the Acropolis, in the heart of the modern-day city. One of the most famous buildings at the Acropolis is the Parthenon, a huge temple built between A.D. 432 and the mid-fifth century to house the statue of the goddess Athena, the protector of the city. In this case study, we will draw the temple, as shown in Figure 4-30, using AS3 code. The main exterior features of the Parthenon will be constructed as sprites in the following manner:

Pediment: This triangular upper part of the front of the temple will be drawn as a color-filled shape.

Frieze: The Doric frieze—the horizontal band near the Parthenon's roof—is composed of panels depicting battles against the Amazons. It will be drawn as a color-filled polygon.

Colonnade: The external colonnade of the temple has 8 columns in the front and 16 columns down the longer 100-foot side. The corner columns were designed larger than the others to harmonize the view of the building from the perspective of the human eye. To enhance the structural integrity of the temple, the trunk

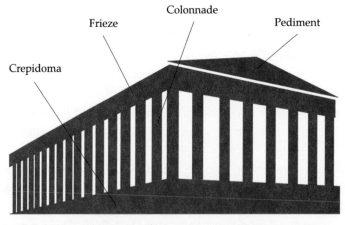

▌ FIGURE 4-30 Main features of the Parthenon drawn in AS3.

of each column swells near the base. We will simplify our drawing by making the columns uniform from top to bottom. We will match the drawing to the real building in terms of the number of columns in the front and down the side, and will maintain the larger dimension of the more prominent corner column.

Crepidoma: The steps at the base of the Parthenon rest on a foundation of three steps, often called the Crepidoma. In reality, there is a slight curvature in the Crepidoma, but we will draw it as a simple polygon with four sides.

To construct this graphic, we first make a rough sketch of the entire temple on grid paper. The grid used in this case study relies on squares measuring exactly 18 × 18 pixels each. This grid drawing will be useful in specifying the dimensions and relevant coordinates delineating the shapes that will be created.

To better understand the AS3 code that follows, the grid drawings for this temple have been subdivided into four parts: pediment, frieze, colonnade, and Crepidoma. These drawings are shown later in this case study in Figures 4-32, 4-33, 4-34, and 4-35, respectively.

Visual Design   This application will not require library symbols, as all graphics will be constructed as sprites during execution. Hence the Timeline will be left entirely empty. There is no animation or interactivity in this application. To accommodate the temple, the Stage size will be set to 700 by 700 pixels.

Program Design   The AS3 code for this application consists of five functions, listed in Table 4-14 and structured hierarchically as shown in Figure 4-31. Because animation and interactivity are not part of this application, events will not be used; thus none of the required functions will be event handlers.

TABLE 4-14 Program Functions

Function Name	Description
parthenonApp()	The constructor and main function of the program. It is responsible for calling all subfunctions that draw the main elements of the Parthenon.
drawPediment()	Draws the pediment.
drawFrieze()	Draws the frieze.
drawColonnade()	Constructs the front columns, the prominent corner column, and the left columns.
drawCrepidoma()	Draws the three steps at the base of the Parthenon.

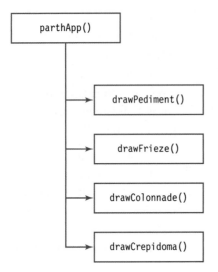

I FIGURE 4-31 Hierarchical structure of the functions used to draw the Parthenon in Case Study 4.

The class document for this application is parthApp. The class package and import library classes are placed at the beginning of the program file. By importing flash. display.* (the graphics library), we automatically import flash.display.Graphics. The last two lines of the parthApp.as AS3 file contain closing curly brackets to close the document class and the package.

```
1   package {
2      import  flash.display.*;
3
4      public class parthApp extends MovieClip {
5

101     }//end of the class parthApp
102 }//end of package
```

The functions used in the application are designed and coded as follows.

Function parthApp() Design   The main function, parthApp(), is the engine behind the construction of the exterior of the Parthenon. Each of the elements in the Parthenon will be constructed as a sprite in a separate function. As shown in lines 7–10, parthApp() calls each of these functions in turn.

```
6   function parthApp() {
7      drawPediment();
8      drawFrieze();
```

```
9       drawColonnade();
10      drawCrepidoma();
11  }
12
```

Function drawPediment() Design   The pediment graphic is constructed as a sprite. As Figure 4-32 shows, it can be drawn by connecting three points and filling the resulting triangle with the color red. This function performs five tasks:

Task 1: Define the sprite as a variable object named Pediment.

Task 2: Move the pen to a starting position at the coordinates (327, 205).

Task 3: Specify the line color for the pediment to be red, with a line thickness of 1. Begin filling in a shape.

Task 4: Connect the three points and end the fill to form the pediment.

Task 5: Add the Pediment sprite to the Stage.

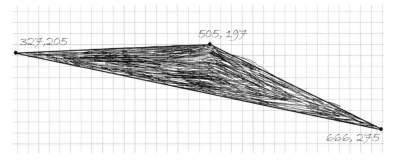

∣ FIGURE 4-32 A grid drawing of the pediment.

```
13  function drawPediment() {
14      //TASK 1:  CREATE THE VARIABLE FOR THE GRAPHIC SPRITE
15      var Pediment:Sprite = new Sprite();
16      //TASK 2:  POSITION THE PEN
17      Pediment.graphics.moveTo(327,205);
18      //TASK 3:  SET THE COLOR TO RED AND LINE THICKNESS TO 1
19      Pediment.graphics.beginFill(0xFF0000);
20      Pediment.graphics.lineStyle(1, 0xFF0000);
21      //TASK 4:  DRAW THREE LINES AND END THE FILL
22      Pediment.graphics.lineTo(505,197);
23      Pediment.graphics.lineTo(666,275);
24      Pediment.graphics.lineTo(327,205);
25      Pediment.graphics.endFill();
26      //TASK 5:  ADD THE GRAPHIC TO THE STAGE
27      addChild(Pediment);
28  }
29
```

Function drawFrieze() Design   The frieze element (Figure 4-33) is constructed as a sprite by connecting six points and filling the interior with red.

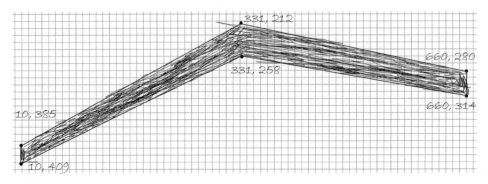

I FIGURE 4-33 A grid drawing of the frieze.

```
30  function drawFrieze() {
31      //TASK : CONNECT SIX POINTS AND FILL IN WITH THE COLOR RED
32      var Frieze:Sprite = new Sprite();
33      Frieze.graphics.moveTo(10,385);
34      Frieze.graphics.beginFill(0xFF0000);
35      Frieze.graphics.lineStyle(1, 0xFF0000);
36      Frieze.graphics.lineTo(331,212);
37      Frieze.graphics.lineTo(660,280);
38      Frieze.graphics.lineTo(660,314);
39      Frieze.graphics.lineTo(331,258);
40      Frieze.graphics.lineTo(10,409);
41      Frieze.graphics.lineTo(10,385);
42      Frieze.graphics.endFill();
43      addChild(Frieze);
44  }
45
```

Function drawColonnade() Design   The colonnade sprite consists of all 24 columns (Figure 4-34). Individual columns are generated as simple rectangular shapes with varying lengths and widths. The one consistent characteristic among the columns is that they all level out at the 500 mark along the *y*-axis. To keep this task simple, the graphics method drawRect() is used to create each column.

Column points

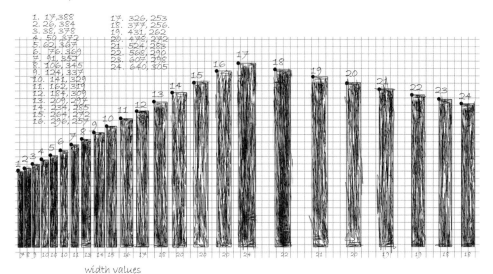

width values

❚ FIGURE 4-34 A grid drawing of the colonnade.

```
46  function drawColonnade() {
47      //TASK 1: CREATE THE SPRITE AND SET THE COLOR TO RED
48      var Colonnade:Sprite = new Sprite();
49      Colonnade.graphics.beginFill(0xFF0000);
50      //TASK 3: CONSTRUCT LEFT COLUMNS 1-16
51      Colonnade.graphics.drawRect(17, 388, 7, 500-388);
52      Colonnade.graphics.drawRect(26, 384, 8, 500-384);
53      Colonnade.graphics.drawRect(38, 378, 9, 500-378);
54      Colonnade.graphics.drawRect(50, 372, 10, 500-372);
55      Colonnade.graphics.drawRect(62, 367, 10, 500-367);
56      Colonnade.graphics.drawRect(76, 360, 10, 500-360);
57      Colonnade.graphics.drawRect(91, 352, 11, 500-352);
58      Colonnade.graphics.drawRect(106, 345, 13, 500-345);
59      Colonnade.graphics.drawRect(124, 337, 14, 500-337);
60      Colonnade.graphics.drawRect(141, 329, 15, 500-329);
61      Colonnade.graphics.drawRect(162, 319, 16, 500-319);
62      Colonnade.graphics.drawRect(184, 309, 17, 500-309);
63      Colonnade.graphics.drawRect(209, 297, 18, 500-297);
64      Colonnade.graphics.drawRect(234, 285, 20, 500-285);
65      Colonnade.graphics.drawRect(264, 272, 20, 500-272);
66      Colonnade.graphics.drawRect(296, 257, 20, 500-257);
67
```

```
68    //TASK 2: CONSTRUCT PROMINENT CORNER COLUMN, 17
69    Colonnade.graphics.drawRect(326, 253, 24, 500-253);
70
71    //TASK 3: CONSTRUCT FRONT COLUMNS 18-24
72    Colonnade.graphics.drawRect(377, 256, 22, 500-256);
73    Colonnade.graphics.drawRect(431, 262, 21, 500-262);
74    Colonnade.graphics.drawRect(478, 272, 20, 500-272);
75    Colonnade.graphics.drawRect(524, 283, 19, 500-283);
76    Colonnade.graphics.drawRect(568, 290, 19, 500-290);
77    Colonnade.graphics.drawRect(607, 298, 18, 500-298);
78    Colonnade.graphics.drawRect(640, 305, 18, 500-305);
79    addChild(Colonnade);
80  }
81
```

Function drawCrepidoma() Design   The Crepidoma graphic is constructed as a sprite by connecting four points and filling the resulting shape with the color red. See Figure 4-35.

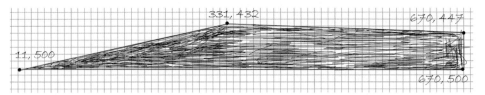

I FIGURE 4-35 A grid drawing of the Crepidoma.

This function performs four tasks:

Task 1: Define the sprite as a variable object named Crepidoma.

Task 2: Set the color for the Crepidoma shape to red. Position the pen at the bottom of the Parthenon to begin drawing the foundation, or Crepidoma.

Task 3: Connect all the points to shape the steps of the Crepidoma.

Task 4: Add the sprite to the Stage.

```
82  function drawCrepidoma() {
83    //TASK 1: DEFINE THE SPRITE
84    var Crepidoma:Sprite = new Sprite();
85
86    //TASK 2: INITIALIZE THE COLOR TO RED AND POSITION PEN
87    Crepidoma.graphics.beginFill(0xFF0000);
88    Crepidoma.graphics.lineStyle(1, 0xFF0000);
89    Crepidoma.graphics.moveTo(11,500);
90
91    //TASK 3: CREATE A SHAPE TO REPRESENT THE STEPS
92    Crepidoma.graphics.lineTo(331,432);
93    Crepidoma.graphics.lineTo(670,447);
```

```
94    Crepidoma.graphics.lineTo(670,500);
95    Crepidoma.graphics.lineTo(11,500);
96    Crepidoma.graphics.endFill();
97
98    //TASK 4: ADD THE CREPIDOMA SPRITE TO THE STAGE
99    addChild(Crepidoma);
100 }
```

4.10 Timer Events and Animation

The first four animations created in the case studies of this chapter have been generated using the ENTER_FRAME event, which simulates a loop using a frame progression. On a reasonably fast computer, these frame-based animations will work smoothly. However, the presentation of a given animation may not be uniform from machine to machine because optimization depends on outside factors such as the browser's Flash player and the speed of the computer. Thus, in the end, the frame rate may not be fully dependable and can affect the quality of play.

As an alternative, you can generate dynamic animations using a timer event, in which movement is tied to a clock rather than the frame rate. A timer event relies solely on the countdown of a timed clock and in some applications may be more consistent from machine to machine. Regardless of which method produces better-quality play, some animations are best done with timer events, such as animated turn-based games that require timed intervals.

The following are the basic components for using a timer.

Task 1: To use a timer event, you must create a Timer object. Two values are specified for its creation: a time delay and a repeat count. The delay time is the amount of time between events being triggered; it is measured in milliseconds. The repeat count value specifies how many times the event will be triggered.

```
var timer:Timer = new Timer(time delay, repeat count);
```

In the statement below, a Timer is created called timeMe. The delay time is 4000 milliseconds, or 4 seconds. In other words, after the clock counts 4 seconds, an event will be triggered. This statement also specifies that after the event is triggered the first time, it will again count to 4 seconds and trigger the event a second time.

```
1   var timeMe:Timer=new Timer(4000, 2);
```

The Timer class is part of the flash.util package.

Task 2: A listener event is registered to the Timer object created in Task 1. This event type is a TimerEvent and the specific event name is TIMER.

In the following statements, a listener event is registered to the Timer object. The timer will begin when the start() method is executed.

```
2   timeMe.addEventListener(TimerEvent.TIMER, sayHello);
3   timeMe.start();
```

Task 3: The TimerEvent event handler in the example may be written as follows:

```
4   function sayHello (event:TimerEvent) {
5      trace("Hello All.");
6   }
```

Take a look at the following two examples.

Example 1

This first example illustrates the basic flow of a timer event.

```
1   package {
2      import flash.display.*;
3      import flash.events.*;
4      import flash.utils.*;
5      public class timerExample extends MovieClip {
6
7         function timerExample () {
8            var atimer:Timer=new Timer(5000, 3);
9            atimer.addEventListener(TimerEvent.TIMER, sayBlue);
10           atimer.start();
11        }
12        function sayBlue (event:TimerEvent) {
13           trace ("blue");
14        }
15     }
16  }
```

Evaluation

Line 4: The library flash.utils.* is imported into the package so that the Timer class can be included.

Line 8: A Timer object named atimer is created to trigger an event every 5000 milliseconds (5 seconds). This will occur exactly three times.

Line 9: A listener event is registered to atimer and the event handler is specified as sayBlue.

Line 10: The atimer begins its countdown. After 5 seconds, the word "blue" is displayed in the output window. After another 5 seconds, "blue" appears again. This is repeated one more time.

The resulting output is

blue
blue
blue

Example 2

This example illustrates an infinite interval, which can be used for endless looping.

```
1   package {
2       import flash.display.*;
3       import flash.events.*;
4       import flash.utils.*;
5
6       public class spriteApp extends MovieClip {
7
8           function spriteApp() {
9               var atimer:Timer=new Timer(500,0);
10              atimer.addEventListener(TimerEvent.TIMER, makeBall);
11              atimer.start();
12          }
13          function makeBall(event:TimerEvent) {
14              var Ball:Sprite=new Sprite();
15              Ball=new Sprite();
16              Ball.graphics.beginFill(0x000000);
17              Ball.graphics.drawCircle(0, 0, 30);
18              Ball.x=Math.random()*400;
19              Ball.y=Math.random()*400;
20              addChild(Ball);
21          }
22      }
23  }
```

Evaluation

The code for this example creates and places a ball sprite on the Stage at regular intervals of $\frac{1}{2}$ second.

Line 9: In this statement, the variable timer named atimer is defined, with its repeat count set to zero. This means that the event will be triggered an infinite number of times, or until the event listener is removed. The delay time is set to 500 milliseconds, which is $\frac{1}{2}$ second. Every $\frac{1}{2}$ second an event will be triggered, continuing an infinite number of times.

Line 10: A listener event is registered to the atimer. The event handler is called makeBall.

Line 11: The `atimer` begins its countdown. After $^1/_2$ second, a ball appears at a random location on the stage. After another $^1/_2$ second, another ball appears. This process is repeated forever during the execution of this application. The creation of balls will occur at $^1/_2$ second delays.

The resulting output after $6^1/_2$ seconds is a stage containing 13 balls positioned randomly.

■ 4.11 Case Study 5: Friction and the Spinning Roulette Wheel

Problem and Analysis   When creating programmatic animation, it is important to understand the effects of friction, the force that slows down or obstructs motion. Friction is present in nearly every activity and should be considered when creating realistic movement. For example, when a ball rolls down a sidewalk, it will slow down and eventually stop because of the friction caused by bumps and cracks on the two surfaces catching on each other.

In this case study, an interactive force is applied to a roulette wheel, which will spin and eventually stop on a number. Several events can be used to create this dynamic animation, such as an ENTER_FRAME event and a timer event. We will use the timer event—not because it is superior, but because it is a useful mechanism to know for creating dynamic animations.

There are two objectives for this case study:

• Explore the concept of friction to create realistic movement.

• Work with a timer event.

Visual Design   The timeline for this application is straightforward: It utilizes a single frame consisting of three layers. The bottom layer holds a MovieClip instance named Wheel, which depicts a roulette wheel with a range of numbers. The middle layer holds a button named SpinBtn, which is required for the user to interactively force the roulette wheel to spin with a random amount of vigor applied to it. The final element of this application is a graphic of a rectangle used for the sole purpose of viewing the final number, which the wheel stops on following a spin. We do not have to name this display object, because it will not be used in the AS3 code. We will, however, need to place it in the top layer of the Timeline to view the numbers as they spin.

Figure 4-36 shows the stage at its initial state and again after a spin.

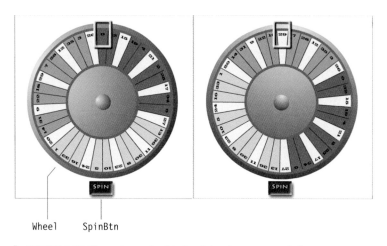

Wheel   SpinBtn

❚ **FIGURE 4-36** The roulette wheel before it has been spun and after.

Program Design   The AS3 code for this application consists of three functions, shown in Table 4-15.

TABLE 4-15 Program Functions

Function Name	Description
spinWheelApp ()	The main function and the constructor of the application. As the constructor, this function executes once the application launches. It has two objectives: 1. Create a velocity property for the MovieClip named Wheel and initialize it. 2. Register a listener event to detect when the user wants to spin the wheel. The event is a mouse event on the button named SpinBtn.
startSpin()	The event handler function that initiates spinning the wheel by taking a single step. This event handler is invoked only when the user clicks the button named SpinBtn.
spinInterval()	The event handler function invoked when the timer starts. This function is called exactly 50 times once the spinning starts. Wheel rotates in increments each time it is called. The velocity of the wheel slows down as friction is applied.

A single constant will be used to apply friction to the wheel. As a result, the wheel's velocity will gradually slow down as it spins, and the wheel will eventually stop spinning altogether.

Here is the complete AS3 code file for this application.

```
1   package {
2      import flash.display.*;
3      import flash.events.*;
4      import flash.utils.*;
5
6      public class spinWheelApp extends MovieClip {
7
8         const FRICTION:Number = .12;
9
10        function spinWheelApp() {
11           Wheel.velocity = 30;
12           SpinBtn.addEventListener(MouseEvent.CLICK,startSpin);
13        }
14
15        function startSpin(event:MouseEvent) {
16           var atimer:Timer = new Timer(150,50);
17           Wheel.velocity = Math.random() * 10 + 20;
18           atimer.addEventListener(TimerEvent.TIMER, spinInterval);
19           atimer.start();
20        }
21        function spinInterval(event:TimerEvent) {
22           Wheel.rotation += Wheel.velocity * 2;
23           Wheel.velocity = Wheel.velocity - Wheel.velocity*FRICTION;
24        }
25     }
26  }
```

Code Explanation

Line 4: flash.util.* is imported so that the Timer class can be used.

Line 8: The constant FRICTION is declared and initialized to 12%. This value will be used to reduce the wheel's spinning velocity by 12% at each timed interval.

Line 11: The MovieClip instance Wheel needs a property for keeping track of its current velocity. This velocity will be recomputed at intervals. This instruction creates the custom property by initializing it to a value.

Line 12: A CLICK mouse event is registered to the button SpinBtn. The function startSpin() executes once this event is triggered.

Line 16: The Timer object named atimer is created and set to execute every 150 milliseconds for a total of 50 times.

Line 17: Compute a random force to be applied to spin the wheel.

Lines 18–19: The TimerEvent TIMER is registered. The clock countdown is started for the intervals.

Line 22: Wheel is rotated by a factor of 2 based on its current velocity.

Line 23: Friction is applied to the current velocity.

◼ Review Questions

1. Define a display object.

2. What are the DisplayObject subclasses?

3. List the main category of events used by AS3.

4. Explain the difference between ROLL_OVER and MOUSE_OVER.

5. List the Timeline methods.

6. Explain the difference between a sprite and a MovieClip.

7. List three examples of display objects.

8. Identify and describe 10 properties that can be inherited by the DisplayObject class.

9. What are acceptable values that can be assigned to the following DisplayObject properties: Visible, scaleX, alpha, and rotation?

◼ Programming Exercises

1. Many games require that dice be rolled. Create a MovieClip representing a single die being rolled.

2. Create a photographic slideshow containing five photographs. Create two buttons that allow the user to interactively move through the photos. The first button should allow the user to move to the next photo in the series, and the second button should display the previous photograph.

3. Write an AS3 program to create the image shown in Figure 4-37, which has a curved mouth.

❙ FIGURE 4-37 Smiley face.

4. Write an AS3 program to create a two-directional arrow.

5. Locate a building of interest and construct a drawing of it using AS3 code.

6. Create an application that allows the user to create word art given 10 words that the user can move around the Stage.

7. Write an AS3 program to create the sprite shown in Figure 4-38.

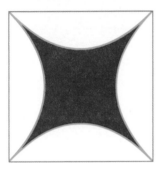

▌ FIGURE 4-38 Sprite shape.

8. Write an application that allows the user to input a birthday message. Using the 3D rotation properties, distort the message into an interesting visual, like that shown in Figure 4-39.

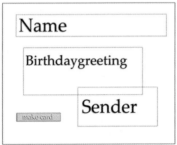

Display objects placed on the Stage

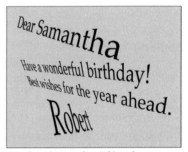

Display objects after AS3 code executes

▌ FIGURE 4-39 Birthday application.

9. Create a programmatic animation that will continuously rotate a collection of text around one of the 3D axes. See Figure 4-40 for an example.

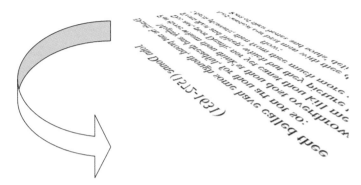

| FIGURE 4-40 Text rotation application.

10. Modify Case Study 5 so that it uses an ENTER_FRAME event instead of a TIMER event.

5 Selective Control and Advanced Animations

Introduction

An important feature of any application program is its ability to make decisions. For example, programmers expect their users to make mistakes. The reality is that to err is human nature, so software must be designed to recover from mistakes. Software, in general, is full of choices for users and is typically designed to allow a user to navigate a path based on these choices. For example, when computing wages for an employee, a decision needs to be made as to whether some of the hours worked will be eligible for an overtime rate. Decision making is a regular characteristic of software applications.

Selective control is a process in which some condition is checked and a decision is made about whether a certain segment of the program code will execute. For example, if an employee works overtime, the calculation to compute his pay may be different than if the same person was a salaried employee. Statements that permit a program to make decisions are called selective control structures. They provide much of the power and simplicity of a programming language and allow us to write meaningful programs. When combined with assignment statements, these selective control structures offer a potent assortment of programming constructions. This chapter looks at the two AS3 selective control structures: `if` statements and `switch` statements.

The foundation of selective control is the subject called Boolean logic. The name "Boolean" is bestowed in honor of the English mathematician George Boole, who pioneered the mathematical theory that now bears his name. A variable of the data type `Bool` can store a value of either true or false. In AS3, as with most programming languages, `true` and `false` are reserved keywords. In this chapter, we will examine relational operators and learn how to form Boolean expressions, also called Boolean test conditions, by using logical operators.

Boolean logic is important to selective control structures because test conditions are defined using Boolean expressions.

▪ 5.1 Boolean Logic

Simply speaking, Boolean logic is used to represent expressions that have two possible values: true or false. These expressions are often constructed with, but not limited to, relational operators, arithmetic operators, and logical operators.

5.1.1 Relational Operators

In arithmetic, number values can be compared using equalities (==) and inequalities (<, >, <=, >=, and so on). All programming languages provide for the comparison of number values. The operators used for comparison are called **relational operators**. Table 5-1 lists the six relational operators used by AS3.

TABLE 5-1 AS3 Relational Operators

Relational Operator	Meaning
==	Is equivalent to
<	Is less than
>	Is greater than
<=	Is less than or equal to
>=	Is greater than or equal to
!=	Is not equivalent to

When two numbers or variable values are compared using a single relational operator, the expression is referred to as a *simple Boolean expression*. Each simple Boolean expression has the Boolean value of true or false according to the validity of the expression. Data of the same general type can be compared; thus numbers can be compared with each other, and strings can be compared with strings. Strings and numbers, however, cannot be compared.

Here are two examples of simple Boolean expressions.

Example 1

Evaluate the value of a simple Boolean expression.

    17 != 5

Evaluation

This Boolean statement expresses that the number 17 is not equivalent to the number 5. This is clearly true.

The value returned by this expression is true.

Example 2

    4 < (3 + 2)

Evaluation

Arithmetic operators, such as +, -, and *, can also be used in simple Boolean expressions. The value returned by this example is true.

5.1.2 Priority Levels of Relational Operators and Arithmetic Operators

The evaluation of an expression that uses both arithmetic operators and relational operators necessitates recognition of priority level. Among arithmetic and relational operators, there are three levels of priority. The relational operators have the lowest priority and are always evaluated last.

Table 5-2 summarizes the priority of these operations. Among arithmetic and relational operators, the relational operators are always evaluated last. Operators of the same priority level are evaluated in order from left to right.

TABLE 5-2 Priority Levels of Relational Operators
Compared with Arithmetic Operators

	Priority	**Operator**
Highest Priority	Level 1	* / %
	Level 2	+ -
Lowest Priority	Level 3	== > < <= >= !=

Example 1

    4 * 5 != 17 + 3

Evaluation

In this example, the expressions on both sides of the relational operator are evaluated first. Because both sides evaluate to 20, this statement evaluates to false.

Example 2

```
14 + 3 * 5 <= 17 + 30 / 4 - 20
```

Evaluation

This example shows an expression that is difficult to evaluate. Although parentheses are not required, sometimes it is a good idea to use them to increase the readability of an expression. Parentheses may also help you avoid using an incorrect expression.

Using precedence priorities, the left side evaluates to 29, while the right side evaluates to 4. Thus this Boolean expression evaluates to false.

5.1.3 Logical Operators

Simple Boolean expressions, such as the ones shown in the previous examples, can be combined to form compound Boolean expressions. This is done by using logical connectives and negation. The logical connectives used by AS3 are && (for AND) and || (for OR). Negation is represented by the symbol ! (for NOT). These three reserved symbols (&&, ||, and !) are called logical operators.

The && Operator (AND)   To understand the && operator, we first define two simple Boolean expressions P and Q. As shown here, && is used to express the conjunction of P and Q. P && Q is true only when P is true and Q is true.

P	Q	P && Q
true	true	**true**
true	false	**false**
false	true	**false**
false	false	**false**

The || Operator (OR)   The logical operator || is used to express the disjunction of two simple Boolean expressions in which the resulting compound expressions are true if either or both of the expressions are true. As shown here, P || Q is true when P is true, Q is true, or both P and Q are true.

P	Q	P || Q
true	true	**true**
true	false	**true**
false	true	**true**
false	false	**false**

The ! Operator (NOT)   The NOT operator ! produces the logical negation of an expression; thus not true is false and not false is true. As shown here, this operator is a unary operator and is not used to join simple Boolean expressions.

P	!P
true	**false**
false	**true**

5.1.4 Priority Levels for All Operators

The priority levels of all operators are listed in Table 5-3. Note that the logical operators do not share the same level of priority. As a unary operator, ! has the highest possible priority among all operators, including the arithmetic and relational operators. It is also important to note that && has a higher priority than ||. As with arithmetic and relational operators, && operators are evaluated from left to right, as are || operators.

TABLE 5-3 Priority Levels of All Operators

	Priority	Operator
Highest Priority	Level 1	!
	Level 2	*, /, %
	Level 3	+, –
	Level 4	==
		>, <
		<=, >=
		!=
	Level 5	&&
	Level 6	||
Lowest Priority	Level 7	=
		+=, –=
		/=, *=, %=

Priority levels are illustrated in the following six examples. For the first four examples, assume that P, Q, and R are Boolean expressions with the values true, true, and false, respectively.

Example 1

```
P && !Q
```

Evaluation

In this example, the logical negation of Q is performed first because ! has the highest priority. The successive steps are shown here.

	P	&&	!Q
Step 1	T	&&	!T
Step 2	T	&&	F
Final value		false	

Note

P and Q are simple expressions. The complete expression P && !Q is referred to as a compound Boolean expression.

Example 2

P && Q || !R

Evaluation

In this expression, the logical negation of R is performed first. Next, the logical AND is performed linking P and Q. Finally, the results of these two operations are linked together with logical OR. The successive steps in the evaluation of the Boolean expression are shown here.

	P	&&	Q	||	!R
Step 1	T	&&	T	||	!F
Step 2	T	&&	T	||	T
Step 3		T		||	T
Final value		true			

Example 3

P && ! (Q || R)

Evaluation

In this example, a set of parentheses is used to alter the order of priority. The logical operation || is first used to link Q and R. This result is negated to produce a value of false and then linked with P using the logical operation &&. The successive steps are as follows.

	P	&&	! (Q	||	R)
Step 1	T	&&	! (T	||	F)
Step 2	T	&&		!T	
Step 3	T	&&		F	
Final value		false			

Example 4

P \|\| Q && R

Evaluation

Because the && operator has a higher priority than \|\|, Q && R is evaluated first, followed by the \|\| logical operation. The successive steps in the evaluation of the Boolean expression are as follows.

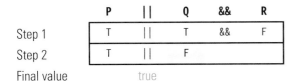

	P	||	Q	&&	R
Step 1	T	||	T	&&	F
Step 2	T	||	F		
Final value		true			

When logical operators are used with relational expressions, parentheses are not required but are often helpful. When complex compound expressions are being evaluated, the logical operators, arithmetic expressions, and relational operators are evaluated during successive passes through the expression. The next set of examples illustrates the evaluation, construction, and common errors found in compound Boolean expressions.

Example 5

Task

Write a Boolean statement expressing that the values stored in the Number variables named n1 and n2 are either both positive or both negative.

Solution

```
n1 > 0 && n2 > 0 || n1 < 0 && n2 < 0
```

Evaluation

The solution requires a compound Boolean statement. The first component expresses that n1 and n2 are both positive. The second component expresses that n1 and n2 are both negative. If the first or second component of the expression is true, then the entire Boolean expression is true. Due to the fact that && is evaluated first, no parentheses are required.

Note

Only if the first component of this statement is false will the second component be tested.

Example 6

Task

Write a Boolean statement expressing that values stored in n1 and n2 are not both zero.

Solutions

a. `n1!= 0 && n2!= 0`

b. `n1 && n2`

Evaluation

There are actually more than two solutions to express this condition. The two shown here are the most clear-cut.

a. This Boolean statement uses !=, the "is not equivalent" operator, to express the condition that both n1 and n2 are not zero.

b. Of the two solutions, this one is the least complicated. It plainly exploits the condition that any number other than zero is considered to be true.

■ 5.2 Introduction to if Statements

Boolean expressions are used to identify whether a condition is true. An if statement provides the mechanism for controlling the execution of program statements based on this condition. This control structure gives AS3 the capacity to make a decision. In other words, programmers can use if statements to examine the existence of a condition and then select the appropriate course of action best suited to that condition. Because it is used in this way, an if statement is referred to as a selection control mechanism.

We begin with the general form of the if statement.

```
if (Boolean expression) {
        statement 1;
        statement 2;
          .
          .
          .
        statement n;
}
```

An if statement begins with the keyword if, written in lowercase, followed by a Boolean expression, which must be enclosed in parentheses. The list of statements to be executed, contained within the {}, is referred to as the set of actions. AS3 requires the set of actions be enclosed in {}. To ensure better readability, the set of action statements should be indented. In the decision structure's simplest form, a specific action, or set of actions, is taken only when a specific condition exists. As shown in Figure 5-1, when the condition is found to be false, the set of actions statements is not performed, but instead is completely bypassed.

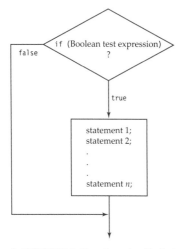

I FIGURE 5-1 Flowchart visually depicting how the if statement works.

The following examples illustrate how the if statement works.

Example 1

```
1   if (day == WEEKEND){
2       trace ( "Wear comfortable jeans.");
3       trace ( "Put on sandals");
4   }
```

Evaluation

The Boolean expression on line 1 tests whether it is a weekend day. If this condition is true, then the set of actions consisting of "Wear comfortable jeans." and "Put on sandals." is executed. As shown in Figure 5-2, if it is not a weekend day, then the condition is false and the program flow follows another path and skips the set of actions.

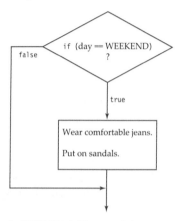

I FIGURE 5-2 Diagram of the if statement flow of control.

Example 2

```
1   var age:int;
2   if (age < 35) {
3       trace ( "You are not old enough to be a U.S. president.");
4   }
5   trace ( "The youngest U.S. president was Kennedy at 42 years old.");
```

Evaluations for Different Values of Age

a. age = 25

In this scenario, the conditional expression on line 2 (age < 35) is true and, therefore, the action statement on line 3 is executed. The statement on line 5 is not located inside the { } and, therefore, is an unconditional statement. Unconditional statements do not depend on a Boolean expression being true or false and will automatically be executed.

The output produced by this segment of code is

You are not old enough to be a U.S. president.
The youngest U.S. president was Kennedy at 42 years old.

b. age = 36

The conditional expression for this given age is false. The action statement is not executed. The unconditional statement will still execute, however.

The output produced by this segment of code is

The youngest U.S. president was Kennedy at 42 years old.

Example 3

What is the problem in the following segment of code?

```
1  var  n1:int = 3;
2  var  n2:int = 7;
3  if (n1 = n2) {
4      trace("The value in n1 is  ", n1);
5  }
```

Evaluation

This example illustrates a common error when writing Boolean expressions: The operator used to express equality is incorrect. The relational operator is == and the assignment operator is =. As with most logic errors, this kind of typographical error can be difficult to identify because it does not hinder the application's ability to run. This error can be detected only during runtime testing of the application.

In this specific example, the Boolean expression on line 3 is an assignment statement. Recall that the number 7 is considered to be a true value because only zero is false. Because true is being assigned to n1, the result is a true expression.

The output produced by this segment of code is

The value in n1 is 7

Example 4

What is the problem in the following segment of code?

```
1  var n1:int = -5;
2  if (3 < n1 < 10) {
3      trace("Blue");
4  }
```

Evaluation

At first glance, the Boolean expression on line 2 appears to be written correctly—but a deceptive logical error is actually present. The goal is to express that the value in n1 is within the range of 3 to 10. The problem is that this mathematical relationship cannot be represented in a programming language without using a logical operator. More to the point, this statement will always be true, no matter what value is stored in n1.

The first operation examines whether 3 is less than n1, which produces a value of false. Because false is represented by a zero, the value zero is used as the operand for the next operation. To show the illogical outcome of this expression, it is necessary to examine the sequence of steps.

$$3 < n1 < 10$$

false

$$0 < 10$$

true

The output produced by this segment of code is

Blue

The correct way to write this condition follows in Example 5.

Example 5

```
1   var  n1:int = -5;
2   if (3 < n1  && n1 < 10){
3       trace("Blue");
4   }
```

Evaluation

Unlike the expression in Example 4, the Boolean expression on line 2 is written correctly. This mathematical relationship begins with an expression of what the lower bound of n1 is. The logical operator && is then used to link the lower bound logical definition with the upper bound definition.

Here is the sequence of steps.

$$3 < n1 \ \&\& \ n1 < 10$$

Step 1

false && n1 < 10

Step 2

false && true

Result   false

No output is produced by this segment of code.

5.3 The if-else Statement

The if statements considered thus far involve selecting a single alternative. Another form of the if statement is one that contains an else clause and, therefore, offers the possibility of selecting one of two alternatives. The correct form and syntax for an if-else statement is

```
if (Boolean expression) {
        set of action statements 1;
}
else {
        set of action statements 2;
}
```

The flow of control when using an if-else statement is as follows:

1. The Boolean expression is evaluated.
2. If the Boolean expression is true, the first set of action statements following the expression is executed and control then exits the entire if-else statement structure.
3. If the Boolean expression is false, the set of action statements belonging to the else clause is executed and control then exits the if-else statement.

The next two examples illustrate how the if-else statement works.

Example 1

```
1   var rain:Boolean = false;
2   if (rain == true){
3       trace ( "Get an umbrella.");
4       trace ( "Wear boots.");
5   } else {
6       trace ( "Store the umbrella.");
7       trace ( "Wear sandals.");
8   }
```

Evaluation

As shown in Figure 5-3, the Boolean expression on line 2 tests whether it is raining. If this condition is true, the block of statements on lines 3 and 4 is executed. If the condition is false, the else clause on lines 6 and 7 will be executed and "Store the umbrella." and "Wear shoes" are output.

The Boolean expression is false. Thus the output produced by this segment of code is

Store the umbrella.
Wear sandals.

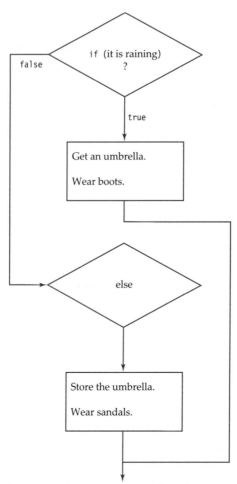

FIGURE 5-3 if-else statement flow of control.

Example 2

```
1    var Num1: Number = 2.2;
2    var Num2: Number = 0;
3    var value:Number;
4
5    if (Num2== 0){
6        trace ( "Error.  Division by Zero ");
7    } else {
```

```
8     value = Num1 / Num2;
9     trace ( value);
10  }
11  trace("exit");
```

Evaluation

This segment of code employs the if-else statement to guard against division by zero. The Boolean expression on line 5 is true; thus the output produced by this segment of code is that shown below. The final statement on line 11 is not dependent on the Boolean expression. Because it is unconditional, it will always execute.

```
Error. Division by Zero
exit
```

5.4 The if-else if-else Statement

Oftentimes, decisions need to be made that involve more than two alternatives. It is possible to use the if-else structure to formulate a selective statement exactly for this purpose. This type of selective statement will take the form if-else if-else if-else, with each clause selecting its own appropriate course of action. This is not a new kind of if statement, but rather a collection of if-else statements.

Here is a generic version of an if statement that contains five alternatives. In this format, statement 1 will execute only if Boolean expression 1 is found to be true, and statement 2 will execute only if Boolean expression 2 is true, and so on. Each if in an else if clause is actually a new if statement and, therefore, is executed only if the conditions defined in all the preceding Boolean expressions are false. Similarly, each else in an else if clause is actually associated with the if of the preceding else if clause (or the first if).

```
if (Boolean expression1) {
      statement 1;
}else if (Boolean expression2) {
      statement 2;
}else if (Boolean expression3) {
      statement 3;
}else if (Boolean expression4) {
      statement 4;
}else {
      statement 5;
}
```

The next three examples examine these kinds of selective statements.

Example 1

```
1   var n1: Number ;
2   if (n1 == 0){
3      trace ( "Zero");
4   } else  if (n1 % 2 == 1){
5      trace ( "Odd ");
6   } else  {
7      trace ( "Even");
8   }
9   trace ( "Number");
```

Evaluations for Different Values of n1

In this example, the value stored in n1 can either be zero, an odd number, or an even number. The if statement uses an if-else if-else format to test each possibility. Each Boolean expression will be tested in sequential order. Once it reaches a condition that is true, it executes the action statement associated with that condition and then exits the structure. The statement trace ("Number"); on line 9 is unconditional and not dependent on any if statement. It will always execute.

a. n1 = 0

   The output produced by this segment of code is

   > Zero
   > Number

b. n1 = 44

   The output produced by this segment of code is

   > Even
   > Number

c. n1 = 57

   The output produced by this segment of code is

   > Odd
   > Number

Example 2

Task

Given the following grading scale, write a segment of code to display the correct grade for an exam score. Assume the value stored in the variable holding the exam score is valid.

Grade	Exam Score
A	Greater than or equal to 90
B	80–89
C	70–79
D	60–69
F	Less than 60

Solution

By using an if-else if-else if-else structure, this task can be greatly simplified. A well-designed selective structure should avoid unnecessary test conditions. For example, the letter grade A is displayed when (score >= 90) is true, as shown in line 2. If this condition is false, it is unnecessary to test for the second part of (score >= 80 && score < 90), because score < 90 is automatically implied. A well designed if-else if-else if-else is written as follows:

```
1   var score: Number;
2   if (score>= 90){
3      trace ( "Grade: A ");
4   } else  if (score>= 80){
5      trace ( "Grade: B ");
6   } else  if (score>= 70){
7      trace ( "Grade: C");
8   } else  if (score>= 60){
9      trace ( "Grade: D");
10  } else  {
11     trace ( "Grade: F ");
12  }
```

Evaluations for Different Values of score

a. score = 55

The only Boolean condition that is true for this scenario is the default test, the else clause. All of the previous Boolean expressions are false.

The output produced by this segment of code is

     Grade: F

b. score = 75

The program will examine each of the Boolean conditions in sequential order. Once it reaches a Boolean condition that is true, it executes the action statement associated with that condition and then exits the structure.

The sequential conditions are evaluated as follows:

Boolean test 1   `if (score >=90)`   false

Boolean test 2   `if (score >=80)`   false

Boolean test 3   `if (score >=70)`   true   `trace ( "Grade: C");`

The output produced by this segment of code is

Grade: C

Example 3

```
1   var score: Number;
2   if (score>= 70){
3      trace ( "Grade: C ");
4   } else  if (score>= 80){
5      trace ( "Grade: B ");
6   } else if (score>= 90){
7      trace ( "Grade: A");
8   }
```

Evaluation

The objective of this segment of code is similar to that of Example 2, which is to display the letter grade that corresponds with the numeric score. However, the order of these conditions creates a logic error such that all scores of 70 or higher are given a grade of 'C' and any score less than 70 will not receive a grade. Upon close examination, you will see that the condition on line 4 is evaluated only if score is less than 70.

There are several ways to solve this problem, two of which are identified here. The first option is of poor quality, however.

Option 1 utilizes independent if statements, even though the Boolean conditions are unmistakably related to each other. This option is inefficient because all test conditions will be evaluated regardless of whether a preceding condition is found to be true. This option should not be considered because of its poor quality.

Option 2 is not only correct, but also of good quality; it is concise and clear. The code and order of the conditions have been refined by eliminating all unnecessary Boolean expressions.

Option 1: Poor Quality

```
1   if (score>= 70 && score < 80){
2       trace ( "Grade: C ");
3   }
4   if (score>= 80 && score < 90){
5       trace ( "Grade: B ");
6   }
7   if (score>= 90){
8       trace ( "Grade: A");
9   }
```

Option 2: Excellent Quality

```
1   if (score >= 90){
2       trace ( "Grade: A ");
3   } else if (score >= 80){
4       trace ( "Grade: B ");
5   } else if (score >= 70 ){
6       trace ( "Grade: C");
7   }
```

▨ 5.5 Case Study 1: The Paddle Game and Collision Detection

In 1972, Atari released a simple video game that featured two elemental objects: a bouncing ball and a paddle to hit the ball with. This game was called Pong. Its enormous popularity eventually led to the beginning of the video game industry. In this case study we will create a similar game, as shown in Figure 5-4.

Objectives of this case study:

1. Explore decision making.

2. Work with concepts of animation.

3. Program basic collision detection.

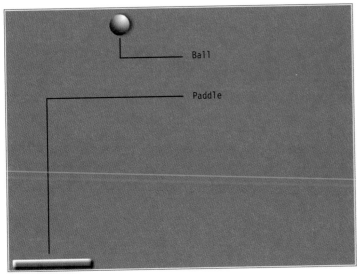

❙ FIGURE 5-4 Paddle game application.

Game Plan

The Paddle game application is a simple version of Pong. It is a single-player game that uses a single paddle and ball. At most, two display objects can be in motion at any given time—the ball and the paddle. The ball will move with a fixed velocity around the stage. When the ball collides with the top, left, or right wall of the stage, it will reverse its direction. The paddle will be controlled by the mouse and can move horizontally across the bottom of the stage. The player must stop the ball from going off the bottom of the stage by hitting it with the paddle.

Once the ball bounces below the bottom of the stage, the ball disappears and the game is over.

Visual Elements

At its most basic level, Pong is a highly instinctive game. This fact is significant for the visual design phase because it indicates that game-play instructions or even elaborate interface elements can be minimized or, as in this case study, skipped altogether. Our paddle game will rely solely on a single screen during the entire game.

The two display objects, Ball and Paddle (shown in Figure 5-4), are both MovieClip instances. The main Timeline is organized using a single layer in a single frame. Both display objects, Ball and Paddle, are placed on the same layer. The frame rate for this animation is set to 30 frames per second, which is fast enough to produce smooth movements.

The display objects, Ball and Paddle, will utilize inherited properties such as height, width, x, and y. In addition, Ball will have two newly constructed properties, xVelocity and yVelocity. Table 5-4 lists all of the properties.

TABLE 5-4 Display Objects and Properties Used in the Paddle Game

Display Object Name	Property
Ball	height: Height of Ball.
	width: Width of Ball.
	x: x-axis position on the Stage.
	y: y-axis position on the Stage.
	xVelocity: A newly constructed property governing the x-axis velocity.
	yVelocity: A newly constructed property governing the y-axis velocity.
Paddle	x: The Paddle MovieClip moves along the x-axis. Only the x-axis position on the Stage will be required.

Collision Detection

To design the algorithm, the details of the collisions need to be established. This game will use three boundary limits of the viewable screen: TOP, LEFT, and RIGHT. TOP, LEFT, and RIGHT represent the topmost, leftmost, and rightmost boundaries, respectively, of where the ball can move in the game area. BOTTOM will not be used in this case study, but will be explored further in an end-of-chapter problem.

To understand boundaries and collisions, we will assume the ball's registration point is located at its center. It is necessary to detect these collisions because the ball's velocity will be reversed once it collides with wall boundaries. As shown in Figure 5-5, the ball collides with TOP when its y position is less than or equal to zero (the topmost edge of the Stage) plus the ball's radius. In a similar fashion, the ball collides with the RIGHT boundary when its x location is equal to or exceeds the width of the Stage minus the ball's radius. Finally, the ball collides with the LEFT boundary when its x location is less than or equal to zero plus the ball's radius.

Ball Radius

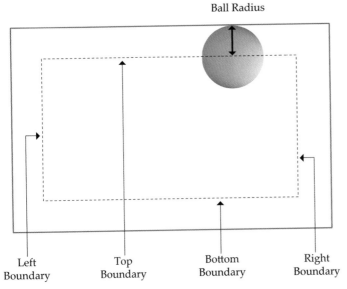

| Left
Boundary | Top
Boundary | Bottom
Boundary | Right
Boundary |

| FIGURE 5-5 The Ball boundaries used for collision detection in the paddle game

Algorithm Design

The AS3 code for this application consists of the class constructor paddleApp(), which initializes the game, and moveBall() and movePaddle(), which control the animation and drive the game. In addition, two auxiliary functions perform the tasks of detecting collisions. Table 5-5 lists all five main functions, and Figure 5-6 illustrates their relationship.

TABLE 5-5 Paddle Game Application Program Functions

Function Name	Description
paddleApp()	The class constructor. After launching, it initializes the Ball and Paddle properties and registers the events for interaction and animation.
moveBall()	Performs the task of animating the ball. This event handler controls the ball's movements by responding to the event ENTER_FRAME looping mechanism. It also guides the collision detection tasks by calling the appropriate functions.
movePaddle()	Responds to the event MOUSE_MOVE. This event handler performs the simple task of visually moving Paddle.
checkBalltoWall()	Checks whether Ball has collided with one of the walls and responds by reversing Ball's velocity.
checkBalltoPaddle()	Checks whether Ball has been struck by Paddle and responds appropriately.

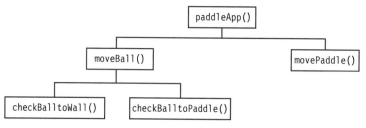

FIGURE 5-6 Relationship of the functions used by the paddle game.

The class package requires the display and events library classes. The last two lines contain closing curly brackets to conclude the paddleApp class and the package.

```
1   package {
2       import flash.display.*;
3       import flash.events.*;
4
5       public class paddleApp extends MovieClip {
```

```
71      }
72  }
```

Constants

The paddle game uses constant values when identifying collisions and reversing the direction of the ball. These constants can be divided into three categories.

The first constant represents the radius of the ball, which is set to 16 pixels. This constant will be used to calculate the boundaries of the area where the ball can freely move.

The second category represents the concrete boundaries: TOP, BOTTOM, LEFT, and RIGHT. As shown in Figure 5-5, the TOP boundary is not zero, but rather the point at which the ball strikes the ceiling, which is the radius of the ball. Lines 9–12 provide constant declarations for these boundaries.

The final constant is REVERSE, which is assigned a value of -1. When the ball's current velocity is multiplied by this constant, the velocity will be negated to reverse the direction.

```
6
7   const BALL_RADIUS:int=16;
8
9   const TOP:Number=BALL_RADIUS;
10  const BOTTOM:Number=stage.stageHeight;
11  const LEFT:Number=BALL_RADIUS;
12  const RIGHT:Number=stage.stageWidth - BALL_RADIUS;
13
14  const REVERSE:int=-1;
15
```

These six functions for this game are designed as follows.

Function paddleApp() Design

The function paddleApp() is immediately executed upon launching the game. Its objective is to simply initialize the elements of the game, which are organized into two tasks.

Task 1: This task performs the initialization of the two dynamic display objects, Ball and Paddle. Both use several inherited properties that will be set to initial values. In addition, Ball will have two newly constructed properties, xVelocity and yVelocity. Table 5-4 lists all of the properties.

Task 2: The second task of this function is to register two listener events. The first registered event listens for the simple movement of the mouse, which will be used to move the paddle. The second registered event is a frame loop that animates the ball by calling moveBall() at regular intervals.

```
16  function paddleApp() {
17     //TASK 1:  INITIALIZE BALL AND PADDLE
18     Ball.height=RADIUS * 2;
19     Ball.width=RADIUS * 2;
20     Ball.x=40;
21     Ball.y=40;
22     Ball.xVelocity=3;
23     Ball.yVelocity=3;
24     Paddle.x=500;
25     Paddle.y=500;
26
27     //TASK 2: REGISTER EVENT LISTENERS TO MOVE BALL AND PADDLE
28     addEventListener(Event.ENTER_FRAME, moveBall);
29     stage.addEventListener(MouseEvent.MOUSE_MOVE, movePaddle);
30  }
31
```

Function movePaddle() Design

The function movePaddle() has one very simple objective—to move the paddle in a horizontal direction along the bottom of the Stage. The y position for Paddle has already been initialized. The x position will be altered as the user moves the mouse. Therefore, Paddle adheres to the position of the mouse along the x-axis.

```
32  function movePaddle(event:MouseEvent) {
33     //TASK : MOVE PADDLE ALONG WITH THE MOUSE ON THE X-AXIS
34     Paddle.x=stage.mouseX;
35  }
36
```

Function moveBall() Design

This function is the event handler for the ENTER_FRAME event registered by paddleApp(). It is also the animation engine that takes the game from static mode to dynamic play by directing the movement of the ball (Task 1) and calling the functions that detect collisions at regular intervals.

In Task 1, Ball is incremented by its fixed velocity along the x- and y-axes. Thus, when the xVelocity property is positive, Ball moves from left to right; otherwise, it moves from right to left. When the yVelocity property is positive, the ball moves toward the bottom of the Stage.

Task 2 examines two types of collisions. The first collision occurs when the ball strikes a wall. The second collision takes place when the ball hits the paddle.

```
37  function moveBall(event:Event) {
38     //TASK 1:  MOVE THE BALL ITS FIXED VELOCITY
39     Ball.x += Ball.xVelocity;
```

```
40      Ball.y += Ball.yVelocity;
41
42      //TASK 2:  CHECK BALL COLLISIONS
43      checkBalltoWall();
44      checkBalltoPaddle();
45  }
46
```

Function `checkBalltoWall()` Design

This function checks for three possible boundary collisions. It is possible for a ball to collide with the top wall and the left wall at the same time, such as when the ball has struck the corner of the Stage. This rationale also applies to the top wall and the right wall. It is not possible, however, for a ball to strike the left and right walls simultaneously. The tasks for this function are to test these specific conditions.

If a ball moves beyond TOP, LEFT, or RIGHT, the ball is positioned at the boundary and the appropriate velocity is reversed. The tactic of positioning Ball at the boundary accomplishes two things:

- It tricks the eye into seeing the ball hit the boundary.
- It forces the ball into the correct location. Because the ball is not allowed to move beyond its boundary, its *x* and *y* coordinates are set to a corrected position.

Note that collision with the BOTTOM boundary is not being tested for. Once the ball has moved beyond the BOTTOM boundary of the Stage, the game is over because the ball is no longer available to hit. How would this be resolved? This issue is revisited in an end-of-chapter programming problem.

```
47  function checkBalltoWall() {
48      //TASK 1:  IF BALL HAS HIT TOP OF THE STAGE, REVERSE ITS DIRECTION
59      if (Ball.y<TOP) {
50          Ball.y=TOP;
51          Ball.yVelocity*=REVERSE;
52      }
53
54      //TASK 2:  IF BALL HAS HIT A SIDE WALL,  REVERSE ITS DIRECTION
55      if (Ball.x<LEFT) {
56          Ball.x=LEFT;
57          Ball.xVelocity*=REVERSE;
58      } else if (Ball.x > RIGHT) {
59          Ball.x=RIGHT;
60          Ball.xVelocity*=REVERSE;
61      }
62  }
63
```

Function `checkBalltoPaddle()` Design

This function uses the display object inherited method called `hitTestObject()`. This method returns true if the referenced object collides with the argument object—in this case, `Paddle` and `Ball`.

```
64  function checkBalltoPaddle() {
65     //TASK :  USE hitTestObject
66     if (Paddle.hitTestObject(Ball)) {
67        Ball.yVelocity*=REVERSE;
68        }
69     }
70  }
```

■ 5.6 Case Study 2: Weight Loss Calculator with Error Detection

Problem

One pound of body weight is equivalent to 3500 calories, regardless of the person's gender or age. Thus, to lose one pound of weight, a person must create a deficit of 3500 calories. This can be done by burning more calories, by reducing the calorie intake, or by implementing a combination of both. The weight loss calculator created in this case study computes the time it will take to drop a given number of pounds using the method of reducing the daily calorie intake by a specific amount. An example run of this application is shown in Figure 5-7.

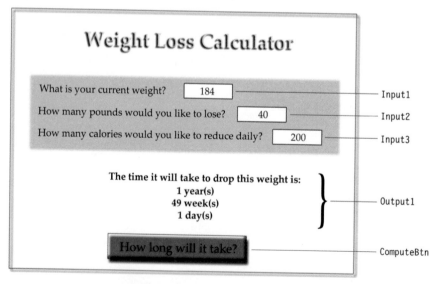

I FIGURE 5-7 Weight loss calculator application.

Problem Analysis

This interactive application provides input text fields for users to supply their current weight, the number of pounds they wish to drop, and the number of calories they will eliminate daily. Once it is determined that the input is valid, the application computes the amount of time it will take to lose the desired weight. This time will be displayed in terms of years, weeks, and days, as opposed to simply days. Examine the following two sentences. The first sentence is easier to assimilate.

Output Option 1: It will take 1 year, 49 weeks, and 1 day to lose the weight.

Output Option 2: It will take 709 days to lose the weight.

This case study has two primary objectives:

1. Explore error detection in the user's input by using an if–else if–else statement.
2. Examine the use of the appendText method. Because the output for this application requires years, weeks, and days to obtain readable results, we will use this method to concatenate several text values.

Visual Design

The visual side of this application requires only one screen for the combined input of weight loss information and the output of the computed results. This interface screen uses a single frame in the Timeline.

In terms of design, it is important that the screen be readable, intuitive, visually appealing, and efficient. The text for this application is the primary source of information. To minimize the possibility of human error, the labels must be worded carefully so that they are easy to understand. The screen is organized from left to right and from top to bottom, and the input text fields are grouped together for effective and quick navigation. Finally, the single interactive button on the screen is labeled and graphically designed so that the user can reasonably understand how to use it.

The visual objects for this application consist of three input text boxes, a single dynamic text box for multipurpose output, and a button that initiates the process to calculate how long it will take to drop the given weight. Figure 5-7 shows the visual blueprint of the completed screen, along with the interactive objects. Table 5-6 lists the objects and describes their specific use.

TABLE 5-6 Visual Objects Used in the Input/Output Screen

Visual Object Name	Type of Object	Description of the Object
Input1	Input text box	Used to input the user's current weight.
Input2	Input text box	Used to input the number of pounds the user wishes to lose.
Input3	Input text box	Used to input the reduction in daily calories.
Output1	Dynamic text box	Used to display all errors that have been encountered during input and the amount of time it will take to lose the weight.
ComputeBtn	Button	Used to start the computation process. This interactive button is labeled "How long will it take?"

Program Design

The AS3 code for this application consists of three algorithms, each represented by a function. The class constructor is named `caloriesApp()`. The other two functions are `validateInput()` and `computeTime()`. Table 5-7 lists the functions used in the application and Figure 5-8 shows the relationship and flow between these functions.

TABLE 5-7 Weight Loss Program Functions

Function Name	Description
caloriesApp()	Controls interactivity. This function is the main function as well as the class constructor.
validateInput()	Identifies input errors. This function reads the input values and tests for a variety of errors.
computeTime()	Computes the time required to lose the weight. The time is then formatted and displayed on the screen.

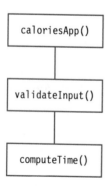

I FIGURE 5-8 Relationship of functions used by the weight loss application.

The package for this program contains flash.display.* and flash.events.*. The application requires three constants for computing the amount of time for the weight loss. These constants (lines 7–9) define the number of days in a year, the number of days in a week, and the number of calories that constitute one pound.

```
1   package {
2       import flash.display.*;
3       import flash.events.*;
4
5       public class caloriesApp extends MovieClip {
6           //CONSTANTS USED FOR WEIGHT LOSS COMPUTATION
7           const DAYS_IN_YEAR:int=365;
8           const DAYS_IN_WEEK:int=7;
9           const CALORIES_PER_LB:int=3500;
10
```

```
63      }
64  }
```

The tasks of each function written for this application are outlined next.

Function caloriesApp() Design

The main algorithm, caloriesApp, is simply the class constructor function that will load immediately once the application is launched. The objective of this function is to construct a listener event that waits for the user to click ComputeBtn. Once this button is clicked, the sub-algorithm validateInput() is called. Prior to clicking the ComputeBtn, the user should have entered the current weight, the number of pounds the user wishes to lose, and the intended reduction in calories.

```
11  function caloriesApp() {
12      //TASK: REGISTER A MOUSE CLICK EVENT TO VALIDATE INPUT AND COMPUTE
13      ComputeBtn.addEventListener(MouseEvent.CLICK, validateInput);
14  }
15
```

Function validateInput() Design

The main goal of the validateInput() function is to validate the user's input. Once it is determined that the input does not contain any errors, the function computeTime() is called to process the weight loss information.

If an error is encountered in an input text box, an appropriate error message is displayed in the text field output1. When validating user input, the isNaN operator allows the application to test whether a variable or expression is **Not a Number**. For example, if the text box named input1, which gathers the user's current weight, contains something other than a number, isNaN() returns true.

Six obvious validation conditions are examined by the code, each one defined as a Boolean expression in an `if` statement:

Validation 1: The current weight must be a number.

Validation 2: The current weight must be greater than zero.

Validation 3: The number of pounds the user wishes to lose must be a number.

Validation 4: The number of pounds must be greater than zero and less than the current weight.

Validation 5: The reduced calories must be a number.

Validation 6: The reduced calories must be greater than zero.

If no errors are found in the input, the `else` default clause calls the function `computeTime()` to compute the amount of time it will take to lose the desired weight.

```
16  function validateInput(event:MouseEvent) {
17      //TASK1: EXAMINE EVERY POSSIBLE INCORRECT INPUT FROM THE USER
18      if (isNaN(Number(input1.text))) {
19          output1.text="Your current weight must be a number.\n";
20      } else if (Number(input1.text) <= 0) {
21          output1.text="Your current weight must be greater than zero.\n";
22      } else if (isNaN(Number(input2.text))) {
23          output1.text="The amount you wish to lose must be a number.\n";
24      } else if (Number(input2.text)>=Number(input1.text)||Number(input2.text)<=0){
25          output1.text="The pounds to lose must be less than your weight.\n" +
26              "and greater than zero.";
27      } else if (isNaN(Number(input3.text))) {
28          output1.text="The reduced calories must be a number.\n";
29      } else if (Number(input3.text)<= 0) {
30          output1.text="The reduced calories must be greater than zero.\n";
31      } else {
32      //TASK: IF INPUT FROM THE USER IS CORRECT, COMPUTE THE TIME TO LOSE WEIGHT
33          computeTime();
34      }
35  }
36
```

Function `computeTime()` Design

The `computeTime()` function is called by `validateInput()` only after it has been established that the input is error free. This function, whose objective is to calculate the time it will take the user to lose the specified weight and display it in a readable fashion, performs four tasks:

Task 1: Read the text from dynamic text boxes for Input1, Input2, and Input3 into the data objects currentWeight, weightLoss, and reducedCals.

Task 2: Compute the time it takes to lose the weight. The time will be in days.

Task 3: For easy readability, convert the total number of days into years, weeks, and days. The % operator is used in these computations.

Task 4: Construct the output display of the time it takes to lose the weight. The output1 text box is used to display this output and a general message along with the six values in the remaining dynamic text boxes.

```
37  function computeTime () {
38     //TASK 1:   READ VALUES FROM INPUT TEXTFIELDS
39     var currentWeight:Number=Number(input1.text);
40     var weightLoss:Number=Number(input2.text);
41     var reducedCals:Number=Number(input3.text);
42
43     //TASK 2:   COMPUTE THE DAYS REQUIRED TO LOSE THE WEIGHT
44     var days:int=int((weightLoss * CALORIES_PER_LB)/reducedCals);
45
46     //TASK 3:   TRANSLATE DAYS INTO YEARS, WEEKS, AND DAYS
47     var years:int=days/DAYS_IN_YEAR;
48     var weeks:int=days%DAYS_IN_YEAR/DAYS_IN_WEEK;
49     days=days%DAYS_IN_YEAR%DAYS_IN_WEEK;
50
51     //TASK 4:   DISPLAY YEARS, WEEKS, AND DAYS TO LOSE WEIGHT
52     output1.text="The time it will take to drop this weight is:\n";
53     if (years>0) {
54        output1.appendText(years + " year(s)\n");
55     }
56     if (weeks>0) {
57        output1.appendText(weeks + " weeks(s)\n");
58     }
59     if (days>0) {
60        output1.appendText(days + " day(s)\n");
61     }
62  }
```

◾ 5.7 The Nested if Statement

The previous section explored if statements that may also contain if-else and else clauses. These clauses provide the option of selecting multiple alternatives. An if statement contains a set of action statements, enclosed in {}, which may also be another if statement—hence the term if statement. The objective of a nested if statement is to improve the efficiency of the code by reducing or eliminating redundant Boolean tests. These refinements occur when compound Boolean expressions are pared down and assembled into a collection of simple Boolean expressions containing nested `if` statements. Oftentimes, use of such nested `if` statements can also boost readability. The next two examples demonstrate nested `if` statements.

Example 1

For this first example, let us consider the childhood game called Rock, Scissors, Paper. In this two-player game, the user plays against the computer. The user selects one of the elements, while the computer is randomly assigned one. The user wins only if her choice dominates the computer's choice. The two players tie if the choices are the same. Otherwise, the user loses. Here are the domination rules:

Rule 1: Rock beats scissors because it can crush it.

Rule 2: Scissors beats paper because it can cut it.

Rule 3: Paper beats rock because it can cover it.

A good solution will display a detailed reason for a win, loss, or tie outcome for the user. There are a total of nine detailed game outcomes.

Two code solutions are provided here to showcase the efficiency of a nested `if` statement.

Rock, Scissors, Paper Game Solution 1

This first solution does not rely on nested statements. Upon close examination, it becomes clear that within each compound Boolean expression is a simple Boolean expression that appears in several compound Boolean expressions. For example, the simple Boolean expression user == ROCK occurs three times, on lines 1, 3, and 5.

```
1   if (user == ROCK && computer == PAPER) {
2      trace ("You lose. Computer chose PAPER, which covers ROCK.");
3   } else if (user == ROCK && computer == SCISSORS) {
4      trace ("SCISSORS can be crushed by ROCK.  Player wins.");
5   } else if (user == ROCK && computer == ROCK) {
6      trace ("You tied with the computer because you both chose ROCK. ");
7   } else if (user == PAPER && computer == SCISSORS) {
8      trace ("PAPER loses because SCISSORS cuts PAPER.  Player loses.");
9   } else if (user == PAPER && computer == ROCK) {
10     trace ("PAPER wins because PAPER covers ROCK.  Player wins.");
11  } else if (user == PAPER && computer == PAPER) {
12     trace ("You both chose PAPER.  Player ties with the computer.");
13  } else if (user == SCISSORS && computer == PAPER) {
14     trace ("PAPER is vulnerable to cutting.  You win.");
```

```
15  } else if (user == SCISSORS && computer == ROCK) {
16     trace ("ROCK loses because PAPER covers ROCK.  Player loses.");
17  } else {
18     trace ("You both chose SCISSORS.  Player ties with the computer.");
19  }
```

Rock, Scissors, Paper Game Solution 2

This second solution utilizes nested if statements to take advantage of the fact that the compound Boolean expressions from Solution 1 can be grouped into three main scenarios:

```
user == ROCK
user == PAPER
user == SCISSORS
```

Within each scenario is a set of subscenarios expressed as nested if statements. For example, when the user chooses Rock, as identified in line 1, there are three possible subscenarios identified on lines 2–8: computer == PAPER, computer == SCISSORS, and computer == ROCK.

The final solution is easier to read and of higher quality due to the elimination of redundant Boolean test expressions.

```
1   if (user == ROCK){ //SCENARIO 1: USER IS ROCK
2      if (computer == PAPER) {
3         trace ("You lose. Computer chose PAPER, which covers ROCK.");
4      } else if (computer == SCISSORS) {
5         trace ("SCISSORS can be crushed by ROCK.  Player wins.");
6      } else {
7         trace ("You tied with the computer. You both chose ROCK. ");
8      }
9   } else if (user == PAPER ) { //SCENARIO 2: USER IS PAPER
10     if (computer == SCISSORS) {
11        trace ("SCISSORS cuts PAPER.  Player loses.");
12     } else if (computer == ROCK) {
13        trace ("PAPER wins because PAPER covers ROCK.  Player wins.");
14     } else {
15        trace ("You both chose PAPER.  Player ties with the computer.");
16     }
17  } else if (user == SCISSORS) {   //SCENARIO 3: USER IS SCISSORS
18     if (computer == PAPER) {
19        trace ("PAPER is vulnerable to cutting.  Player wins.");
```

```
20    } else if (computer == ROCK) {
21        trace ("ROCK loses because PAPER covers ROCK.  Player loses.");
22    } else {
23        trace ("You both chose SCISSORS.  Player ties.");
24    }
25 }
```

Example 2

In this example, we examine a segment of AS3 code that issues facts about a user's age. Depending on the user's age, multiple conditions need to be examined and one or more age-appropriate pieces of information displayed based on the following facts.

Fact 1: Any person age 5 or younger is considered to be a child.

Fact 2: All persons older than age 5 and younger than age 13 are considered to be kids.

Fact 3: Kids younger than age 8 go to elementary school.

Fact 4: Kids age 8 and older go to middle school.

Fact 5: All persons from the age of 13 through 19 are called teenagers.

Fact 6: Teenagers younger than age 16 cannot drive a car.

Fact 7: Teenagers of age 16 and older may drive a car if they pass a driving test.

Fact 8: Any person who is not a child, kid, or teenager is considered to be an adult.

Two solutions are used to showcase the efficiency of a nested if statement.

Age-Appropriate Facts Solution 1

The first solution does not use nested statements. Because multiple statements can be true, this solution is split into two independent if statements. Suppose the user is 13 years old. He is a teenager and he cannot drive.

```
1 //ARE YOU A CHILD, KID, TEENAGER, OR ADULT?
2 if (age <= 5) {
3     trace ("You are a child.");
4 } else if (age < 13) {
5     trace ("You are a kid.");
6 } else if (age <= 19) {
7     trace ("You are a teenager.");
8 } else {
```

```
9      trace ("You are an adult.");
10  }
11
12  //WHAT YOU CAN (OR CANNOT) DO AT YOUR CURRENT AGE
13  if (age < 13 && age > 5) {
14      trace ("You are in school.");
15  } else if (age <= 19 && age >= 16) {
16      trace ("You can drive.");
17  } else if (age < 16)
18      trace ("You cannot drive yet.");
19  } else {
20      trace ("You are an adult.");
21      trace ("You can run for president.");
22  }
```

Age-Appropriate Facts Solution 2

This solution uses a single nested if statement in which the user is categorized into one of the following groups:

Child   Kid   Teenager   Adult

By using nested if statements, multiple conditions can be examined. This code solution is concise, efficient, and easy to read.

```
1   if (age <= 5) {                           // A CHILD
2       trace ("You are a child.");
3   } else if (age < 13) {                    // A KID
4       trace ("You are a kid.");
5       trace ("You should be in school.");
6   } else if (age <= 19) {                   // A TEENAGER
7       trace ("You are a teenager.");
8       if (age <= 16) {
9           trace ("You can drive.");
10      } else {
11          trace ("You cannot drive yet.");
12      }
13  } else {                                  // AN ADULT
14      trace ("You are an adult.");
15  }
```

■ 5.8 Case Study 3: The Virtual Pet Fish

Problem

The virtual fish in this case study has a single requirement for survival—food. Our fish will never starve, however, because there is a constant source of food in the tank.

The fish exhibits three possible states: playing, hungry, and eating. While the fish is playing, it is in a constant state of motion, moving around the tank seeking out its toy, and burning off calories. Once it becomes hungry, the fish immediately moves toward the food source. When it locates its food, the fish eats until its stomach is full, at which point it again seeks out its toy to burn off calories until it is hungry again, and the cycle continues.

There are three objectives for this case study:

1. Use nested `if` statements to monitor and respond to the three possible conditions of the fish: `isHungry`, `isEating`, and `isAtPlay`.

2. Build custom properties to identify individual fish attributes.

3. Work with basic game mathematics to create realistic motion.

Problem Analysis and Visual Design

The primary goal of this application is to create a display object that behaves like a simple-minded pet fish in a virtual fish tank. This pet fish will need a minimal amount of artificial intelligence that allows it to evaluate its current condition as it plays, becomes hungry, or generally swims around the tank. Once it understands its current condition, it then responds with an appropriate change in behavior.

The display object on the stage that represents the pet fish is a `MovieClip` instance named `Fish`. In addition to `Fish`, two other `MovieClip` instances are found in this virtual environment: `Toy` and `Food`. These three display objects are shown in the fish tank environment in Figure 5-9.

`Fish`'s behavior will be controlled by basic artificial intelligence constructed as a set of nested `if-else` `if-else` statements, more appropriately called rules. These rules will utilize a set of properties, shown in Table 5-8, created specifically for this purpose.

The artificial intelligence rules for controlling `Fish` are as follows:

Rule 1: If `Fish` is playing with its toy (`isAtPlay == true`), rotate and move `Fish` toward `Toy`. Burn a calorie by reducing the amount of food in `Fish`'s stomach and check whether it is hungry.

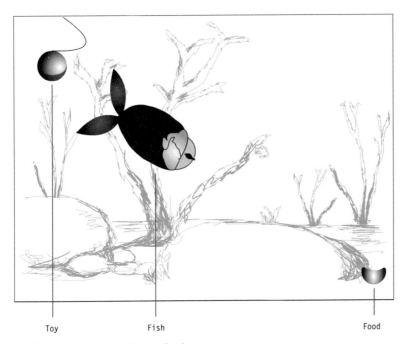

FIGURE 5-9 Virtual pet fish application.

Rule 2: If Fish is hungry (isHungry == true), rotate and move Fish toward Food. Check whether it has reached its food.

Rule 3: If Fish is eating (isEating == true), check whether its stomach has reached its limited capacity for food.

TABLE 5-8 Properties Constructed for Fish

Fish Property	Type of Property	Description of Property
isHungry	Boolean, dynamic value	True if Fish is hungry; false otherwise. If Fish is hungry, it is not eating or playing.
isAtPlay	Boolean, dynamic value	True if Fish is playing with, or seeking to play with, its toy.
isEating	Boolean, dynamic value	True if Fish is currently eating; false otherwise. If Fish is eating, it is not hungry and not playing.
velocity	Number, static value	Fish's normal traveling velocity. This static value will not change throughout the program.
capacity	Number, static value	The amount of food Fish can eat before it is full.
inStomach	Number, static value	The current amount of food in Fish's stomach.

Algorithmic Design

The program for this game consists of the five functions described in Table 5-9. Figure 5-10 shows the relationship between these functions.

TABLE 5-9 Program Functions Used by the Virtual Pet Fish Application

Function Name	Description
virtualPetApp()	The main function as well as the class constructor. It executes immediately when the application begins. This function is responsible for initializing the Fish properties and registering the main listener event ENTER_FRAME.
makeItLive()	The event handler for the listener event ENTER_FRAME. It is also the engine that drives the artificial intelligence of the pet fish by monitoring its three possible conditions—isHungry, isAtPlay, and isEating—and responds with a call to the appropriate function that carries out the required behavior.
goPlay()	Called when Fish is seeking out its toy and playing.
findFood()	Dictates how Fish will locate its food.
eatFood()	Called when Fish is eating its food. This function dictates how the pet eats and finishes eating.

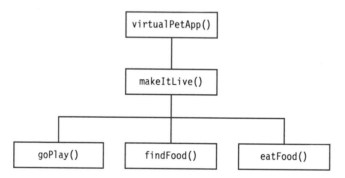

FIGURE 5-10 Relationship structure of functions used by the virtual pet fish application.

This program does not require any game constants. The package contains the libraries flash.display.* and flash.events.*.

```
1  package {
2      import flash.display.*;
3      import flash.events.*;
4
```

```
5      public class virtualPetApp extends MovieClip {
6
```

⋮

```
89     }
90   }
```

The tasks of each function written for this application are outlined next.

Function virtualPetApp() Design

The function virtualPetApp(), which is the class constructor, has the sole task of initializing Fish and registering the event listener ENTER_FRAME to enable a looping mechanism. Its instructions are organized into three tasks:

Task 1: Set Fish's initial behavioral conditions. Initially Fish is playing with its toy. Because it is not currently hungry and not eating, both these conditions are set to false.

Task 2: Set Fish's attributes that govern its velocity and the physical properties that will dictate hunger. Its normal traveling velocity is set to 10. Its capacity, which is the amount of food it can eat to satisfy its hunger, and the current amount of food in its stomach are both set to 50.

Task 3: Register the listener event ENTER_FRAME with the function makeItLive() as the event handler.

```
7    function virtualPetApp() {
8       //TASK 1: SET THE INITIAL CONDITION OF THE FISH TO PLAY
9       Fish.isHungry=false;
10      Fish.isAtPlay=true;
11      Fish.isEating=false;
12
13      //TASK 2: SET THE INITIAL PROPERTIES OF THE PET FISH
14      Fish.velocity=10;//ITS NORMAL TRAVELING VELOCITY.
15      Fish.capacity=50;//HOW MUCH CAN IT EAT BEFORE IT'S FULL
16      Fish.inStomach=50;//THE CURRENT AMOUNT OF FOOD IN FISH
17
18      //TASK 3:  USE AN ENTER_FRAME LISTENER TO MAKE PET ALIVE
19      addEventListener(Event.ENTER_FRAME,makeItLive);
20   }
21
```

Function makeItLive() Design

Function makeItLive() is the event handler that executes at regular intervals when called by the event listener for ENTER_FRAME. This function takes the static fish and makes it dynamic by responding with appropriate function calls based on the current condition of Fish.

By using an `if–else if–else if` structure, the function can identify when `Fish` is hungry, playing with its toy, or eating.

```
22  function makeItLive (event:Event) {
23     //EXAMINE AND RESPOND THE CONDITIONS: isHungry, isAtPlay, isEating
24     if (Fish.isAtPlay) {
25        goPlay();
26     } else if (Fish.isHungry) {
27        findFood();
28     } else if (Fish.isEating) {
29        eatFood();
30  }
31
```

Function `goPlay()` Design

The `goPlay()` function directs the behavior of `Fish` while its current state is playing with its toy. This function is subdivided into five tasks:

Task 1: Burn a calorie by reducing the amount of food in the fish's stomach by decrementing this amount by one.

Task 2: Compute the distance `Fish` must travel to get to its toy. This distance must be computed along both the x-axis and the y-axis.

Task 3: Turn `Fish` in the direction of its toy. To accomplish this task, the angle must first be computed. This is done by using the arctangent function `Math.atan()`, which produces a result in radians. Because rotation requires a value in degrees, the conversion from radians to degrees is performed by multiplying the angle by `180 / Math.PI`.

Task 4: Move `Fish` toward `Toy`. To create the illusion of elegant dynamic movement, the fish must be able to gradually slow down as it nears its toy, as opposed to barreling into the toy and stopping abruptly. This can easily be done by dividing the distance to be traveled by the fixed velocity, which eases `Fish` to its final destination.

Task 5: Check whether `Fish` is hungry again. This code assumes `Fish` is hungry if it has less than 25 units of food in its stomach. If `Fish` is found to be hungry, the `isAtPlay` property is set to false and the `isHungry` property is set to true.

```
32  function goPlay() {
33     //TASK 1:  BURN A CALORIE
34     Fish.inStomach–;
35
36     //TASK 2: COMPUTE THE DISTANCE TO TOY
37     var xDistance:Number=Toy.x-Fish.x;
38     var yDistance:Number=Toy.y-Fish.y;
```

```
39
40    //TASK 3: ANGLE THE FISH TOWARD ITS TOY
41    var Angle:Number=Math.atan2(yDistance,xDistance);
42    Fish.rotation=Angle*180/Math.PI;
43
44    //TASK 4: MOVE FISH CLOSER TO ITS TOY
45    Fish.x+=xDistance/Fish.velocity;
46    Fish.y+=yDistance/Fish.velocity;
47
48    //TASK 5: CHECK IF THE FISH IS HUNGRY
49    if (Fish.inStomach < 25) {
50        //SUBTASK 1: SET THE FISH TO HUNGRY
51        Fish.isAtPlay=false;
52        Fish.isHungry=true;
53    }
54  }
55
```

Function `findFood()` Design

The `findFood()` function is divided into four tasks:

Task 1: Compute the distance `Fish` must travel to locate `Food`.

Task 2: Turn `Fish` in the direction of `Food`.

Task 3: Move `Fish` toward `Food` by traveling distance divided by velocity. `Fish` will ease toward its final destination.

Task 4: Check whether `Fish` has located `Food`. This code assumes `Fish` has located `Food` once its horizontal distance is less than 5 and its vertical distance is less than 3. At this point, the `isEating` property is set to true and the `isHungry` property is set to false.

```
56  function findFood() {
57      //TASK 1: CALCULATE DISTANCE TO ITS FOOD
58      var xDistance:Number=Food.x-Fish.x;
59      var yDistance:Number=Food.y-Fish.y;
60
61      //TASK 2: TURN FISH TOWARD ITS FOOD
62      var Angle:Number=Math.atan2(yDistance,xDistance);
63      Fish.rotation=Angle*180/Math.PI;
64
65      //TASK 3: MOVE THE FISH TOWARD ITS FOOD
66      Fish.x+=xDistance/Fish.velocity;
67      Fish.y+=yDistance/Fish.velocity;
68
69      //TASK 4: CHECK IF THE FISH HAS LOCATED ITS FOOD
70      if (xDistance < 5 && yDistance < 3) {
71          //SUBTASK: SET THE STATE OF THE FISH TO EATING
```

```
72          Fish.isHungry=false;
73          Fish.isEating=true;
74      }
75  }
76
```

Function eatFood() Design

The eatFood() function is divided into two tasks:

Task 1: Increment the amount of food in Fish's stomach.

Task 2: Check whether Fish's stomach is full. This code assumes Fish is full when the amount of food in its stomach has reached capacity. At this point, the isEating property is set to false and the isAtPlay property is set to true.

```
77  function eatFood() {
78      //TASK 1:  FISH CONSUMES A CALORIE OF FOOD
79      Fish.inStomach++;
80
81      //TASK 2: CHECK IF THE FISH IS FULL
82      if (Fish.inStomach >= Fish.capacity) {
83          //SUBTASK: SET THE STATE OF THE FISH TO PLAYING
84          Fish.isEating=false;
85          Fish.isAtPlay=true;
86      }
87  }
88
```

■ 5.9 The switch Statement

In addition to the if statement, there is another selective control structure available—the switch statement. The switch statement is not strictly necessary, but can in some cases make for more concise and readable code.

As seen in the previous sections, one of the most commonly seen patterns in programming is a series of if–else if–else statements that test a single value against a series of values. For example, the following code segment displays the string "Freshman," "Sophomore," "Junior," or "Senior," depending on the value of year:

```
if (year == 1) {
   trace("Freshman");
}else  if (year == 2 {
   trace("Sophomore");
}else if (year == 3) {
   trace("Junior");
}else {
   trace("Senior");
}
```

This structure is important in programming because it provides us with a mechanism to solve all multiway selective-type problems. Because multiway selection statements can sometimes be difficult to follow, many languages provide an alternative method of handling this concept—the switch statement.

In AS3, switch statements are often used when several options depend on the value of a single variable or expression, as in the previous example. The typical form of the switch statement is shown next. The words switch, case, break, and default are reserved keywords.

```
switch (variable) {

    case value1 : statement list1;
        break;

    case value2 : statement list2;
        break;
        .
        .
        .
    case valueN : statement listN;
        break;

    default : statement listDefault;
}
```

1. The value of variable is determined.

2. The first matching value with a case is found. The statements following the matching case are executed.

   Note: break and default statements are optional. If a break statement occurs, control is transferred to the first statement following the end of the switch statement; otherwise, the execution of statements continues. In general, a case should end with a break statement.

3. If no matching value is found, then the default statement list is executed.

The following code segment is a rewrite of the if statement that displays "Freshman," "Sophomore," "Junior," or "Senior," depending on the value of year. This segment illustrates the switch statement. Each of the statement lists in a switch statement usually ends with a break statement. The effect of the break in these statements causes a transfer of control to the end of the switch statement.

```
switch  (year) {
    case   1:
        trace("Freshman");
        break;
    case   2:
        trace("Sophomore");
        break;
    case   3:
        trace("Junior");
        break;
```

```
     default  :
        trace("Senior");
  }
```

The next three examples illustrate how the switch statement works.

Example 1

```
1   var Num:Number;
2   switch (Num){
3      case 0 : trace ("ZERO");
4         break;
5      case 1 : trace ("ONE or");
6      case 2 : trace ("TWO");
7         break;
8      default :trace("NO MATCHES!");
9   }
10  trace ("DONE");
```

Evaluations for Different Values of Num

a. Num = 0

In this scenario, the value of Num is matched with the first case in line 1. The trace statement executes, and a break is encountered on line 4, ending the switch statement. Line 11 is an unconditional statement that displays the text "DONE."

The output produced by this segment of code is

    ZERO
    DONE

b. Num = 1

The value of Num has found a match with the second case statement, 1, on line 5. The trace statement on the same line executes, but no break is encountered; hence, all instructions are executed until a break is found, or the switch statement terminates on its own. In this case, a break statement is found on line 7.

The output produced by this segment of code is

    ONE or
    TWO
    DONE

c. Num = 4

No matching values for Num are found. The default statement on line 8 is executed.

The output produced by this segment of code is

NO MATCHES!
DONE

Example 2

```
1   var Digit:int;
2   switch (Digit){
3      case 0 : trace ("ZERO");
4         break;
5      case 1 :
6      case 3 :
7      case 5 :
8      case 9 : trace ("ODD");
9         break;
10     case 2 :
11     case 4 :
12     case 6 :
13     case 8 : trace ("EVEN");
14  }
```

Evaluation

The switch statement in this segment of code illustrates the capture of multiple matches.

a. Digit = 3

When Digit contains the value 3, a match is found in the third case statement on line 6. There are no statements to execute, but more importantly, there is no break statement to terminate the switch statement. This means any instructions from lines 6 through 8 are executed until a break is encountered on line 9.

The output produced by this segment of code is

ODD

b. Digit = 8

In this scenario, a match is found in the final case statement on line 13. There is no break statement following this final statement list because there are no statements to execute, so the switch statement will terminate automatically. As shown in this example, default statements are optional.

The output produced by this segment of code is

```
EVEN
```

Example 3

```
1    var P:int;
2    var Q:int;
3    switch (P){
4       case 0 : switch (Q){
5          case 3: P = P + Q; break;
6          default: P = P - Q;
7          }
8          break;
9       case 1 :
10      case 3:
11      case 5 : switch (Q){
12         case 2:
13         case 6: P = P * Q; break;
14         case -4:
15         case -6: P = Q * Q;
16         }
17   }
18   trace ("P = ", P );
19   trace ("Q = ", Q );
```

Evaluation

This segment of code illustrates a nested switch statement. Like if statements, switch statements may contain multiple layers of alternatives.

a. P = 0, Q = 3

A match is found for P in the first case statement on line 4. The nested switch statement switch (Q) is executed, and a match is found in case 3 on line 5. The statement P = P + Q is executed, followed by the break on line 8.

The output produced by this segment of code is

```
P = 3
Q = 3
```

b. P = 1, Q = -3

When P contains the value 1, a match is found in the second case statement on line 9. There is no break statement to terminate the switch statement, so all statements will be executed until a break is encountered. In this case, the nested switch (Q) statement in case 5 on line 11 will execute. No match is found within the nested `switch` statement, and the values in `P` and `Q` will not be altered.

The output produced by this segment of code is

```
P = 1
Q = -3
```

5.10 Case Study 4: Airship Flight Simulator

Problem

In this case study, we construct a simple top-view flight simulator for an airship. Airships were once luxury passenger aircraft that experienced a period of grandeur in Europe during the 1920s and 1930s. These magnificent aircraft, which were designed to fly wealthy passengers across oceans and continents, often featured opulent lounges, fine accommodations, dining rooms, and even smoking rooms. The largest passenger airship in history, as well as the most disastrous, was the *Hindenburg*.

Three objectives are addressed in this case study:

1. Use `switch` statements to respond to keyboard control of the airship.

2. Use a timer to create smooth animations as the airship flies to a higher or lower altitude over the world below.

3. Work with basic game math to reposition the world below as the airship changes direction and flies overhead.

Game Plan and Analysis

The flight simulator for this case study, shown in Figure 5-11, will be kept simple in terms of the rules of engagement and the game play parameters. For example, the airship will not be permitted to land or crash. Four essential characteristics govern how this simulator will perform:

1. The airship will be constrained to a static location at Stage center. The world below will move as the airship flies overhead. There are two reasons for the restricted movement of the airship. First, an anchored airship will not run the risk of flying off the Stage. It will be possible for the airship to change direction. Second, and most important, the user can expect a uniform perspective, thereby creating the illusion of being aboard, or at least linked to, the airship. This consistent perspective will make the navigation more user friendly.

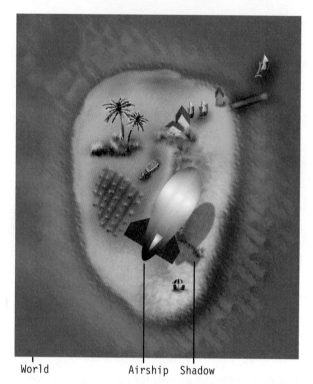

World   Airship   Shadow

❙ FIGURE 5-11 Airship flight simulator application.

2. The dynamic world below the airship will be stored as a separate MovieClip instance. Using an ENTER_FRAME event, this world will be continuously repositioned and scaled to reveal a new view from the moving airship.

3. The airship will have a fixed velocity. The user will not have access to this velocity.

4. The user can guide the airship by simply pressing the up, down, left, or right arrow keys. These keys will change the direction and elevation of the airship. The up arrow will be used to climb to a higher altitude. The down arrow key will be used to decrease elevation, but not beyond a set minimum altitude. The left and right arrow keys allow the airship to change direction by turning left or right a set number of degrees.

Visual Design

The flight simulator requires three MovieClip instances as shown in Figure 5-11: Airship, Shadow, and World. Both Airship and Shadow are simple vector drawings created in Flash, with Shadow representing the shadow the airship casts over the world below. For this example, the MovieClip instance named World was created in Adobe

Photoshop and then imported into Flash. This is not a requirement and could just as easily been done in Flash using the vector drawing tools.

The simulator application relies solely on a single frame, representing a single screen. There are no instructions or buttons. The Timeline is organized using three layers. The bottom layer holds World, the middle layer holds Shadow, and the top layer contains Airship. This animation is set to a rate of 60 frames per second, which is fast enough to create the illusion of a smooth flight—a hallmark of these luxurious airships.

Program Design

The algorithm for this game application will use Airship, Shadow, and World to create the animations necessary for visualizing an aircraft in virtual flight. These animations will rely on a select set of inherited display object properties. In addition, the MovieClip instance Airship will utilize the constructed properties Velocity and Altitude. Table 5-10 provides a comprehensive explanatory list of all the display object properties required for the visualization of the flight simulator.

TABLE 5-10 Properties Constructed for the Airship Flight Simulator Application

Display Object Name	Property
Airship	rotation: Airship's turn amount dictated by the left and right arrow keys. Note: The x and y position of Airship will remain static throughout execution; however, the ability to turn left or right will be permitted.
	Velocity: Airship's traveling Velocity. This newly constructed property will be used to compute the visual adjustments made to the World. These adjustments will ultimately create the illusion of movement from the perspective of the airship looking below as it travels.
	Altitude: Elevation gains and losses of Airship. This property is used to make alterations to the velocity for the airship. The lower the airship, the faster it appears to fly because the World is magnified.
Shadow	alpha: The level of transparency for the airship's shadow. Creates a three-dimensional impression of an overhead airship.
	scaleX, scaleY: The scale of the shadow projected by the airship. Used to create the illusion of three-dimensionality. This value is altered only when the elevation of the airship changes. As the airship descends closer to the surface, the shadow's scale increases. As the airship moves farther away, the shadow's scale decreases.
World	x, y: World is the only display object whose x and y positions will be altered during runtime.
	scaleX, scaleY: As with Shadow, the scale of World will be altered when the elevation of Airship changes.

This flight simulator application will consist of five functions: `airshipApp()`, `adjustWorld()`, `checkControlKey()`, `zoomHigher()`, and `zoomLower()` (described in Table 5-11). Figure 5-12 shows the relationship between these functions.

TABLE 5-11 Airship Flight Simulator Program Functions

Function Name	Description
`airshipApp()`	Sets the game elements and adds event listeners. The main function of the application, it is also the constructor function and executes immediately when the application is launched.
`adjustWorld()`	Adjusts `World`'s location as the airship moves. This function is an event handler that is triggered by the `ENTER_FRAME` event. It executes at regular intervals.
`checkControlKey()`	Examines the control keys (up, down, left, and right), and responds to them.
`zoomHigher()`	Creates a visual animation that uses scaling to impart the illusion of the airship climbing in altitude. This function is an event handler triggered by a timer event.
`zoomLower()`	Creates a visual animation that shows the airship decreasing in altitude. Scaling is used to trick the eye. Like `ZoomHigher()`, this function is an event handler triggered by a timer event.

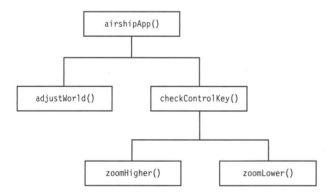

FIGURE 5-12 Relationship of functions used in the airship flight simulator application.

The first line of this `airshipApp.as` AS3 file consists of the class `package`. The required library classes to be imported are `display`, `events`, and `utils`. The `utils` library classes are needed for the timer event. The final curly brackets, located on the last two lines of the file, conclude the `airshipApp` class and the package.

```
1   package {
2       import flash.display.*;
3       import flash.events.*;
4       import flash.utils.*;
5       public class airshipApp extends MovieClip {
```

```
103     }
104 }
```

Game Constants

Two categories of constant values are needed. The first category defines game constants. The first constant is RADIANS, which will be used in the game mathematics. Recall that Flash trigonometric functions use radians instead of degrees as units. The other constants include the airship's cruising altitude and minimum and maximum flying altitudes. Line 12 contains the constant ALTITUDE_AMT, which specifies the altitude increase and decrease amounts when the user presses the up and down arrow control keys. The constant TURN specifies the turn amount in degrees for maneuvering left or right when the user presses the left and right arrow keys.

```
6        //GAME CONSTANTS
7        const RADIANS:Number=Math.PI/180;
8        const MIN_ALTITUDE:Number=30;
9        const CRUISING_ALTITUDE:Number=50;
10       const MAX_ALTITUDE:Number=70;
11       const CRUISING_VELOCITY:Number=.3;
12       const ALTITUDE_AMT:Number=0.1;
13       const TURN:Number=4;
```

The last category of constants defines the flight control keys. These constants represent the specific ASCII key values used to direct the airship right and left and to adjust its altitude.

```
14       //FLIGHT CONTROL CONSTANTS
15       const RIGHTARROW:Number=39;
16       const LEFTARROW:Number=37;
17       const UPARROW:Number=38;
18       const DOWNARROW:Number=40;
```

Timer Variable

In addition to the constants, there will be a global variable, atimer, that stores a timer object. This variable is used by the functions checkControlKey(), zoomHigher(), and zoomLower() to smooth the scaling animation of World as the airship gains or losses altitude. This variable object is made global so that all three functions that use it will have unfettered access to the variable. Chapter 8 discusses the alternative to creating global variables such as `atimer`.

```
19  //TIMER VARIABLES
20  var atimer:Timer;
```

The functions for this application are designed as follows.

Function `airshipApp()` Design

The main algorithm, `airshipApp()`, is a constructor that loads immediately once the application is launched. The objective of this function is to set the initial properties of the elements on the Stage and add event listeners for the control keys and adjustments made to the `World` at every frame loop.

> Task 1: Initialize the properties of `Airship`. The two properties `Velocity` and `Altitude` are constructed when they are initialized.

> Task 2: Initialize the properties of `Shadow`. The initial scale of `Shadow` is set to 25% of the size of the airship and 25% opacity.

> Task 3: Initialize the position and scale of `World`.

> Task 4: Register the event listeners for the ENTER_FRAME event and the KEY_DOWN event. The keyboard event listener waits for the user to interactively control the altitude and direction of the airship.

```
21  function airshipApp() {
22     //TASK 1:  SET AIRSHIP PROPERTIES TO INITIAL VALUES
23     Airship.x=Airship.y=350;
24     Airship.Altitude=CRUISING_ALTITUDE;
25     Airship.Velocity=CRUISING_VELOCITY;
26
27     //TASK 2:  SET AIRSHIP SHADOW PROPERTIES TO VALUES
28     Shadow.alpha=.25;
29     Shadow.scaleY=.25;
30     Shadow.scaleX=.25;
31
32     //TASK 3:  SET VILLAGE PROPERTIES TO INITIAL VALUES
33     World.x=World.y=350;
34     World.scaleY =.25;
35     World.scaleX=.25;
36
37     //TASK 4: ADD EVENT LISTENERS
38     stage.addEventListener(Event.ENTER_FRAME, adjustWorld);
39     stage.addEventListener(KeyboardEvent.KEY_DOWN, checkControlKey);
40  }
41
```

Function `adjustWorld()` Design

This function is an event handler that is called at every frame loop. Its primary objective is to adjust the location of the world below. Its complete set of tasks is as follows:

Task 1: Adjust the velocity of the airship to make the world below appear to move faster at low altitudes and slower at high altitudes. This small trick has a nuanced effect in creating a more realistic simulation.

Task 2: Change the world's x and y positions on the stage. As shown in Figure 5-13, the calculation of this altered world is based on the velocity and rotation of the airship. For example, as `Airship` changes direction by turning to the right, `World` will shift to the left.

The trigonometric functions `sin()` and `cos()` are used to compute the correct angle (in radians) in which to shift the world below. The radian value is needed to use the `sin()` and `cos()` functions.

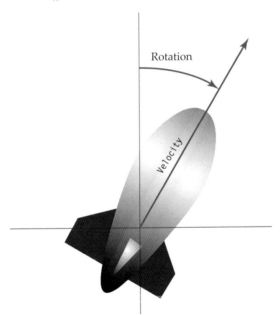

| **FIGURE 5-13** Angle and velocity diagram of the airship.

```
42  function adjustWorld(event:Event) {
43      //TASK 1:  ADJUST THE VELOCITY OF THE AIRSHIP ACCORDING TO ALTITUDE
44      Airship.Velocity=CRUISING_VELOCITY-.01*(Airship.Altitude-CRUISING_ALTITUDE);
45
```

```
46   //TASK 2: CHANGE WORLD'S LOCATION RELATIVE TO THE AIRSHIP
47   var toRadians:Number=Math.PI/180;
48   World.x += (Airship.Velocity)*Math.sin(Airship.rotation*toRadians);
49   World.y -= (Airship.Velocity)*Math.cos(Airship.rotation*toRadians);
50 }
51
```

Function checkControlKey() Design

This function, an event handler, has the simple task of examining the input from the user and responding. Using a switch statement makes this code more readable.

Responses to individual arrow keys occur by changing Airship's rotation and altitude as follows:

> LEFTARROW or RIGHTARROW: Rotate Airship and Shadow the appropriate number of degrees defined by the constant TURN.

> UPARROW: Increase the altitude of Airship. If the maximum altitude has not been exceeded, activate a timer to decrease, in gradual measure, the scale of World. The timer is set to execute four times, for 40 milliseconds each time. The animation generated by this timer creates the illusion of the airship moving farther away.

> DOWNARROW: Decrease the altitude of Airship. If the altitude has not gone below the minimum, a timer animation is triggered to create the illusion of the airship moving closer to the world below.

```
52
53 function checkControlKey(event:KeyboardEvent) {
54    //TASK : EXAMINE AND RESPOND TO INPUT FROM USER
55    switch (event.keyCode) {
56       case RIGHTARROW :
57          Airship.rotation+=TURN;
58          Shadow.rotation+=TURN;
59          break;
60       case LEFTARROW :
61          Airship.rotation-=TURN;
62          Shadow.rotation-=TURN;
63          break;
64       case UPARROW :
65          //AIRSHIP INCREASES ITS ALTITUDE
66          Airship.Altitude+=ALTITUDE_AMT;
67          if (Airship.Altitude > MAX_ALTITUDE) {
68             Airship.Altitude=MAX_ALTITUDE;
69          } else {
70             atimer=new Timer(40,4);
```

```
71              atimer.addEventListener(TimerEvent.TIMER, ZoomHigher);
72              atimer.start();
73            }
74            break;
75        case DOWNARROW :
76            //AIRSHIP DECREASES ITS ALTITUDE
77            Airship.Altitude-=ALTITUDE_AMT;
78            if (Airship.Altitude < MIN_ALTITUDE) {
79                Airship.Altitude=MIN_ALTITUDE;
80            } else {
81                atimer=new Timer(40,4);
82                atimer.addEventListener(TimerEvent.TIMER, ZoomLower);
83                atimer.start();
84            }
85    }
86  }
87
```

Function ZoomHigher() Design

This function responds to the up arrow key. The display objects representing the world below and the airship's shadow are scaled down in size by small increments using a timer.

```
88  function ZoomHigher(event:TimerEvent) {
89     var newSize:Number;
90     newSize=World.scaleY-.0001;
91     World.scaleY=World.scaleX=newSize;
92     Shadow.scaleY=Shadow.scaleX=newSize;
93     atimer.removeEventListener(TimerEvent.TIMER, ZoomHigher);
94  }
95
```

Function ZoomLower() Design

This function has the simple task of incrementing the size of World and Shadow.

```
96  function ZoomLower(event:TimerEvent) {
97     var newSize:Number;
98     newSize=World.scaleY+.0001;
99     World.scaleY=World.scaleX=newSize;
100    Shadow.scaleY=Shadow.scaleX=newSize;
101    atimer.removeEventListener(TimerEvent.TIMER, ZoomLower);
102 }
```

■ 5.11 Case Study 5: Billiards Physics

In this case study, we explore several important physical concepts in the game of billiards. Our focus is a pared-down game that revolves around a user hitting a cue ball with a cue stick.

Algorithm Design

Three display objects will be used by the ActionScript 3.0 code: Stick, CueBall, and RedBall. In addition, a table and an image of a green cloth will provide visual boundaries to aid the player in the game (Figure 5-14). We assume both balls on the billiard table are of the same mass. The frame rate for this application is set to 30 frames per second for smooth animations.

In addition to delving into the mechanisms behind aiming the cue stick and striking a ball with it, four important physical concepts are explored in this algorithm:

1. Velocity vectors
2. Friction
3. Impulse
4. Conservation of momentum

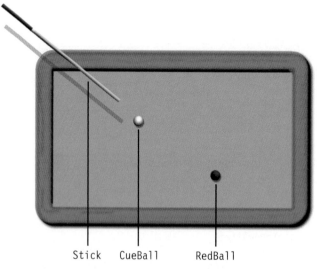

Stick   CueBall   RedBall

I FIGURE 5-14 Billiards application.

Velocity Vector

The velocity of a given ball is the speed at which it moves in a given direction. Figure 5-15 shows the velocity vectors indicating both direction and speed for two balls. Notice that the red ball moves from left to right at nearly half the speed of the cue ball sitting to the right. The velocity vector of a given ball can be deconstructed into its velocity along the *x*-axis and its velocity along the *y*-axis. In this case study, we will refer to these velocities as xVelocity and yVelocity, respectively.

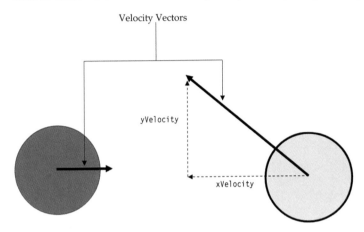

| FIGURE 5-15 Velocity vectors for two balls in motion.

Friction

One important element of billiards is the green felt table cloth, which provides traction as well as friction. Friction is the resistance the ball encounters as it rolls over the surface of the table cloth, causing it to slow down. The velocity of a moving ball is constantly changing due to the force of friction. Friction will be applied to moving balls in this case study.

Impulse

Impulse is the change in momentum of an object. In other words, it refers to the hit and the resulting transference of velocity from one object to the object it has impacted.

In this game, the user attempts to strike the cue ball with the stick. Once hit, the cue ball moves with similar velocity and direction. Thus the momentum from the stick is transferred to the cue ball, forcing it to move across the billiards table with an initial velocity.

Conservation of Momentum

Momentum is a conserved quantity. The total momentum during and following a collision will be the same. For example, when one ball hits another, the first ball imparts velocity to the second through momentum. As shown in Figure 5-16, when the cue ball hits the red ball, the red ball, which is initially at rest, is transferred a good deal of speed; simultaneously, the velocity of the cue ball decreases. Together, the new velocities add up to the momentum before impact. Notice that after impact, the red ball moves in the direction of the impulse, which is the line joining the center of the two balls.

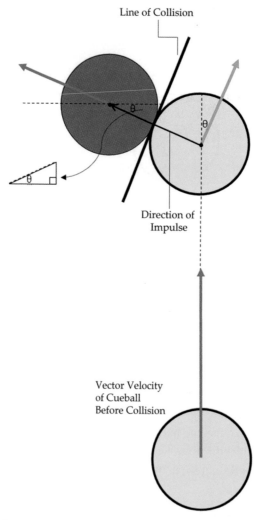

Line of Collision

θ

θ

θ

Direction of
Impulse

Vector Velocity
of Cueball
Before Collision

❙ FIGURE 5-16 Momentum before and after the collision of two balls in motion.

The theory of conservation of momentum, along with the initial velocity vectors of the colliding balls, can be used to compute the trajectories after impact. The line of collision is drawn at a tangent to both balls at the point of contact. This line is perpendicular to the line of impulse, which passes through the center of the two balls at the point of contact. Using geometry, we can see that the line of collision also makes an angle θ with the vertical, and the line of impulse makes an angle θ with the horizontal. This behavior follows the geometric principle that the angle of incidence will equal the angle of reflection.

As you will notice soon in the AS3 code, the physics of billiards is complex. To develop such a game, programmers need to be proficient in trigonometry and the practical usage of the physics.

Interactive Cue Stick Functionality

The cue stick is the user's only tool for interaction. Placing a strict restriction in its functionality so that it aims solely at the cue ball will provide a better gaming experience for the user. The stick is flexible only in its ability to follow the mouse cursor, which enables the user to direct a shot from any angle. As Figure 5-17 illustrates, trigonometry is used to compute the angle of rotation, θ, for the stick.

```
θ = Math.atan2(dy, dx);
```

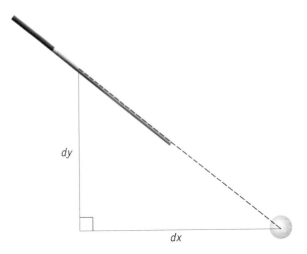

I FIGURE 5-17 The billiards stick shooting the cue ball from angle θ.

Algorithm Functions

The AS3 code for this application consists of the class constructor `billiardsApp()`, which initializes the game, and `aimStick()`, `startShoot()`, and `billiardsEngine()`, which control the animation and drive the game. In addition, three auxiliary functions perform the tasks completing a shot and responding to movement and collisions. Table 5-12 lists the seven functions and Figure 5-18 illustrates their relationship.

TABLE 5-12 billiardsApp Program Functions

Function Name	Description
billiardsApp()	The class constructor. After launching, it initializes the visual element properties and registers the events for interaction and animation.
aimStick()	Performs the task of aiming the cue stick at the cue ball. This event handler imposes a strict and constant aim on the cue ball by responding to the ENTER_FRAME event.
startShoot()	An event handler that responds to the event MOUSE_DOWN. This function starts the task of allowing the user to shoot the cue ball. It also initiates the event handler, finishShoot(), for completing the shot. Finally, it initializes collision detection tasks by calling the appropriate functions.
finishShoot()	An event handler that responds to the event MOUSE_UP. This function ends the task of the user shooting the cue ball.
billiardsEngine()	Drives the game of billiards by calling appropriate functions to move the balls and check for and respond to collisions.
moveBall()	Moves an individual ball, computes the decrease in velocity from frictional force, and responds to ball and table wall collisions.
checkCollision()	Checks for a collision between the two balls. If a collision has occurred, it responds by computing the new trajectories.

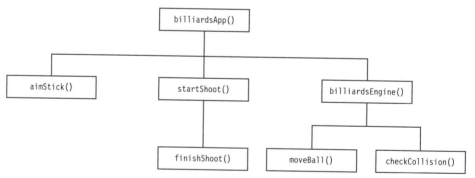

❙ FIGURE 5-18 Relationship of the functions used by the billiards game.

Game Constants

Billiards will utilize many of the same constants required by the game of Pong. The game of Pong used constant values when identifying collisions and reversing direction of the ball. These constants can be divided into three categories for the billiards game. The first represents the radius of the ball, which is set to 16 pixels. This constant is used to calculate the boundaries within which the ball can freely move. The second category represents the concrete boundaries of the table—TOP, BOTTOM, LEFT, and RIGHT. As in the Paddle game, the TOP boundary is not zero, but rather the point at which the ball strikes the top rail of the table, which is the radius of the ball. Lines 12–15 are constant declarations for these boundaries.

The final constant is REVERSE, −1. When the ball's current velocity is multiplied by this constant, the velocity is negated to reverse the ball's direction.

The package requires the display and events library classes. The final lines contain closing curly brackets to conclude the billiardsApp class and the package.

```
1   package {
2       import flash.display.*;
3       import flash.events.*;
4
5       public class billiardsApp extends MovieClip {
6           // GAME CONSTANTS
7           const REVERSE:Number=-1;    //REVERSE DIRECTION OF MOVING OBJECTS
8           const DIAMETER:Number=20;   //DIAMETER OF THE BILLIARD BALLS
9           const FRICTION:Number=.96;  //FRICTION OF THE BALLS ON THE TABLE
10          const MINSPEED:Number=.1;   //A BALL IS CONSIDERED STOPPED
11
12          const LEFT:Number=285;      //LEFT OF THE TABLE
13          const RIGHT:Number=734;     //RIGHT OF THE TABLE
14          const TOP:Number=241;       //TOP OF THE TABLE
15          const BOTTOM:Number=480;    //BOTTOM OF THE TABLE
16
```

```
157     }
158 }
```

The initial velocity vector of the cue ball is used to compute the resulting velocity vectors for both balls following a collision. Thus, if the ball hits the side of the table at an angle of 25 degrees, it will rebound at that angle.

Function billiardsApp() Design

This function initializes the ball properties and registers an event to wait for the user to use the cue stick.

```
17  function billiardsApp() {
18      //TASK 1:  SET THE VELOCITIES OF EACH BALL TO ZERO
19      CueBall.width=DIAMETER;
20      CueBall.height=DIAMETER;
```

```
21        RedBall.width=DIAMETER;
22        RedBall.height=DIAMETER;
23
24        //TASK 2:  POSITION BALLS ON THE TABLE
25        CueBall.x=400;
26        CueBall.y=350;
27        RedBall.x=600;
28        RedBall.y=350;
29
30        //TASK 3:  SET THE VELOCITY OF EACH BALL TO ZERO
31        CueBall.xVelocity=0;
32        CueBall.yVelocity=0;
33        RedBall.xVelocity=0;
34        RedBall.yVelocity=0;
35
36        //TASK 4:  ALWAYS AIM THE STICK AT THE CUE BALL
37        stick.addEventListener(Event.ENTER_FRAME,aimStick);
38
39        //TASK 5:  WAIT FOR USER TO START TO SHOOT MOUSE DOWN
40        stick.addEventListener(MouseEvent.MOUSE_DOWN,startShoot);
41        //TASK 6:  AT EVERY FRAME, CHECK IF A BALL SHOULD MOVE
42        addEventListener(Event.ENTER_FRAME,gameEngine);
43    }
44
```

Function `aimStick()` Design

Aiming the stick requires positioning its tip at the cue ball. The angle of the stick can be adjusted by moving it along with the mouse. The angle is computed using right triangle properties.

```
45    function aimStick(event:Event) {
46        //ROTATES THE ANGLE OF THE CUE STICK TO POINT AT THE WHITE BALL
47        var dx:Number=CueBall.x-mouseX;
48        var dy:Number=CueBall.y-mouseY;
49        var angle:Number=Math.atan2(dy,dx);
50        stick.rotation=angle*180/Math.PI;
51        stick.x=mouseX;
52        stick.y=mouseY;
53    }
54
```

Function `startShoot()` Design

This function begins the process of shooting the cue ball with the stick. If the ball has successfully been hit, the event handler function `FinishShoot()` is called to complete the task.

```
55  function startShoot(event:MouseEvent) {
56     //TASK 1:  LOCATE THE DISTANCE BETWEEN THE STICK AND THE BALL
57     var dx:Number=CueBall.x-mouseX;
58     var dy:Number=CueBall.y-mouseY;
59     var dist:Number=Math.sqrt(dx*dx+dy*dy);
60
61     //TASK 2:  IF WITHIN SHOOTING DISTANCE,
62     //          WAIT FOR THE USER TO FINISH THE SHOT
63     if (dist > 110) {
64        //TASK 3: STORE THE STARTING POSITION OF THE SHOT
65        stick.startx=stick.x;
66        stick.starty=stick.y;
67        stick.addEventListener(Event.ENTER_FRAME,FinishShoot);
68     }
69  }
70
```

Function FinishShoot() Design

This function is the event handler for completing a shot. The velocity of CueBall is computed based on the distance of the stick and the ball when the process began.

```
71  function FinishShoot(event:Event) {
72     //TASK 1:  COMPUTE DISTANCE BETWEEN STICK AND CUE BALL
73     var dx:Number=CueBall.x-stick.x;
74     var dy:Number=CueBall.y-stick.y;
75     var dist:Number=Math.sqrt(dx*dx+dy*dy);
76
77     //CHECK IF THE STICK HAS JUST HIT THE WHITE BALL
78     if (dist < 110) {
79        //TASK 2:  COMPUTE THE NEW VELOCITY OF THE WHITE BALL
80        CueBall.xVelocity=(stick.x-stick.startx)/4;
81        CueBall.yVelocity=(stick.y-stick.starty)/4;
82        //TASK 3:  THE FINISH SHOOT OPERATION IS DONE
83        stick.removeEventListener(Event.ENTER_FRAME,FinishShoot);
84     }
85  }
86
```

Function gameEngine() Design

This function is the event handler for the ENTER_FRAME event registered by the application constructor billiardsApp(). It is also the animation engine that takes the game from static mode to dynamic play by directing the movement at regular intervals. In addition, this function is responsible for directing collision detection between the two balls on the Stage.

```
87  function gameEngine(event:Event) {
88     //TASK 1: MOVE EACH BALL ON STAGE
89     moveBall(CueBall);
90     moveBall(RedBall);
91
92     //TASK 2: CHECK IF BALLS HAVE COLLIDED
93     checkBalltoBall();
94  }
```

Function moveBall() Design

This function moves an individual ball, applies friction, and checks for collisions along the table walls. The object Ball is a parameter: It is a variable that represents either the CueBall or the RedBall. By utilizing this variable, this function is written to perform the tasks for either ball.

```
95  function moveBall(Ball) {
96     //TASK 1: MOVE THE GIVEN BALL ITS FIXED SPEED
97     Ball.x+=Ball.xVelocity;
98     Ball.y+=Ball.yVelocity;
99
100    //TASK 2:  APPLY FRICTION TO THE  BALL
101    Ball.xVelocity*=FRICTION;
102    Ball.yVelocity*=FRICTION;
103
104    //TASK 3: IF A WALL IS HIT, CHANGE  DIRECTION
105    if (Ball.x > RIGHT) {
106       Ball.xVelocity*=REVERSE;
107       Ball.x=RIGHT;
108    } else if (Ball.x < LEFT) {
109       Ball.xVelocity*=REVERSE;
110       Ball.x=LEFT;
111    }
112    if (Ball.y > BOTTOM) {
113       Ball.yVelocity*=REVERSE;
114       Ball.y=BOTTOM;
115    } else if (Ball.y < TOP) {
116       Ball.yVelocity*=REVERSE;
117       Ball.y=TOP;
118    }
119
120    //TASK 4: DETERMINE IF THE BALL HAS STOPPED MOVING
121    var speed:Number;
122    speed = Ball.xVelocity*Ball.xVelocity+Ball.yVelocity*Ball.yVelocity;
123    speed = Math.sqrt(speed);
```

```
124          if (speed < MINSPEED) {
125              Ball.xVelocity=0;
126              Ball.yVelocity=0;
127      }
128 }
```

Function `checkBalltoBall()` Design

This function is called to compute the resulting velocities and angles when the balls have collided with each other.

```
129 function checkBalltoBall() {
130     //TASK 1:  COMPUTE THE DISTANCE BETWEEN THE TWO BALLS
131     var dx:Number=CueBall.x-RedBall.x;
132     var dy:Number=CueBall.y-RedBall.y;
133     var dist:Number=Math.sqrt(dx*dx+dy*dy);
134
135     // HAVE THE BALLS COLLIDED?
136     if (dist < DIAMETER) {
137         //TASK 2: COMPUTE THE ANGLE OF COLLISION
138         var angle=Math.atan2(dy,dx);
139
140         //TASK 3:  COMPUTE THE COSINE AND SINE OF THE ANGLE OF COLLISION
141         var cosineAngle=Math.cos(angle);
142         var sinAngle=Math.sin(angle);
143
144         //TASK 4:  COMPUTE THE VELOCITIES ALONG THE ANGLE OF COLLISION
145         var xVelocity2=cosineAngle*CueBall.xVelocity+sinAngle*CueBall.yVelocity;
146         var yVelocity1=cosineAngle*CueBall.yVelocity-sinAngle*CueBall.xVelocity;
147         var xVelocity1=cosineAngle*RedBall.xVelocity+sinAngle*RedBall.yVelocity;
148         var yVelocity2=cosineAngle*RedBall.yVelocity-sinAngle*RedBall.xVelocity;
149
150         //TASK 5:  ASSIGN NEW TRAJECTORIES FOR BOTH BALLS
151         CueBall.xVelocity=cosineAngle*xVelocity1-sinAngle*yVelocity1;
152         CueBall.yVelocity=cosineAngle*yVelocity1+sinAngle*xVelocity1;
153         RedBall.xVelocity=cosineAngle*xVelocity2-sinAngle*yVelocity2;
154         RedBall.yVelocity=cosineAngle*yVelocity2+sinAngle*xVelocity2;
155     }
156 }
```

Review Questions

1. What is a logical expression?

2. Give an example of a simple Boolean expression.

3. Give an example of a compound Boolean expression. How does a compound Boolean expression differ from a simple Boolean expression?

4. Identify the three logical operators and describe how they work.

5. What is the if statement used for?

6. List and briefly describe the six relational operators provided by AS3.

7. What value is used to represent false in the computer?

8. What value is used to represent true in the computer?

9. How does a switch statement differ from an if statement?

■ Exercises

Evaluate the following logical expressions. Provide an answer of true or false.

1. (!0)

2. (5 + 4 < 3 && 7 + 3 <= 20)

3. (int (3.9) != 3)

4. (!(7 == 7))

5. (3 % 2)

6. (!1 || !0)

7. (3 != 2 || 7 == 7 && 10 < 9)

Determine the output for each of the following program segments. Assume that n1 and n2 have the following assignments prior to the execution of each if operation:

```
var n1:Number = 2;
var n2:Number = 3;
```

8.
```
if (n1 < n2){
     trace ( "n1 = " , n1 );
     trace ( "n2 = " , n2 );
}
```

9.
```
if (n1 == '2'){
     trace ( "n1 = " , n1 );
}
```

10.
```
if (n1){
     trace ( "The value of n1 is nonzero." );
}
```

11.
```
if (n1 == n2 - 1){
     var temp:Number = n2;
     n2 = n1;
     n1 = temp;
     trace ( "n1 = " , n1 );
     trace ( "n2 = " , n2 );
}
```

```
12. if ((n1 < n2) && ( n2 != 10)){
        var sum:int = n1 + n2;
        trace ( "n1 = " , n1 );
        trace ( "n2 = " , n2 );
        trace ( "Sum = " , sum );
    }

13. if ((n1 > n2) || ( n1 - n2 < 0)){
        n1 += 1;
        n2 -= 1;
        trace ( "n1 = " , n1 );
        trace ( "n2 = " , n2 );
    }

14. if (n1 > n2){
        n1 += 1;
    }else{
        n2 -= 1;
        trace ( "n1 = " , n1 );
        trace ( "n2 = " , n2 );
    }

15. if (n1 < n2){
        n1 += 1;
    }else{
        n2 -= 1;}
        trace ( "n1 = " , n1 );
        trace ( "n2 = " , n2 );

16. if (!(n1 > n2)){
        n1 += 1;
    }else{
        n2 -= 1;
        trace ( "n1 = " , n1 );
        trace ( "n2 = " , n2 );
    }

17. if ((n1 > n2) || ( n1 * n2 < 0)){
        n1 +=1;
        n2 -= 1;
        trace ( "n1 = " , n1 );
        trace ( "n2 = " , n2 );
    }
    trace ( "n1 = " , n1 );
    trace ( "n2 = " , n2 );

18. if (n1 < n2){
        n1 +=1;
        n2 -= 1;
        trace ( "n1 = " , n1 );
        trace ( "n2 = " , n2 );
    }
```

```
trace ( "n1 = " , n1 );
trace ( "n2 = " , n2);
```

19. Write an if statement that displays "not zero" when the value of variable num1 (a Number) is nonzero.

20. Write an if statement that displays "BLUE" when both num1 and num2 (Number variables) are positive or both negative.

21. Write an if statement that displays "IN RANGE" when num1 (a Number variable) is between −10 and 10.

22. Rewrite the following segment of code in the most efficient way possible.

```
if ((n1 < n2) && (n1 == 0)){
    trace ( "ORANGE");
}
if ((n1 < n2) && ( n1 != 0)){
    trace ( "APPLE");
}
if (n1 >= n2){
    trace ( "BANANA");
}
```

23. Write an if statement that displays "Out of Range" if the input text box entry input0 is negative or is greater than 100.

24. Write an efficient if statement to assign num3 the following values:

    8, if num1 is less than 1.5

    7, if 1.5 <= num1 < 2.5

    6, otherwise

25. Write a segment of AS3 code to do the following:

    a. Assume values exist for variables num1, num2, and num3 (all uints).

    b. If num3 is a 1, calculate and display the sum of num1 and num2.

    c. Otherwise, output the difference of num1 and num2.

26. Write a switch statement that does the following:

    a. Increases balance (a Number variable) by adding amount (a Number variable) to it if the value of transaction (a String variable) is "Deposit".

    b. Decreases balance by subtracting amount from it if the value of transaction is "Withdrawal".

    c. Display the value of balance if the value of transaction is "Display".

    d. Display "Illegal transaction" otherwise.

Projects

1. The city of Flowerville bills its residents for water consumption. The charges are based on usage according to the following table:

Water Used	Rate
First 200 cubic meters	$5.00 minimum cost
Next 430 cubic meters	$0.10 per cubic meter
Next 570 cubic meters	$0.07 per cubic meter
More than 1000 cubic meters	$0.02 per cubic meter

   Create an application that computes the charges for a given amount of water usage. Provide error detection capabilities to identify incorrect input by the user.

2. Write an application that allows the user to enter a date and then determine its validity. If the date is invalid, an error message should be displayed explaining precisely where the error is. If the date is valid, the program should compute the day of the year. During leap years, there are 29 days in February. During non-leap years, there are exactly 28 days. To be a leap year, the year must be evenly divisible by 4. However, not all years evenly divisible by 4 are leap years. Years whose last two digits are zero are century years; for example, 1800, 1900, and 2000 are century years. Century years are leap years only if they are evenly divisible by 400. Thus the years 1600 and 2000 are leap years; 1700, 1800, and 1900 are not leap years.

   Example date 1:
   Day: 1   Month: 13   Year: 2001
   Display: This date has an error. 13 is an invalid month.
   Example date 2:
   Day: 12   Month: 3   Year: 3012
   Display: This is day number 72 of the leap year 3012.

3. Write an interactive application that plays the game of Rock, Paper, Scissors. In this game, the user will play against the computer. Provide buttons for the user to choose "rock," "paper," or "scissors." Your program must be able to generate a random choice for the computer. The winner is the one whose choice dominates the other.

4. Rewrite the Paddle Game in Case Study 1 so that when the ball falls through the BOTTOM of the stage, the listener event moving the ball is eliminated.

5. Enhance the Paddle Game further by keeping track of how many successful hits the user makes. Make the game more challenging by increasing the velocity of the ball with each successful hit.

6. Modify the pet fish application to have the fish die after a set number of feedings and rotate and float to the top of the tank.

7. Modify the pet fish application to have the fish randomly select two toys to play with.

8. Make enhancements to the pet fish application from Case Study 3.

    a. Add animation to each stage of its life—eating, sleeping, and moving. Use a `switch` statement.

    b. Introduce an obstacle to the fish tank that requires the fish to navigate around it.

    c. Decrease the food size as the pet fish feeds.

    d. Add a predator object to the aquarium.

6 Repetition

Introduction

The basic control structures used in writing programs are **sequence**, **selection**, and **repetition**. Sequential control refers to the execution of a sequence of statements in the order in which they appear so that each statement is executed exactly once. Selective control structures (the `if` and `switch`) statements, specify that a group of statements is to be executed selectively, based on the value of some condition. Repetition—the topic of this chapter—controls a segment of code so that it can be executed repeatedly.

> **Note**
>
> It is important that an iterative control structure not be confused with the inherent looping nature of Flash's Timeline. As we saw in previous chapters, Flash updates the Stage at the end of a frame. For example, once Flash executes and displays frame 1, it will then attempt to move to frame 2. If there is only one frame in the Timeline, or if a `gotoAndStop()` instruction is used to hold the playhead on a specified frame, the playhead will loop within that frame over and over again.

Much of the power of computer programs comes from use of the third control structure—repetition, also referred to as **iteration**. The iteration control structures, called **loops**, allow the repetition of the same calculation or sequence of instructions over and over based on the value of a condition.

In ActionScript 3.0, loops are implemented using the `for`, `while`, and `do-while` statements. These three iterative structures, which are also used in C++ and Java, test a condition to determine when to exit the loop. The differences among these structures relate to their anatomy and the point at which they test a given condition. A loop structure can be classified as pre-test or post-test. If a loop examines a Boolean condition before the loop body is executed, it is called a pre-test. If the Boolean condition is examined after the loop body, it is a post-test.

In this chapter, we examine the three iterative looping structures `for`, `while`, and `do-while`.

■ 6.1 for Loops

Although the selective control structures if and switch are powerful mechanisms, they are by themselves not potent enough to solve all computing problems. Applications commonly perform the same set of instructions over and over. We begin by examining several tasks that can be solved using iteration and introduce the most common of the repetition structures: the for loop.

Task 1   Suppose we are asked to write a small segment of code that would display the word "BLUE" 25 times in a dynamic text box named output. Without knowing how to use a looping structure, we might solve this problem by writing the following collection of instructions:

```
output.text  = "BLUEBLUEBLUEBLUEBLUE";
output.text += "BLUEBLUEBLUEBLUEBLUE";
output.text += "BLUEBLUEBLUEBLUEBLUE";
output.text += "BLUEBLUEBLUEBLUEBLUE";
output.text += "BLUEBLUEBLUEBLUEBLUE";
```

This code gets the job done, but tediously so.

Task 2   Suppose we are now asked to edit the code so that "BLUE" is displayed 200,000 times instead of 25 times. At this point we would be forced to find a better method—specifically, an iterative control structure such as the for loop.

Unlike the other iterative structures, the for loop is designed to be used when we know precisely how many times a group of statements is to be repeated. This structure is also referred to as a counting loop or a fixed iterative loop because it is most often used to count the fixed number of times a given set of statements will be executed.

For example, in Task 2 the text "BLUE" will be added to the text box exactly 200,000 times. By establishing a counter, we can keep track of how many times "BLUE" is added to the text box and stop when it reaches its goal of 200,000. This is called a fixed condition. Although programmers can write variable conditions for loops, we will begin with the general form of the for loop.

The for loop is considered a single executable statement.

```
for (counter variable declaration; Boolean test condition; counter modification) {
        list of statements to be executed in the loop;
}
```

The information contained within the parentheses is referred to as the heading of the loop. The three elemental statements that initialize the counter variable test the counter variable for exiting the loop, and update the counter variable are incorporated into the heading of the for loop.

The list of instructions executed within the loop structure is placed within open and closed curly brackets, {}, and referred to as the body of the loop. Statements in the body are indented for readability.

The following examples illustrate how the for statement works.

Example 1

```
1   for (var count:int = 1; count <= 3; count++) {
2       trace ("BLUE");
3   }
```

Evaluation

The heading of the for loop and the body act as follows (see Figure 6-1):

1. The first statement in the for heading (line 1) is the declaration and initialization of the loop counter variable, count. This variable is simply used to control the number of repetitions in the loop and is initialized to 1.

2. The goal of this for loop is to process the statement trace ("BLUE"); exactly three times. To do so, a Boolean test expression is placed as the second statement in the for loop heading to determine whether count has reached its goal of 3, producing exactly three iterations. The for loop is a pre-test loop, which means that this test condition must be true before an iteration can be executed. When count <= 3 is false, the loop has reached its goal and terminates.

3. The loop statement trace ("BLUE"); is executed.

4. At the end of an iteration, the third statement in the heading, count++, is executed. This statement is the counter modification. It ensures that the loop counter is modified, such as incrementing it, so that it eventually reaches its concluding value. The modification will occur at the end of every iteration.

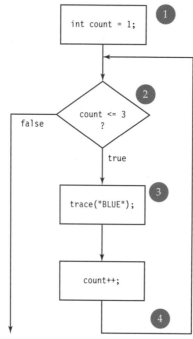

Exit the loop

▌ FIGURE 6-1 Diagram of the for loop behavior.

Example 2

```
1    for (var i:int = 1; i <= 5; i++){
2        trace ( "Hello\n");
3    }
```

Evaluation

This code segment is an example of a simple counting loop that repeats exactly five times. A for loop is generally a fixed iterative loop that is used when it can be determined in advance how often the loop body should be repeated.

In this example, the loop counter called i is used to control how many times the loop body executes. The first statement in the header, var i:int = 1;, initializes the loop counter to the value of 1. This statement is performed only once. As a pre-test loop, the Boolean test condition i <= 5; will be evaluated at the start of every iteration. If the test condition is true, the loop statement trace("Hello\n"); will be executed. If the test condition is false, the for loop will terminate. At the end of an iteration, the modification statement i++; will be executed.

The hand-traced table shows the details of each iteration.

	i	i <= 5	Loop Body: trace ("Hello\n");	i++
Iteration 1	1	true	Hello	2
Iteration 2	2	true	Hello	3
Iteration 3	3	true	Hello	4
Iteration 4	4	true	Hello	5
Iteration 5	5	true	Hello	6
	6	false		

As shown in the hand-traced table, the output produced by this segment of code is

```
Hello
Hello
Hello
Hello
Hello
```

Example 3

```
1   for (var k:int = 5; k <= 25; k += 5){
2       trace (k);
3   }
```

Evaluation

In Example 1, we examined a loop that counted up in increments of 1. On some occasions, however, we would like to count by a factor of 2 or more.

This segment of code is an example of a counting loop that displays the multiples of 5 beginning with 5 and ending with 25. The loop counter, k, is initialized to the first multiple, 5. The pre-test condition requires that the loop body be repeated until k exceeds 25. At the end of each iteration, k is incremented by 5. As the hand-traced table shows, there are 5 iterations of this loop.

	k	k <= 25	Loop Body: trace (k);	k += 5
Iteration 1	5	true	5	10
Iteration 2	10	true	10	15
Iteration 3	15	true	15	20
Iteration 4	20	true	20	25
Iteration 5	25	true	25	30
	30	false		

The output produced by this segment of code is

```
5
10
15
20
25
```

Example 4

```
1   var sum:uint = 0;
2   var n:uint = 5;
3   for (var i:uint = 1; i <= n; i++) {
4       sum += i;
5   }
6    trace ("The sum is " + sum);
```

Evaluation

Although calculating the sum of the integers from 1 to 100 is not a particularly important computation, a generalization of this problem (called the summation problem) has many applications in computing. The segment of code in this example calculates the sum of the integers from 1 to n, where n contains an integer value of 5.

$$sum = 1 + 2 + \cdots + n$$

When validating output for larger values of n, it is best to rely on the following well-known summation formula:

$$1 + 2 + 3 + \cdots + n = n(n+1)/2$$

The body of the for loop (line 4), simply adds consecutive integers, keeping a running sum as it repeats. The first two variable declarations, sum and n, are used to store the running sum and the final integer n, respectively. The loop counter, i, starts with 1, and the loop will repeat as long as the value of i is less than or equal to n. By hand-tracing the loop structure, we can see that a running sum of the numbers from 1 through 5 is computed. The final sum is displayed once the loop terminates, along with our calculated known value.

i	i <= n	Loop Statements: sum += i;	i++
Iteration 1	1	true	sum contains 1	2
Iteration 2	2	true	sum contains 3	3
Iteration 3	3	true	sum contains 6	4
Iteration 4	4	true	sum contains 10	5
Iteration 5	5	true	sum contains 15	6
	6	false		

The output produced by this segment of code is

```
The sum is 15
```

Example 5

```
1   var k:int = 5;
2   for (; k >= 1; k -= 2){
3       trace (k);
4   }
```

Evaluation

The for loop is known for its flexibility. In this example, the loop counter is neither declared nor initialized within the for header structure. A loop counter, or control variable, can be declared elsewhere in the code. Notice that the first element in the for statement is replaced with a semicolon; this semicolon is required and indicates the element is missing.

After further inspection, we can see that this loop displays the odd numbers from 5 through 1. The variable k, which is initialized to 5, is used as the pre-test condition for iterations. Each iteration requires that k be greater than or equal to 1. At the end of each iteration, k is decremented by 2.

k	k >= 1	Loop Body: trace (k);	k -= 2
Iteration 1	5	true	5	3
Iteration 2	3	true	3	1
Iteration 3	1	true	1	−1
	−1	false		

The output produced by this segment of code is

```
5
3
1
```

Example 6

```
1   var i:int = 25;
2   for (; i < 6; i++){
3      trace ("Apples");
4   }
```

Evaluation

This example illustrates **zero-trip behavior**. The body of a pre-test loop, such as the `for` loop, may be executed zero or more times. Because the pre-test condition here, `i < 6`, is false to begin with, zero iterations will occur. In other words, the loop will terminate before the loop body can be executed.

	i	i < 6	Loop Body: trace ("Apples");	i++
No repetitions	6	false		

No output is produced during the execution of this loop.

Example 7 Infinite Loop

```
1   for (;;) {
2      trace ("Apples");
3   }
```

Evaluation

Many modern programming languages provide a general loop statement that is not restricted to being either a pre-test or post-test loop. ActionScript, along with C++, Java, and some other languages, allows the programmer to construct a special case of the general looping construct. In this particular example, the Boolean test condition has been removed, which means that the loop will never terminate. In addition, the initialization expression and the modification statement have been removed from the header. This loop is referred to as an infinite or forever loop. We will examine this looping construct further in the next example.

Loop Statement: trace ("Apples");
Iteration 1   Apples
Iteration 2   Apples
Iteration 3   Apples
.
.
.

The text "Apples" will be output an infinite number of times.

Example 8 Decimal to Binary Conversion

```
1   var binary:uint = 0;
2   var bit:uint;
3   var position:uint=1;
4   var number:uint=13;
5   for (;;) {
6       bit = number % 2;
7       binary += bit*position;
8       number = number / 2;
9       if (number == 0){
10          break;
11      }
12      position *= 10;
13  }
14  trace (number + "base ten equals " + binary + "in binary.");
```

Evaluation

An infinite loop is executed infinitely many times, unless it contains a **break**. When a break statement is encountered, execution of the loop will terminate and execution will continue with the next statement after the loop.

The terminating statement is usually an if statement combined with a break statement, as shown on lines 9–11. This pairing of these two statements is called an if-break combination. Just as a break statement within a switch statement transfers control to the statement following the switch, so does a break statement inside a loop transfer control to the statement following the loop. Repetition will continue as long as the condition in the if-break combination is false—repetition terminates when the condition becomes true. For this reason, it is called a *termination condition* instead of a *loop condition*.

This code example computes the binary representation of the number 13 by using successive division by 2. The termination condition will occur when the division produces a zero on line 9. The binary representation is constructed a bit at a time using the positional system. For example, the number positions of the digits in the binary number 1101 are

$$
\begin{array}{cccc}
1 & 1 & 0 & 1 \\
2^3 & 2^2 & 2^1 & 2^0
\end{array}
$$

binary += bit * position;	number = number / 2;	(number == 0)
1	6	false
01	3	false
101	1	false
1101	0	true: break

The output produced by this segment of code is

13 base ten equals 1101 in binary.

6.2 Case Study 1: Fibonacci Flowers

Problem

Images play a significant role in much of what we see on computers today. Creating artwork algorithmically is an interesting endeavor, as well as an efficient method for producing remarkably detailed designs. Algorithmic artwork is an ideal application for looping because it allows us to build complex visual images by constructing simple elements repeatedly. We will apply this technique to the creation of the Fibonacci flower containing 44 petals shown in Figure 6-2.

Stage center

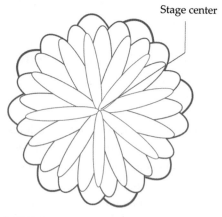

I FIGURE 6-2 Flower consisting of 44 generated petals using the Golden Ratio.

Problem Analysis

Mathematicians, computer scientists, and graphic designers make frequent use of the Golden Ratio, which is derived from the Fibonacci series. Leonardo Fibonacci was an Italian mathematician who created the sequence of numbers in which each term is the sum of the two preceding terms. The first 14 terms in the sequence are as follows:

Term 1:	1	First term
Term 2:	1	Second term
Term 3:	2	= 1 + 1
Term 4:	3	= 1 + 2
Term 5:	5	= 2 + 3
Term 6:	8	= 3 + 5
Term 7:	13	= 5 + 8
Term 8:	21	= 8 + 13
Term 9:	34	= 13 + 21
Term 10:	55	= 21 + 34
Term 11:	144	= 34 + 55
Term 12:	233	= 55 + 144
Term 13:	377	= 144 + 233
Term 14:	610	= 233 + 377

An important aspect of this sequence is the ratio produced when dividing successive terms. For example, when the 9th term is divided by the 10th term, the ratio of 0.61802575 is produced. When the 13th term is divided by its previous term, the result is 0.61803444. As the terms become larger and larger, the ratio between two successive terms converges to approximately 0.6180339. This so-called Golden Ratio is considered to be extraordinary because of its common occurrence in nature.

The Golden Ratio is useful in giving computer-generated images the appearance of natural harmony. In creating a flower, such as the one in Figure 6-2 composed of 44 petals, the Golden Ratio can be used to repeatedly offset the angle of each petal. Both the Golden Ratio and the number of petals will be stored as constants in this application.

Each petal generated is 6% wider and 1% longer that the previous one. In addition, the angle of rotation is increased by 360 multiplied by the Golden Ratio. This outcome is illustrated in the first two petals of the flower shown in Figure 6-3. The second petal is slightly wider and longer and offset at an angle of 223° (360 * 0.6180339).

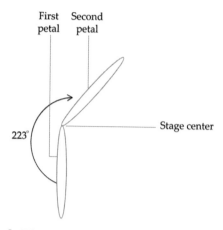

I FIGURE 6-3 The first two petals generated by the Fibonnaci flower algorithm.

The data objects required for this application focus on altering the width, height, and rotation of each petal as it is generated. Table 6-1 shows the complete list of data objects. Generating the Fibonacci flower will require three sets of constant values. The first set identifies the Stage center, from which all petals will radiate. The second set refers to the Golden Ratio constants—in particular, the `Golden_Angle`, which will be used to compute the angle of rotation. The last set of constant values identifies the rate of growth for the width and the height and stores the total number of petals to be generated.

TABLE 6-1 Data Objects for the Fibonacci Flower

Data Object	Description	Data Type	Object Type
XCENTER	The center of the Stage along the x-axis.	Number	Constant
YCENTER	The center of the Stage along the y-axis.	Number	Constant
GROW_WIDTH	The rate of growth in width of each petal in the flower is set to 6%.	Number	Constant
GROW_HEIGHT	The rate of growth in height is set to 1%.	Number	Constant
GOLDEN_RATIO	The limiting ratio of successive Fibonacci (i.e., 0.6180339).	Number	Constant
GOLDEN_ANGLE	360*GOLDEN_RATIO	Number	Constant
TOTAL_PETALS	The number of petals in the flower is initially set to 44.	Number	Constant
PetalObj	PETAL is the name of the symbol in the library. PetalObj is the display object representing a newly constructed PETAL.	PETAL	Variable

TABLE 6-1 Data Objects for the Fibonacci Flower (continued)

Data Object	Description	Data Type	Object Type
newWidth	The calculated width of the new petal. The value of this variable is initially set to 1 and recomputed each time a flower petal is generated.	Number	Variable
newHeight	The calculated height of the new petal. As with newWidth, the initial value of this variable is set to 1 and recomputed for each petal generated.	Number	Variable
angle	The number of degrees by which the new petal will be rotated. The angle of rotation for the first flower petal is set to zero. After each petal is generated, angle is incremented by GOLDEN_ANGLE.	Number	Variable

Visual Design

The visual side of this application will require a simple petal as shown in Figure 6-4. This element will be created in Flash and stored as a MovieClip symbol with the class linkage ID of PETAL. The linkage ID will allow the ActionScript 3.0 program to generate multiple instances of PETAL during runtime. The Timeline and Stage will remain empty.

| FIGURE 6-4 The PETAL MovieClip with the registration at the top of the graphic.

Program Design

The AS3 code for this application consists of a single function, the main function flowerApp(), which generates the entire flower once the application is launched.

The package for this program contains flash.display.*. Because the application does not require interactivity, the events class is not included.

```
1   package {
2       import flash.display.*;
3
4       public class flowerApp extends MovieClip {
5
⋮
48      }
49  }
```

Constants

The constants for this application are declared globally on lines 6–19.

```
6       // CONSTANTS FOR THE CENTER OF THE STAGE
7       const XCENTER:Number=stage.stageWidth/2;
8       const YCENTER:Number=stage.stageHeight/2;
9
10      // GOLDEN RATIO CONSTANTS
11      const GOLDEN_RATIO:Number=.618033989;
12      const GOLDEN_ANGLE:Number=360*GOLDEN_RATIO;
13
14      // CONSTANTS FOR PETAL GROWTH
15      const GROW_WIDTH:Number=GOLDEN_RATIO*.06;
16      const GROW_HEIGHT:Number=GOLDEN_RATIO*.01;
17
18      // NUMBER OF PETALS IN THE FLOWER
19      const TOTAL_PETALS:int=44;
20
```

The design for the function flowerApp() is described next.

Function flowerApp() Design

The main algorithm, flowerApp(), is also the class constructor function that will generate the flower without any interaction from the user.

The specific tasks within the loop that generates 44 individual petals are as follows:

Task 1: Create a new petal and set its height and width to a given percent value. Position it in the center of the Stage and rotate it by a given angle.

Task 2: Add the petal to the stage. Use setChildIndex() to position it under the other existing petals.

Task 3: In preparation for the next petal to be generated, compute the new width, height, and angle.

```
21  function flowerApp() {
22    //DECLARE AND INITIALIZE VARIABLES FOR A GENERIC PETAL
23    var petalObj:PETAL;
24    var newWidth:Number=1;
25    var newHeight:Number=1;
26    var angle:Number=0;
27
28    //CREATE INDIVIDUAL PETALS TO FORM A FLOWER
29    for (var i:int = 1; i <= TOTAL_PETALS; i++) {
30      //TASK 1: CREATE THE PETAL AND SET ITS PROPERTIES
31      petalObj=new PETAL;
32      petalObj.scaleX*=newWidth;
33      petalObj.scaleY*=newHeight;
34      petalObj.x=XCENTER;
35      petalObj.y=YCENTER;
36      petalObj.rotation=angle;
37
38      //TASK 2: ADD THE PETAL TO THE BOTTOM OF THE OTHER PETALS
39      addChild(petalObj);
40      setChildIndex(petalObj, 0);
41
42      //TASK 3: COMPUTE THE SIZE AND ANGLE FOR THE NEXT PETAL
43      newWidth+=newWidth*GROW_WIDTH;
44      newHeight+=newHeight*GROW_HEIGHT;
45      angle+=GOLDEN_ANGLE;
46    }
47  }
```

Further enhancements can be made to the final flower by adding color, utilizing the alpha property, and generating several types of petals such as the petal graphics seen in Figure 6-5. The flower shown in Figure 6-6 is constructed using these different petals.

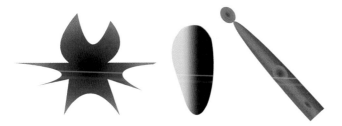

┃ FIGURE 6-5 Movie clip symbols of individual petal creations.

FIGURE 6-6 Fibonacci flower made from multiple complex petals with transparency.

■ 6.3 while Loops

As shown in the previous section, a for loop is a fixed iterative loop that is used when it can be determined in advance how often a segment of code needs to be repeated. For some computing problems, a fixed iterative loop is inappropriate given that a segment of code may need to be repeated an unknown number of times. This type of loop, called a variable condition loop, is used most often when conditions change within the body of the loop. In this case, the condition controlling the loop must be variable rather than constant. Such conditions often involve sentinel values, Boolean flags, input from the user, or arithmetic expressions.

The while loop is a variable condition loop that uses a pre-test condition. Here is the general form of the while loop:

```
while ( Boolean test expression ) {
    list of statements to be executed in the loop;
}
```

The Boolean expression contained within the parentheses is evaluated in exactly the same manner as a Boolean expression used in an if-else statement. The difference lies in how the expression is used. As we have seen, when the expression is true (has a nonzero value) in an if-else statement, the statement following the expression is executed repeatedly as long as the expression continues to have a nonzero value. Thus, somewhere in the while statement, there must be a statement that alters the value of the tested expression.

As with a for loop, the instructions performed in the while loop are referred to as the body of the loop and should be indented for readability.

The following examples illustrate how the while statement works.

Example 1

```
1   var count:int = 1;
2
3   while (count <= 3) {
4       trace ("BLUE");
5       count++;
6   }
```

Evaluation

The while loop in this example behaves as shown in Figure 6-7. Notice that the variable count, declared on line 1, is not part of the while loop.

1. As a pre-test loop, the first action of this structure is the evaluation of the Boolean test condition. This step determines whether the loop body is executed or the loop is terminated. The test condition must be true before an iteration can be executed. When the Boolean text condition is false, the loop is terminated and the loop body statements are not executed.

2. After each execution of the body, the loop branches back to the Boolean test condition in the while loop.

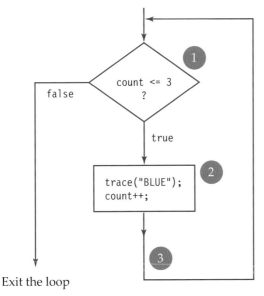

Exit the loop

I FIGURE 6-7 Diagram of the while loop behavior.

Example 2

```
1   var  x:int  = 2;
2   while  (x < 300){
3       trace (x);
4       x *= x;
5   }
```

Evaluation

The condition (x < 300) controls the execution of the loop. The placement of this loop condition before the body of the loop is significant because it means that when a while loop is executed, this condition is evaluated *before* the body of the loop is executed.

The control loop variable x is initially set to 2. The pre-test condition is true because x is less than 300. The body is executed, and the condition is retested. The condition is changed within the loop body by the statement x *= x. The condition will eventually become false and the loop will terminate.

The four iterations of this loop are hand-traced here.

	x	x < 300	Loop Statement: trace (x);	x *= x;
Iteration 1	2	true	2	x = 4
Iteration 2		true	4	x = 16
Iteration 3		true	16	x = 256
Iteration 4		true	256	x = 65536
		false		

The output produced by this segment of code is

```
2
4
16
256
```

Example 3

```
1   var  n:int  = 0;
2   var sum:uint = 0;
3
4   while  (sum <= 50){
5       trace (sum);
6       n++;
7       sum += n;
8   }
```

Evaluation

This example illustrates a summation problem that uses a Boolean condition to determine the point when a running sum exceeds 50. The `while` loop body adds consecutive integers in increments of 1, as it displays the running sum. The iterations of this loop are shown in the hand-traced table.

	n sum	sum <= 50	Loop Statements: trace (sum);	n++; sum += n;
Iteration 1	n = 0 sum = 0	true	0	n = 1 sum = 1
Iteration 2		true	1	n = 2 sum = 3
Iteration 3		true	3	n = 3 sum = 6
Iteration 4		true	6	n = 4 sum = 10
Iteration 5		true	10	n = 5 sum = 15
Iteration 6		true	15	n = 6 sum = 21
Iteration 7		true	21	n = 7 sum = 30
Iteration 8		true	30	n = 8 sum = 38
Iteration 9		true	38	n = 9 sum = 47
Iteration 10		true	47	n = 10 sum = 57
		false		

Example 4

```
1   var  x:int  = 44;
2   while  (x < 10){
3      trace (x);
4      x++;
5   }
```

Evaluation

The while loop is a pre-test loop and, therefore, can also be a zero-trip loop. This example illustrates zero-trip behavior. The Boolean condition is false before the loop body can be iterated and is terminated at the start. Thus the program makes zero trips through the body of the loop.

x	x < 10	Loop Statement: trace (x);	x++
44	false		

No output is produced by this segment of code.

Example 5

```
1   var  x:int ;
2   while  (x != 4){
3       trace (x);
4       x++;
5   }
```

Evaluation

The Boolean test condition does not have a value prior to entering the loop. Because x has not been initialized, this segment of code will not work.

No output is produced because this segment of code contains an error.

Example 6

```
1   var  x:int  = 5;
2   while (x){
3       trace (x);
4       x--;
5   }
```

Evaluation

The condition can be any expression that has a Boolean value. Standard examples include relational operators and Boolean variables. Because x contains a number value, it can be translated into a value of true or false. A false is zero and true is anything other than zero.

	x	(x)	Loop Statements: trace (x);	x--;
Iteration 1	5	true	5	4
Iteration 2	4	true	4	3
Iteration 3	3	true	3	2
Iteration 4	2	true	2	1
Iteration 5	1	true	1	0
	0	false		

The output produced by this segment of code is

```
5
4
3
2
1
```

Example 7

```
1   var  x:int  = 1;
2   while  (x < 100){
3       trace (x);
4   }
5   trace ("Hello\n");
```

Evaluation

A provision must be made for changing the loop control condition in the body of the loop. If no such changes are made, the loop condition will remain true, a condition called an infinite loop. The instruction trace ("Hello\n"); never executes.

	x	x < 100	Loop Statement: trace (x);
Iteration 1	1	true	1
Iteration 2	1	true	1
Iteration 3	1	true	1
Iteration 4	1	true	1
Iteration 5	1	true	1
⋮	⋮	⋮	⋮

This segment of code produces an output of infinitely many 1's. The loop never exits.

■ 6.4 Case Study 2: Processing an XML File

There are many computing situations that require processing data from an external file—a condition that cannot efficiently rely on the looping nature of Flash's Timeline.

This case study illustrates a common use of `while` loops: reading and processing a set of exam score values stored in an XML file. Because entering large sets of data from the keyboard is tiresome, data is often stored in files that can be read by the program. Sometimes it is not possible or practical to determine beforehand how many data values are stored in the file. In this situation, a general loop, such as a `while` loop, should be used rather than a counting loop. A common method for processing a data file is the use of a sentinel-controlled loop that reads an **end-of-file flag**. As each data item is read, the end-of-file condition is examined to determine if the loop should be terminated.

This case study analyzes exam scores, as shown in Figure 6-8. We will read a series of test scores from an XML file and compute the average score, count the number of failing scores, and construct a bar chart to illustrate the percentages of scores that are A's, B's, C's, D's, and F's.

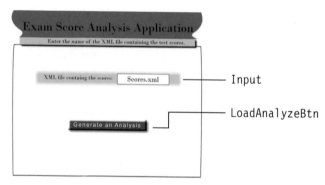

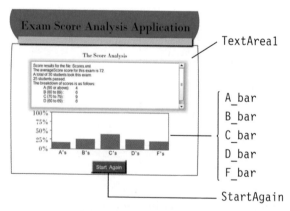

I FIGURE 6-8 Input and Output layouts for the exam score analysis application.

Problem Analysis

There are two considerations for this case study. The first involves the format of the file that contains the exam scores. The second consideration is how to use ActionScript 3.0 to access this specific data.

File Input Format

An XML (Extensible Markup Language) file is designed for the purpose of storing and distributing data across the Internet. This type of file uses a textual format to represent data structures. For example, the following file stores information about students who have taken an exam, including their names, their ID numbers, and the scores they received on the test. To represent a data element opening and closing tags are used. For example, in the following XML file, the first student, Boris Baca, is identified by the unique number 565677785 and scored a 71% on the exam. The tag that begins with <score> and ends with </score> is used to identify an individual score. In this case study, we will access only the data stored in the score tag construct.

XML File

```
<name>Baca, Boris</name>        <ID>565677785</ID>    <score>71</score>
<name>Cooke, Jane</name>        <ID>46564486</ID>     <score>64</score>
<name>Davis, Sue</name>         <ID>68633867</ID>     <score>56</score>
<name>Epston, Xavier</name>     <ID>77656868</ID>     <score>46</score>
<name>Green, Caitlin</name>     <ID>34600869</ID>     <score>34</score>
<name>Habe, Katie</name>        <ID>22689860</ID>     <score>56</score>
<name>Incret, Thom</name>       <ID>11634561</ID>     <score>98</score>
<name>Jones, Keenan</name>      <ID>25687462</ID>     <score>93</score>
<name>Kartner, Andy</name>      <ID>38600863</ID>     <score>82</score>
<name>Meene, Amber</name>       <ID>39600164</ID>     <score>81</score>
<name>Novine, Jenna</name>      <ID>29611265</ID>     <score>64</score>
<name>Smith, Mack</name>        <ID>60622845</ID>     <score>66</score>
```

ActionScript 3.0 Data Access

XML files allow for straightforward access using ActionScript 3.0. The XML files containing the exam scores will be opened and read by this application using the ActionScript XML class. There are three steps in this process:

Step 1. Create an instance of the XML class to load and process data in a given XML file.

Step 2. Load the XML file to gain access to the individual exam scores contained in the file. A URLRequest object will be used in this task to initiate the download of the XML file.

Step 3. A URLLoader object will be used to load all of the data from the URLRequest. This data must be loaded before it is made accessible to the ActionScript 3.0

program. Once the XML file has completed loading, its data elements can then be processed by the rest of the ActionScript 3.0 code.

Visual Elements

This application will utilize two interface screens. Figure 6-8 shows the completed screens and identifies the interactive visual objects. The input screen is the first screen the user will see; it requires only the name of the XML file to be processed. No other input data are needed from the user.

Once the user clicks the LoadAnalyzeBtn button, an analysis of the exam scores found in the XML file will appear in the output screen. The analysis will consist of a text explanation and a bar chart.

With the use of Flash's Timeline, the input screen is represented on frame 1, and the output screen on frame 2. Visual objects for this application consist of an input text field for the user to specify the XML file to be processed, a UI scrolling TextArea component to hold an easy-to-read explanation of the analysis, graphics for the bar chart, and buttons to begin the processing or return to input.

Algorithm Design

The variables used by this algorithm focus on accessing data from the XML file and computing the average score, as well as the number of A's, B's, C's, D's, and F's assigned to the scores. The evaluation of A's, B's, C's, D's, and F's will be stored as constants. Table 6-2 shows the complete list of variable data objects with identifier names and data types.

TABLE 6-2 Data Objects for the XML File Processing Application

Data Object	Description	Data Type	Object Type
dataXML	An instance of the XML class containing functionality that allows for the processing of data stored in the file	XML	Variable
scoresURL	An instance of the URLRequest class; used to request the downloaded information	URLRequest	Variable
scoresLoader	An instance of URLLoader, containing functionality for initiating the URL downloads	URLLoader	Variable
aScore	An individual score retrieved from the XML data file	uint	Variable
howManyScores	The number of scores processed so far from the XML file	uint	Variable

TABLE 6-2 Data Objects for the XML File Processing Application (continued)

Data Object	Description	Data Type	Object Type
sum	A running sum of scores read from the XML file	uint	Variable
howManyPassed	Total number of passing test scores	uint	Variable
averageScore	The average test score	uint	Variable
howManyAs	The number of test scores evaluated as A's	uint	Variable
howManyBs	The number of test scores evaluated as B's	uint	Variable
howManyCs	The number of test scores evaluated as C's	uint	Variable
howManyDs	The number of test scores evaluated as D's	uint	Variable
howManyFs	The number of test scores evaluated as F's	uint	Variable

The code for this application consists of the class constructor scoreAnalysisApp(), which initializes the application, and the functions LoadXMLScores() and analyze-Scores(), which load and process the given XML file. Table 6-3 lists the four functions used in this application and Figure 6-9 illustrates their relationship.

TABLE 6-3 Score Analysis Application Functions

Function Name	Description
scoreAnalysisApp()	The class constructor. After launching, this function pauses the playhead at frame 1 to allow the user to enter the name of the XML score file to be processed. This function initiates the loading of the XML file.
LoadXMLScores()	Performs the task of loading the XML file. This function initiates the process of analyzing scores once the XML file has been loaded.
analyzeScores()	An event handler that responds to the completion of the XML file load. This function uses a while loop to process every score in the XML file and produce an analysis.
returnToInput()	Returns the user to frame 1 to process another XML input file. This function is an event handler for a button click.

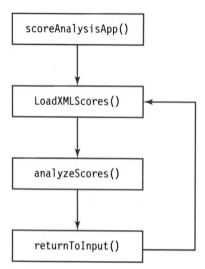

▎ FIGURE 6-9 Relationship of the functions used by the score analysis application.

The class package requires the display, events, net.URLLoader, and net.URLRequest library classes. The last two lines contain closing curly brackets to conclude the score-AnalysisApp class and the package.

```
1   package {
2       import flash.display.*;
3       import flash.events.*;
4       import flash.net.URLLoader;
5       import flash.net.URLRequest;
6
7       public class scoreAnalysisApp extends MovieClip {
8
```

```
107     }
108 }
```

Constants

The constants for this application define grades for A, B, C, D, and F grades.

```
9          //CONSTANTS
10         const GRADE_A:Number=90;
11         const GRADE_B:Number=80;
12         const GRADE_C:Number=70;
13         const GRADE_D:Number=60;
14
```

The four functions for this application are designed as follows.

Function scoreAnalysisApp() Design

The function scoreAnalysisApp() executes immediately upon launching the application. Its objective is to hold the playhead on frame 1 for user input of the XML file to be processed. The second task of this function is to register a listener event for a mouse click of LoadAnalyzeBtn to activate the sub-algorithm LoadXMLScores().

```
15     function scoreAnalysisApp() {
16         //TASK 1:  HOLD AT  FRAME 1 FOR INPUT
17         gotoAndStop(1);
18         //TASK 2:  LISTEN FOR THE USER TO LOAD XML FILE AND ANALYZE
19         LoadAnalyzeBtn.addEventListener(MouseEvent.CLICK,LoadXMLScores);
20     }
21
```

Function LoadXMLScores() Design

This function is organized around four tasks. Its primary objective is to successfully load the XML file.

Task 1: Input from the user is complete at this point. Therefore, the event listener for the LoadAnalyzeBtn button found on the input screen is removed.

Task 2: Construct a URLRequest for the input XML file specified by the user.

Task 3: Using the URLRequest, create a URLLoader. This loader will be used to load the external XML file. This URLLoader method will download data from a URL.

Task 4: Register a listener event to execute the function analyzeScores() once the URLLoader has completed loading the XML file.

```
22     function LoadXMLScores(event:MouseEvent) {
23         //TASK 1:  REMOVE THE BUTTON CLICK LISTENER EVENT
24         LoadAnalyzeBtn.removeEventListener(MouseEvent.CLICK,LoadXMLScores);
25         //TASK 2:  ASSIGN THE XML FILE TO THE URLRequest
26         var scoresURL:URLRequest=new URLRequest(Input1.text);
27         //TASK 3:  LOAD THE URLRequest
28         var scoresLoader:URLLoader=new URLLoader(scoresURL);
29         //TASK 4:  REGISTER AN EVENT TO INDICATE COMPLETED LOADING
30         scoresLoader.addEventListener(Event.COMPLETE, analyzeScores);
31     }
32
```

Function analyzeScores() Design

This function is the engine behind the application. It is responsible for processing all the scores found in the XML file, constructing an analysis, and displaying the analysis in the form of text and a bar chart. There are seven tasks, the most important of which is Task 2, outlined here:

While (score data can be retrieved from the XML file) {

   a. Retrieve a score from the XML file and store it in variable aScore.

   b. Increment HowManyScores.

   c. Compute a new value for sum.

   d. Determine whether the score is an A, B, C, D, or F and add it to the grade count.

}

```
33  function analyzeScores(event:Event) {
34    //TASK 1: DECLARE THE VARIABLES USED FOR ANALYSIS
35    var fileName:String = Input1.text;
36    var dataXML:XML=XML(event.target.data); //XML object to retrieve data
37    var aScore:uint;
38    var HowManyScores:uint=0;
39    var sum:uint=0;
40    var howManyPassed:uint=0;
41    var averageScore:uint;
42
43    var howManyAs:uint=0;
44    var howManyBs:uint=0;
45    var howManyCs:uint=0;
46    var howManyDs:uint=0;
47    var howManyFs:uint=0;
48
49    //TASK 2 : READ DATA FROM XML FILE
50    while (HowManyScores < dataXML.child("*").length()) {
51      //SUBTASK A: RETRIEVE A SCORE FROM THE XML FILE
52      aScore=Number(dataXML.score[HowManyScores++]);
53
54      //SUBTASK B: KEEP A RUNNING SUM OF THE SCORES
55      sum+=aScore;
56
57      //SUBTASK C: COUNT WHETHER THE SCORE IS AN A, B, C, D, OR F
58      if (aScore>=GRADE_A) {
59        howManyAs++;
60      } else if (aScore >= GRADE_B) {
61        howManyBs++;
62      } else if (aScore >= GRADE_C) {
63        howManyCs++;
64      } else if (aScore >= GRADE_D) {
65        howManyDs++;
```

```
66            } else {
67               howManyFs++;
68            }
69         }
70         //TASK 3: COMPUTE INFORMATION TO BE OUTPUT
71         howManyPassed=howManyAs+howManyBs+howManyCs+howManyDs;
72         averageScore=sum/HowManyScores;
73
74         //TASK 4: GO TO AND HOLD ON FRAME 2 FOR OUTPUT
75         gotoAndStop(2);
76
77         //TASK 5:  DISPLAY THE GRADE  INFORMATION IN THE SCROLLABLE TEXT AREA
78         TextArea1.text = "Score results for the file: " + fileName +
79                       "\nThe averageScore score for this exam is " +
80                       averageScore + ". \n" +"A total of " + HowManyScores +
81                       " students took this exam.\n" +howManyPassed +
82                       " students passed.";
83
84         TextArea1.text += "\nThe breakdown of scores is as follows:" +
85            "\n\t\tA (90 or above) : \t" + howManyAs +
86            "\n\t\tB (80 to 89) : \t\t" + howManyBs +
87            "\n\t\tC (70 to 79) : \t\t" + howManyCs +
88            "\n\t\tD (60 to 69) : \t\t" + howManyDs +
89            "\n\t\tF (59 or below) : \t\t" + howManyFs;
90
91         //TASK 6: COMPUTE THE BARS IN THE BAR CHART
92         A_bar.scaleY=howManyAs/HowManyScores;
93         B_bar.scaleY=howManyBs/HowManyScores;
94         C_bar.scaleY=howManyCs/HowManyScores;
95         D_bar.scaleY=howManyDs/HowManyScores;
96         F_bar.scaleY=howManyFs/HowManyScores;
97
98         //TASK 7:  LISTEN FOR THE USER TO TRY ANOTHER SET OF SCORES
99         StartAgainBtn.addEventListener(MouseEvent.CLICK,returnToInput);
100 }
101
```

Function `returnToInput()` Design

The objective of this function is to simply return to frame 1 so that the user can input a new XML file for processing.

```
101 function returnToInput(event:MouseEvent) {
102    //TASK 1:  RETURN TO THE INPUT SCREEN ON FRAME 1
103    gotoAndStop(1);
104    //TASK 2:  LISTEN FOR THE USER TO PROCESS A NEW SET OF SCORES
105    LoadAnalyzeBtn.addEventListener(MouseEvent.CLICK,LoadXMLScores);
106 }
```

6.5 do-while Loops

In the last section, we saw that the while statement provides a general (i.e., noncounting) loop that evaluates its loop condition prior to executing the statement it controls. We also saw that such pre-test loops are useful in solving problems where zero-trip behavior is required.

In some repetition problems, however, zero-trip behavior is not appropriate. To solve these problems, many languages provide a post-test loop called a do-while loop.

The general form of the do-while loop is as follows:

```
do {
        list of statements to be executed in the loop;
} while (Boolean test expression);
```

Both do and while are keywords. The Boolean test expression contained within the parentheses is the loop condition. The while clause at the end of the statement appears after the body of the loop, which means that this condition is evaluated at the end of the loop. The syntax of the do-while statement differs from that of the while statement and is designed to indicate clearly that it is a post-test loop. Another, less obvious difference between the while and do-while loops is that the do-while loop must be terminated with a semicolon. In contrast, it is an error to terminate a while loop with a semicolon. This difference is often a source of programming errors for first-time programmers.

The fact that the loop condition is evaluated after the body of the loop has been executed guarantees that the body of the loop will be executed at least once. For this reason, post-test loops are said to exhibit **one-trip behavior**, whereas pre-test loops are said to exhibit zero-trip behavior.

The following examples illustrate the use of the do-while statement.

Example 1

```
1   var count:int = 1;
2
3   do  {
4       trace ("BLUE");
5       count++;
6   } while (count <= 3);
```

Evaluation

This example illustrates a simple do-while loop that displays the text BLUEBLUEBLUE in the output window. This loop will perform as shown in Figure 6-10 and will act as follows:

1. As a post-test loop, the first action of this structure is the execution of the statements contained in the body of the loop (lines 4–5).

2. At the end of the iteration, the Boolean condition is tested (line 6).

3. As a post-test loop, the Boolean test condition must be true before another repetition can be executed. When the Boolean test condition is false, the loop is terminated.

As with a while loop, all loop control variables, such as the one shown in line 1, are declared outside the do-while loop.

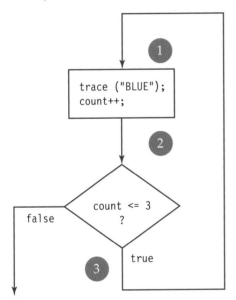

Exit the loop

I FIGURE 6-10 Diagram of the do-while loop behavior.

Example 2

```
1   var  i:uint  = 1;
2   do  {
3        trace (i++);
4   } while (i <= 5);
5
```

Evaluation

Like the previous example, this segment of code uses the do-while loop as a fixed counting loop. The loop control variable, i, is initialized to 1. In this post-test loop, the Boolean test condition i <= 5; will be evaluated at the end of every iteration. If the test condition is true, the loop will begin again. If the test condition is false, the do-while loop will terminate. The trace(i++); statement will be executed first within the body of the loop. This statement performs two tasks: display the variable stored in i and then increment i. The hand-traced table shows the details of each iteration.

	Loop Statement: trace (i++);	i	i <= 5
Iteration 1	1	2	true
Iteration 2	2	3	true
Iteration 3	3	4	true
Iteration 4	4	5	true
Iteration 5	5	6	false

The output produced by this segment of code is

```
1
2
3
4
5
```

Example 3

```
1    var  k:uint  = 100;
2    do  {
3        trace (k);
4        k -= 2;
5    } while (k <= 5);
```

Evaluation

This segment of code illustrates the one-trip nature of the do-while loop. Because a do-while loop is executed at least once, whereas a while loop may be skipped if the initial value of the Boolean expression is false, do-while loops are generally used less frequently than while loops.

In this example, the loop counter k is initialized to 100. Because the Boolean test condition, which is found to be false, is not evaluated until after the loop body executes, a single iteration will occur.

Loop Statement: trace (k);	k -= 2	k <= 5
Iteration 1 100	98	false

The output produced by this segment of code is

100

Example 4

```
1   const ACCURACY:Number=0.0001;
2   var oldSqrt:Number;
3   var newSqrt:Number=10;
4   var number:Number=110;
5   do {
6      oldSqrt=newSqrt;
7      newSqrt = .5 * (oldSqrt + number / oldSqrt);
8      trace(newSqrt.toPrecision(7));
9   } while (Math.abs(newSqrt - oldSqrt) >= ACCURACY);
```

Evaluation

An early algorithm for approximating square roots is the Babylonian method, which is named after the Babylonians, who are credited with its discovery. This method starts with an approximation and then obtains successively better approximations until the desired degree of accuracy is achieved.

In this example, the do-while loop attempts to compute the square root of 110. Logically, we know that the square root is between 10 and 11, so we can begin with 10 or 11 as our first approximation. By the third iteration, the solution computes 10.4880885 as the square root of 110 with an accuracy of 0.0001.

	Loop Statement: oldSqrt = newSqrt;	trace(newSqrt);	newSqrt - oldSqrt >= ACCURACY
Iteration 1	oldSqrt = 10 newSqrt = 10.5000000	10.5000000	0.5 >= 0.0001 true
Iteration 2	oldSqrt = 10 newSqrt = 10.4880952	10.4880952	0.011904761904762 >= 0.0001 true
Iteration 3	oldSqrt = 10 newSqrt = 10.4880885	10.4880885	0.000006756391545 >= 0.0001 false

The output produced by this segment of code is

10.5000000
10.4880952
10.4880885

The square root of 110 is 10.4880885.

Example 5

```
1   var sum:int = 0;
2   do {
3      sum += i++;
4      trace (sum);
5   } while (i <= 5);
```

Evaluation

This example computes the sum of the first five integers using a do-while loop. The loop control variable, i, is initialized to 1. In this post-test loop, the Boolean test condition i <= 5; will be evaluated at the end of every iteration. Once inside the loop, sum is computed, i is incremented, and sum is displayed. At the end of the loop, the test condition (i <= 5) is evaluated. If it is true, the loop executes again. If the test condition is found to be false, the do-while loop terminates.

	Loop Statements: sum += i;	trace ("sum");	i++	i < 6
Iteration 1	sum contains 1	1	2	true
Iteration 2	sum contains 3	3	3	true
Iteration 3	sum contains 6	6	4	true
Iteration 4	sum contains 10	10	5	true
Iteration 5	sum contains 15	15	6	false

The output produced by this segment of code is

1
3
6
10
15

6.6 Case Study 3: Graphing Population Growth

The goal of this case study is to explore the use of looping for constructing graphs. Specifically, we will chart the population growth for the United States and China, as shown in Figure 6-11.

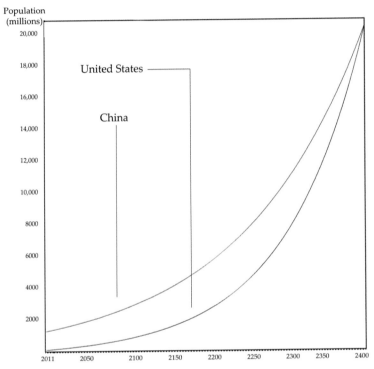

I FIGURE 6-11 The growth of the populations in the United States and China.

Problem and Analysis

In 2011, the United States' average annual percent change in population was approximately 0.98%. This population growth rate was the result of a surplus of births over deaths and the balance of migrants entering the country. This rather high percentage exceeds that of any country in Europe other than Ireland. Growth rate is an important factor in determining the changing needs of a country's populace for infrastructure, resources, and jobs. In the same year, China's average annual percent change in population was approximately 0.66%.

For this problem, we will play with the idea that the population growth rates for the United States and China will remain constant. Using the fixed population growth rates, we will attempt to compute the year in which the size of the U.S. population will exceed the size of the Chinese population. The application will also chart this growth.

This problem requires the storage of growth rates as well as current populations for China and the United States. These figures will be stored as constants and used to compute population sizes and to build the charts. A looping structure will be required to compute the new population sizes and assign them to variables for every year controlled by the loop. Given that it would be informative to graph the population growth for each of these nations, the program will also require variables for plotting lines. Table 6-4 shows the complete list of data objects with identifier names and general numeric types.

TABLE 6-4 Data Object Requirements for the Population Growth Application

Data Object	Description	Data Type	Object Type
`INIT_YR`	The starting year of 2011.	`uint`	Constant
`US_GROWTH_RATE`	The constant growth rate of the United States; initialized to 0.98%.	Number	Constant
`CHINA_GROWTH_RATE`	The constant growth rate of China; initialized to 0.66%.	Number	Constant
`US_INIT`	The initial population of the United States in the year `INIT_YR`. This constant is initialized to 306, representing 306 million people.	Number	Constant
`CHINA_INIT`	The initial population of China in the year `INIT_YR`. This constant is set as 1300, or 1300 million people.	Number	Constant
`BASELINE`	The baseline for the plotted graph. This is the lowest y-axis position on the visual document.	Number	Constant
`year`	The year of any given iteration.	`uint`	Variable
`chinaPOP`	China's population in any given year.	Number	Variable
`usPOP`	The U.S. population in any given year.	Number	Variable
`FinalPopulation`	The final population when the U.S. population exceeds the Chinese population.	Number	Global Variable
`finalYear`	The year that the U.S. population exceeds the Chinese population.	`uint`	Global Variable
`graphYscale`	The size of the height area for plotting the y coordinate.	Number	Global Variable
`graphXscale`	The width of the horizontal area for plotting the x coordinate.	Number	Global Variable
`x0`	The point on the x-axis for an x, y coordinate.	Number	Variable
`y0`	The point on the y-axis for an x, y coordinate.	Number	Variable

Visual Design

This case study will not use the Timeline, nor will it rely on display objects built in Flash. Because no interactions will occur, the event system will not be needed.

Algorithm Design

The structure for this program, shown in Figure 6-12, will consist of the main algorithm `population()` (also the constructor), the `computeYearAndFinalPOP` algorithm, the `plotChinaPopulation` algorithm, and the `plotUSPopulation` algorithm.

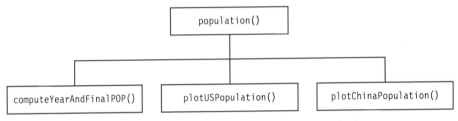

▌FIGURE 6-12 Relationship of functions used by the population growth application.

The required class `package` is placed at the beginning of the file. The `flash.display` library class is the only class needed for the application. The document class is named `population`. The class constants and global variables derived from the problem analysis and listed in Table 6-5 are declared first.

The last two lines of the AS3 file contain closing curly brackets to close the document class and the package.

```
1    package {
2        import flash.display.*;
3        public class population extends MovieClip {
4            //CONSTANT DECLARATIONS
5            const US_GROWTH_RATE:Number=.0098;
6            const CHINA_GROWTH_RATE:Number=.0063;
7            const US_INIT:Number=306;
8            const CHINA_INIT:Number=1300;
9            const INIT_YR:uint=2011;
10           const BASELINE:Number=US_INIT;
11           //GLOBAL VARIABLE DECLARATIONS
12           var graphYscale:Number;
13           var graphXscale:Number;
14           var FinalPopulation:Number;
15           var finalYear:Number;
```

```
⋮

71       }
72   }
```

The four functions used in the application are designed and coded as described next.

Function population() Design

The main algorithm, population(), is the class constructor function. This function is initiated once the application is executed.

The role of this function is to control the execution of main tasks.

```
16    function population() {
17        computeYearAndFinalPOP();
18        plotUSPopulation();
19        plotChinaPopulation();
20    }
21
```

Function computeYearAndFinalPOP() Design

This function is the main engine behind the application. It computes the number of years it takes the U.S. population to exceed China's population and calculates the final population sizes for both nations. In addition, the variable for storing the graphing scale is computed.

```
22    function computeYearAndFinalPOP() {
23        //TASK 1:  SET THE INITIAL YEAR AND THE INITIAL POPULATIONS
24        var year:uint=INIT_YR;
25        var chinaPOP:Number=CHINA_INIT;
26        var usPOP:Number=US_INIT;
27        //TASK 2: LOOP UNTIL THE U.S. SURPASSES CHINA's POPULATION
28        do {
29            year++;
30            chinaPOP+=chinaPOP*CHINA_GROWTH_RATE;
31            usPOP+=usPOP*US_GROWTH_RATE;
32        } while (chinaPOP > usPOP);
33        //TASK 3: ASSIGN THE FINAL POPULATION AND YEAR
34        FinalPopulation=usPOP;
35        finalYear=year;
36        //TASK 4: COMPUTE THE SCALE WITH WHICH TO CONSTRUCT THE FINAL GRAPH
37        graphYscale=stage.stageHeight/FinalPopulation;
38        graphXscale=stage.stageWidth/(finalYear - INIT_YR);
39    }
40
```

Function plotUSPopulation() Design

This function plots the size of the U.S. population until it exceeds the size of the Chinese population. It employs a fixed loop structure to iterate from 1 to finalYear, recalculating usPOP at each iteration. The variables x0 and y0 are used to draw individual line segments.

```
41    function plotUSPopulation() {
42        //TASK 1: INITIALIZE THE POPULATION FOR THE U.S.
43        var usPOP:Number=US_INIT;
44        //TASK 2: SET THE FIRST DRAWING POINT AND THE LINE STYLE
45        var x0:Number=0;
46        var y0:Number=(US_INIT - usPOP ) * graphYscale + stage.stageHeight;
47        graphics.moveTo(x0,y0);
48        graphics.lineStyle(1);
49        //TASK 3: ITERATE FROM 1 TO THE FINAL YEAR; POPULATION IS RECALCULATED
50        for (var i:int = 1; i <= (finalYear - INIT_YR); i++) {
51            x0=i*graphXscale;
52            usPOP+=usPOP*US_GROWTH_RATE;
53            y0 = (US_INIT - usPOP ) * graphYscale + stage.stageHeight;
54            graphics.lineTo(x0,y0);
55        }
56    }
57
```

Function plotChinaPopulation() Design

This function plots the population for China in the same manner as the function plotUSPopulation().

```
58    function plotChinaPopulation() {
59        var chinaPOP:Number=CHINA_INIT;
60        var x0:Number=0;
61        var y0:Number=(US_INIT - chinaPOP )*graphYscale+stage.stageHeight;
62        graphics.moveTo(x0,y0);
63        graphics.lineStyle(1, 0xFF0000);
64        for (var i:int = 1; i <= (finalYear - INIT_YR); i++) {
65            x0=i*graphXscale;
66            chinaPOP+=chinaPOP*CHINA_GROWTH_RATE;
67            y0 = (BASELINE - chinaPOP ) * graphYscale + stage.stageHeight;
68            graphics.lineTo(x0,y0);
69        }
70    }
```

6.7 Nested Loops

At this point, we have examined three loop structures. Each has been discussed with respect to syntax, semantics, form, writing style, and use in programs. Because each loop is treated as a single statement, it is possible to have a loop serve as one of the statements in the body of another loop. When this happens, the loops are said to be nested.

Loops can be nested to any depth; that is, a loop can be present within a loop within a loop and so on. Also, any of the three types of loops can be nested within any other type of loop.

Example 1

```
1   for (var row:int = 1; row <= 5; row++) {
2       for (var col:int = 1; col <= 3; col++) {
3           trace ( row * col);
4       }
5   }
```

Evaluation

This segment of code prints out the product of the row and column numbers of a 3 by 5 array. Thus 3rd row and 4th column = 3 * 4 = 12. For each value of row, the inner loop found in lines 2–4 is executed.

When row is 1, col will be initialized to 1 and will loop in increments of 1 until it exceeds 3. The hand-traced table when row = 1 will look as follows:

row = 1	col <= 3	trace (row * col);	col++
Iteration 1	col = 1 true	1	2
Iteration 2	col = 2 true	2	3
Iteration 3	col = 3 true	3	4
Iteration 4	col = 4 false		

The same loop is repeated when row is 2. The hand-traced table when row = 2 will look as follows:

row = 2	col <= 3	trace (row * col);	col++
Iteration 1	col = 1 true	2	2
Iteration 2	col = 2 true	4	3
Iteration 3	col = 3 true	6	4
Iteration 4	col = 4 false		

The complete output from these nested loops is

```
1
2
3
```

```
2
4
6

3
6
9

4
8
12

5
10
15
```

■ 6.8 Case Study 4: An ASCII Bull's Eye

ASCII artwork—that is, text-based art that utilizes keyboard characters to piece together pictures—is more fun than practical. However, it can be useful in illustrating how to use a nested loop to explore a virtual coordinate system.

In this case study we will create an algorithmic ASCII bull's eye like the one shown in Figure 6-13.

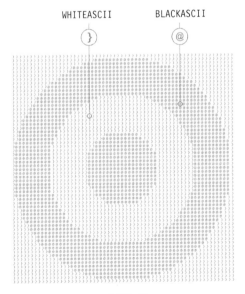

▌ FIGURE 6-13 An ASCII bull's eye.

Virtual Coordinate System

The most complex aspect of this algorithm is a nested counting loop that will be used to construct a virtual *x*, *y* coordinate system. The bull's eye contains three rings: a center dark circle, followed by a light ring, another dark ring, and finally a light area.

The light ring areas are made with the ASCII text '}' and the dark ring areas are made with the ASCII text '@'.

As seen in Figure 6-14, when we divide the stage into an *x*- and *y*-axis coordinate system, in which the *x*-axis and the *y*-axis meet in the center at (0, 0), the distance from the center to any *xy* point in the coordinate system can be computed using the Pythagorean Theorem as follows:

```
distance = Math.sqrt(X * X + Y * Y);
```

If this distance falls within the range of the light ring, we will display a '}'; otherwise, we will display a '@'.

Distance along the *y*-axis

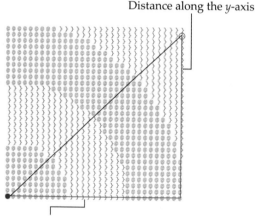

Distance along the *x*-axis

▌ FIGURE 6-14 The computed distance from (0, 0) to a given ASCII character in the bull's eye.

The graphic requirements for the bull's eye are two MovieClip objects: one containing the '}' and the other containing the '@'. Each of these MovieClips will be created with a linkage ID: WHITEASCII for '}' and BLACKASCII for '@'.

The algorithm will need two sets of coordinate values. The first set of coordinate variables will represent the coordinate system natural to the Flash environment; it is required for positioning the ASCII characters on the stage. The uppermost point on a Flash stage is (0, 0). Because the full size of the bullseye image is 600 by 600 pixels, the lower-right point of the stage is (600, 600).

To compute the distance from the center of the image, thereby identifying which ASCII character to draw, we will use the *x*, *y* coordinate system where (0, 0) is the center. These two variables will be designated X and Y (in uppercase letters).

Table 6-5 shows the complete list of data objects with identifier names and general numeric types.

TABLE 6-5 Data Objects for the ACSII Bull's Eye

Data Object	Description	Data Type	Object Type
ASCIIsize	The size of the ASCII character. Width and height are equal.	uint	Constant
blackObj	BLACKASCII is the name of the symbol in the library that represents the ASCII character '@'. blackObj is the display object representing a newly constructed BLACKASCII.	BLACKASCII	Variable
whiteObj	WHITEASCII is the name of the symbol in the library that represents the ASCII character '{'. whiteObj is the display object representing a newly constructed WHITEASCII.	WHITEASCII	Variable
xPosition	The x position on the Stage.	int	Variable
yPosition	The y position on the Stage.	int	Variable
X	The point along the x-axis.	int	Variable
Y	The point along the y-axis.	int	Variable
distance	The computed distance from (0, 0) to any x, y point.	Number	Variable

Visual Design

The visual side of this application will require two simple ASCII characters created in Flash and stored as MovieClip symbols with the class linkage IDs of BLACKASCII and WHITEASCII. The linkage IDs will allow the ActionScript 3.0 program to generate multiple instances of the ASCII elements during runtime. The Timeline and Stage will remain empty.

Program Design

The AS3 code for this application will consist of three functions. The main function, bullseye(), directs the generation of the entire ASCII image once the application is launched. The relationship between these functions is shown in Figure 6-15.

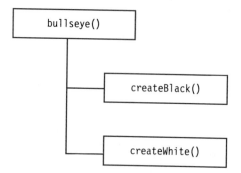

I FIGURE 6-15 Relationship of functions used by the ASCII bull's eye application.

The package for this program contains flash.display.*. Because the application does not require interactivity, the event class is not included. Constants and variables declared globally are derived from the problem analysis.

```
1   package {
2      import flash.display.*;
3
4      public class bullseye extends MovieClip {
5         //CONSTANT AND GLOBAL VARIABLE DECLARATIONS
6         const ASCIIsize:Number=10;
7         var blackObj:BLACKASCII;
8         var whiteObj:WHITEASCII;
9         var xPosition:Number=0;
10        var yPosition:Number=0;
11
```

```
56     }
57  }
```

Function bullseye() Design

In this application, the constructor bullseye() is also the engine behind the ASCII art. Using a nested for loop, this function constructs the individual ASCII elements based on the virtual *x, y* coordinate system.

```
12  function bullseye() {
13     //TASK 1: CONSTRUCT THE VIRTUAL COORDINATE SYSTEM
14     for (var Y:int = 30; Y >= -30; Y--) {
15        for (var X:int = -30; X <= 30; X++) {
16           //TASK 2: FOR ALL XY POINTS, COMPUTE DISTANCE FROM (0,0) CENTER
17           var distance:Number=Math.sqrt(X*X+Y*Y);
18           //TASK 3: IDENTIFY IF BLACK OR WHITE IS CREATED
19           if (distance < 10)
```

```
20              createBlack();
21          else if (distance < 20)
22              createWhite();
23          else if (distance < 30)
24              createBlack();
25          else
26              createWhite();
27      }
28      xPosition=0;
29      yPosition+=ASCIIsize;
30  }
31 }
32
```

Function createBlack() Design

The objective of createBlack() is to generate and position a dark-colored ASCII character on the Stage.

```
33    function createBlack (){
34       //TASK 1:  CREATE AN OBJECT USING THE LINKAGE ID FOR BLACKASCII
35       blackObj=new BLACKASCII;
36       //TASK 2:  SET THE PROPORTIONS AND POSITION OF THE NEW ASCII CHILD
37       blackObj.width=blackObj.height=ASCIIsize;
38       blackObj.x=xPosition;
39       blackObj.y=yPosition;
40       //TASK 3:  ADD THE ASCII CHILD TO THE STAGE
41       addChild(blackObj);
42       //TASK 4: SET THE ATTRIBUTES FOR THE NEXT BLACKASCII
43       xPosition+=ASCIIsize;
44    }
45
```

Function createWhite() Design

The objective of createWhite() is to generate and position a light-colored ASCII character on the Stage.

```
46  function createWhite (){
47     whiteObj=new WHITEASCII;
48     whiteObj.width=whiteObj.height=ASCIIsize;
49     whiteObj.x=xPosition;
50     whiteObj.y=yPosition;
51     //ADD THE WHITEASCII INSTANCE
52     addChild(whiteObj);
53     //SET THE ATTRIBUTES FOR THE NEXT WHITEASCII
54     xPosition+=ASCIIsize;
55  }
```

There are very interesting possibilities for creating patterns using looping structures. For example, the image in Figure 6-16 can be produced by simply nesting an additional loop in the current case study. This added loop repeatedly adds the ASCII character '{' and rotates it in the amount of the Golden Ratio, introduced in Case Study 1 in this chapter.

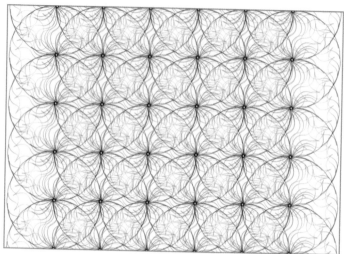

I FIGURE 6-16 Enhanced ASCII art piece using a nested loop.

6.9 Case Study 5: Graphing a Mathematical Function

Problem and Analysis

Oftentimes, it is necessary to produce scientific graphs in an application, such as the function $f(x) = x^2$ illustrated in Figure 6-17. This case study uses two coordinate systems—the one inherent to the Flash Stage and a virtual coordinate system, initially explored in Case Study 4.

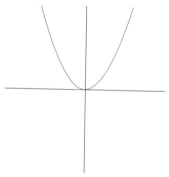

I FIGURE 6-17 Plot: $f(x) = x^2$.

To construct a graph, the virtual coordinate system is used, in which the center point is located at (0, 0). The values for this graph are then translated to the Flash coordinate system for the actual plotting of points of the mathematical function. The values representing the location on the Stage are stored in the variables xPosition and yPosition. The values representing the location on the virtual coordinate system are stored in the variables X and Y. To eliminate an abrupt beginning and ending locations of the graph, the xPosition and yPosition values will begin at -50, just off the upper-left corner of the Stage. Table 6-6 shows the complete list of data objects with identifier names and general numeric types.

TABLE 6-6 List of Data Objects Used in the Mathematical Function Application

Data Object	Description	Data Type	Object Type
xPosition	The x position on the Stage	int	Variable
yPosition	The y position on the Stage	int	Variable
X	The point along the x-axis	int	Variable
Y	The point along the y-axis	int	Variable

Algorithm Design

The structure for this program consists of the functions graphApp(), drawAxisLines(), plotFunction(), and plotPoint(). The document class is also graphApp. graphApp() is the main function that calls both drawAxisLines() and plotFunction(). It is designed as a constructor. drawAxisLines() simply draws the lines of the x, y coordinate system, while plotFunction() uses a nested loop that simulates the traversing of all x, y coordinates in a system from X = -35 to 35 and Y = -350 to 350. Finally, plotPoint() is called to plot an individual point in the mathematical function. Figure 6-18 shows the relationship between these functions.

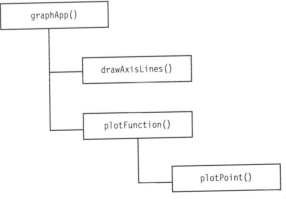

| **FIGURE 6-18** Relationship of functions used by the plotting application.

The class package requires only the display library class. The last two lines contain closing curly brackets to conclude the graphApp class and the package.

```
1    package {
2        import flash.display.*;
3
4        public class graphApp extends MovieClip {
5
6            var xPosition:Number=-50;
7            var yPosition:Number=-50;
8
```
⋮
```
49       }
50   }
```

Function graphApp() Design

The constructor function, graphApp(), controls the plotting of $f(x) = x^2$.

```
9    function graphApp () {
10       drawAxisLines();
11       plotFunction();
12   }
13
```

Function drawAxisLines() Design

This function draws two lines of the coordinate system—the x- and y-axes. This visual will aid in interpreting the final graph.

```
14   function drawAxisLines() {
15       //TASK 1: DRAW THE X-AXIS
16       graphics.moveTo(0,stage.stageHeight/2);
17       graphics.lineStyle(1);
18       graphics.lineTo(stage.stageWidth,stage.stageHeight/2);
19
20       //TASK 2: DRAW THE Y-AXIS
21       graphics.moveTo(stage.stageWidth/2,0);
22       graphics.lineStyle(1);
23       graphics.lineTo(stage.stageWidth/2,stage.stageHeight);
24   }
25
```

Function plotFunction() Design

As the plotting engine of the algorithm, this function utilizes a nested loop to construct the virtual coordinate system. It calls the function plotPoint() to individually draw and connect each point in the graph.

```
26  function plotFunction() {
27      //TASK 1:  POSITION THE PEN AT THE INITIAL POINT OFF THE STAGE
28      graphics.moveTo(-350, -350);
29      //TASK 2:  USE A NESTED LOOP TO CONSTRUCT THE VIRTUAL COORDINATE SYSTEM
30      for (var X:Number = -35; X <= 35; X++) {
31          for (var Y:int = 350; Y >= -350; Y--) {
32              //TASK 3:  COMPUTE THE POINT USING THE FUNCTION Y = X²
33              if (Y==X*X) {
34                  plotPoint();
35              }
36              yPosition++;
37          }
38          //TASK 4:  AFTER PLOTTING ONE ROW, START A NEW ROW
39          yPosition=-50;
40          xPosition+=10;
41      }
42  }
43
```

Function plotPoint() Design

This function uses Flash's Graphics library to connect the points in the graph.

```
44  function plotPoint() {
45      graphics.lineStyle(.5, 0xFF0000);
46      graphics.lineTo(xPosition,yPosition);
47      graphics.moveTo(xPosition,yPosition);
48  }
```

▣ Review Questions

1. Why is the for loop called a fixed iterative loop?

2. Why is the for loop known as a pre-test loop? Explain. Which types of loops are the do-while and while loops?

3. Why is the for loop called a zero-trip loop? What are the do-while and while loops called?

4. When is a for loop a better choice than a while loop? When is a while loop a better choice than a do-while loop?

5. What output is produced by the following segments of code:

   a. ```
      for (var i:int = 1; i < 5; i++){
            trace('A');
      }
      ```

   b. ```
      for (var i:int = 1; i <= 3;){
            trace('A');
      ```

```
        }
    c. for (var x:int = 3; x >= -1; x--){
            trace(x);
        }

    d. for (var i:int = 0; i >= 3; i++ ){
            trace(i);
        }

    e. for (var i = 1:int; i <= 10; i += 2){
            trace(i);
        }

    f. for (var i:int = 1; i <= 10; i ++){
            trace(i);
            i++;
        }
```

6. What output is produced by the following segments of code? Assume the variable
   i and the constant MAX have been defined as follows:

```
        var i:int = 0;
        const MAX:int = 4;
```

```
    a. while (i <= 5){
            trace('A');
            i++;
        }
```

```
    b. while (i <= 2){
            trace('A');
        }
```

```
    c. i = MAX - 1;
       while (i > MAX){
            i= i- 2;
            trace(i) ;
       }
```

```
    d. i = MAX - 1;
       do {
           i-= 2;
       }while (i > MAX);
       trace(i);
```

```
    e. i = MAX - 1;
       do {
           trace(i);
       }
       while (i >= 3);
```

```
f. do{
       i++
       trace(i);
       i++;
   }
   while (i <= 10);
```

Exercises

1. Write a program that will generate all of the three-digit odd whole numbers that exist.

2. Generate all possible five-digit sequential numbers, where a sequential number is considered to be any five consecutive digits.

3. Determine all the prime numbers less than 100.

4. Write an interactive program that requires the user to input two integers, X and Y—positive or negative. Calculate X * Y without using the multiplication operator.

5. The Fibonacci sequence of numbers is defined as follows:

$F(0) = 1$

$F(1) = 1$

$F(n) = F(n - 1) + F(n - 2)$ for $n > 1$

This says that the first two numbers in the sequence are 1 and 1. Then, each subsequent Fibonacci number is the sum of the two previous numbers in the sequence. Thus the first 9 Fibonacci numbers are

1, 1, 2, 3, 5, 8, 13, 21, 34

Write an interactive program that will prompt the user for a number, x, between 100 and 550 and compute and display all the Fibonacci numbers less than x.

6. Write a simple program that uses nested for loops to print the following multiplication table:

	1	2	3	4	5	6	7	8	9
1	1								
2	2	4							
3	3	6	9						
4	4	8	12	16					
5	5	10	15	20	25				
6	6	12	18	24	30	36			
7	7	14	21	28	35	42	49		
8	8	16	24	32	40	48	56	64	
9	9	18	27	36	45	54	63	72	81

7. Write a program that creates a monthly calendar. The application should receive as input from the user the month and the year. Verify that the input is correct and that leap years are considered. The monthly calendars must be correct. For example, if the user enters **December 1969**, the following calendar will be constructed:

S	M	T	W	T	F	S
	1	2	3	4	5	6
7	8	9	10	11	12	13
14	15	16	17	18	19	20
21	22	23	24	25	26	27
28	29	30	31			

7 Arrays, Stacks, and Character Strings

Introduction

Many software applications require the creation and manipulation of lists of objects. In this chapter, we explore the concepts behind processing lists of data.

List processing involves the use of a data structure called an **array**. Simply put, an array is a variable that holds a collection of elements. Every modern programming language supports arrays for list processing, but they differ in the ways in which arrays are implemented. In AS3, an array can conveniently grow and shrink during the execution of a given program.

In the first sections of this chapter, we introduce arrays along with the concept of indexing. We explore the built-in properties and methods associated with this data structure and see how arrays are used to solve common programming problems.

AS3 also has an inherent ability to use arrays for the creation of stacks and queues. A stack is a list in which objects are added and removed strictly from the back of the list. A queue, by comparison, is a list that behaves similarly to lines that are formed in places like supermarkets or banks, where people wait their turn for service. With waiting lines, new people go to the back of the line and service is rendered to them when they reach the front of the line. This chapter looks at the implementation and application of these two list structures.

The principles of strings and arrays are very similar, although with AS3 there are several fundamental differences that will be explored. In the last part of this chapter, we introduce string and character processing capabilities.

7.1 Introduction to Arrays

Until now, we have not explored the idea of controlling a significant collection of display objects on the Stage or manipulating large numbers of variable data. Arrays are crucial to programming because they lend themselves to applications that require a sizable number of objects that will be processed repeatedly.

An array is a general type of variable that resembles a list and is used to store objects of any type. At its essence, it is a collection of sequential memory locations. The convenience of an array is that it allows programmers to store and manipulate an entire list of objects as a single entity. Each object within the array can be accessed by identifying its position within the list.

7.1.1 The Basics

Why use an array structure? What does an array structure look like?

An array structure is used to store a collection of data, such as numbers, strings, and display objects.

To better understand this concept, we begin with a simple example.

Example

Consider a program in which 10 quiz scores must be stored. Once these scores are stored, we assume they need processing in several ways, such as computing the average score and displaying those scores that are greater than the computed average. We will explore these processing tasks a little later.

Solution

By using an array, we can store 10 quiz scores as a single entity. The AS3 instruction that creates the array holding the quiz scores will look as follows:

```
1   var quizScores:Array = new Array(90,89,77,78,67,75,74,77,68,69);
```

In this declaration, this single variable is named `quizScores` and is defined as an array. The keyword `new`, which has been explored in earlier chapters, is used in this case to create an array data structure. The list of numeric values (shown in parentheses) represents the 10 quiz scores, which we will assume are the input values. With this declaration, the entire list of quiz scores is stored as a single entity and the identifier name `quizScores` represents the entire body of quiz scores.

Each individual value in `quizScores` will occupy an individual memory cell in an uninterrupted sequence. The term **cell** refers to an individual memory location. The first quiz score in the array is positioned at cell 0 in the sequence, so the last quiz score is positioned at cell 9 in the sequence. The following is a visualization of the memory cells allocated to store the list of quiz scores. The cell position in an array is called an index. We examine this concept next.

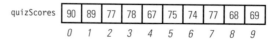

7.1.2 Processing an Array: Indexed Array Elements

To process a list of data, it is necessary to understand the concept of indexing. Arrays are called indexed data structures because individual cells can be accessed by an index. Each cell is identified by its index position in the array. Even though an array is a list of objects referenced by a single name, each object is an individual variable positioned in a sequence. The first object of any array is always positioned at the zero index, the second object is positioned at index 1, and so forth. The last index of any cell in an array is always one less than the number of elements in the list.

The syntax for accessing a cell requires a set of brackets to hold the index, as follows:

```
arrayName[indexNumber]
```

The following example illustrates the basic use of indexing in assignment statements.

Example 1

Task 1: Create an array named list1 that contains six cells, all initialized to zero.

Instruction

```
1   var list1:Array = new Array(0,0,0,0,0,0);
```

Visualization

list1, along with the cell indices, is visualized as follows:

list1	0	0	0	0	0	0
index	0	1	2	3	4	5

Task 2: Place the number −99 in the cell at index 4.

Instruction

```
2   list1 [4] = -99;
```

Visualization

list1	0	0	0	0	-99	0
index	0	1	2	3	4	5

The next four examples feature additional array indexing.

Example 2

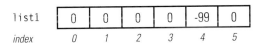

```
1   var list2:Array = new Array(10, 7, 6, 3);
2   var num:int = list2[0]
3   trace(list2 [num / 2 - 3]);
```

Evaluation

This code segment illustrates that an index can also be an expression as long as it results in an unsigned integer. The expression [num / 2 - 3] results in an index of 2.

list2

10	7	6	3
0	1	2	3

num

10

The output produced by this segment of code is 6.

Example 3

```
1   var list3:Array = new Array(1, 8, 4, 9);
2   trace(list3 [-1]);
```

Evaluation

An error occurs in the trace statement. There is no such cell index as −1.

Example 4

```
1   var list4:Array = new Array(6,7,8,9,10,11,12);
2   for (var i:int = 0;  i < 7; i++){
3     if (list4 [i]%2 == 1) {
4        list4 [i] = list4 [i] * 2;
5     }
6   }
7
```

Evaluation

This example illustrates list processing. The initial values in list4 are as follows:

list4

6	7	8	9	10	11	12
0	1	2	3	4	5	6

The for loop examines the value within each cell. If the value is odd, it is doubled. A for loop is often used to navigate an array structure because its loop control variable can easily serve as a roaming index. The final values in list4 are as follows:

list4 | 6 | 14 | 8 | 18 | 10 | 22 | 12 |
       0   1   2   3   4   5   6

Example 5

Processing Task

Given the array quizScores, which holds 10 quiz scores, compute the average quiz score. Display all the scores greater than the average.

Solution

Solving this processing task requires two passes through the array. The first pass (lines 6–9) uses a looping structure that accesses and sums each quiz score stored in the list. Once the scores are summed, the average is computed by dividing the sum by 10.

The final pass through the array (lines 12–15) uses another for loop to examine each score in the array and display it if it is larger than the average.

```
1  var quizScores:Array = new Array(90,89,77,78,67,75,74,77,68,69);
2  var sum:int = 0;
3  var average:Number;
4
5  //PASS 1: COMPUTE THE AVERAGE
6  for (var i:int = 0; i < 10; i++) {
7     sum += quizScore[i];
8  }
9  average = sum / 10;
10
11  //PASS 2: DISPLAY ALL SCORES ABOVE THE AVERAGE
12  for (var i:int = 0; i < 10; i++) {
13     if ( quizScore[i] > average) {
14        trace (quizScore[i]);
15     }
16  }
```

7.1.3 Other Ways to Create an Array

ActionScript provides multiple ways to create arrays. As illustrated in the examples in the previous section, the Array() constructor function can be used to create an instance of an array object. The general syntax used to declare an array initialized to a list of elements is shown here. Reserved AS3 keywords are identified in bold.

var *listName:**Array** = **new Array***(list of elements);*

The keywords new and Array are not always required. For example, the following declarations of the array listNum create equivalent array structures:

```
var listNum: Array = new Array(2, 3, 5);
var listNum = new Array(2, 3, 5);
var listNum: Array = [2, 3, 5];
```

Populating the array at declaration time is not essential. In fact, it is often necessary to begin with an empty array and then add or subtract elements during the execution of the program.

The following three definitions are all valid methods for creating an array that contains no elements:

```
var listNum: Array = new Array();
var listNum = new Array();
var listNum: Array = [];
```

A fourth method can be used to create an array of a specific size by indicating the number of cells. Do not confuse this process with that for creating an array holding a single value.

```
var listNum = new Array(number of cells);
```

7.1.4 Populating and Determining the Size of an Array

Populating an array can also be done in a variety of ways. One method is to use direct assignments in which a value is assigned to a given array cell. For example, the set of instructions that follows creates an empty array and then populates it using direct assignment statements. In this case, the value 22 is placed in the first cell and the value 33 is placed in the second cell of the listNum array.

```
var listNum:Array = new Array();
listNum[0] = 22;
listNum[1] = 33;
```

The length property of the Array class can be used to report the number of cells in a given array.

We illustrate some of these properties in the following examples.

Example 1

```
1   var aList = new Array(7);
2   trace("The length of aList is " + aList.length);
```

Evaluation

Here, a new array is created with seven cells reserved. Each of the reserved cells initially will contain an undefined value. In the visualization below, the question mark indicates an *undefined* value.

```
aList    | ? | ? | ? | ? | ? | ? | ? |
           0   1   2   3   4   5   6
```

The `trace` statement will display the number of cells in `aList`. Notice that the last index of the array is 6; however, the length of the array is 7. The first index of every array is zero. The length of an array starts with 1.

The output produced is

The length of aList is 7

Example 2

```
1   var aList = new Array(3);
2   aList[3] = 22;
3   trace("The length of aList is "+ aList.length);
```

Evaluation

This example illustrates the dynamic nature of the `Array` class.

Line 1: Initially, `aList` is declared with a size of three cells, each holding an undefined value.

Line 2: Directly assigning a value to a nonexistent cell index will add an element at that index. In this case, the array will grow to hold four cells.

```
aList    | ? | ? | ? | 22 |
           0   1   2   3
```

Line 3: The output produced is

The length of aList is 4

Example 3

Task

Create an array that contains all the numbers from 0 to 200.

Solution

Entering all 200 numbers during initialization of the array would be cumbersome. An equally poor approach would be to use direct assignment—a technique that requires 201 assignment statements. The best option, by far, is to employ a loop structure to automate the insertion process. Arrays and loop structures are often used in combination. Specifically, an empty array is created and then the `for` loop populates it.

```
1    var numberList:Array = new Array();
2    for (var i:int = 0; i <= 200; i ++;) {
3        numberList [i] = i;
4    }
```

Example 4

Task

In ActionScript, an array is not restricted to a single data type. Thus, unlike with C# and C++ arrays, ActionScript allows a mixture of value types and display objects in a single array. Figure 7-1 shows a Flash movie containing four different types of display objects on the Stage. The first display object is a member of the SimpleButton class. The instances Ball1 and Ball2 are both members of the MovieClip class, and Input1 is a member of the TextField class. Write a definition for an array that stores the different display objects in Figure 7-1.

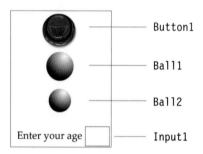

Button1

Ball1

Ball2

Enter your age ☐   Input1

I FIGURE 7-1 Flash Stage containing display objects.

Solution

```
1    var objectList:Array = new Array(Button1, Ball1, Ball2, Input1);
```

Example 5

Arrays in ActionScript provide a way of creating memory as needed by a program. In this example, the numList array declaration begins with an empty structure, and memory is then allocated as needed.

```
1    var numList:Array = new Array();
2    numList [0] = 33;
3    numList [3] = 66;
4
5    trace(numList.length);
6    for (var i:int = 0; i <= numList.length; i++) {
7        trace(numList [i]);
8    }
```

Evaluation

Line 2: The first cell of the array is allocated with a direct assignment.

Line 3: Using direct assignment again, a cell at index 3 is created.

Line 5: The length of this array is 4. Due to the gap between index 0 and the last index 3, two additional cells of memory were allocated in line 3.

```
listNum   33   ?   ?   66
           0   1   2   3
```

Lines 6–8: The output produced by the for loop is

```
33
undefined
undefined
66
```

7.1.5 Built-in Methods of Arrays

In AS3, an array is a versatile data structure, partly due to the collection of built-in operations, or methods, provided by the Array class. These operations, which are listed in Tables 7-1, 7-2, and 7-3, provide valuable functionality in manipulating and organizing the contents of a given array.

Array Operations Category 1: Growing and Shrinking the Array   Operations in this category deal with adding elements to and removing elements from an array. As Table 7-1 shows, an array structure is dynamic and can easily grow and shrink in AS3.

TABLE 7-1 Addition and Deletion Operations

Method	Description
push()	Used to add an element to the end of an array.
pop()	Used to remove an element from the end of an array.
unShift()	Used to add an element to the beginning of an array.
shift()	Used to remove the first element of an array.
splice(index, howMany)	Used to remove an element from the middle of an array. The two values required for this method are index and howMany: index refers to the start position from which elements will be removed; howMany refers to the number of cells to be removed.

Array Operations Category 2: Searching and Sorting the Elements Within the Array   Since the beginning of computing, computer scientists and mathematicians have devoted considerable effort to solving the problem of how best to sort the contents of and search for an element within an array. The concepts involving sorts and searches are considered crucial knowledge for programmers.

In AS3, an understanding of these concepts is not required because the Array class provides a useful collection of methods to perform these operations efficiently. Even without an understanding of how these methods are programmed, they can be called on to do the work for us. Nevertheless, the notion of a search is such a common task in computer science that we offer an algorithm for it at the end of this section.

Four Array operations for sorting and searching arrays are available, as listed in Table 7-2.

TABLE 7-2 Sorting and Searching Array Operations

Method	Description
indexOf(element)	Searches for an element in the array and returns its index number. If an element is not found, a −1 is returned.
reverse()	Alters the array by reversing the existing order of its contents.
sort()	Alters the array by using sorting algorithms to sort the contents of the array in a specified way, such as alphabetical or numeric order.
sortOn()	Sorts elements based on common attributes.

Array Operations Category 3: Building Arrays from Existing Arrays   The operations in this category are used in situations where new arrays need to be built to store the combined elements from several arrays or a subset of a single array. AS3 provides these operations, shown in Table 7-3, as a convenience.

TABLE 7-3 Operations to Build New Arrays

Method	Description
concat()	Returns a new array that is the combination of two existing arrays. Takes one array and merges it with a second existing array to create a new array. See Example 4 for its usage syntax.
slice(startIndex, endIndex)	Returns a new array. Requires two parameters, the start index and an end index. Returns a new array containing a copy of the elements "sliced" from the existing array. The slice begins with the element at startIndex and ends with the element just before endIndex.

Example 1

```
1   var listNum: Array = new Array(2,3);
2   listNum.push(4);
3   listNum.unShift(1);
```

Evaluation

Using the push() operator, a new cell is added to the end of the array and holds the value 4. Using the unShift() operator, a new cell is added to the beginning of the array and holds the value 1.

Before push() and unShift()

listNum

2	3
0	1

After the Operations

listNum

1	2	3	4
0	1	2	3

Example 2

```
1   var listNum: Array = new Array(1,2,3,4);
2   listNum.pop();
3   listNum.shift();
```

Evaluation

Using the pop() operator, the last cell in the array is removed. Using the shift() operator, the first cell in the array is removed.

Before pop() and shift()

listNum

1	2	3	4
0	1	2	3

After the Operations

listNum

2	3
0	1

Example 3

```
1   var listNum: Array = new Array(1,2,3,4);
2   listNum.reverse();
3   listNum.splice(2,1);
```

Evaluation

Using the reverse() operation, the order of elements is reversed. In addition, the splice() operation removes the cell located at index 2.

Before reverse() and splice()

listNum

1	2	3	4
0	1	2	3

After the Operations

listNum

4	3	1
0	1	2

Example 4

```
1   var listNum1:Array = new Array(1,2,3,4);
2   var listNum2:Array = new Array(5,6,7,8);
3   var listNum3:Array = new Array();
4
5   listNum3 = listNum1.concat(listNum2);
```

Evaluation

Using the concat() operation, the elements in listNum1 and listNum2 are merged and placed in listNum3. Following this operation, listNum1 and listNum2 are left intact.

Before concat()

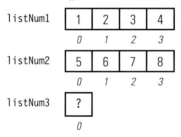

listNum1

1	2	3	4
0	1	2	3

listNum2

5	6	7	8
0	1	2	3

listNum3

?
0

After the Operation

listNum

1	2	3	4	5	6	7	8
0	1	2	3	4	5	6	7

7.1.6 The Linear Search Algorithm

An important problem in list processing is searching list elements for a specified item. For example, we may want to search a dictionary for a specific word to retrieve its definition or pronunciation.

The Array class provides the operation `indexOf` precisely for this purpose. If an item is found, the function will return the index; otherwise, it returns a −1. Here are two examples of this operation in action.

Example 1

```
1   var list:Array = new Array(22,33,44,55,66,77,88,99);
2   var found:int = list.indexOf(44)
3   trace(found);
```

Evaluation

The number 44 is located at index 2. The output is 2.

Example 2

```
1   var list:Array = new Array(22,33,44,55,66,77,88,99);
2   var found:int = list.indexOf(43)
3   trace(found);
```

Evaluation

The number 43 is not located in the array. The output is −1.

The Algorithm   Knowing how to write the code to conduct a linear search is a useful skill in programming. A linear search of a list of cells begins with the first item in the array and searches sequentially until either the desired item is found or there are no cells left to search.

The following segment of ActionScript 3.0 code is an illustration of this method for searching.

```
1  var findValue = ?;
2  var list:Array = new Array(22,33,44,55,66,77,88,99);
3
4  var found:int = -1;
5  for (var i:uint = 0; i < list.length; i++) {
6     if (list[i] == findValue){
7        found = i;
8        break;
9     }
10    if (i == list.length){
11       found = -1;
12    }
13 }
14
15 trace("found at index" + found);
```

The linear search technique is important because it can be used for any list, including those whose elements have some special organization or arrangement.

7.1.7 The Selection Sort Algorithm

Sorting is the problem of arranging the items in a list so that they are in either ascending or descending order. One of the reasons that sorting is crucial is that it imposes some kind of order on a list, making it possible to perform certain other list operations more efficiently. For example, searching for the smallest value in a very large list is easier and less time-consuming when the list is sorted.

The Array class provides several member functions, to perform sorting operations, such as `sort()`, `sortOn()`, and `reverse()`. The following example illustrates a simple sort.

Example

```
1   var list:Array = new Array(42,33,24,55,76,67,98,99);
2   list.sort(2);
3   trace(list.toString());
```

Evaluation

The argument for the sort member function indicates the starting index—in this case, the second index or third cell. The operation `toString()` is another `Array` operation that simply returns a single string containing all the values in the array.

The output is

42, 33, 24, 55, 67,76, 98, 99

The Algorithm   Aside from ActionScript's built-in sorting functions, literally dozens of sorting methods of varying complexity and efficiency have been developed. This section examines one of the simplest sorting methods, called the **selection sort**. Although it is not an efficient sorting method for large lists, this technique does perform reasonably well for small lists and is easy to understand.

The basic idea underlying the selection sort is to process a list by making a number of passes through the list, correctly positioning one item on each pass. For example, one approach is to

1. Find the smallest value in the list and move it to the first cell.

2. Find the second smallest item in the list and move it to the second cell.

3. Find the third smallest item in the list and move it to the third cell.

. . . And so on, until all the cell values are in ascending order.

To illustrate, imagine the following list is to be sorted in ascending order.

| 99 | 44 | 22 | 102 | 33 |

99	44	22	102	33
22	44	99	102	33
22	44	99	102	33
22	33	99	102	44
22	33	99	102	44
22	33	44	102	99
22	33	44	102	99
22	33	44	99	102

Task 1. Locate the smallest value in the list, 22.

Task 2. Swap 22 with the value in the first cell.

Task 3. Locate the second smallest value in the list, 33.

Task 4. Swap 33 with the value in the second cell.

Task 5. Locate the third smallest value in the list, 44.

Task 6. Swap 44 with the value in the third cell.

Task 7. Locate the fourth smallest value in the list, 99.

Task 8. Swap 99 with the value in the fourth cell.

After a maximum of four swaps, the list of five elements is sorted.

A crucial step in sorting is to find the smallest item in a list of cells, or a portion of the list. This searching problem can be solved using an approach similar to the linear search. Searching for the smallest value in a list of cells requires an index at which to begin the search. The following algorithm is a general solution.

For each cell in the range 0 up to (length −1):

- Locate the index position of the smallest element in the sublist and store it as smallest.
- Swap the element located at smallest with the current cell.

The following segment of ActionScript code is the implementation of this algorithm. This code can be refined in several ways. Please see the exercises at the end of this chapter for further exploration.

```
1   var listN:Array=new Array(99,44,22,102,33);
2   var size=listN.length;
3   for (var cell:int=0; cell < size - 1; cell++) {
4      //LOCATE THE SMALLEST VALUE IN THE LIST SUBSET
5      var smallest:int=cell;
6      for (var i:int=cell+1; i<size; i++) {
7         if (listN[i]<listN[smallest]) {
8            smallest=i;
9         }
10     }
11
12     //SWAP THE SMALLEST VALUE WITH THE CURRENT CELL
13     var temp:int=listN[cell];
14     listN[cell]=listN[smallest];
15     listN[smallest]=temp;
16  }
17
18  trace(listN.toString());
```

■ 7.2 Case Study 1: Multiple-Ball Paddle Game

Problem and Analysis

The objective of this case study is to work with a more dynamic paddle ball game. This game differs from the previous paddle game in that users can add as many balls as they wish to their environment (Figure 7-2). Programmatically, this means that we must be able to compute the new location and velocity for each ball at any given moment. Just as crucial, we must determine whether a collision has occurred between a ball and the paddle and one of the walls.

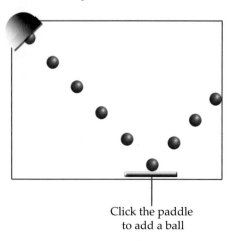

Click the paddle
to add a ball

I FIGURE 7-2 Multiple-ball paddle game application.

The optimal approach to this problem is to use an array structure to store each ball in the list of balls as the user adds it. Once a ball falls through the floor, it will need to be removed from the Stage as well as from the list.

The goals for this case study are as follows:

1. Employ a ball dispenser that allows the user to add balls interactively to the game.

2. Work with an array structure to process the animation and computations for each ball.

3. Work with the Array class operations, push(), shift(), and splice().

4. See first-hand how to remove a ball from the visual environment and the array structure.

Visual Design

This paddle ball game will be called PaddleAppII. As in the paddle ball case study, this game requires a paddle and the ability to detect collisions. There is one major change in the game—namely, the ability to add as many balls as the user wishes. This change will result in three main alterations in the visual design and the featured display objects:

1. The paddle must be made clickable. This gives the user the ability to add a ball to the environment by simply clicking the paddle.

2. The library symbol representing Ball must be exported as a class. Recall that whenever a MovieClip is created in real time, AS3 requires it to be exported with a base class of flash.display.MovieClip.

3. A non-interactive graphic is placed in the upper-left corner of the Stage that represents the ball dispenser. Once the user clicks the paddle, a new ball will appear at this location. There is no need to name this visual graphic, as it will not be used for anything other than visual effect.

By making the paddle a clickable MovieClip, the user can dispense balls with ease. Table 7-4 identifies each display object that the interface screen and the program will require.

TABLE 7-4 Visual Objects Used in the Input/Output Screen

Visual Object	Type of Object	Description of the Object
Ball	Class: Ball Base class: flash.display.MovieClip	MovieClip graphic of a ball.
Paddle	MovieClip	A clickable MovieClip that allows the user to both hit balls and create new balls with ease.

Program Design

The ActionScript 3.0 code for this application will consist of the class constructor PaddleAppII(), which initializes the game and registers the event listeners; the event handlers; and playGame(), which controls the animation and is the engine that drives the game.

Unlike in the previous version of the paddle game, the playGame() function will perform all game tasks involving moving the balls, detecting collisions, and removing balls from the game once they have fallen through the floor. The rationale behind this approach will be explained in the discussion of playGame(). Table 7-5 lists all four functions.

TABLE 7-5 PaddleAppII Program Functions

Function Name	Description
PaddleAppII()	As the constructor, sets up a listening system so that the user can move the paddle, dispense balls, and play the game.
dispenseBall()	Creates new balls as indicated by user clicking the paddle.
movePaddle()	Enables the paddle to move horizontally along with the mouse.
playGame()	Moves all balls in the game and checks for collisions; also deletes balls that fall through the bottom of the Stage.

The first lines of the ActionScript file construct the required class package and import the necessary library classes. Both the flash.events and flash.display library classes are required. The class document is named PaddleAppII() and, therefore, will share the same name as the file and public class. The last two lines of the ActionScript file contain closing curly brackets to close the document class and the package.

```
1  package {
2     import  flash.display.*;
3     import  flash.events.*;
4
5     public class PaddleAppII extends MovieClip {
6
```

⋮

```
80     }
81  }
```

Game Constants and the Array Variable Structure for Storing the Balls

This new paddle game will use constant values when identifying collisions and reversing the direction of the ball. In addition to the constants, an array structure for storing all active balls must be defined. This array, ballList, is initially declared as an empty list. The location where this array is defined is important. Notice that it is not placed within a program function, which ensures its global availability. The list of balls will be accessible to all functions in the program.

```
7   //CONSTANT DECLARATIONS
8   const BALL_RADIUS:int=16;
9   const TOP:Number=BALL_RADIUS;
10  const BOTTOM:Number=stage.stageHeight;
11  const LEFT:Number= BALL_RADIUS;
12  const RIGHT:Number=stage.stageWidth - BALL_RADIUS;
13  const REVERSE:int=-1;
14
```

```
15  //GLOBAL ARRAY DECLARATION
16  var ballList:Array=new Array();
17
```

The four functions in this program are designed as follows.

Function PaddleAppII() Design

The main algorithm, PaddleAppII(), is simply the class constructor function that loads immediately once the application is launched. The objective of this function is to construct three listener events. The first event allows the user to move the paddle. The second listener event, found on line 20, makes the paddle clickable, so it will dispense a ball each time it is performed. The last listener event, found on line 21, is the looping mechanism that drives the game.

```
18  function PaddleAppII(){
19      stage.addEventListener(MouseEvent.MOUSE_MOVE,movePaddle);
20      Paddle.addEventListener(MouseEvent.CLICK,dispenseBall);
21      stage.addEventListener(Event.ENTER_FRAME,playGame);
22  }
23
```

Function movePaddle() Design

As with the previous version of this game, this event handler moves the paddle as the user moves the mouse along the x-axis.

```
24  function movePaddle(event:MouseEvent) {
25      Paddle.x=stage.mouseX;
26  }
27
```

Function dispenseBall() Design

This event handler adds balls not only to the Stage for the user to visualize, but also to the globally defined array called ballList. Several of the displayObject inherited properties are set to identify an initial location on the stage and fix the dimensions. In addition to the inherited properties, two custom properties are created, xVelocity and yVelocity, to govern the speed at which the balls will move. Line 38 uses the push() operation to add balls to the array by pushing them to the back of the list.

```
28  function dispenseBall(event:MouseEvent) {
29      var ballObj:Ball;
30      ballObj=new Ball;
31      ballObj.x=55;
32      ballObj.y=55;
33      ballObj.height=RADIUS*2;
34      ballObj.width=RADIUS*2;
```

```
35      ballObj.xVelocity=3;
36      ballObj.yVelocity=3;
37      addChild(ballObj);
38      ballList.push(ballObj);
39  }
40
```

Function playGame() Design

The playGame() function has four main actions, all involving individual balls. These actions occur at regular loop intervals governed by the ENTER_FRAME event. From the user's perspective, balls are animated by being repositioned on the Stage; collisions with the paddle and the walls are detected and responded to; and once a ball falls through the floor, it is removed from view. These major tasks are executed for every ball in the array. To perform this list processing, a simple for loop is used.

Splitting up these tasks into separate functions would involve multiple for loops. The main reason for having playGame() perform all of these tasks is to simplify the list processing. In later chapters, we explore another approach.

For every ball in the array, the following tasks are performed:

Task 1: Move the ball at index i by its fixed velocity.

Task 2: Check whether the ball has collided with a wall or ceiling. Reverse the direction of the ball in this case.

Task 3: Use the built-in function hitTestObject() to check whether the ball has collided with the paddle. Reverse the direction of the ball's velocity in this case.

Task 4: If the ball has fallen through the floor, remove it from the game. This requires three subtasks:

a. The ball is removed from the stage. This is done by using removeChild().

b. The ball object is removed from the array cell by assigning it a null value.

c. The array cell is deleted from the array. This is done with a shift if the cell is at index 0; otherwise, splice is used and the index is decremented.

```
41  function playGame(event:Event) {
42      //FOR EACH BALL IN THE ARRAY
43      for (var i:uint=0; i<ballList.length; i++) {
44          //TASK 1: MOVE THE BALL BY ITS FIXED VELOCITY
45          ballList[i].x+=ballList[i].xVelocity;
46          ballList[i].y+=ballList[i].yVelocity;
47
48          //TASK 2: CHECK FOR A BALL-TO-WALL COLLISION
49          if (ballList[i].y<TOP) {
50              ballList[i].y=TOP;
```

```
51          ballList[i].yVelocity*=REVERSE;
52        }
53        if (ballList[i].x<LEFT) {
54          ballList[i].x=LEFT;
55          ballList[i].xVelocity*=REVERSE;
56        } else if (ballList[i].x>RIGHT) {
57          ballList[i].x=RIGHT;
58          ballList[i].xVelocity*=REVERSE;
59        }
60
61        //TASK 3: CHECK FOR A BALL-TO-PADDLE COLLISION
62        if (Paddle.hitTestObject(ballList[i])) {
63          ballList[i].yVelocity*=REVERSE;
64          ballList[i].y=Paddle.y-RADIUS*2;
65        }
66        //TASK 4: CHECK IF BALL FALLS THROUGH THE FLOOR
67        if (ballList[i].y>BOTTOM) {
68          removeChild(ballList[i]);
69          ballList[i]=null;
70
71          if (i==0) {
72            ballList.shift();
73          } else {
74            ballList.splice(i,1);
75            i--;
76          }
77        }
78      }
79    }
```

7.3 Multidimensional Arrays

Up to this point, we have examined one-dimensional arrays, using them to store a list of values. ActionScript also allows arrays of more than one dimension. For example, a two-dimensional array can be used to store a data set whose values are arranged in rows and columns. Similarly, a three-dimensional array is an appropriate storage structure when the data needs to be arranged along rows, columns, and ranks. When several characteristics are associated with the data, still higher dimensions may be useful, with each dimension corresponding to one of these characteristics.

As an introduction, consider the pixels of a small JPEG image. Imagine an image that can be displayed as 400 rows of pixels, with 600 pixels per row. The standard way to describe the image is in terms of horizontal rows and vertical columns, with the rows numbered from 0 through 399 and the columns numbered from 0 through 599. Figure 7-3 shows the possible two-dimensional structure for an image with the upper-left corner positioned at row 0 and column 0. The row and column indices provide a way to uniquely identify a pixel. Such an image can be modeled using a two-dimensional array. Accessing a cell in a two-dimensional array requires the use of two indices—one for the row and one for the column.

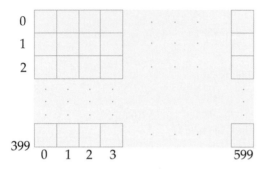

I FIGURE 7-3 A graphic image is an array of rows and columns representing pixels.

Example 1

As a first example of accessing a cell in a two-dimensional array, we will examine a simple multiplication table for the numbers 0 through 4. Let us assume an empty two-dimensional array, named `table`, has already been declared. Now we want to insert the appropriate multiplied values into the cells.

In this example, we wish to write an assignment statement to place the product of 3 * 2 in the appropriate cell, row 3, column 2.

```
table [3][2] = 6;
```

The resulting table is

```
table
```

```
          0   1   2   3   4
      0 ┌───┬───┬───┬───┬───┐
        │   │   │   │   │   │
      1 ├───┼───┼───┼───┼───┤
        │   │   │   │   │   │
      2 ├───┼───┼───┼───┼───┤
        │   │   │   │   │   │
      3 ├───┼───┼───┼───┼───┤
        │   │   │ 6 │   │   │
        └───┴───┴───┴───┴───┘
```

Example 2

This example illustrates list processing of multidimensional arrays. Using the same multiplication table from Example 1, the following segment of code places all the correct products in appropriate cells.

```
1  for (var row:int = 0; row <= 4; row++) {
2     for (var col:int = 0; col <= 4; col++) {
3        table [row][col] = row * col;
4     }
5  }
```

Evaluation

Using a nested for loop, the entire array structure is examined row by row. Within each row, every entry can be explored with the inner loop, which uses an index to move from column to column. The resulting table looks as follows:

table

	0	1	2	3	4
0	0	0	0	0	0
1	0	1	2	3	4
2	0	2	4	6	8
3	0	3	6	9	12

7.3.1 Declaring and Populating Multidimensional Arrays

In ActionScript 3.0, several approaches may be used to solve the problem of declaring a multidimensional array. For fixed arrays initialized during declaration, the approach is similar to the declaration of a single-dimension array.

For the declaration of dynamic multidimensional arrays, we must consider the concept of an **array of arrays**. In other words, a multidimensional array is fundamentally an array whose elements are other arrays.

To explore this idea further, consider a vacation spreadsheet in which the costs for three days are stored in an array. The spreadsheet array uses rows to store the costs of each day and keeps track of specific costs such as transportation (column 0), food (column 1), and entertainment (column 2).

	Transportation	Food	Entertainment
day1Costs	30	40	60
day2Costs	30	40	50
day3Costs	30	42	55

Examine the three approaches to creating this array. Each approach produces the same result.

Example 1

In the earlier part of this chapter, we saw that a one-dimensional array can be initialized when it is declared. Multidimensional arrays may also be initialized using this same technique. For example, we might initialize the vacation spreadsheet array named costs as follows:

```
1    var costs: Array = {[30, 50, 60],
2                         [35, 55, 50],
3                         [30, 60, 40]};
```

Evaluation

This form of declaration improves the readability of the array contents, and permits the values to be grouped using brackets. It is clear that the list used to initialize costs has three rows, each of which contains three numbers.

It is also correct to write this statement in a single line.

```
1    var costs:Array = {[30, 40, 60],   [30, 40, 50],   [30, 42, 55]};
```

Example 2

The second approach to this problem capitalizes on the fact that the multidimensional array is three arrays, with each array storing three cell values.

The costs for each day can, therefore, be viewed as a one-dimensional array. The resulting two dimensional array consists of these three one-dimensional arrays.

The three individual array declarations can be declared as follows:

```
1    var   day1Costs:Array = new Array(30, 40, 60);
2    var   day2Costs:Array = new Array(30, 40, 50);
3    var   day3Costs:Array = new Array(30, 42, 55);
```

These three arrays will serve as cell values in the multidimensional array, costs.

```
4    var costs:Array = new Array(day1Costs, day2Costs, day3Costs);
```

Example 3

The third approach is useful when a multidimensional array needs new arrays added to it. For example, imagine the vacationers have decided to spend more days away and, therefore, wish to expand their spreadsheet array to include the costs for these additional days. This solution uses a loop structure to add the additional days onto the back of the array.

```
1    var numDays:int = 3;
2
3    var costs:Array = new Array();
```

```
4    for (var row:int = 0; row < numDays; row++) {
5         costs[row] = new Array(30,40,50);
6    }
```

Evaluation

Line 1: The number of rows in the array represents the number of days on vacation.

Line 3: The main array is declared.

Lines 4–6: The for loop is used to add complete days to the spreadsheet array. An individual array declaration representing each day is placed in a single cell.

7.4 Case Study 2: Prey and Predator—A Logic Board Game

Problem and Analysis

Logic board games have been around for a very long time. Aside from their entertainment value, they are popular ways to test one's skills at problem solving. In this case study, we will create a turn-based game called Prey and Predator. A turn-based game is one in which the player takes a turn followed by the opponent taking a turn. Tictac-toe is an example of a turn-based game.

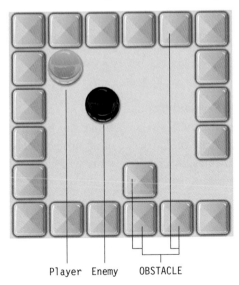

Player   Enemy   OBSTACLE

❙ FIGURE 7-4 The Prey and Predator game application.

At the start of this game, a "board" is displayed on stage containing a collection of square checkers and two round checkers (Figure 7-4). The square checkers represent obstacles blocking a pathway. The black circular checker is the enemy and the blue circular checker represents the user, or rather the player of the game.

The player is first to take a turn, using the arrow keys to move the blue circular checker up or down a single square on the keyboard as long as there are no obstacles in his way. Once the player has taken his turn, the enemy will compute his next move. To win the game, the player must navigate around the board obstacles, avoid colliding with the enemy, and successfully exit through the single opening on the board. When it is the enemy's turn, he will actively hunt down the player. If a collision with the enemy occurs, the player is defeated.

There are two main objectives for this case study:

1. Work with a two-dimensional array to store data about the board, such as the location of obstacles and the exit.

2. Explore the intelligence component of the enemy.

Board Data

Before we examine the visual design of the game, we need to analyze how the board will be used to store game data. Figure 7-4 shows the configuration of display objects at the start of a game. The obstacle checkers are placed around the periphery of the board, with one exception—the exit door. To make the game challenging, but not impossible to play, an obstacle checker is also placed in the interior of the board. Consider that each individual square on this 6 × 6 board may contain one of the following:

- An Obstacle checker (coded as 1)
- Is Empty (coded as 2)
- An Exit (coded as 3)

A two-dimensional array named codeBoard will be used to store the data. Specifically, the data for the board shown in Figure 7-4 will look like the grid that follows. The 1's are placed in the array to indicate the presence of an obstacle. The 2's indicate the square is empty, and the 3 indicates the exit. This array will be useful in positioning the display objects on the Stage and determining the moves made by the player and the enemy.

1	1	1	1	1	1
1	2	2	2	2	1
1	2	2	2	2	1
1	2	1	2	2	1
1	2	2	2	2	3
1	1	1	1	1	1

Visual Design

The game is designed to use a Stage size of 600 pixels in height and width. This will allow for 6 rows and 6 columns of 100 square pixels each. The display objects placed on the Stage before runtime are `Player` and `Enemy`, as shown in Figure 7-4. During runtime, a collection of obstacles is generated using an exported symbol in the Library called `OBSTACLE`. Table 7-6 lists the visual objects required for this game application.

TABLE 7-6 Visual Objects Used in the Checkerboard Chase Game Application

Visual Object	Type of Object	Description of the Object
Player	Instance of a `MovieClip`	Blue round checker piece placed directly on the Stage and named Player.
Enemy	Instance of a `MovieClip`	Black round checker piece placed on stage and named Enemy
OBSTACLE	Class: OBSTACLE Base class: `flash.display.MovieClip`	Symbol in the Library used to create obstacle checkers to be placed on the Stage during runtime. An export link is required for this symbol.

The Timeline for this game will utilize two layers, one holding the `Player` checker and the other holding the `Enemy` checker. This is a simple version of a game that can be enhanced in a variety of ways. To keep things as simple as possible, a single frame is used for the entire game; see Figure 7-5.

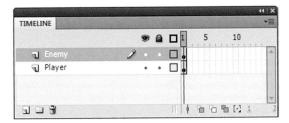

FIGURE 7-5 The Timeline of the Prey and Predator game application.

Program Design

The main tasks of this game are as follows:

1. Construct the two-dimensional board and fill the screen with `Obstacle` checkers.

2. In a series of turns:

   a. Wait for the `Player` to make his move and then position his checker in the appropriate spot on the stage.

b. Compute the best counter move for the Enemy and reposition his checker on the stage.

3. Test whether the Player wins or loses with each turn. The game will end with a win or loss.

These tasks will be performed using four functions: boardGameApp(), drawBoard(), playerMoves(), and enemyMoves(). These functions are briefly described in Table 7-7.

TABLE 7-7 Board Game Functions

Function Name	Description
boardGameApp()	The constructor function that serves to initialize the game.
drawBoard()	Called by the constructor, boardGameApp(), to create the crucial game element—the two-dimensional logic board. This board is represented as an array structure.
playerMoves()	An event handler that responds to the arrow keys on the keyboard. This function moves the Player graphic based on the key pressed.
enemyMoves()	Called after the Player has made a move. This function contains the intelligence behind the Enemy and governs his movements.

The first lines of the ActionScript file are used to construct the required class package and import the necessary library classes. On line 5, the document class is declared. The last two lines of the ActionScript file contain closing curly brackets to close the class and the package.

```
1   package {
2       import flash.display.*;
3       import flash.events.*;
4
5       public class boardGameApp extends MovieClip {
6
```
⋮
```
126     }
127 }
```

Game Constants and Variables

Three sets of constants are used for this game. The first set is used to identify the control keys for moving the Player checker around the stage. The second set refers to general board information. The last set establishes the code indicators for the board.

```
7    //ARROW KEYS CONTROLLING PLAYER MOVEMENTS
8    const RIGHT:Number=39;    //ASCII VALUE FOR RIGHT ARROW KEY
9    const LEFT:Number=37;     //ASCII VALUE FOR LEFT ARROW KEY
10   const UP:Number=38;       //ASCII VALUE FOR UP ARROW KEY
11   const DOWN:Number=40;     //ASCII VALUE FOR DOWN ARROW KEY
12
13   //BOARD INFORMATION
14   const SQUARE:int=100;     //BLOCK SIZE IN SQUARE PIXELS
15   const COLUMNS:int=6;      //NUMBER OF COLUMNS ON BOARD
16   const ROWS:int=6;         //NUMBER OF ROWS ON BOARD
17
18   //CODES FOR THE BOARD
19   const anOBSTACLE:int=1;   //CODE INDICATOR FOR AN EXIT CELL
20   const isEMPTY:int=2;      // CODE INDICATOR FOR AN EMPTY CELL
21   const anEXIT:int=3;       // CODE INDICATOR FOR A CELL OBSTACLE
```

The two-dimensional array, boardCodes, is used to store the information about the logic board. This array, along with the constants, will be declared globally. Thus all the functions in the document class have access to them. Notice that the fixed code values in boardCodes match the configuration of Figure 7-4. The game relies on this two-dimensional logic board, which will be used to compute movements and determine when a game ends.

```
22   //TWO-DIMENSIONAL ARRAY CONTAINING CELL CODES
23   var boardCodes: Array = [
24                      [1,1,1,1,1,1],
25                      [1,2,2,2,2,1],
26                      [1,2,2,2,2,1],
27                      [1,2,1,2,2,1],
28                      [1,2,2,2,2,3],
29                      [1,1,1,1,1,1]
30                      ];
31
```

The four functions for this application are designed as follows.

Function boardGameApp() Design

The constructor function, boardGameApp(), initializes the game elements. It has three tasks:

Task 1: Call the function drawBoard() to create the OBSTACLE display objects and position them on the Stage.

Task 2: Position Player and Enemy on the Stage. Both of these display objects already exist. Player will always start in row 1, column 1. Enemy will be placed in row 4 but its column position can vary between 3 and 4, as calculated in line 40.

Task 3: Registering a KEY_DOWN listener event to wait for the arrow keys to be pressed. The final initialization task, this task is required to set the game in motion.

```
32  function boardGameApp() {
33     //TASK 1: CONSTRUCT THE LOGIC BOARD
34     drawBoard();
35
36     //TASK 2: POSITION THE GAME PLAYERS ON THE BOARD
37     Player.x=SQUARE;
38     Player.y=SQUARE;
39     Enemy.x=4*SQUARE;
40     Enemy.y = (Math.ceil(Math.random() * 2) + 2) * SQUARE;
41
42     //TASK 3: CONSTRUCT THE LISTENER EVENT TO ALLOW PLAYER A TURN
43     stage.addEventListener(KeyboardEvent.KEY_DOWN, playerMoves);
44  }
45
```

Function drawBoard() Design

The function drawBoard() will use the new mechanism to create obstacle checkers and place them in the appropriate spots on the Stage. Obstacles will be based on the coded two-dimensional array boardCodes and their positions will be computed using the row and column of the array.

```
46  function drawBoard() {
47     //TASK 1: DEFINE THE VARIABLE FOR THE OBSTACLE DISPLAY OBJECT
48     var Obstacle:OBSTACLE;
49
50     //TASK 2: FOR EVERY CELL CONTAINING AN OBSTACLE, PLACE ONE ON STAGE
51     for (var row:int = 0; row < ROWS; row++) {
52        for (var col:int = 0; col < COLUMNS; col++) {
53           //TASK 3: CHECK IF THE CODE INDICATES AN OBSTACLE
54           if (boardCodes[row][col]==anOBSTACLE) {
55              Obstacle=new OBSTACLE  ;
56              Obstacle.x=col*SQUARE;
57              Obstacle.y=row*SQUARE;
58              addChild(Obstacle);
59           }
60        }
61     }
62  }
```

Function playerMoves() Design

The function playerMoves() performs the general tasks of validating the player's move and then repositioning the blue circular checker in the appropriate square. This function is an event handler triggered by pressing a key on the keyboard and will respond to only the arrow keys. The specific tasks are as follows:

Task 1: Locate the player's row and column position on the logic board.

Task 2: Use a switch statement to identify which arrow key was used to control the player's movement. Validate the player's move. In other words, if the cell the player wishes to move to is not blocked by an obstacle, then move the player's checker to the appropriate adjacent square.

Task 3: Check whether the player's checker has successfully reached the exit. This is done by computing the blue checker's current row and column position on the board and determining whether it holds the isEXIT code.

Task 4: If the player has *not* successfully reached the exit, the enemy takes a turn.

```
64  function playerMoves(event:KeyboardEvent) {
65      if (event.keyCode==UP||event.keyCode==LEFT||
66      event.keyCode==RIGHT||event.keyCode==DOWN) {
67          //TASK 1: COMPUTE THE PLAYER'S ROW AND COLUMN ON THE BOARD
68          var col:int=Player.x/SQUARE;
69          var row:int=Player.y/SQUARE;
70          //TASK 2: MOVE THE PLAYER'S CHECKER BASED ON THE ARROW KEY SELECTED
71          switch (event.keyCode) {
72              case RIGHT :
73                  if (boardCodes[row][col+1]!=anOBSTACLE) {
74                      Player.x+=SQUARE;
75                  }
76                  break;
77              case LEFT :
78                  if (boardCodes[row][col-1]!=anOBSTACLE) {
79                      Player.x-=SQUARE;
80                  }
81                  break;
82              case DOWN :
83                  if (boardCodes[row+1][col]!=anOBSTACLE) {
84                      Player.y+=SQUARE;
85                  }
86                      break;
87              case UP :
88                  if (boardCodes[row-1][col]!=anOBSTACLE) {
89                      Player.y-=SQUARE;
90                  }
91          }
92
93          //TASK 3: CHECK IF PLAYER HAS REACHED THE EXIT
94          col=Player.x/SQUARE;
95          row=Player.y/SQUARE;
```

```
96      if (boardCodes[row][col]==anEXIT) {
97          trace("Player wins. Game over.");
98          stage.removeEventListener(KeyboardEvent.KEY_DOWN, playerMoves);
99      } else {
100     //TASK 4: ENEMY MAKES A MOVE
101         enemyMoves();
102     }
103   }
104 }
```

Function enemyMoves() Design

The function enemyMoves() embodies the predatory intellect of the enemy. Using the location of the player's checker, the enemy will make a move with a goal of catching this piece. This function performs three tasks:

Task 1: Compute the enemy's row and column location on the board. This information will be used to identify where the obstacles are positioned so that the enemy's checker does not move into an already occupied cell.

Task 2: Compute the enemy's move. This segment of code identifies four scenarios and tests whether the player and the enemy fit within one of them. These scenarios govern the move.

Task 3: Test whether the enemy's checker has reached the player's checker. The game ends in this case.

```
105 function enemyMoves() {
106     //TASK 1: COMPUTE THE LOCATION OF ENEMY ON THE BOARD
107     var col:int=Enemy.x/SQUARE;
108     var row:int=Enemy.y/SQUARE;
109
110     //TASK 2: THE PREDATORY INTELLIGENCE OF THE ENEMY.  COMPUTE A MOVE.
111     if (Enemy.x<Player.x&&boardCodes[row][col+1]==isEMPTY) {
112         Enemy.x+=SQUARE;
113     } else if (Enemy.x > Player.x && boardCodes[row][col-1] == isEMPTY) {
114         Enemy.x-=SQUARE;
115     } else if (Enemy.y < Player.y && boardCodes[row+1][col] == isEMPTY) {
116         Enemy.y+=SQUARE;
117     } else if (Enemy.y > Player.y && boardCodes[row-1][col] == isEMPTY) {
118         Enemy.y-=SQUARE;
119     }
120
121     // TASK 3: CHECK IF ENEMY DEFEATS (COLLIDES WITH) PLAYER
122     if (Enemy.x*SQUARE==Player.x*SQUARE&&Enemy.y*SQUARE==Player.y*SQUARE) {
123         stage.removeEventListener(KeyboardEvent.KEY_DOWN, playerMoves);
124         trace("Player is defeated. Game over");
125     }
126   }
```

■ 7.5 Stacks and Queues

In ActionScript, arrays are versatile in that they can be used to implement special types of lists such as stacks and queues. Both of these structures have applications in classic computer science problems as well as in problems requiring artificial intelligence. They can also be used in game programming to implement solutions for puzzles. The case study following this section illustrates the use of a stack for constructing a maze.

7.5.1 Stacks

We begin this section with a discussion of the data structure called the **stack**. Conceptually, a stack is a list with very strict rules placed on its behavior. Unlike a typical array, elements in a stack may be added or removed only from the back of the list. In computer science circles, the back of the list is usually referred to as the top of the stack.

When an element is added to a stack, it must be pushed onto the back of the list. When an element is removed, it must be popped off the back of the list. As a consequence, elements at the bottom of the stack have been in the stack the longest. The top element of the stack is the last element added to the stack. Because elements are added and removed strictly from the back of the list (the top), it follows that the item that is added last will be removed first. For this reason, a stack is also called a **last in, first out (LIFO)** data structure.

To best understand the idea behind stacks, consider a collection of books, one stacked on top of the other, as shown in Figure 7-6. The second book on the pile can be removed only once the book on top of it has been removed. The last book added to the stack will be the first to be removed (LIFO). After removing this top book, the second book now becomes the top book, or the top element of the stack.

Top of the stack

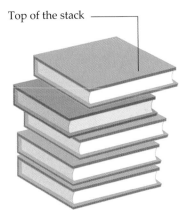

I FIGURE 7-6 The last book added to a stack is the first book removed—LIFO (last in, first out).

With ActionScript, a stack can easily be implemented using an array structure. Stacks begin with zero elements, initialized to an empty state. The top of the stack is the last element in the array. Two array operations are used for accessing elements on a stack:

- push(): Adds an item to the back of the list.
- pop(): Removes an item from the back of the list.

The basic nature of a stack structure is illustrated in the next three examples.

Example 1

```
1   var  stack:Array = new Array();
```

Evaluation

A stack is created just as an array would be. A stack begins as an empty structure, which means it is nothing more than an array with a length of zero.

In this example, the variable stack is initialized to an empty state.

Example 2

```
1   var  stack:Array = new Array();
2   stack.push(3);
3   stack.push(4);
4   trace("Top of the stack is ", stack.length − 1);
```

Evaluation

In this example, two elements have been added to the stack. The top of the stack is the index of the last element. To keep track of the top of the stack, we can use the Array property length and subtract one. The trace statement outputs the number 1.

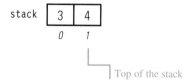

Example 3

Task

For this example, consider a stack that contains five elements. Write code to access the second element in stack.

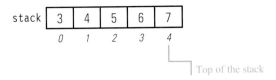

Top of the stack

Solution

This example illustrates that stacks are arrays with access restricted at one end—the back of the list. To gain access to the value in the second cell, the three elements ahead of it, or on top of the stack, must be removed. The following code segment uses the pop() operation to remove the element at the end of the array.

```
1   stack.pop();
2   stack.pop();
3   stack.pop();
4   trace("Top of the stack is ", stack.length - 1);
```

7.5.2 Queues

A queue is similar to a stack with the exception of its access point. With a queue, an item can be added only to the back of the list, while the removal of an item can occur only from the front of the list. Notice that this behavior mimics human lines formed at places such as grocery stores and banks. For this reason, a queue is also called a **first in, first out (FIFO)** data structure.

A queue is created in the same way an array would be. Like arrays, queues usually begin in an empty state.

Two operations are used for accessing elements in a queue:

- push(): Adds a new item to the back of the queue list.
- shift(): Removes the first item from the queue list.

Example 1

Task

For this example, consider a queue that contains five elements. Write code to access the second element in the queue.

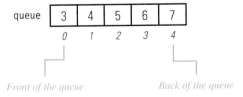

Front of the queue   Back of the queue

Solution

Queues are restricted lists, which means that elements are added to the back and removed from the front. To access the value in the second cell, the first element ahead of it must be removed. The following code segment uses the `shift()` operation to remove the element at the front of the array.

```
1    queue.shift();
```

This results in the following queue:

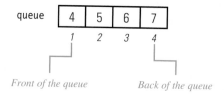

Front of the queue   *Back of the queue*

■ 7.6 Case Study 3: Optional—Generating a Perfect Maze

Problem

In this case study, we will write a program that will create a random two-dimensional "perfect" 9 × 9 maze. A "perfect" maze is one in which there is exactly one path between any two given cells (Figure 7-7). In computer science terms, it is called a minimal spanning tree over a set of cells. The task of carving out a path from one cell to the next is based on the concept of a depth-first search, which uses a stack data structure.

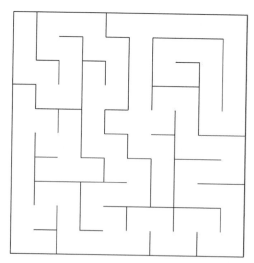

I FIGURE 7-7 A noncircular maze has exactly one path between any two cells.

The objective of this case study is to explore how a stack can be used with a depth-first search to navigate a noncircular path from cell to cell. To do so, we will rely on an algorithm called a backtracker.

The Backtracker

Creating a perfect maze involves building the maze cell by cell while making sure that no loops exist and that no cell ends up isolated. The backtracker algorithm belongs to a class of algorithms that share a common operational goal:

- Begin with an array of maze cells with all the walls intact.
- Choose a starting cell.
- Repeatedly select a random adjacent cell in the maze—one that has been unvisited—and open the wall between the two. Continue to do this until every cell has been "visited" and a wall has been eliminated during the visit.

A perfect maze contains no circular paths: Every cell is connected to every other cell by exactly one path. The various algorithms differ in how the cells are selected and whether they use recursion instead of an iterative loop. The following algorithm uses an iterative loop and a stack.

How the Backtracker Algorithm Works

We examine this process more closely for creating a perfect maze containing nine cells arranged in three rows and three columns.

Step 1:   Initialize the process. Begin with a two-dimensional array representing the maze cells. As shown in Figure 7-8, all cell walls are initially intact. An empty stack is also constructed. The stack is used to ensure that no loops exist in the path and that no cell ends up isolated.

0	1	2
3	4	5
6	7	8

I FIGURE 7-8 No cells have been visited in the initial array.

Step 2:   This is the beginning of the backtracker procedure. As shown in Figure 7-9, the starting cell is selected. For convenience in this example, the starting cell will be cell number 0. This first cell is marked as `visited`, and pushed onto the stack. The stack now holds the first cell visited.

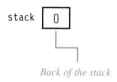

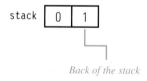

I FIGURE 7-9 Cell 0 is visited.

Step 3:   Choose a random adjacent cell that has not yet been visited. In this case, the possible adjacent cells are 1 and 3. We assume that cell 1 has been randomly selected.

The east wall of cell 0 is eliminated. As shown in Figure 7-10, cell 1 is marked as `visited` and pushed onto the stack.

I FIGURE 7-10 Cell 1 is visited.

Step 4:   The possible adjacent cells to cell 1 are 2 and 4. We assume that cell 4 has been randomly selected. The south wall of cell 1 is eliminated. As shown in Figure 7-11, cell 4 is marked as visited and pushed onto the stack.

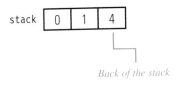

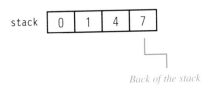

I **FIGURE 7-11** Cell 4 is visited.

Step 5:   The possible adjacent cells visit from to cell 4 are 3, 7, and 5. We assume that cell 7 has been randomly selected. The south wall of cell 4 is eliminated. As shown in Figure 7-12, cell 7 is marked as visited and pushed onto the stack.

I **FIGURE 7-12** Cell 7 is visited.

Step 6:   The possible adjacent cells to visit from cell 7 are 6 and 8. We assume that 6 has been randomly selected. The west wall of cell 7 is eliminated. As shown in Figure 7-13, cell 6 is marked as `visited` and pushed onto the stack.

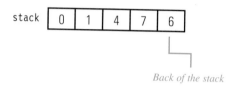

Back of the stack

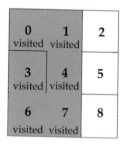

I FIGURE 7-13 Cell 6 is visited.

Step 7:   Cell 3 is the only possible adjacent cell to visit from cell 6. The north wall of cell 6 is eliminated. As shown in Figure 7-14, cell 3 is marked as `visited` and pushed onto the stack.

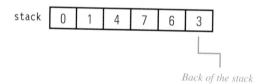

Back of the stack

I FIGURE 7-14 Cell 3 is visited.

Step 8: At this point, there are no valid adjacent cells to cell 3 that can be visited. All cells can be visited only once. The stack will be used for backtracking to a cell that has unvisited neighbors.

Backtrack 1
3 is popped from the back of the stack and rejected as having no valid neighbors.

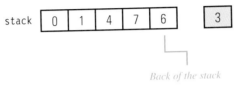

Backtrack 2
6 is popped from the back of the stack and also rejected as having no valid neighbors.

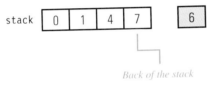

Backtrack 3
7 is popped from the back of the stack and found to have valid neighbors. Backtracking ends.

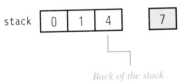

Step 9: Cell 8 is the only possible adjacent cell to visit from cell 7.

The east wall of cell 7 is eliminated. As shown in Figure 7-15, cell 8 is marked as visited and pushed onto the stack.

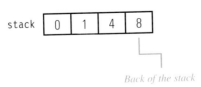

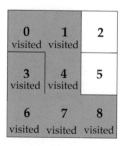

FIGURE 7-15 Cell 8 is visited.

Step 10: Cell 5 is the only possible adjacent cell to visit from cell 8. The north wall of cell 8 is eliminated. As shown in Figure 7-16, cell 5 is marked as visited and pushed onto the stack.

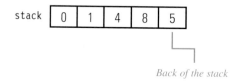

Back of the stack

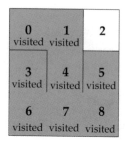

FIGURE 7-16 Cell 5 is visited.

Step 11: Cell 2 is the only remaining cell to be visited in the algorithm. It is also the only possible adjacent cell to visit from cell 5. The north wall of cell 5 is eliminated. Cell 2 is marked as visited and a perfect maze has been completed. As Figure 7-17 shows, there is exactly one path between any two given cells.

FIGURE 7-17 Cell 2 is visited. All cells have been visited.

Visual Design

The visual design for this application is simple. There are no library symbols required, and frames in the Timeline will not be used because there is no animation or interactivity.

The Stage dimensions are set to 520 × 520 pixels to accommodate a maze containing 10 rows and 10 columns of cells, which are sized at 50 pixels in each dimension. An offset of 10 pixels on each side, top and bottom, of the maze will place it in the center of the Stage.

Algorithmic Design

The ActionScript code for this application consists of four functions as described in Table 7-8. Figure 7-18 shows the relationship between these functions.

TABLE 7-8 Maze Program Functions

Function Name	Description
mazeApp()	The main function as well as the class constructor. It executes immediately once the application launches. mazeApp() calls all other functions.
initialization()	Adds a MazeCell MovieClip for each cell in the maze. Initializes all of the cells in the maze with all walls intact.
backtracker()	Uses the backtracker method to carve out a maze.
drawMazeCells()	Identifies the configuration needed for each cell and draws it in real time.

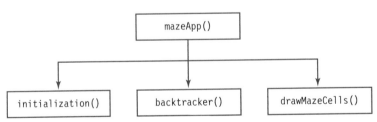

I FIGURE 7-18 The relationship structure of functions for the maze application.

The first lines of the ActionScript file construct the required class package and import the flash.display library class. The flash.events library class is not needed for this application because there are no animations or interactive components.

```
1    package {
2        import  flash.display.*;
3
```

```
4     public class mazeApp extends MovieClip {
5
```

```
⋮
```

```
167      }
168 }
```

Constants

The constants required for this application primarily describe the dimensional components of the maze. The constant OFFSET is used to nudge the maze over and down 10 pixels so it does not butt up against the edge of the Stage. Lines 7–11 provide the constant declarations.

The remaining declaration, in line 14, is the maze array. This single-dimension array is declared globally. Thus it is not part of a specific function and, therefore, is accessible to all functions in the package. The size of this array is set to N_CELLS.

```
6   //CONSTANTS
7   const COLS:int=10;              //MAZE COLUMNS
8   const ROWS:int=10;              //MAZE ROWS
9   const N_CELLS:int=COLS*ROWS;    //NUMBER OF CELLS ON MAZE BOARD
10  const SIZE:int=50;              //SIZE OF MAZE CELL DRAWN ON THE STAGE
11  const OFFSET:int=10;            //BUFFER AROUND THE MAZE
12
13  //THE MAZE ARRAY TO HOLD EACH MAZE CELL DISPLAY OBJECT
14  var maze:Array = new Array(N_CELLS);
15
```

The four functions for this maze generator are designed as follows.

Function mazeApp() Design

The main algorithm, mazeApp(), is the class constructor function and controls the entire flow of the program. It calls the three functions in turn to perform the major tasks in generating the maze.

```
16  function mazeApp() {
17     initialization();
18     backtracker();
19     drawMazeCells();
20  }
21
```

Function initialization() Design

The initialization() function prepares the maze array for the backtracking algorithm. It has the general task of adding all the maze cells to the Stage and the maze array and setting their initial properties. Before we examine the specific tasks performed by this function, we take a look at the required custom properties declared for each cell instance.

ID   Uniquely identifies each cell in the maze. ID will match the index of the maze array.

visited   Holds a true or false value. Has this cell been visited during backtracking?

north   Holds a true or false value. Does the north wall exist?

south   Holds a true or false value. Does the south wall exist?

east   Holds a true or false value. Does the east wall exist?

west   Holds a true or false value. Does the west wall exist?

Task 1: Creates a variable named mazeCellObj. This variable is a display object that is a member of the subclass MovieClip. A MovieClip class is used because it is flexible and able to accommodate the needed custom properties.

Task 2: Set all the custom properties for the mazeCellObj instance. Also set the location of the display object. The computation of the location is based on the row, column, size, and offset.

Task 3: Place the mazeCellObj object in the maze array. Increment the index of the array by one.

Note

The child mazeCellObj has not yet been added to the stage. This step will be done last, after all the graphic drawing occurs.

```
22  function initialization() {
23     var cellID:int=0;
24     for (var r=0; r<ROWS; r++) {
25        for (var c=0; c<COLS; c++) {
26
27           //TASK 1: GENERATE A DISPLAY OBJECT FOR MAZE CELL
28           var mazeCellObj:MovieClip=new MovieClip;
29
30           //TASK 2: SET THE PROPERTIES OF THE MAZE CELL
31           mazeCellObj.x=c*SIZE+OFFSET;
32           mazeCellObj.y=r*SIZE+OFFSET;
33           mazeCellObj.ID=cellID;
34           mazeCellObj.visited=false;
35           mazeCellObj.north=true;
36           mazeCellObj.south=true;
37           mazeCellObj.east=true;
38           mazeCellObj.west=true;
```

```
39
40              //TASK 3: PLACE MAZE CELL DISPLAY OBJECT IN ARRAY
41              maze[cellID]=mazeCellObj;
42              cellID++;
43          }
44      }
45  }
46
```

Function backtracker() Design

This function is the heart of the maze generation program—it is the implementation of the backtracker algorithm. It performs two tasks:

Task 1: Set the initial values for the backtracker algorithm. The first variable is the empty stack. The remaining variables keep track of how many cells have been visited and the current cell on the top of the stack. The first maze cell visited is at index 0 of the maze array.

Task 2: Using a while loop, this task continues to carve out the maze until all the cells have been visited. This task is divided into three parts: A, B, and C. Part A strings together a list of all the walls that are available to be eliminated. Part B randomly chooses one of the walls from that string and eliminates it. Part C will occur only if there are no walls to eliminate, in which case the backtracking of the stack will occur.

```
47  function backtracker() {
48      //TASK 1: CREATE BACKTRACKER VARIABLES AND INITIALIZE
49      var stack:Array=new Array();
50      var visitedCells:int=1;      //How many cells are visited
51      var cell:int=0;              //Start position will be the first cell in the maze
52      maze[cell].visited=true;     //Mark this first cell as visited
53      stack.push(cell);            //Push the cell onto the stack
54
55      //TASK 2: BACKTRACKING
56      //PART A: FOR EACH CELL
57      //    BUILD A STRING CONTAINING A LIST OF WALLS,
58      //    (N, S, E, W) THAT CAN BE ELIMINATED
59
60      var possibleWalls:Array=new Array();
61      while (visitedCells<N_CELLS) {
62          //NOTE: A CELL CANNOT BE REVISITED
63          possible=[];
64          if (maze[cell].west&&cell%COLS!=0) {
65              if (! maze[cell-1].visited) {
66                  possibleWalls.push("W");
67              }
68          }
```

```
69        if (maze[cell].east&&cell%COLS!=COLS-1) {
70          if (! maze[cell+1].visited) {
71            possibleWalls.push("E");
72          }
73        }
74        if (maze[cell].south&&cell<COLS*ROWS-COLS) {
75          if (! maze[cell+COLS].visited) {
76            possibleWalls.push("S");
77          }
78        }
79        if (maze[cell].north&&cell>=COLS) {
80          if (! maze[cell-COLS].visited) {
81            possibleWalls.push("N");
82          }
83        }
84
85        //PART B:  IF possibleWalls CONTAINS WALLS TO REMOVE,
86        //          GENERATE A RANDOM WALL FROM THE POSSIBLE WALLS,
87        //          ELIMINATE THE WALL, AND MARK THE NEW CELL AS VISITED
88        if (possibleWalls.length>0) {
89          howManyWalls=possibleWalls.length-1;
90          randomWall=possibleWalls[Math.round(Math.random()*howManyWalls)];
91          //OPEN THE WALL FOR THE CELL AS WELL AS THE WALL OF THE OTHER CELL
92          switch (randomWall) {
93            case "N" :
94              maze[cell].north=false;
95              maze[cell-COLS].south=false;
96              cell-=COLS;
97              break;
98            case "S" :
99              maze[cell].south=false;
100             maze[cell+COLS].north=false;
101             cell+=COLS;
102             break;
103           case "E" :
104             maze[cell].east=false;
105             maze[cell+1].west=false;
106             cell++;
107             break;
108           case "W" :
109             maze[cell].west=false;
110             maze[cell-1].east=false;
111             cell--;
112             break;
113         }
114         maze[cell].visited=true;
115         stack.push(cell);  //PUSH CELL ONTO THE STACK
116         visitedCells++;    // ANOTHER CELL VISITED
117       } else {
```

```
118        //PART C:  IF NO WALLS CAN BE REMOVED,
119        // BEGIN BACKTRACKING; POP THE STACK
120        top=stack.pop();
121        if (top==cell) {
122           cell=stack.pop();//POP THE STACK - REVERSE
123           stack.push(cell);
124        }
125     }
126   }
127 }
128
```

Function drawMazeCell() Design

The drawMazeCell() function draws each individual cell and places it on the Stage. The drawing relies on the property values for north, east, south, and west that are assigned to each wall in a given maze cell.

```
129 function drawMazeCell() {
130    var xPos:int;
131    var yPos:int
132    for (var i=0; i<N_CELLS; i++) {
133       //TASK 1: GET THE POSITION OF THE CELL MOVIECLIP
134       xPos = maze[i].xPos;
135       yPos = maze[i].yPos;
136
137       //TASK 2: SET THE GRAPHIC LINE STYLE AND MOVE THE PEN
138       maze[i].graphics.lineStyle(1, 0x000000);
139       maze[i].graphics.moveTo(xPos,yPos);
140
141       //TASK 3: DRAW THE CELL
142       //DRAW THE NORTH WALL IF IT EXISTS
143       if (maze[i].north) {
144          maze[i].graphics.lineTo(xPos+SIZE, yPos);
145       }else {
146          maze[i].graphics.moveTo(xPos+SIZE, yPos);
147       }//DRAW A CONNECTING EAST WALL IF IT EXISTS
148       if (maze[i].east) {
149          maze[i].graphics.lineTo(xPos+SIZE, yPos+SIZE);
150       }else {
151          maze[i].graphics.moveTo(xPos+SIZE, yPos+SIZE);
152       }//DRAW A CONNECTING SOUTH WALL
153       if (maze[i].south) {
154          maze[i].graphics.lineTo(xPos, yPos+SIZE);
155       }else {
156          maze[i].graphics.moveTo(xPos, yPos+SIZE);
```

```
157     }//DRAW A CONNECTING WEST WALL
158     if (maze[i].west) {
159         maze[i].graphics.lineTo(xPos, yPos);
160     }else {
161         maze[i].graphics.moveTo(xPos, yPos);
162     }
163     //TASK 3: USE addChild TO PLACE THE MAZE CELL ON STAGE
164     addChild(maze[i]);
165  }
166 }
```

■ 7.7 Strings

The `String` class is a data type in ActionScript that can be used to define and manipulate character string variables. String values are similar to arrays in that individual characters are located at an index position. For example, the declaration for the variable `word`

```
var word:String = "Media";
```

is represented as follows:

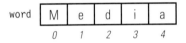

As with arrays, the length of a string can be determined by the property `length`. The instruction

```
trace(word.length);
```

outputs the value 5.

Arrays and strings primarily differ in their accessibility. To access a single value in the string, we must use the operation `charAt()`. For example, to display the character located at index 2, we would use the instruction

```
trace(word.charAt(2));
```

which outputs the character d.

As with arrays, the `String` class contains a large number of operations in the form of method functions. In addition, the relation operators can be used to compare strings. Table 7-9 lists the main operations that can be used with strings, where the operations have been categorized by functionality.

TABLE 7-9 Commonly Used String Methods

Operations for Returning Values	Description
length	Returns the number of characters in the string.
charAt(index)	Returns the character at an index location.
charCodeAt(index)	Returns the ASCII character code.
indexOf(substring)	Returns the index of the first occurrence of a matching substring.
lastIndexOf(substring)	Returns the index of the last occurrence of a matching substring.
search()	Returns the index of a matching substring.

Operations for Adding and Removing Characters	Description
+	Adds additional characters or words to the end of a string.
slice(start index, end index)	Removes the characters from the start index to the end index.

Operations for Modifying Strings	Description
replace(substring1, substring2)	Replaces the first matching substring1 with the specified substring2.
toLowerCase()	Returns the string in lowercase.
toUpperCase()	Returns the string in uppercase.

Operations That Create a String Subset	Description
substr(start index, length)	Returns a new string containing a substring of an existing string.
substring(start index, end index)	Returns a new string containing a substring of an existing string.

Operators for Comparing Strings	Description
<, <=, >, >=, !=, ==	Relational operators can be used with strings. Characters are evaluated from left to right.

The following examples illustrate String functionality.

Example 1

```
1   var sentence:String = "The Farmer takes a Wife.";
2   trace("The length of sentence is " + sentence.length);
3   trace(sentence.toLowerCase());
4   trace(sentence.toUpperCase());
```

Evaluation

The output displayed is

> The length of sentence is 24
> the farmer takes a wife.
> THE FARMER TAKES A WIFE.

Example 2

```
1   var sentence:String = "The Farmer takes a Wife.";
2   sentence += "\nThe Wife takes a Child.";
3   trace (sentence);
4   trace ("Child begins at index number ", sentence.indexOf("Child"));
```

Evaluation

The addition operator, +, is used to concatenate strings. The escape sequence \n
will add a newline character to the string.

> The output displayed is

> The Farmer takes a Wife.
> The Wife takes a Child.
> Child begins at index number 42

Example 3

Task

Display the ASCII value for each uppercase vowel in the alphabet.

Solution

```
1   var vowels:String = "AEIOU";
2   for (var i:int = 0; i < vowels.length; i++) {
3      trace (vowels.charAt(i) + " is the ASCII value " + vowels.charCodeAt(i));
4   }
```

Evaluation

The vowels are stored as a string. A loop structure is used to access each vowel
as if it were an item in an array list.

The output displayed is

A is the ASCII value 65
E is the ASCII value 69
I is the ASCII value 73
O is the ASCII value 79
U is the ASCII value 85

Example 4

```
1   var word:String = "Mississippi";
2   var letter:String = "i"
3   trace (word);
4   word=word.replace(letter,"y");
5   trace (word);
```

Evaluation

This example uses the operation `replace` to make a letter substitution in the string "Mississippi." The natural (incorrect) assumption is that `replace` will perform a substitution for all occurrences of a matching substring or letter. It is important to note that only the *first* occurrence of a match will be replaced.

The output displayed is

Mississippi
Myssissippi

Example 5

Task

Create a list of names and sort them in ascending order.

Solution

```
1   var names:Array = new Array();
2   names.push("Xavier");
3   names.push("Mike");
4   names.push("Bullwinkle");
5   names.push("Ann");
6   names.push("Yvette");
7
8   names.sort();
9   trace(names.toString());
```

Evaluation

Relational operators can be used with strings in the same way as with numeric values. A beneficial aspect of this approach is that strings stored in an array can be sorted. In this code segment, a collection of names are added to an array. The names are identified as strings by simply using double quotes.

The output displayed is

Ann,Bullwinkle,Mike,Xavier,Yvette

7.8 Case Study 4: Word Scramble Game

Problem and Analysis

Various forms of word games have been around for centuries and have long been a source of fascination and entertainment. The word game in this application is called Word Scramble; it is a stripped-down version of a popular word game named Jumble.

This Word Scramble game begins by taking a word from an embedded dictionary, scrambles the letters, and presents the result to the player. For every scrambled word, a hint is also displayed. As shown in Figure 7-19, the player must rearrange the letters and enter the correct unscrambled word. Players may check their answers by clicking the button labeled "Check your answer." At any time during the game, the player may go to another word.

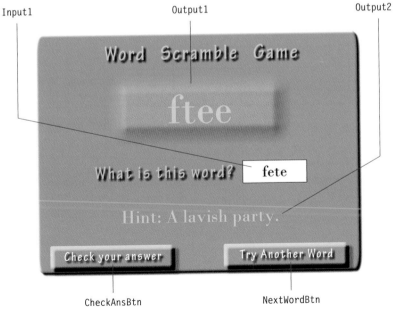

FIGURE 7-19 The Word Scramble game.

The objectives of this case study are as follows:

1. Use a two-dimensional array to store dictionary information.

2. Use the `replace` operation from the `String` class to scramble letters in a given word.

3. Strip an input text string of extraneous characters. This objective is an important precaution.

Visual Design

The Word Scramble game will use a single frame in a multilayered Timeline to hold all the visual elements. Five interactive display objects are required for this game, shown in Figure 7-19 and listed in Table 7-10. These objects include text fields for input and output, and two buttons for the user to control the play of the game.

Other elements can easily be added to the visual design to enhance the enjoyment of the game.

TABLE 7-10 Visual Objects Used in the Input/Output Screen

Visual Object Name	Type of Object	Description of the Object
Output1	Dynamic text box	Displays the scrambled word.
Input1	Input text box	Player enters a word.
Output2	Dynamic text box	Displays a hint or definition of the word in play.
CheckAnsBtn	Button	An interactive button to test the player's answer.
NextWordBtn	Button	An interactive button to let the player choose another word from the dictionary.

Program Design

The ActionScript code for this application consists of five functions, shown in Table 7-11. Figure 7-20 shows the relationship between these functions.

TABLE 7-11 Program Functions

Function Name	Description
scrambleApp()	Activates the application. This is the constructor function that gets the game started.
constructDictionary()	Adds the word and hint content to the dictionary program data structure. This function is simply an initialization task.
prepareWord()	Prepares a word for play.
checkWord()	Determines whether the user's input matches the word. This function is an event handler that responds to a click of the button named CheckAnsBtn.
getAnotherWord()	Identifies the next word in the dictionary that will be played. This function is an event handler that responds to a click of the button named NextWordBtn.

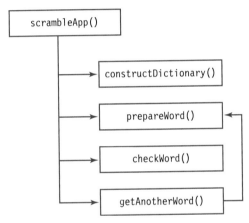

FIGURE 7-20 The relationship structure of functions of the Word Scramble game.

The class package begins with the imported library classes. The flash.display and flash.events library classes are necessary for working with the display objects and button interactivity. The last two lines of the ActionScript file contain closing curly brackets to close the document class and the package.

```
1   package {
2       import flash.display.*;
3       import flash.events.*;
4
5       public class scrambleApp extends MovieClip {
6
    ⋮
80      }
81  }
```

Game Constants and Variables

Two global constants are needed for this application. The first constant indicates the number of words stored in the dictionary. The second, and more important, constant is the escape sequence representing the RETURN character. This character will eventually be stripped from all word answers input by the player.

```
7   //GAME CONSTANTS
8   const HOWMANYWORDS:uint=4;
9   const RETURN:String="\r";
10
```

Two global variables are also used in this game. As global variables, they will be made available to all functions. The first variable is dictionary, a two-dimensional array storing the words and hint content. The second global variable, whichWord, is used to identify which word is currently in play. Notice that it has been initialized to index 0, the first word in the dictionary.

```
11  //GLOBAL GAME VARIABLES
12  var dictionary:Array=new Array();
13  var whichWord:uint=0;
14
```

The five functions used in the application are designed and coded as follows.

Function scrambleApp() Design

The main algorithm, scrambleApp(), is the class constructor function and is initiated once the application is executed. This function is used to initialize the game and begin playing with the first word. There are four tasks:

Task 1: Call constructDictionary() to build the embedded dictionary.

Task 2: Start the game by preparing the first word. prepareWord() is called to do all the work involved in displaying a scrambled word and its hint to the player.

Task 3: A listener event is registered for when the player wishes to check an answer. The event handler for this event is checkWord().

Task 4: A listener event is registered for when the player wishes to try another word from the dictionary. The event handler for this event is getAnotherWord().

```
15  function scrambleApp() {
16  //TASK 1: BUILD THE DICTIONARY HOLDING THE WORDS AND HINTS
17  constructDictionary();
18
19  //TASK 2: SCRAMBLE AND PREPARE THE FIRST WORD
20  prepareWord();
```

```
21
22  //TASK 3: LISTEN FOR USER TO CHECK ANSWER
23  CheckAnsBtn.addEventListener(MouseEvent.CLICK, checkWord);
24
25  //TASK 4: LISTEN FOR USER TO PLAY WITH ANOTHER WORD
26  NextWordBtn.addEventListener(MouseEvent.CLICK, getAnotherWord);
27  }
28
```

Function constructDictionary() Design

The constructDictionary() function simply constructs the two-dimensional array that represents the dictionary. Each row in the array will represent a word, and every word will be accompanied by a hint. The first column of any given row is the word and the second column is the hint. Each cell in this two-dimensional array will hold a String data type.

Note that as part of a two-dimensional array, each row is essentially an independent array holding the word and its hint.

```
29  function constructDictionary() {
30     dictionary=[
31                ["fete", "A lavish party."],
32                ["net", "Take-home pay."],
33                ["ham", "It's often smoked."],
34                ["alto", "Quartet voice."]
35                ];
36  }
37
```

Function prepareWord() Design

The prepareWord() function is the engine that performs the work of scrambling the word. This function has three tasks:

Task 1: Declare the variables that will be used to scramble the word in play. Scrambling a string requires an auxiliary variable, scrambled. This variable will be used in Task 2. The global variable whichWord is used to access words from the dictionary.

Variable Name	Data Type	Description
word	String	Holds the word in play.
hint	String	Holds the hint in play.
scrambled	String	Is initially empty. This auxiliary variable will be used to build a random string containing the letters in word.

Task 2: A loop structure is used to build the scrambled string by randomly selecting a letter from word, placing it in scrambled, and then eliminating it from word. Scrambling will be complete when word is empty. The operation replace is used to remove a letter by replacing it with an empty string, "".

Task 3: The scrambled word, scrambled, is placed in the text field Output1 and its hint is placed in the text field Output2.

```
38  function prepareWord() {
39      //TASK 1: GET THE WORD AND HINT FROM THE DICTIONARY
40      var word:String=dictionary[whichWord][0];
41      var hint:String=dictionary[whichWord][1];
42      var scrambled:String="";
43
44      //TASK 2: SCRAMBLE THE LETTERS IN THE WORD
45      while (word.length > 0) {
46          var letter:String=word.charAt(Math.floor(Math.random()*word.length));
47          scrambled+=letter;
48          word=word.replace(letter,"");
49      }
50
51      //TASK 3: DISPLAY THE SCRAMBLED WORD AND SHOW A HINT
52      Output1.text=scrambled;
53      Output2.text="Hint: "+hint;
54  }
55
```

Function checkWord() Design

The checkWord() function is an event handler that is triggered once the player decides to check an answer. Two main tasks are performed by this function:

Task 1: The answer entered by the player is first copied into the variable string word. It is important to note that frequently an Enter or Return character is intercepted in a text field along with a string. To guard against this possibility, the replace() operation is used to strip it off.

Task 2: Check whether word matches the word in play. The word in play is accessed by whichWord from dictionary. A response to the correct or incorrect answer is displayed in the Output2 text field.

```
56  function checkWord(event:MouseEvent) {
57      //TASK 1: WORD INPUT AND STRIP OFF THE INTERCEPTED RETURN
58      var word:String=Input1.text;
59      word=word.replace(RETURN,"");
60
61      //TASK 2: CHECK IF THE USER'S WORD MATCHES THE DICTIONARY WORD
```

```
62    if (word==dictionary[whichWord][0]) {
63        Output2.text="Correct";
64    } else {
65        Output2.text="Sorry, the correct word is "+dictionary[whichWord][0];
66    }
67 }
68
```

Function getAnotherWord() Design

The getAnotherWord() function is an event handler triggered by the player once the player decides to try another word. This function is divided into three tasks:

Task 1: Increment whichWord. Use a modulus of HOWMANYWORDS in case the index exceeds the number of words in the dictionary.

Task 2: Refresh the screen by clearing out the input and output text fields.

Task 3: Call the function prepareWord() to scramble the letters and display the new word and its hint.

```
69 function getAnotherWord(event:MouseEvent) {
70    //TASK 1: INCREMENT THE WORD INDEX TO THE NEXT WORD
71    whichWord = (whichWord + 1) % HOWMANYWORDS;
72
73    //TASK 2: CLEAR OUT THE OUTPUT AND THE INPUT TEXT BOX DISPLAYS
74    Input1.text="";
75    Output1.text="";
76
77    //TASK 3: SCRAMBLE AND PREPARE THE NEW WORD
78    prepareWord();
79 }
```

▨ Review Questions

1. What is an array and why is it useful?

2. Show three ways to create the following array:

   list | 3 | 2 | 1 |

3. True or False: The elements within a given array can be any combination of data types.

4. Given the following array, what does the statement trace(list.length); display?

   list | 3 | 2 | 1 |

5. Explain the difference between pop() and push().

6. Explain the difference between unShift() and shift().

7. How do the array methods sort() and sortOn() differ?

8. What does the method splice() do? Which values are required for it to perform its intended operation?

9. Both concat() and slice() return new arrays. Describe the arrays they return.

10. Write a variable definition for an array called num[] that stores the numbers 3, 4, and 5. What is the index of the first element in this array?

11. Write a variable definition for an array called ballGraphics[] that stores instances of a Ball MovieClip. Assume Ball is also the name of the Linkage ID.

12. Consider an array that contains 200 elements. What is the index of the last element in the array?

13. What is the index of the last element of the following array?

arr1 | 10 | 3 | 1 | −1 | 7 | 19 | 24

14. Write ActionScript 3.0 code that swaps the first element in the following array with the last element.

Before: arr2 | 17 | 4 | 6 | 2 | 3 | 1 | −1 | 7 | 19 | 24

After: arr2 | 24 | 4 | 6 | 2 | 3 | 1 | −1 | 7 | 19 | 17

15. Write ActionScript 3.0 code that doubles the values of all elements in the following array.

Before: arr3 | 3 | 4 | 6 | 2 | 3 | 1 | −1 | 7 | 19 | 24

After: arr3 | 6 | 8 | 12 | 4 | 6 | 2 | −2 | 14 | 38 | 48

16. Write ActionScript 3.0 code that defines an array arr4[] and initializes 25 of its cells to zero.

17. Consider the following array definition and code segment. What are the contents of the array named `arr2[]` after the code segment executes?

Before: arr2 | 17 | 4 | 6 | 2 | 3 | 1 | −1 | 7 | 19 | 24 |

```
1   for (var i:int= 3; i < 8; i++){
2      if ( i % 2 ==0){
3         arr2 [ i ] = 2 * i;
4      }
5      else {
6         arr2 [ i ] = i;
7      }
8   }
```

18. Consider the following array definition and code segment. What is displayed after the code segment executes?

Before: arr5 | 22 | 4 | 16 | 12 | 24 | 2 | −2 | 3 | 4 | 52 |

```
1   var sum:int = 0;
2   for (var i:int= 0; i <= 9; i+=2){
3      sum += arr5[i];
4   }
5   trace ( sum);
```

19. Explain the selection sort algorithm.

20. Consider the following matrix. Write the ActionScript 3.0 code to declare it.

1	2	3
4	5	6
7	8	9

21. What is the difference between a stack and a queue?

22. Which array operations are used to alter the contents of a stack, such as adding elements to the top of the stack and removing the top element of the stack?

23. When working with string data, what does the operation `replace()` do?

24. Explain the difference between the String methods `charAt()` and `charCodeAt()`.

25. Which String operation returns the index of a matching substring?

■ Programming Exercises

1. Create an application that allows the user to enter a paragraph of text. Write ActionScript code to count the occurrence of letters. For example:

Input

The information thus gained was a relief, but only partially so. For both Clyde and Roberta there was no real relief now until this problem should be definitely solved. And although within a few moments after he had obtained it, he appeared and explained that at last he had secured the name of someone who might help her.

Output

A: 25

B: 6

C: 2

D: 14

E: 35

F: 8

G: 3

H: 20

I: 16

J: 0

K: 0

L: 16

M: 7

N: 17

O: 19

P: 6

Q: 0

R: 14

S: 11

T: 23

U: 6

V: 1

W: 6

X: 1

Y: 4

Z: 0

2. Graphic patterns created using dynamic motion can be very interesting. Write an application that draws 10 MovieClips shaped as balls. Place each of these balls in an array. Assign each ball a velocity property and initialize that property to a unique sequential value. For example, the first ball can be given a velocity of 1, the second ball a velocity of 2, the third ball a velocity of 3, and so on. Position the balls on the Stage so that they form a vertical line on the left side of the Stage. Use an ENTER_FRAME event to move each ball to the right side of the Stage at their assigned velocity. Once a ball has hit the left or right Stage wall, its direction should be reversed.

3. Create an application that allows the user to interactively construct Tetris-like blocks. These blocks will fall from the top of the Stage. Once they hit the bottom of the Stage, they should be deleted.

4. Add two character elements to the maze application from Case Study 3. The first character element should represent the user. When the application begins, position the user's character on a cell and allow it to interactively move to other cells in the maze. The second character element should represent the opponent—the computer. Calculate and store the path from the opponent's location to the exit of the maze. Add a Go button, such as the one shown in Figure 7-21, so that the user can race against the opponent in an attempt to make it to an exit cell the fastest.

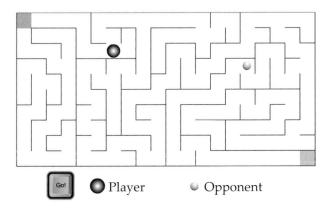

FIGURE 7-21 A maze race.

5. Consider a chessboard with eight rows and columns. Write an application that allows the user to position a bishop on a square on the board and computes all the

possible moves, as seen in Figure 7-22, starting at the intersection of the specified row and column.

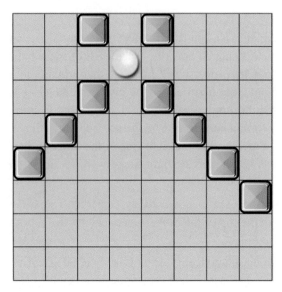

❙ FIGURE 7-22 The moves of a bishop on a chess board.

8 Functions in Depth

Introduction

Up to this point, we have designed functions that perform a specific task as part of a larger program. These functions execute a set of instructions that can also involve changing global variable values, but their uses have been restricted in that they do not return values. The type of programming we have done thus far is called procedural programming; it is particularly useful for facilitating program design. For example, when a task has to be performed more than once, an appropriate function is designed, written, and then called whenever it is needed. In previous case studies, the larger program has been divided into smaller tasks. Several tasks are assigned to a function and are performed when the function is called.

In addition to procedural programming, we have worked with standard built-in functions, such as `Math.sin(angle)`, `Math.cos(angle)`, and `Math.sqrt(n)`. These functions focus on data. To wit, data is required in the form of parameters for these functions to perform their tasks. In addition, data is returned by these functions to the calling function. In this chapter, we explore data functions in depth.

Finally, we take a rather brief look at the concept of recursion in this chapter. A recursive function is a function that calls itself. We will examine recursion in general and more specifically its use in constructing complex graphical shapes called fractals.

■ 8.1 User-Defined Functions with a Focus on Data

It is easy to envision the need for functions that return data and that are not on the list of standard functions available in ActionScript. As seen in previous chapters, a function provides a way for programmers to perform a set of related tasks that are grouped together and called by a single name. This concept is the same for functions that return values.

We begin with a simple example to illustrate such a function. Consider a program that requires the frequent computation of the area of a rectangle. To write this program efficiently, it would be convenient to design a function named `areaRectangle()` that receives data for the width and length of a generic rectangle and then calculates and returns the computed area. The assignment and function call might look as follows:

```
var area:Number = areaRectangle(W, L);
```

In this statement, the variable area is declared as a Number data type and initialized to the value returned by the function areaRectangle(). Within the parentheses of the function call are the variables W and L. They are the **arguments** supplied to the function; they are needed for it to calculate the correct area.

Many problems from mathematics, physics, and game programming would require this type of function, but such methods appear in other applications as well. For example, in an interior paint design application, it might be useful to have a function that determines a customer's bill given the size of one room, the number of paint coats, and the cost per gallon of paint used. Similarly, a hotel might like a function to compute the room charge for a visitor given the type of accommodation (standard, luxury suite, and so on) and various other options. Functions such as these are not standard functions. In AS3, however, we can easily create such data-focused functions to pass values to and return the result of computations.

The general form for a function such as this is

```
function functionName (parameter list): return type{

    return value;
}
```

This syntax format has three significant elements:

- The parameter list, which corresponds to a list of arguments.
- A return type specification to describe the type of data returned. This will be discussed in the next section.
- A return statement. This will be discussed in the next section.

8.1.1 Parameters and Arguments

Parameters are used so that values of variables may be passed from one function to another. A parameter is nothing more than a variable that receives the argument that has been passed by a calling function.

To reiterate, the values that are passed to a function are referred to as **arguments** and are used to send data in one direction to the calling function. The variables that receive the data are parameters.

In the assignment statement

```
var num1:int = Math.floor(3.25);
```

the literal value 3.25 is the argument that is passed to the function `Math.floor()`. `Math.floor()` is equipped with a parameter that will receive this value. Once it performs the required calculation, it will return a value, which is then assigned to `num1`.

The parameter list for any function must match the number of corresponding arguments used when the function is called. Thus, if a function is designed to receive three parameter values, its call must contain three arguments.

Example 1

Code Segment

```
1   var num1:int = 3;
2   num2 = playFunc(num1);
```

Evaluation

In these two lines of code, the value stored in the variable `num1` is the argument that is passed to the function `playFunc()`. Once `playFunc()` returns a value, that value will be assigned to the variable `num2`.

Example 2: Literal Arguments

This example illustrates a complete program containing a data function named `areaRectangle()`. It also shows literal arguments passed to a function.

```
1   package {
2       import flash.display.*;
3
4       public class exampleApp extends MovieClip {
5
6           function exampleApp () {
7               var area = areaRectangle(4, 5);
8               trace ("The area of this rectangle is ", area);
9           }
10
11          function areaRectangle(W:Number, L:Number):Number {
12              return W * L;
13          }
14      }
15  }
```

Evaluation

Line 7: The function call to `areaRectangle()` is the expression in this assignment statement. The two arguments in the function call are the literal values 4 and 5. When the function `areaRectangle()` is called, these arguments will be passed to the function.

Line 11: This function declaration contains two parameters, W and L, that correspond with the two arguments on line 7. The return class for the function `areaRectangle()` is a Number data type. In other words, this function will return a number.

Line 12: The area for the rectangle is computed and returned to the calling instruction in line 7.

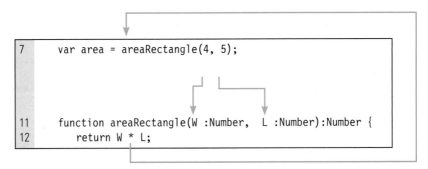

The output produced by this code is

The area of this rectangle is 20

Example 3

This complete program example illustrates that parameter identifiers are not required to match the identifiers of the corresponding argument.

```
1   package {
2       import flash.display.*;
3       public class exampleApp extends MovieClip {
4           function exampleApp (){
5               var W: Number=2;
6               var X: Number=3;
7               var Y: Number=4;
8               var Z: Number=funcA(W, X, Y);
9
10              trace("The value in Z is ", Z);
11          }
12
13          function funcA (A: Number, B: Number, C: Number):Number {
14              return C /A + B*10;
15          }
16      }
17  }
```

Evaluation

Line 8: The function call to `funcA()` is made in this assignment statement. The identifier names in this argument list are W, X, and Y.

Line 13: The function declaration for `funcA()` contains three parameters. The identifier names of these parameters are A, B, and C. Even though the identifier names do not match, the passing of arguments to the parameters will work correctly.

Fundamentally, parameters are variables for which new memory locations are allocated. When `funcA()` is called, the number of parameters must correspond with the number of arguments, as values will be passed in sequence. In other words, the first argument will be passed to the first parameter, the second argument will be passed to the second parameter, and so on.

Line 14: The return value, `C/A + B*10`, is computed (4/2 + 3*10 = 32), returned to the calling instruction in line 7, and assigned to Z.

```
8          var  Z: Number = funcA(W, X, Y);



13         function funcA(A: Number, B: Number, C: Number):Number {
14             return C /A + B*10;
```

The output produced by this code is

The value of Z is 32

Example 4: Multiple Function Calls

```
1   package {
2   import flash.display.*;
3      public class exampleApp extends MovieClip {
4          function exampleApp () {
5              var r1:Number=areaRectangle(5.0,6.0);
6              var r2:Number=areaRectangle(7.0,3.0);
7              var r3:Number=areaRectangle(8.0,4.0);
8
9              trace("The area of r1 is " + r1);
10             trace("The area of r2 is " + r2);
11             trace("The area of r3 is " + r3);
12         }
13         function areaRectangle(W:Number, L:Number):Number {
14             return W * L;
15         }
16     }
17 }
```

Evaluation

Once a function is defined, it can be called any number of times. In this example, the function areaRectangle() is called three times, each time passing a different set of argument values.

The output produced by this code is:

```
The area of r1 is 30.0
The area of r2 is 21.0
The area of r3 is 32.0
```

8.1.2 Return Data Types

A **return data type** identifies the type of data a function must return. When a function returns a value, it is returning an object; as a consequence, it is important to indicate the data type of the object that will be returned. An error will occur if the function returns an incompatible data object.

As we have seen in previous chapter examples, on some occasions, a function does not return anything. This type of function is referred to as a **void** function. A function uses a void return type to indicate that it does not return a value. From this point on, all functions, non-void and void, will be written to include the appropriate return data types.

Example 1

The return data type in this example is an int. The parameter list consists of three String data types. The objective of this function is to compute the length of all three strings added together. This length, an integer value, will be returned.

Parameter list   Return data type

```
function sizeIt(A:String, B:String, C:String):int {

    var D:String = A + B + C;

    return D.length;
}
```

Example 2

For this example, consider a MovieClip symbol BALL in the Library with an export linkage.

```
1   package {
2      import flash.display.*;
3      public class exampleApp extends MovieClip {
4         function exampleApp () :void{
5            var Ball:BALL = makeBall();
6            trace ("The size of Ball is ", Ball.width);
7         }
8         function makeBall():BALL {
9            var hold:BALL = new BALL();
10           hold.x = 20;
11           hold.y = 30;
12           hold.width = 200;
13           hold.height = 100;
14           addChild(hold);
15           return hold;
16        }
17     }
18  }
```

Evaluation

This example shows that a return object is not restricted to the AS3 primitive data types. The return data type can also be a display object, such as a MovieClip.

Line 4: The constructor function is a void function; it does not return a value.

Line 5: The function call to makeBall() occurs in this assignment statement.

Line 8: The function declaration for makeBall() contains no parameters and returns a BALL display object.

Lines 9–15: An instance of BALL named hold is created. Once hold's properties are initialized, it is then physically added to the Stage. On line 15, this instance is returned to the calling function.

Example 3

```
1   package {
2      import flash.display.*;
3      public class exampleApp extends MovieClip {
4         function exampleApp ():void {
5            rectangleInfo (12.5,  5.5);
6         }
7
8         function rectangleInfo(W:Number, L:Number):void {
9            trace("The width of the rectangle is " , W);
10           trace("The length of the rectangle is ", L);
11           trace("The area of the rectangle is ", W*L);
12           trace("The perimeter of the rectangle is ", W*2+L*2);
```

```
13          }
14      }
15  }
```

Evaluation

This example illustrates the use of a void function call. A void function performs a task but does not return a value to the calling function. Because no data is returned, this type of function can never be part of an expression within an assignment statement and cannot be used in a `trace` statement.

The function `rectangleInfo()` contains a parameter list consisting of `W:Number` and `L:Number`. It performs the task of displaying the width, length, area, and perimeter of a given rectangle.

Example 4

```
1   package {
2       import flash.display.*;
3       public class exampleApp extends MovieClip {
4           function exampleApp ():void {
5               int tossDice = tossDie() + tossDie();
6           }
7
8           function tossDie ():int {
9               return Math.floor(Math.random() * 6) + 1;
10          }
11      }
12  }
```

Evaluation

This example illustrates the use of multiple non-void function calls within the same expression. The function `tossDie()` has an empty parameter list and returns an `int` data type. It is called twice to generate a dice toss.

8.1.3 The return Statement and Termination of a Function

The specific purpose of a `return` statement is to force a function to terminate and return a value. For example, in the function

```
function sum(A:int, B:int):int {
    return A + B;
}
```

the sum of A plus B is returned and the function terminates.

Functions with a `void` return type do not normally include `return` statements. Because nothing is returned in a void function, it will automatically terminate once the closing curly bracket, }, is encountered. However, a `return` statement with no argument may be used in a void function to execute an early termination. For example, in the function

```
function sayHello(n1:int):void {
   if (n1 == 0) {
      return;
   }
   trace (n1);
}
```

an early return is performed only if `n1` is equal to zero; otherwise, the function will terminate at the final closing curly bracket, }.

The next four examples illustrate return errors and early termination options.

Example 1: Error—Functions Can Return Only a Single Object

```
1   package {
2      import flash.display.*;
3      public class exampleApp extends MovieClip {
4         function exampleApp ():void {
5            var dice:int = tossDie();    }
6
7         function tossDie ():int {
8            return Math.floor(Math.random() * 6) + 1;
9            return Math.floor(Math.random() * 6) + 1;
10        }
11     }
12  }
```

Evaluation

A function can return only one object. This example shows a logic error in which the function `tossDie()` attempts to return two values. The first `return` statement on line 8 will terminate the function.

Example 2: Error—Non-void Functions Must Return a Value

```
1   package {
2      import flash.display.*;
3      public class exampleApp extends MovieClip {
4         function exampleApp():void {
5            var n2:int = func1 (0);
6         }
7         function func1(n1:int):int {
8            trace("Bananas are yellow. ");
9         }
10     }
11  }
```

Evaluation

All non-void functions must be terminated with a `return` statement. In this example, the function `func1()` does not return a value and will not terminate properly.

Example 3: Error—Non-void Function with Potentially No Return

```
1   package {
2      import flash.display.*;
3      public class exampleApp extends MovieClip {
4         function exampleApp ():void {
5            var x:int = func1 (2);
6            trace("X is " + x);
7         }
8         function func1(n1:int):int {
9            if (n1 == 0) {
10              return 7;
11           } else if (n1 == 1) {
12              return 8;
13           }else  if (n1 == 2) {
14              return 9;
15           }
16        }
17     }
18  }
```

Evaluation

This example illustrates the problems associated with `return` statements that run the risk of not executing. On lines 9–14, three test conditions are examined, but if none is found to be true, no `return` statement will be executed and the function cannot terminate. The correction is to supply a `return` statement in a final `else` clause.

Function Correction

```
function func1(n1:int):int {
   if (n1 == 0) {
      return 7;
   }else if (n1 == 1) {
      return 8;
   }else if (n1 == 2) {
      return 9;
   }else {
      return -1;
   }
}
```

Example 4: Detecting Errors

```
1   package {
2       import flash.display.*;
3       public class exampleApp extends MovieClip {
4           function exampleApp ():void {
5               func1 (0);
6               func1 (2);
7               trace("The sky is blue.");
8           }
9           function func1(n1:Number):void {
10              if (n1 == 0) {
11                  return;
12              }
13              for (var i:int = 1; i< 10; i++){
14                  trace (i / n1);
15              }
16          }
17      }
18  }
```

Evaluation

The function `func1()` is a void function that contains a `return` statement used specifically to perform an early termination in the case of an error. Line 10 tests whether the parameter `n1` has a value of zero. When the result is true, the function immediately returns control back to the function `exampleApp()`, by using the `return` statement with no value (line 11). This technique can be used as a means of error detection when a certain parameter is considered unacceptable or, as in this case, will result in division by zero (line 14).

8.2 Local and Global: The Scope of Variables

A **local variable** is a variable that is defined within a function. This type of variable is defined only for use within the function block; it has no meaning outside the respective function. Once the function terminates, the variable's memory will be deallocated.

A **global variable** is a variable that can be used by all functions of a given program. To be made global, a variable must be defined outside any specific function. By definition, a globally declared variable is not linked to one function but rather is made available to all functions defined within a package.

The **scope** of a variable identifier refers to those sections of the program in which a given variable is accessible. A global variable defined at the beginning of a class definition has the widest scope, because it is accessible to all functions within that package. In contrast, a local variable declared within, and linked to, a specific function has very limited scope because it is available only within the function that defined it.

The general rule for declaring variables is the opposite of the rule that applies to constants. While constants should be declared prior to all functions, variables are normally declared locally within functions. One exception to this rule occurs when several functions need to share a common variable or data structure, such as an array.

Examples illustrating the scope of variables follow.

Example 1

```
1   package {
2      import flash.display.*;
3      public class exampleApp extends MovieClip {
4         var n1:Number = 1;
5
6         function exampleApp ():void {
7            var n2:Number = 2;
8            func1(n2);
9            trace("n1 = ",n1);
10           trace("n2 = ",n2);
11        }
12        function func1(n2:Number):void {
13           n1= 3;
14           n2 = 4;
15        }
16     }
17  }
```

Evaluation

Line 4: The variable n1 is defined as a global variable. It is not declared within any specific function.

Line 7: The variable n2 is defined as a local variable. Unlike n1, n2 is declared within the function exampleApp() and, therefore, its scope is local and accessible only to this function.

Line 12: The function func1() has a single parameter named n2. The parameter n2 shares the same name as the local variable n2, but they are not the same. In fact, they reside at different locations in memory.

Line 13: The global variable n1 is reassigned the value 3. Because it is a global variable, this operation is allowed.

Line 14: The parameter variable n2 is assigned the value 4. This assignment will not affect the value stored in the local variable n2 within the function exampleApp(). It is important to remember that they are two separate variables that happen to share the same name.

The output produced by this code is

```
n1 = 3
n2 = 2
```

Example 2

```
1   package {
2      import flash.display.*;
3      public class exampleApp extends MovieClip {
4         function exampleApp() :void{
5            var X:int = 3;
6            var Y:int = 4;
7            var Z:int = 5;
8            func1 (X, Y, Z);
9            trace("X = ", X);
10           trace("Y = ", Y);
11           trace("Z = ", Z);
12        }
13        function func1(Z:int, X:int, Y:int):void {
14           trace("X = ", X);
15           trace("Y = ", Y);
16           trace("Z = ", Z);
17        }
18     }
19  }
```

Evaluation

This example reiterates the idea that parameters are actually local variables for which new memory locations are allocated.

Lines 5–7: The local variables X, Y, and Z are defined and initialized.

Line 8: The function func1() is called with the arguments X, Y, and Z passed in that order.

Line 13: The value parameters indicate a local copy of the values passed. Note the order of the parameters:

1. Z receives the value 3.

2. X receives the value 4.

3. Y receives the value 5.

Lines 9–11: As local variables, X, Y, and Z will remain intact upon the termination of func1().

The output produced by this code is

```
X = 4
Y = 5
Z = 3
X = 3
Y = 4
Z = 5
```

Example 3

```
1   package {
2      import flash.display.*;
3      public class exampleApp extends MovieClip {
4         function exampleApp():void {
5            var Y:Number=3;
6            func1(Y);
7            trace("Y = ", Y);
8         }
9         function func1(Z:Number):void {
10           var Y:Number=5;
11           trace("Z = ", Z);
12           trace("Y = ", Y);
13        }
14     }
15  }
```

Evaluation

This example shows that the same local variable identifier can be used in many functions.

Line 5: The local variable Y is defined and initialized. This variable is local to exampleApp().

Line 6: The function func1() is called and the argument Y is passed.

Line 9: The parameter Z receives the value 3 passed by the function call on line 6.

Line 10: The local variable Y is defined and initialized to 3. This variable is local to func1(). The local variable in exampleApp() is a different variable and, therefore, will not be altered.

The output produced by this code is

```
Z = 3
Y = 5
Y = 3
```

■ 8.3 Case Study 1: Paint Job Cost Application

Problem Analysis

Carol and Bob's Paint Store would like an Internet application that allows visitors to determine how many gallons of paint are required to paint a single room in their home.

The number of gallons will be based on a single coat of paint covering four walls and the ceiling.

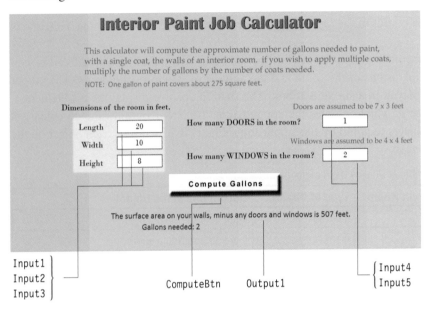

Users will be able to provide the dimensions of the room as well as the number of doors and windows. The input for the dimensions of the room will be the length, width, and height of the room. In addition, the user will provide the number of doors and windows in the room; their area will not be included in the area to be painted. A door will be given a standard measurement of 7 × 3 feet. All windows will be given a standard measurement of 4 × 4 feet.

The application will assume one gallon of paint will cover approximately 275 square feet. The output will consist of the number of gallons needed and the computed surface area to be painted.

This application must perform the following general tasks:

1. Provide input boxes for the user to enter the dimensions of the room and the number of windows and doors.

2. Provide the user with a button to start the calculation process.

3. Once the calculation process has begun, get the input values from the text boxes and store the data in local variables.

4. Call a function to compute the costs.

5. Call a function to display the costs.

Visual Design

This application will require only one screen for the combined input of room information and the output of the calculated paint results. Only one frame in the Timeline is needed.

This interactive application will provide input text boxes in which the user can enter the dimensions of the room and the number of windows and doors. The output will be displayed in a single text box. The final interactive display object element is the ComputeBtn, which initiates the computation. Table 8-1 outlines the complete set of visual objects required by this application. Figure 8-1 identifies each object on the interface screen.

TABLE 8-1 Visual Objects Used in the Input/Output Screen

Visual Object Name	Type of Object	Description of the Object
Input1	Input text box	Input data for room length
Input2	Input text box	Input data for room width
Input3	Input text box	Input data for room height
Input4	Input text box	Input data for the number of doors in the room
Input5	Input text box	Input data for the number of windows in the room
Output1	Dynamic text box	Output box displaying the computed gallons of paint needed and the surface area to be painted
ComputeBtn	Button	Interactive button to start the computation process

Algorithmic Design

The ActionScript code for this application, located in file paintJobApp.as, consists of six functions, as described in Table 8-2. Figure 8-2 shows the relationships among these functions.

TABLE 8-2 Paint Application Program Functions

Function Name	Details
`paintJobApp()`	Parameters: None Return type: `void` Description: This function is the main function as well as the class constructor. As a class constructor, it launches when the application begins.
`calculate()`	Parameters: Event Return type: `void` Description: The event handler function that is initiated once the user clicks the `ComputeBtn`. This function is the engine behind the application and is responsible for calling all other functions.
`inputIsValid()`	Parameters: `L:Number` Length of the room `W:Number` Width of the room `H:Number` Height of the room `drs:Number` Number of doors in the room `wnds:Number` Number of windows in the room Return type: `Boolean` Description: Validates the input entered by the user.

`computeWallSurface()`	Parameters: The dimensions of the room
	`Length:Number`
	`Height:Number`
	`Width:Number`
	
	Return type: `Number`
	
	Description: Computes the surface area for four walls and the ceiling

`computeDoorWindowArea()`	Parameters: The number of doors and windows in the room
	`doors:Number`
	`windows:Number`
	
	Return type: `Number`
	
	Description: Computes the area that includes the doors and the windows.

`displayPaintInfo()`	Parameters:
	`wallArea:Number`
	`dr_wndArea:Number`
	`gallons:Number`
	
	Return type: `void`
	
	Description: Displays the computed number of gallons needed and the surface area to be covered.

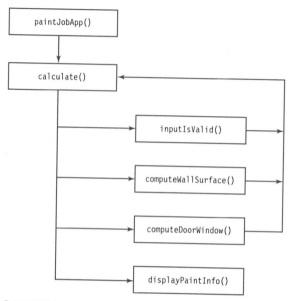

| FIGURE 8-2 Relationship structure of functions for the paint job application.

The required class `package` contains the imported libraries `flash.display` and `flash.events.*`. The last two lines of the ActionScript file contain closing curly brackets to close the `paintJobApp` class and the package.

```
1    package {
2        import flash.display.*;
3        import flash.events.*;
4
5        public class paintJobApp extends MovieClip {
6
```

```
85        }
86    }
```

The three constants required for this application are assumptions regarding the surface area covered by a gallon of paint and the size of a standard window and door. As specified in the problem analysis, windows are on average 4 feet by 4 feet, or 16 square feet. Doors are typically 7 feet by 3 feet, or 21 square feet. One gallon of paint will cover approximately 275 square feet of surface area.

```
7    //CONSTANTS USED IN THE APPLICATION
8    const WINDOW_AREA:int=16;
9    const DOOR_AREA:int=21;
10   const GAL_PER_FT:int=275;
11
```

The six functions for this application are designed as follows.

Function paintJobApp() Design

The class constructor, paintJobApp(), performs two basic tasks. First, it places the number 0 in each of the input text boxes. This helps to ensure the user will understand the expectation of numbers. Second, it constructs a listener event that waits for the user to click ComputeBtn. Once this button is clicked, the algorithm calculate() is called.

```
12
13  function paintJobApp():void {
14      //TASK 1: FILL THE INPUT TEXT BOXES WITH ZEROS
15      Input1.text="0";
16      Input2.text="0";
17      Input3.text="0";
18      Input4.text="0";
19      Input5.text="0";
20
21
22      //TASK 2: LISTEN FOR A MOUSE CLICK EVENT
23      ComputeBtn.addEventListener(MouseEvent.CLICK,calculate);
24
25  }
26
```

Function calculate() Design

The calculate() function performs four tasks:

Task 1: Store the values from the input text fields into the declared variables.

Task 2: Call the function inputIsValid() to test the validity of the user's input.

Task 3: If the input is valid, call the appropriate functions to compute the wall surface area and the door and window surface area. On line 40, compute the number of gallons needed to paint the walls and the ceiling, minus the doors and windows.

Task 4: The final function call to function displayPaintInfo() is made only when the input is valid.

```
27  function calculate(event:MouseEvent):void {
28      //TASK 1: STORE INPUT VARIABLES
29      var Length:Number=Number(Input1.text);
30      var Width:Number=Number(Input2.text);
31      var Height:Number=Number(Input3.text);
32      var doors:Number=Number(Input4.text);
33      var windows:Number=Number(Input5.text);
34
```

```
35    //TASK 2: CHECK VALIDITY OF VARIABLES
36    if (inputIsValid(Length,Width,Height,doors,windows)) {
37        //TASK 3: IF VALID, COMPUTE SURFACE AREAS AND GALLONS NEEDED
38        var wallSurfaceArea:int=computeWallSurface(Length,Height,Width);
39        var door_windowSurface:int=computeDoorWallSurface(doors,windows);
40        var gallons=Math.ceil((wallSurfaceArea-door_windowSurface)/GAL_PER_FT);
41
42        //TASK 4: IF VALID, DISPLAY PERTINENT INFORMATION
43        displayPaintInfo(wallSurfaceArea, door_windowSurface, gallons);
44    }
45 }
46
```

Function inputIsValid() Design

The function inputIsValid() is called by calculate() to test the validity of the input provided by the user. The parameters in this function represent the dimensions of the room and the number of doors and windows. If each condition within the if-else if statement is false, this function will return true, indicating that all input has been entered correctly.

```
47  function inputIsValid(L:Number, W:Number,
48                        H:Number, drs:Number, wnds:Number):Boolean {
49      if (isNaN(L)||isNaN(W)||isNaN(H)) {
50          output1.text="Room dimensions must be numbers.\n";
51          return false;
52      } else if (L <= 0 || W <= 0 || H<= 0) {
53          output1.text="Room dimensions must be greater than zero.\n";
54          return false;
55      } else if (isNaN(drs)|| isNaN(wnds)) {
56          output1.text="The number of windows and doors must be a number.\n";
57          return false;
58      } else if (drs < 0 || wnds< 0) {
59          output1.text="The number of windows and doors cannot be negative.\n";
60          return false;
61      } else {
62          return true;
63      }
64 }
65
```

Function computeWallSurface() Design

This function computes the surface area for the walls and ceiling. The return value is a Number, and the parameter list consists of three variables that have been passed the dimensions of the room.

```
65   function computeWallSurface(Length:Number,Height:Number,Width:Number):Number {
66       return 2* Length * Height + 2 * Width * Height + Length * Width;
67   }
68
```

Function computeDoorWallSurface() Design

This function computes the surface area covered by the doors and windows. The
return value is a Number, and the parameter list consists of two variables indicating the
number of doors and windows in the room.

```
69   function computeDoorWallSurface(doors:Number,windows:Number):Number {
70       return doors * DOOR_AREA + windows * WINDOW_AREA;
71   }
72
```

Function displayPaintInfo() Design

The function displayPaintInfo() is a void function that simply displays the results in
a text field on the screen. The use of an if statement allows the function to identify an
input error when the computed surface area is less than or equal to zero.

```
73   function displayPaintInfo(wallArea:Number, dr_wndArea:Number,
74                            gallons:Number):void {
75       if (wallArea-dr_wndArea>0) {
76           output1.text="Wall surface area minus any doors and windows is ";
77           output1.appendText(String(wallArea - dr_wndArea));
78           output1.appendText(" feet.  \n\t\tGallons needed: ");
79           output1.appendText(String(gallons));
80       } else {
81           output1.text="There is an error in your input. The computed ";
82           output1.appendText("surface area is less than or equal to zero.");
83       }
84   }
```

▓ 8.4 Arrays as Reference Parameters

Arrays behave differently from non-list-type variables when it comes to passing them
as arguments to a function.

In AS3, variables, other than arrays, are always passed by value. The value of a
typical argument variable is passed to the function and assigned to the target parameter variable. The movement of this type of passed argument occurs in only one
direction—to the function. This action preserves the integrity of the argument variable. The sole reason for this restriction is that arguments and value parameters are
separate memory locations, so any changes made to the parameter variables will not
affect the original argument variables.

Because arrays can be quite large, it would not be practical to have them passed in the same manner as a typical variable argument. Doing so would require the allocation of a large amount of memory for a value parameter. In addition to this inefficiency, an extensive copy would be required once a parameter "receives" the argument value. For this reason, arrays are not passed by value, but rather by **reference**. A reference parameter in a function is simply an **alias** for the actual variable argument. When a reference parameter is used in a function, a value is not received by the calling function; rather, its location, or address, in memory is provided. By passing the memory address of the array, the entire array can be accessed without having to allocate many cells of new memory and copy the array contents. Thus arrays are said to be **passed by reference** rather than by value.

When array parameters are used, any change of values in the function produces a corresponding change of values in the original array. This characteristic should prompt the programmer to exercise caution when working with these parameters. Oftentimes, out of convenience, arrays are declared globally within a package. This convention makes them available to all functions within the package; thus passing them as parameters is unnecessary and added work. However, the notion of referencing an array should be understood. The next two examples look at referencing.

Example 1

```
1   public class exampleApp extends MovieClip {
2
3       function exampleApp():void {
4           var listArr:Array = new Array(1,2,3);
5           changeArr1(listArr);
6           trace(listArr.toString());
7       }
8
9       function changeArr1(listArr:Array):void {
10          listArr[0] += 1;
11          listArr[1] += 1;
12          listArr[2] += 1;
13      }
14  }
15 }
```

Evaluation

This complete program illustrates the behavior of an array passed by reference.

Line 4: The array listArr containing three cells is created and initialized to 1, 2, and 3.

Line 5: The function changeArr1 is called and the argument passed is the array listArr.

Line 9: The reference parameter is listArr.

Lines 10–12: The value in each cell of the array is incremented by one.

Line 6: Upon returning from the function, the values in the array are displayed.

The output produced by this code is

2,3,4

Example 2

```
1    public class exampleApp extends MovieClip {
2
3        function exampleApp():void {
4            var listArr:Array = new Array(1,2,3);
5            changeArr2(listArr);
6            trace(listArr.toString());
7        }
8        function changeArr2(Arr:Array):void {
9            Arr[0] += 1;
10           Arr[1] += 1;
11           Arr[2] += 1;
12       }
13   }
14 }
```

Evaluation

This example is similar to the previous example with one exception—the parameter in the function changeArr() is named Arr. This illustrates the notion of aliasing. The reference parameter Arr is merely an alias for the actual array variable—listArr.

The output produced by this code is exactly the same as the previous example:

2,3,4

8.5 Case Study 2: Deck of Cards Experiment

Problem Analysis and Visual Design

This case study is not an application, but rather an examination of the mechanisms needed when working with a deck of cards to simulate a card game. Quite often, card game programs must be able to provide functionality for shuffling the contents of a deck of cards, dealing a card, flipping a dealt card over, and identifying its rank and suit.

A clicked card is flipped.
Its rank and suit are displayed.

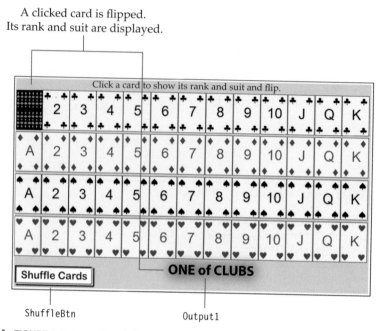

ShuffleBtn   Output1

⎮ FIGURE 8-3 A complete deck of cards displayed in rows and columns on the stage.

The goal of this case study is to experiment with a deck of cards, as shown in Figure 8-3, and to construct a set of functions that will eventually lead to, and simplify, the development of a card game. The notable areas explored in this case study are as follows:

Card representation: All cards are represented by the same MovieClip symbol named CARD. This exported symbol consists of a set of 53 frames; each frame holds one of the 52 cards and the last frame holds an image of the back of the card. Thus frame 1 features the image of an ace of clubs, frame 2 is the image of two of clubs, and so on.

Card properties: Instances of a given card are embodied with properties for storing card information such as card rank, suit, and value.

Deck representation: An array data structure is used to hold a complete deck of 52 cards, or display objects. An additional array data structure is used as an index identifying the location of the cards within the deck. This greatly simplifies development, as we will need to construct a deck only once, and we can control the shuffling and dealing of cards using the index.

Shuffling a deck: The shuffling of an array of cards requires the random rearrangement of the deck array. This program keeps the deck intact while shuffling an index array.

Card Representation

To implement a card game, the first requirement is a deck of cards. This means 52 bitmap images, each of which represents a card, are imported into the Library. The downloadable Flash file of this case study contains the complete set of 52 bitmaps.

In this case study, all cards in the deck are represented by the same MovieClip symbol, CARD. CARD is an export symbol that can be used to generate instances of cards during the execution of the application.

The MovieClip symbol CARD will contain 53 frames, of which the first 52 occupy bitmap images of the cards in the deck; see Figure 8-4. Frame 53, the last frame, is occupied by an image representing the common back of a nonspecific card. This display object will serve for the back of any card. The position of the playhead will indicate which card it is.

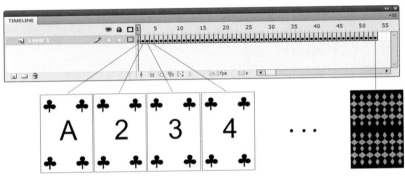

I FIGURE 8-4 Deck of cards represented using a timeline containing 53 frames.

Screen Design

This application is not a game. It simply allows us to explore a representation of cards and the shuffling of a deck, which will require only one frame in the Timeline.

Once the application is launched, 52 cards are generated in sequential order, placed in the deck, and displayed in 4 rows and 13 columns on stage. An interactive button is made available for the user to shuffle the deck. When it is clicked, the cards on display will be repositioned on the stage according to their new locations within the shuffled deck.

As shown in Figure 8-3, the display objects placed directly on the stage are Output1, a dynamic text field, and ShuffleBtn. Output1 will be used to display the rank and suit of a card clicked on stage.

Program Design

Before embarking on the details of the program design phase of this case study, it should be stated that the arrays required to represent our deck of cards will serve our purposes better if they are given a global scope. Much of this reasoning has to do with the simple fact that card games require access to a deck of cards in every aspect of the game. The functions used by this case study are outlined in Table 8-3 and the relationship between the functions is shown in Figure 8-5.

TABLE 8-3 Deck Application Program Functions

Function Name	Details
deckApp()	Parameters: None
	Return type: void
	Description: Performs rudimentary initialization of the experiment. This is the constructor function.
constructDeck()	Parameters: None
	Return type: void
	Description: Fills the data structures representing the deck with cards.
displayDeckGraphics()	Parameters: None
	Return type: void
	Description: Refreshes the entire display of cards.
shuffleDeck()	Parameters: Event
	Return type: void
	Description: Performs the random shuffling of cards in the deck.
cardClicked()	Parameters: Event
	Return type: void
	Description: Identifies the card that has been clicked by the user.
flipCard()	Parameters: Card:CARD
	Return type: String
	Description: Turns a given card over and returns its rank and suit.

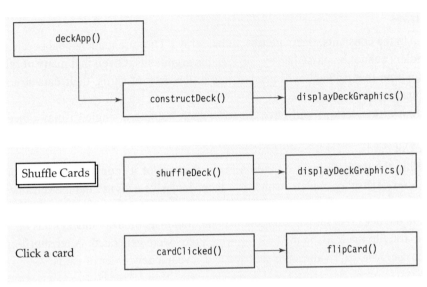

| FIGURE 8-5 The relationship structure of functions in the deck application.

The class package imports two libraries, flash.display.* and flash.events.*. The document class is declared on line 5 as deckApp.

```
1   package {
2       import flash.display.*;
3       import flash.events.*;
4
5       public class deckApp MovieClip {
6
```
⋮
```
113     }
114 }
```

Constants

The five constants employed by this program will be used to describe the rank and suit of a given card, as well as its dimensions for placement on the Stage.

```
7   //CONSTANTS
8   const OFFSET:int=45;
9   const CARDWIDTH:int=80;
10  const CARDBACK:int=54;
11  const SUITS:Array=new Array("CLUBS","DIAMONDS", "SPADES", "HEARTS");
12  const RANKS:Array=new Array("ACE","TWO", "THREE",
13                              "FOUR","FIVE","SIX",
14                              "SEVEN", "EIGHT","NINE",
15                              "TEN", "JACK", "QUEEN", "KING");
```

Global Arrays

In addition to the constants, there are two global arrays. They are made global because event handlers cannot be passed arrays or variable arguments. Given that many of the functions within this package will need access to the deck of cards, their data structures are made global.

The first array, deck[], will have 52 cells, each holding a single display object representing the visual of a card. The second array, deckIndexes[], will store the order of the deck of cards.

Shuffling the deck requires a random rearrangement of its contents. Rather than shuffling a set of display objects, which is a labor-intensive activity, the index values in deckIndexes[] are shuffled instead. These indexes are then used to reference the specific card in the deck. As shown in Figure 8-6, the initial set of array indexes has been assigned to refer to the cards in the order in which they were generated. After shuffling occurs, the deckIndexes[] values are shuffled and reveal a new order of cards.

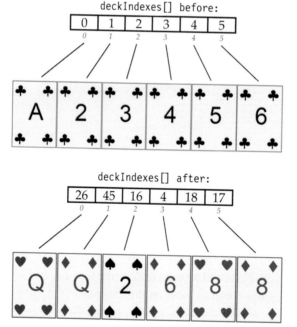

I FIGURE 8-6 The before and after values of a shuffled deck of cards.

```
16  //GLOBAL ARRAYS
17  var deck:Array = new Array();
18  var deckIndexes:Array = new Array();
19
```

The six functions of this case study are designed as follows.

Function deckApp() Design

This class constructor has the essential task of initializing the application upon launch. The first and most important task is to call the necessary function to construct the deck. The second task is simply the registration of an interactive mouse event for the ShuffleBtn so that the user can shuffle the deck at will.

```
20  function deckApp():void {
21     //TASK 1: FUNCTION CALLS TO BUILD THE DECK AND DECK INDEX
22     constructDeck(deck, deckIndexes);
23
24     //TASK 2: REGISTER EVENT FOR BUTTON TO SHUFFLE THE DECK
25     shuffleBtn.addEventListener(MouseEvent.CLICK, shuffleDeck);
26  }
27
```

Function constructDeck() Design

The constructDeck() function creates 52 individual cards and places them in the appropriate deck array. Each card is assigned a rank, suit, and value, and then placed on the Stage. The suit and rank of a given card are based on the fact that every suit contains 13 cards. In anticipation of our use of this application to eventually construct a blackjack game, card ranks range from 1 through 13, while a card's value can range from 1 through 10. The jack, queen, and king will each have a value of 10.

```
28  function constructDeck():void {
29     var cardObj:Card;
30     for (var i:uint = 0; i < 52; i++) {
31        //TASK 1: CREATE THE CARD DISPLAY OBJECT AND SET ITS SCALE
32        cardObj=new CARD;
33        cardObj.scaleX=cardObj.scaleY=.4;
34
35        //TASK 2: ASSIGN THE SUIT, VALUE, AND RANK
36        cardObj.Suit=SUITS[Math.floor(i/13)];
37        cardObj.Value=i%13+1;
38        cardObj.Rank = RANKS[cardObj.Value-1];
39        if (cardObj.Value>10) {
40           cardObj.Value=10;
41        }
42        //TASK 3: ALL CARDS ARE INITIALLY PLACED FACE UP
43        cardObj.faceUp=true;
44
45        //TASK 4: ASSIGN THE FRAME THAT HOLDS THE FACE IMAGE
46        cardObj.frameIndex=i+1;
47        cardObj.gotoAndStop(i+1);
48
49        //TASK 5: REGISTER AN EVENT LISTENER FOR THE CARD
50        cardObj.addEventListener(MouseEvent.CLICK,cardClicked);
51
```

```
52        //TASK 6: ADD CARD TO BOTH ARRAYS
53        deck.push(cardObj);
54        deckIndexes.push(i);
55
56        //TASK 7: ADD THE DISPLAY OBJECT TO THE STAGE
57        addChild(cardObj);
58      }
59      //TASK 8: CALL FUNCTION TO DISPLAY CARDS IN A READABLE FORMAT
60      displayDeckGraphics();
61  }
62
```

Function displayDeckGraphics() Design

The displayDeckGraphics() function is a void function that fills the Stage with four rows of cards. After a deck shuffle has been performed, this function is used to refresh the Stage with newly positioned cards that reveal the random location of each card in the deck. Rows hold 13 cards (line 71). Columns are offset so as not to push the first column too close to the left wall of the stage (line 72).

```
63  function displayDeckGraphics():void {
64      var row:uint=1;
65      var col:Number=0;
66      var cardIndex:uint;
67      for (var i:Number=0; i < 52; i++) {
68          //TASK 1: SELECT THE CARD IN THE INDEXED ARRAY
69          cardIndex=deckIndexes[i];
70          //TASK 2: COMPUTE AND ASSIGN THE ROW AND COLUMN POSITION
71          row=Math.floor(i/13)*120+2*OFFSET;
72          col=i%13*CARDWIDTH+OFFSET;
73          deck[cardIndex].y=row;
74          deck[cardIndex].x=col;
75          //TASK 3: MAINTAIN THE FLIPPED STATUS OF THE CARD
76          if (deck[cardIndex].faceUp) {
77              deck[cardIndex].gotoAndStop(deck[cardIndex].frameIndex);
78          }
79      }
80  }
81
```

Function shuffleDeck() Design

The shuffleDeck() function is an event handler that responds to the user clicking the shuffle button on the Stage. The objective of this function is to randomize the elements in the indexed array while leaving the deck array intact. Once a complete shuffle occurs, the deck of cards is redisplayed (line 92).

Randomizing the array deckIndexes is done using a loop. The instructions in the loop perform the following steps:

> Lines 85–86: Two random numbers, representing card indexes between 0 and 51, are computed.
>
> Lines 87–89: The two card indexes are swapped within the array.

```
82  function shuffleDeck(event:MouseEvent):void {
83      //TASK 1: SHUFFLE THE INDEXES
84      for (var swap:uint=0; swap < 52; swap++) {
85          var cardI1:uint=Math.floor(Math.random()*52);
86          var cardI2:uint=Math.floor(Math.random()*52);
87          var hold:uint=deckIndexes[cardI1];
88          deckIndexes[cardI1]=deckIndexes[cardI2];
89          deckIndexes[cardI2]=hold;
90      }
91      //TASK 2: REFRESH THE CARDS ON DISPLAY
92      displayDeckGraphics(deck, deckIndexes);
93  }
94
```

Function cardClicked() Design

The cardClicked() function is an event handler that responds to one of the cards being clicked. Its objective is to simply identify the card the user selected and pass it to the function flipCard, which will then flip the card. A specific card that was clicked can be identified using the mechanism event.currentTarget (line 97). The String value returned by the function flipCard() is displayed in the dynamic text field Output1.

```
95   function cardClicked(event:MouseEvent):void {
96       //TASK 1: IDENTIFY THE CARD THAT WAS CLICKED
97       var theCard = (event.currentTarget);
98
99       //TASK 2: CALL A FUNCTION TO FLIP THIS CARD
100      Output1.text = flipCard(theCard);
101  }
102
```

Function flipCard() Design

This function returns a String value. It receives a card display object, the sole parameter, and flips it either face up or face down depending on its current state. Flipping a card requires a gotoAndStop() MovieClip operation to move and hold the Timeline playhead for a given card on a frame that reveals either the card's face (line 108) or the back of the card (line 105).

The card Rank and Suit are concatenated into a string and returned.

```
103  function flipCard(theCard:CARD):String {
104      if (theCard.faceUp) {
105          theCard.gotoAndStop(CARDBACK);
106          theCard.faceUp=false;
107      } else {
108          theCard.gotoAndStop(theCard.frameIndex);
109          theCard.faceUp=true;
110      }
111      return theCard.Rank + " of " + theCard.Suit;
112  }
```

■ 8.6 Case Study 3: Game of Blackjack

Problem Analysis and Visual Design

The game of blackjack is a popular casino card game that is also known as twenty-one. In this case study, we will simplify the game by ignoring betting and any except the simplest of casino rules. Our goal is to examine the main characteristics and implement the basic rules of the game itself.

To start the game, the player requests cards to be dealt by clicking the Deal button on the Stage. Two cards are then dealt to both the player and the dealer. The dealer receives the first card face down, so as to be hidden from the player, and the second face up. To win the game, the player must get cards whose values sum as close to a total of 21 as possible, but do not exceed 21, and not less than the value of the dealer's hand. If the player exceeds 21, he or she immediately loses. By clicking the Hit button on the Stage, the player can add cards to his or her hand.

The player goes first and signals she is done adding cards to her hand by clicking the Stay button. At this point the player ends her turn, and the dealer then takes his turn by adding extra cards to his hand to get as close to 21 as possible. If the sum of the dealer's cards exceeds 21, the player wins. If the player and the dealer tie, the hand is a draw.

Figure 8-7 shows a typical game using a single layout screen. The dealer's hand is located on the top. The player's hand is placed on the lower part of the table. Visually, this game is constructed using a single frame in the Timeline. A total of five display objects are placed directly in frame 1 of this layout screen. They are outlined in Table 8-4 and shown in Figures 8-7 and 8-8. Additional graphics, sounds, and special animated effects can be added for game enhancement.

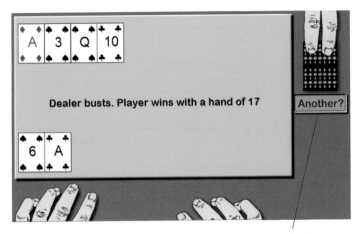

AnotherBtn
(Initiates a new game)

FIGURE 8-7 The game of blackjack.

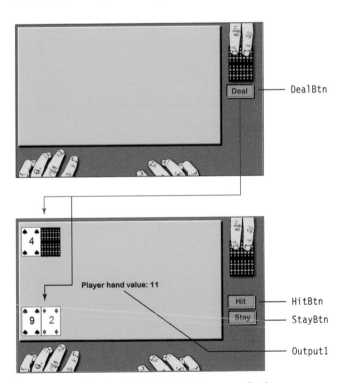

FIGURE 8-8 The visuals of the blackjack game application.

TABLE 8-4 Visual Objects Used on the Layout Screen

Visual Object Name	Type of Object	Description of the Object
DealBtn	Button	Activates a new game by dealing the first cards
HitBtn	Button	Allows the player to add cards to his or her hand
StayBtn	Button	Signals the player is done adding cards. Forces the dealer to take a turn
Output1	Dynamic text box	Displays the total in the player's hand and the result of a game
AnotherGameBtn	Button	Clears the table and prepares for a new game

Program Design

The implementation of the blackjack game requires a continuation of the array structures and functionality, listed in Table 8-5 and illustrated in Figure 8-9, for storing and shuffling the deck of cards. In addition, array structures are used to store the player's and dealer's hands.

TABLE 8-5 Blackjack Program Functions

Function Name	Description
blackjackApp()	Parameters: None
	Return type: void
	Description: Performs rudimentary game functions.
constructDeck()	Parameters: None
	Return type: void
	Description: Fills the data structures representing the deck with cards.
initializeGame()	Parameters: None
	Return type: void
	Description: Starts a new game of blackjack. This function is called before every game is played.
shuffleDeck()	Parameters: None
	Return type: void
	Description: Performs the random shuffling of cards in the deck.

TABLE 8-5 Blackjack Program Functions (continued)

Function Name	Description
`dealInitialHands()`	Parameters: `MouseEvent` Return type: `void` Description: Deals two cards to the dealer and two cards to the player.
`dealCard()`	Parameters: `who:uint` Identifies who is to be dealt a card, either the player or dealer. `facing:uint` Identifies whether the card is facing up or down. Return type: `void` Description: Deals one card from the top of the deck to either the player or the dealer.
`activateHit()`	Parameters: `MouseEvent` Return type: `void` Description: Adds a card from the deck to the player's hand.
`activateStay()`	Parameters: `MouseEvent` Return type: `void` Description: Activates the player's stay and forces the dealer to take a turn to determine the winner.
`callWinner()`	Parameters: None Return type: `void` Description: Compares the hands of the player and dealer and determines the winner.
`computeHandValue()`	Parameters: `hand:Array` Represents either the player or dealer hand. Return type: `uint` Description: Given a hand of cards, computes the total value of that hand.
`anotherGame()`	Parameters: `MouseEvent` Return type: `void` Description: Initiates a new game of blackjack.

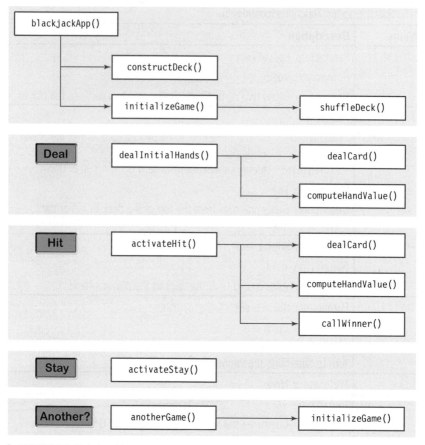

| FIGURE 8-9 Relationship structure of functions of the blackjack game.

The ActionScript 3.0 code is stored in the file blackjackApp.as. The required class package and import library classes are placed at the beginning of the file. The flash. display library class is the base class needed for the main function blackjackApp(), and the flash.events library class is necessary for all button interactivity. The last two lines of the ActionScript file contain closing curly brackets to close the document class and the package.

```
1   package {
2
3       import flash.display.*;
4       import flash.events.*;
5
6       public class blackjackApp extends MovieClip {
⋮
225     }
226 }
```

The constants for this game are listed here:

```
8   //GAME CONSTANTS
9   const OFFSET:uint=60;      //STAGE BUFFER
10  const CARDWIDTH:int=80;    //WIDTH OF ALL CARDS
11  const CARDBACK:int=54;     //FRAME HOLDING CARDBACK
12  const PLAYER:uint=1;       //IDENTIFIES THE PLAYER
13  const DEALER:uint=0;       //IDENTIFIES THE DEALER
14  const FACEUP:uint=1;       //CODE FOR FACE UP
15  const FACEDOWN:uint=1;     //CODE FOR FACE DOWN
16
17  //GLOBAL ARRAYS
18  var deck:Array = new Array();         //DECK OF CARDS
19  var deckIndexes:Array = new Array();  //INDEXES TO THE CARDS
20  var playerHand:Array = new Array();   //HOLDS THE PLAYER HAND
21  var dealerHand:Array = new Array();   //HOLDS THE DEALER HAND
22
```

The functions used in the application are designed and coded as follows.

Function blackjackApp() Design

The main function, blackjackApp(), is the class constructor function. This function, which is initiated once the application is executed, performs all rudimentary one-time game functions.

```
23  function blackjackApp():void {
24      //TASK 1: CALL FUNCTION TO BUILD THE DECK OF CARDS
25      constructDeck();
26
27      //TASK 2: PLAY THE GAME
28      initializeGame();
29      DealBtn.addEventListener(MouseEvent.CLICK, dealInitialHands);
30      HitBtn.addEventListener(MouseEvent.CLICK, activateHit);
31      StayBtn.addEventListener(MouseEvent.CLICK, activateStay);
32      AnotherGameBtn.addEventListener(MouseEvent.CLICK, anotherGame);
33  }
34
```

Function constructDeck() Design

This function is similar to the constructDeck() function in Case Study 2, with two exceptions:

1. The card's face value is the only requirement for blackjack. Therefore, this function is not designed to store the card's rank and suit.

2. Array parameters representing the deck of cards are not required and, therefore, are not used in this function.

```
35  function constructDeck():void {
36     var cardObj:Card;
37     for (var i:uint=0; i < 52; i++) {
38        //TASK 1: CREATE CARD AND SET ITS SCALE AND LOCATION OFFSTAGE
39        cardObj=new Card;
40        cardObj.scaleX=cardObj.scaleY=.4;
41        cardObj.x=-42;
42
43        //TASK 2: ASSIGN THE VALUE OF THE CARD
44        cardObj.faceValue=i%13+1;
45        if (cardObj.faceValue>10) {
46           cardObj.faceValue=10;
47        }
48        //TASK 3: ASSIGN THE FRAME THAT HOLDS THE FACE IMAGE
49        //         TURN CARD FACE DOWN
50        cardObj.frameIndex=i+1;
51        cardObj.gotoAndStop(54);
52
53        //TASK 4: ADD CARD TO THE DECK ARRAY
54        deck.push(cardObj);
55        deckIndexes.push(i+1);
56
57        //TASK 5: ADD THE DISPLAY OBJECT TO THE STAGE
58        addChild(cardObj);
59     }
60  }
61
```

Function initializeGame() Design

The initializeGame() function is divided into five tasks, all with the objective of
beginning a fresh game of blackjack. The table is cleared of cards, cards are moved
off screen, the deck is shuffled, hands are emptied, and the player is shown only the
buttons that are relevant for a new game.

```
62  function initializeGame():void {
63     //TASK 1: SET THE GAME DISPLAY OUTPUT TO EMPTY
64     Output.text="";
65
66     //TASK 2: MOVE ALL CARDS PREVIOUSLY DEALT OFF THE MAT
67     for (var i:uint=0; i < 52; i++) {
68        deck[i].x=-42;
69        deck[i].gotoAndStop(54);
70     }
71     //TASK 3: CALL TO SHUFFLE THE DECK
72     shuffleDeck();
73
74     //TASK 4: CLEAR OUT THE PLAYER AND DEALER HANDS FOR A FRESH GAME
75     playerHand=[];
```

```
76      dealerHand=[];
77
78      //TASK 5: SET UP VISIBILITY FOR BUTTONS; DEAL BUTTON IS USED FIRST
79      DealBtn.visible=true;
80      HitBtn.visible=false;
81      StayBtn.visible=false;
82      AnotherGameBtn.visible=false;
83  }
84
```

Function shuffleDeck() Design

The shuffleDeck() function is subdivided into the two tasks shown here.

```
85  function shuffleDeck():void {
86      //TASK 1: START WITH A FRESH DECK; INITIALIZE THE DECK INDEXES
87      deckIndexes=[];
88      for (var i:uint=0; i < 52; i++) {
89          deckIndexes.push(i);
90      }
91
92      //TASK 2: SHUFFLE THE INDEXES
93      for (var swap:uint=0; swap < 52; swap++) {
94          var cardI1:uint=Math.floor(Math.random()*52);
95          var cardI2:uint=Math.floor(Math.random()*52);
96          var hold:uint=deckIndexes[cardI1];
97          deckIndexes[cardI1]=deckIndexes[cardI2];
98          deckIndexes[cardI2]=hold;
99      }
100 }
101
```

Function dealInitialHands() Design

The dealInitialHands() function calls on the function dealCard() to deal cards to both the player and the dealer. In addition to showing the total value of the player's cards, the buttons on the Stage are hidden or shown, depending on the next stage of the game.

```
102 function dealInitialHands(event:MouseEvent):void {
103     //TASK 1: DEAL TWO CARDS TO PLAYER AND DEALER
104     dealCard(PLAYER, FACEUP);
105     dealCard(PLAYER, FACEUP);
106     dealCard(DEALER, FACEUP);
107     dealCard(DEALER, FACEDOWN);
108
109     //TASK 2: SHOW PLAYER'S TOTAL VALUE; CALL A WINNER IF PLAYER HITS 21
110     Output.text="Player hand value: "+String(computeHandValue(playerHand));
111     if (computeHandValue(playerHand)==21) {
112         callWinner();
```

```
113    } else {
114    //TASK 3: HIDE DEAL BUTTON AND SHOW THE HIT AND STAY BUTTONS
115        DealBtn.visible=false;
116        StayBtn.visible=true;
117        HitBtn.visible=true;
118    }
119 }
120
```

Function dealCard() Design

```
121 function dealCard(who:uint, facing:uint):void {
122    //TASK 1: POP THE TOP CARD OFF THE DECK OF INDEXES
123    var cardIndex:int=deckIndexes.pop();
124
125    //TASK 2: IF IT'S THE PLAYER, MOVE CARD TO THE LOWER PART OF THE MAT,
126    //               FLIP IT FACE UP, AND ADD IT TO THE PLAYER HAND
127    if (who==PLAYER) {
128        deck[cardIndex].x=deck[cardIndex].width*playerHand.length+OFFSET;
129        deck[cardIndex].y=400;
130        deck[cardIndex].gotoAndStop(deck[cardIndex].frameIndex);
131        playerHand.push(cardIndex);
132    } else {
133    //TASK 3: IF IT'S THE DEALER, MOVE CARD TO THE HIGHER PART OF THE MAT,
134    //               FLIP FACE UP OR FACE DOWN, AND ADD IT TO THE DEALER HAND
135        deck[cardIndex].x=deck[cardIndex].width*dealerHand.length+OFFSET;
136        deck[cardIndex].y=87;
137        if (facing==FACEUP) {
138            deck[cardIndex].gotoAndStop(deck[cardIndex].frameIndex);
139        }
140        dealerHand.push(cardIndex);
141    }
142 }
143
```

Function activateHit() Design

Each time the HitBtn is clicked by the player, the activateHit() function is called to add a card to the player's hand. The game is over if the total value of the player's hand has exceeded 21.

```
144 function activateHit(event:MouseEvent):void {
145    //TASK 1: DEAL A CARD FOR PLAYER
146    dealCard(PLAYER, FACEUP);
147    var playerValue:uint=computeHandValue(playerHand);
148    Output.text="Player hand value: "+String(playerValue);
149
150    //TASK 2: CHECK IF BUSTED OR A 21.  IMMEDIATE LOSE OR WIN
151    if (playerValue>21) {
```

```
152        StayBtn.visible=false;
153        HitBtn.visible=false;
154        callWinner();
155    } else if (playerValue == 21) {
156        callWinner();
157    }
158 }
159
```

Function activateStay() Design

The activateStay() function is initiated once the player clicks the button labeled "Stay" to end his or her turn. This function executes the tasks required in the dealer taking a turn.

```
160 function activateStay(event:MouseEvent):void {
161    //TASK 1: HIDE THE HIT AND STAY BUTTONS AND EVENT LISTENERS
162    HitBtn.visible=false;
163    StayBtn.visible=false;
164
165    //TASK 2: TURN OVER THE SECOND CARD IN DEALER's HAND
166    var cardIndex:uint=dealerHand[1];
167    deck[cardIndex].gotoAndStop(deck[cardIndex].frameIndex);
168
169    //TASK 3: IF DEALER HAS LESS THAN 16, ADD A CARD TO THE HAND
170    while (computeHandValue(dealerHand) < 16){
171        dealCard(DEALER, FACEUP);
172
173    }//TASK 4: DETERMINE THE WINNER
174    callWinner();
175 }
176
```

Function callWinner() Design

The callWinner() function utilizes the computeHandValue() function to compute the value for any hand of cards.

```
177 function callWinner():void {
178    //TASK 1: COMPUTE THE VALUE OF THE PLAYER AND DEALER HANDS
179    var playerValue=computeHandValue(playerHand);
180    var dealerValue=computeHandValue(dealerHand);
181
182    //TASK 2: DETERMINE THE WINNER AND DISPLAY THE RESULTS
183    if (playerValue==21) {
184        Output.text="Player hits 21.  You win!";
185    } else if (playerValue>21) {
186        Output.text="You lose. Player busts with a hand of " + playerValue;
187    } else if (dealerValue > 21) {
188        Output.text="Dealer busts. Player wins with a hand of " + playerValue;
```

```
189      } else if (playerValue == dealerValue) {
190         Output.text="You've tied with the dealer.";
191      } else if (playerValue > dealerValue) {
192         Output.text="Player wins with a hand of " + playerValue;
193      } else {
194         Output.text="You lose.  Dealer has a hand value of " + dealerValue;
195      }
196
197      //TASK 3: MAKE VISIBLE THE BUTTON FOR PLAYING ANOTHER GAME
198      AnotherGameBtn.visible=true;
199 }
200
```

Function computeHandValue() Design

The function computeHandValue() receives a hand of cards as an argument. It then computes the total value of the cards and returns that value as an unsigned integer.

```
201 function computeHandValue(hand:Array):uint {
202    var handValue:uint=0;    //INITIALIZE HAND TO ZERO
203    var noAces:Boolean=true; //ASSUME THERE ARE NO ACES
204
205    //TASK 1: EXAMINE EACH CARD AND SUM THE VALUE
206    for (var i:uint=0; i < hand.length; i++) {
207       var cardIndex:uint=hand[i];
208       var cardValue:uint=deck[cardIndex].faceValue;
209       handValue+=cardValue;
210       if (cardValue==1) {
211          noAces=false;
212       }
213    }
214
215    //TASK 2: IF AN ACE WAS FOUND, CHOOSE THE 1 OR 11 VALUE TO ADD
216    if (!noAces && handValue+10<=21) {
217       handValue+=10;
218    }
219    return handValue;
220 }
221
```

Function anotherGame() Design

The anotherGame() function has the sole task of calling initializeGame(), which will begin a new game of blackjack.

```
222 function anotherGame(event:MouseEvent):void {
223    initializeGame();
224 }
```

■ 8.7 Recursion

Only a few problems are likely to be solved using the concept of recursion, which is discussed briefly in this section. In special circumstances, however, recursion can sometimes allow programmers to express complicated programs in a very simple fashion. This leads to some elegant and simple, yet powerful programs. The importance of this technique is the ease in translating a complicated problem into something minimal.

Before deciding on recursion as a mechanism for solving a problem, this benefit should be carefully weighed against its many potential drawbacks, such as large memory consumption and possibly slow execution. These disadvantages will be further discussed following the examples in this section.

A function is **recursive** if it calls itself. Recursive problems are solved by having a subtask call itself as part of the solution. Recursion is a phenomenon that we often use in everyday life, but perhaps have not noticed.

Examine the image in Figure 8-10. What we see is a man standing next to a portrait of a man standing next to a portrait and so on, until the portraits containing portraits become too small to be seen.

| FIGURE 8-10 Recursive portrait.

All recursive problems are defined using two elements:

• A recursive element in which the function calls itself.

• One or more primitive states. All recursive problems must terminate at some point; this point of termination is often referred to as a primitive state.

Many mathematical problems use recursion in their definitions. Consider the definition of $n!$ (n factorial) for a positive nonzero integer n.

Recursive element: $n! = n * (n - 1)!$ when n is greater than 1.

Primitive state: $n = 1$ when n is 1.

Therefore $5! = 5 * 4 * 3 * 2 * 1$. This can also be written as

$$5! = 5 * 4! = 5 * 4 * 3! = 5 * 4 * 3 * 2! = 5 * 4 * 3 * 2 * 1! = 5 * 4 * 3 * 2 * 1$$

Each recursive term, such as 4!, 3!, and 2!, was defined by using the previous term or terms. Once the primitive state has been encountered, the end of the recursion is met. At this point, the steps are reversed for returning values, as shown in Figure 8-11.

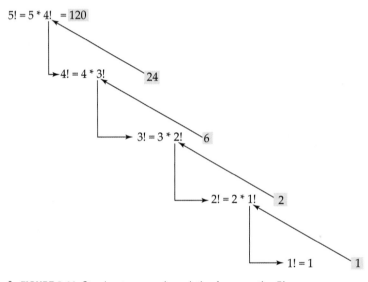

| FIGURE 8-11 Step-by-step recursive solution for computing 5!.

Consider the ActionScript recursive function for computing $n!$.

```
1   function factorial(n:Number):Number {
2       if (n == 1) {
3           return 1;
4       } else {
5           return n * factorial(n-1);
6   }
```

In this function, the condition on line 2 checks for the primitive state. Once the primitive state is encountered, the function returns a 1 and terminates the recursion. Line 5 contains the recursive element, which is executed when the primitive state is not found. Once the primitive state has been reached, the return assignments are made in reverse.

This process, which is triggered when the function call `trace(factorial(5))` is executed, is illustrated in Figure 8-12.

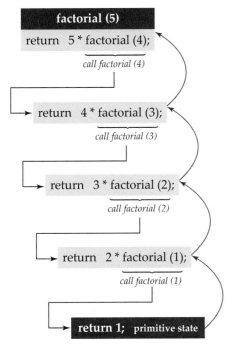

| FIGURE 8-12 The recursive process for the function call `factorial(5)`.

The Drawbacks and Benefits of Recursion   Many recursive functions can be written using loop control structures. For example, the factorial recursive function could have been written without the use of recursion as follows:

```
1  function factorial(n:Number):Number {
2     var value:int; = 1;
3     for (var i:Number=1; i <= n; i++) {
4        value *= i;
5     }
6     return value;
7  }
```

In principle, most recursive functions can be rewritten in a nonrecursive manner. The difference is that in many cases, a recursive process requires more time and memory resources.

Simplicity, brevity, and elegance are the three beneficial traits often associated with a recursive algorithm. On the downside are two additional characteristics often associated with recursive algorithms: memory hog and slow. Recursion generally requires more memory and processor time than equivalent nonrecursive iteration. In fact, recursion should never be used if a solution to a problem is easier to obtain using nonrecursive methods. A loop structure will usually require less execution time and use memory more efficiently, as illustrated in the following example.

Example

The Fibonacci sequence begins with the two terms 1 and 1. The third term is computed as the sum of terms 1 and 2. The fourth term is computed as the sum of terms 2 and 3. Thus each term in the Fibonacci sequence is computed as the sum of the previous two.

Computing the *n*th term in the sequence is a simple recursive process.

Recursive element: `fibonacci(n)` = `fibonacci(n-1)` + `fibonacci(n-2)`, when n is greater than 2

Primitive state: `fibonacci(n)` = 1, when n is either the first or second term, 1 or 2

Consider the recursive function for computing `fibonacci(n)`:

```
1   function fibonacci (n:Number):Number {
2       if (n == 1 || n == 2) {
3           return 1;
4       } else {
5           return  fibonacci (n-1) + fibonacci (n-2);
6   }
```

This is a simple solution to evaluate. Both the primitive state and the recursive element are easily constructed. However, the larger the term n, the more memory will be consumed. This can be seen on line 5, which is actually two recursive calls. Recursion in this case is a highly inefficient choice.

Now consider the nonrecursive function for computing `fibonacci(n)`:

```
1   function fibonacci(n:Number):Number {
2       var f1:int; = 1;
3       var f2:int; = 1;
4       if (n ==1 || n == 2) {
5           return 1;
6       } else {
7           for (var i:=3; i <= n; i++) {
8               var fn = f1 + f2;
9               f1 = fn;
10              f2 = f1;
11          }
12      return fn;
13  }
```

This solution is not nearly as elegant as the recursive one, but it is more efficient. Any two previous terms are stored using the variables f1 and f2. The loop structure on lines 7–11 continually adds the previous two terms to build the next term. Once a new term is computed, the previous terms are shifted.

8.8 Case Study 4: A Recursive Fractal

Problem and Analysis

This case study uses recursion to draw a well-known and interesting fractal pattern known as the C-curve. A fractal is a geometric pattern that can be subdivided into many smaller imitations, called self-similar copies, of the larger pattern. Thus, if you enlarge any small portion of the fractal, it will have the same structure as the larger complete work. Figure 8-13 shows the construction of the C-curve at different levels of elaboration. Mathematical fractals, such as the C-curve, typically have simple recursive definitions.

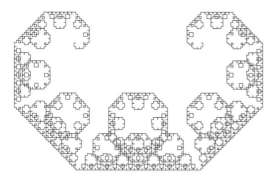

| FIGURE 8-13 The C-curve fractal.

Computer-generated objects that depict elements commonly found in nature are often reproduced using fractals. This approach reflects the fact that elements such as rivers, trees, coastlines, clouds, snowflakes, and so on, have self-similar characteristics that approximate fractals.

This case study will not use the Timeline, nor will it rely on display objects built in Flash. Because no user interactions will occur, the event system will not be needed.

How the C-Curve Is Built

The construction of the C-curve is illustrated at four levels in Figure 8-14. This fractal starts with a straight line drawn from the point (X1, Y1) to the point (X2, Y2). This basic line will occur at the primitive state. This primitive state refers to level 0 of the fractal.

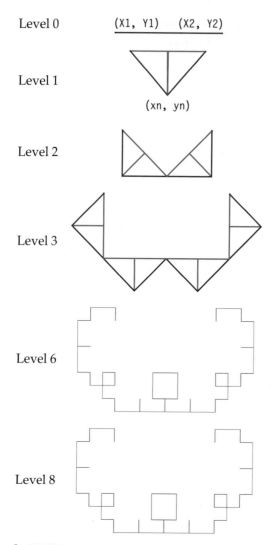

Level 0   (X1, Y1)   (X2, Y2)

Level 1

(xn, yn)

Level 2

Level 3

Level 6

Level 8

I FIGURE 8-14 Levels of recursion in the C-curve.

At the first level of the fractal, an isosceles right triangle is built using the line at level 0 as its hypotenuse. The line at level 0 is then replaced by the other two sides of this triangle. Line 1 is drawn from the point (X1, Y1) to the point (xn, yn). Line 2 is drawn between points (xn, yn) and (X2, Y2).

The point at (xn, yn) can be computed as follows:

```
xn = (X1 + X2)/2 + (Y1 - Y2)/2
yn = (X2 - X1)/2 + (Y1 + Y2)/2
```

At the second level, the two new lines are used to form the foundation for another right-angled isosceles triangle. At this level, the two lines constructed at level 1 are replaced by the other two sides of their respective triangle.

At the next level, each straight line in the curve is again replaced by the other two sides of a right-angled isosceles triangle.

After each subsequent level, the curve consists of $2n$ line segments, where n represents the level. Each line drawn gets smaller and smaller than the original line.

The recursive definition for constructing the C-curve fractal is as follows:

Primitive state: Level = 0   Draw a line from (X1, Y1) to (X2, Y2)

Recursive element: Level > 0   cCurve(X1, Y1, xn, yn, Level - 1);

                                   cCurve(xn, yn, X2, Y2, Level - 1);

Program Design

The ActionScript code for this application consists of two functions. The class constructor, pattern(), makes the initial call to the recursive function cCurve(). The pattern contains 12 levels of construction. Lines 18–21 draw the simple line from point (X1, Y1) to point (X2, Y2) when the primitive state is reached for level 0.

The recursive element of the function occurs in lines 23–26. The point (xn, yn) of the isosceles triangle is computed and the function calls itself to construct these lines.

```
1   package {
2       import flash.display.*;
3
4
5       public class pattern extends MovieClip {
6           const COLOR:int=0x0000FF;
7
8           function pattern():void {
9               var X1:int=200;
10              var Y1:int=200;
11              var X2:int=600;
12              var Y2:int=200;
13              var level:int=12;
14              cCurve(X1, Y1, X2, Y2, level);
15          }
16
17          function cCurve(X1:int, Y1:int, X2:int, Y2:int, level:int):void {
18              if (level==0) {
19                  graphics.moveTo(X1,Y1);
20                  graphics.lineStyle(2, COLOR);
21                  graphics.lineTo(X2, Y2);
22              } else {
```

```
23              var xn:int = (X1 + X2)/2 + (Y1 - Y2)/ 2;
24              var yn:int = (X2 - X1) / 2 + (Y1 + Y2)/2;
25              cCurve(X1, Y1, xn, yn, level-1);
26              cCurve(xn, yn, X2, Y2, level-1);
27          }
28        }
29      }
30  }
```

■ Review Questions

1. What is the purpose of a function in an ActionScript 3.0 program?

2. Identify the main parts of a function definition.

3. What is a parameter?

4. Explain the role of reference parameters.

5. Explain the difference between an argument in a function call and a parameter in a function.

6. What is the purpose of a `return` statement in a function?

7. What is a void function?

8. Explain the concept of recursion.

9. Name the two elements found in a recursive function.

10. What is a primitive state?

11. Which of the following are invalid function headings? Explain why they are invalid.

   a. `function func1():num1, num2`

   b. `function func2(num1:void, num2:void)`

   c. `function func3(num1:uint, num2:uint):uint`

   d. `function func4(void)`

   e. `function func5(num1):String`

   f. `function func6(nums:Array):uint`

12. Write an appropriate function heading for the following functions:

   a. Compute the average cost of three concert tickets.

   b. Convert a test (numeric) score to a letter grade.

   c. Compute the hypotenuse of a right triangle given the other two sides of the triangle.

   d. Calculate the smallest score in an array of test scores.

13. Explain the difference between a local variable and a global variable.

Programming Exercises

1. Write a function that returns the minimum value in an array of numbers.

2. Write a function that removes the maximum value in an array of numbers.

3. Write a program that uses a function with an iterative structure, such as a `for` loop, to generate a Fibonacci term.

   The first two terms in the sequence are 1 and 1. The third term is computed by adding the first and second terms. The fourth term is computed by adding the second and third terms. Each term can be computed by adding the two subsequent terms in the sequence.

   This sequence is defined as follows:

   $$F_0 = 1$$
   $$F_1 = 1$$
   $$F_2 = 1$$
   $$F_n = F_{n-1} + F_{n-2}, \text{ for } n > 1$$

   Also write a program that uses a recursive function to generate a term. Time how long it takes each of the programs to run. Why does the recursive function take so long?

4. Create an online quiz application, such as the one shown in Figure 8-15, on any topic that interests you. This application should ask the user at least five multiple-choice questions constructed by data from an XML file with a tag structure as follows:

   ```
   <question>What is the most populous state in the United States?</ques-
   tion>
   <answers>
      <answer>Texas</answer>
      <answer>New York</answer>
      <answer>Arkansas</answer>
      <answer>California</answer>
   </answers>
   <correct>California has the largest population of all fifty states.</cor-
   rect>
   ```

   Use non-void functions to generate individual text fields for questions and multiple-choice answers. In addition, provide a function that stores the possible answers in an array and randomly shuffles them. In this way, the quiz can be taken several times, with multiple-choice answers appearing in random order.

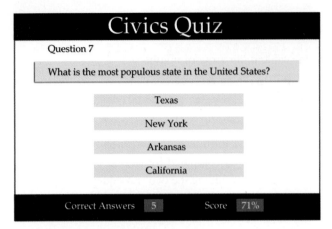

Civics Quiz

Question 7

What is the most populous state in the United States?

Texas

New York

Arkansas

California

Correct Answers   5   Score   71%

FIGURE 8-15 An XML quiz application.

5. Write a program that plays a game of craps.

What is "craps"? From 1900 through the 1940s, craps was a very popular game. It was a tough guy's game. Soldiers, sailors, and leisure gamblers liked the game because dice are small, you can carry them anywhere, and a game can last 10 minutes or all night. Any number of people can play, and the dice (and money) can disappear in a moment if a mortar shell comes arcing over or a police officer suddenly walks past.

By the 1990s, however, craps had nearly disappeared. The majority of gamblers preferred to play slots and video poker; fewer than 4% of gamblers play dice. But an interesting trend has developed in the last few years: Gamblers are rediscovering this dice game.

In a game of craps, a player—the craps shooter—throws a pair of dice. If the first throw (called the come-out roll) adds up to 2, 3, or 12, the player loses. If the come-out roll adds up to 7 or 11, the player wins. Otherwise, the player must continue throwing the dice until he or she matches the come-out roll (which means the player wins the game) or a 7 (which means the player loses).

Guidelines

- Each die can have a random value from 1 to 6. The value of a throw is the added value of the two dice.
- A player can bet any amount from $1 to the amount of money on hand. Players cannot bet more money than they have.
- Create a function to handle a throw of the dice (by calculating the contents of two random dice and reporting the result).
- Give the player a fixed amount to start. The game is over when the player has no money left to bet with.

9 | Classes, Inheritance, and Polymorphism

Introduction

This chapter examines the principles of object-oriented programming (OOP) and how they apply to AS3 applications. All applications in previous chapters of this textbook have been constructed using a single document class. This chapter uses multiple document classes, which are organized into packages and rely heavily on the concept of encapsulation, one of the principles of OOP design. The previous eight chapters of this text have emphasized that objects and classes are inherent in AS3 as well as Flash multimedia elements.

A further understanding of classes and objects is essential to developing object-oriented programs that require multiple document classes. This means that each class will be packaged in a separate ActionScript 3.0 document. Multiple-class documents in an application are not always required or necessarily advantageous. However, for complex and large applications, the principles of OOP can be used to greatly simplify the tasks of writing, testing, and maintaining programs. In addition, once classes are created, they can be reused by other AS3 applications.

In this chapter, the focus shifts to four central OOP concepts: encapsulation with information hiding, inheritance, composition, and polymorphism.

9.1 Class Terminology and Implementation

OOP is a programming methodology based on objects and classes. The fundamental concept underlying OOP is the encapsulation of characteristics and behaviors into self-contained classes. A class is the blueprint or model that is used to create objects, or rather instances of a class. Every object used in an object-oriented program comes from a class.

To use a common metaphor for OOP, the parent (class) makes the child (object), by providing the attributes and behaviors that form the basis for the child. Although the child objects are created from the parent class, each child object is distinct and is entirely self-contained.

Classes, whether they are built into the language or custom created by the programmer, typically contain two components:

Properties: A set of data attributes assigned to an object.

Behaviors: The set of operations, called **methods** or **member functions**, that the object is capable of performing. For example, the Number class in AS3 contains a set of methods common to all its members, such as toString and toPrecision, which provide programmers with a mechanism for formatting numbers.

9.1.1 Data Abstraction

To completely understand the nature of a class, it is essential to consider **data abstraction**. A class is an **abstraction**, whereas an object is a real entity. For example, a ball MovieClip symbol that exists in the library is merely an abstraction for the real BallObj that is physically seen and interacted with on the Stage. Another good illustration of this principle is the Array class.

An array organizes a collection of data elements in a linear sequence. However, arrays are more than just collections of data elements. In AS3, Array is a class with which we associate a set of functions. The functionality of an Array, in the form of methods, allows programmers to manipulate a given linear data structure. In the segment of code below, the variable arrNum is defined as a member of the Array class and initialized to a sequence of four data elements. On line 2, the method sort() is used to organize the elements in increasing order.

```
1   var arrNum:Array = new Array(2,3,5,4);
2   arrNum.sort ();
```

On an abstract level, we understand the essence of what sort() does, but we do not know the complex details of how it does so. Arrays are easy to understand and use because the operations are easily abstracted. We can use all the functionality provided by the Array class without needing to know the exact set of instructions used to accomplish the task. In this way, data abstraction hides the details that would be irrelevant or distracting. A member function, or method, is an abstraction in that it simplifies a complex task.

Data abstraction can also be defined as the separation of behavior from actual data. The primary benefits of data abstraction are its simplicity, ease of use, and information hiding. Information hiding is discussed in the next section.

9.1.2 Encapsulation: Data Attributes and Behaviors

Encapsulation is simply the idea of packaging the class components of data attributes and behavior in a well-defined programming unit. A class is encapsulated in that it is a collection of data members and related operations that are combined into a distinct building block representing a complete abstract entity. A class in AS3 provides for encapsulation by packaging both data attributes and member functions into a single ActionScript 3.0 document file.

The next two examples illustrate encapsulation.

Example 1 A class representing a car

In this example, a class named Car is structured to represent the basic attributes of a car object to be used in a programmatic animation.

A given car can have many characteristics, so it is important to isolate the attributes that are essential to the applications that will use it. For example, the make, model, and year of a car will be unimportant in animation applications. The Car class in this example will require attributes that focus less on description and more on functionality.

A general set of basic attributes relevant to animation might include the following items:

1. The current velocity of the car
2. The maximum velocity the car can attain
3. The minimum velocity of the car before it is considered stopped
4. The acceleration when the gas pedal is pressed
5. The deceleration when the brake pedal is pressed
6. The turning radius of the car—that is, the angle in which it can turn

In addition to this collection of attributes, a class constructor function will be included in the package to initialize these attributes. Class constructors must be given the same name as the class document. Thus the constructor for this example will be named Car.

Solution

The class Car will be packaged in a separate document class. Because the name of the class is Car, it is a requirement that the AS3 file also be named Car, with an extension of .as. The AS3 file bearing the name Car.as might be coded as shown here.

Car.as

```
1  package {
2      import flash.display.*;
3
4      public class Car extends MovieClip {
5          private var Velocity:Number;
```

```
6        private var maxVelocity:Number;
7        private var minVelocity:Number;
8        private var acceleration:Number;
9        private var brakeAmt:Number;
10       private var turnRadius:Number;
11
12       public function Car () {
13          //TASK: INITIALIZE THE CLASS ATTRIBUTES
14          velocity = 0;
15          maxVelocity = Math.random() * 40 + 40;
16          minVelocity = 2;
17          acceleration = Math.random() * 10;
18          brakeAmt = Math.random() * 10;
19          turnRadius = Math.random() * 90 + 90;
20       }
21    }
22 }
```

Note the use of the keywords `public` and `private`. The term `public` makes a class element available to other documents, while `private` does not. This distinction will be explained later in this chapter.

Example 2 A class representing a village resident

Consider a Flash application in which an interactive village must be populated with individual inhabitants generated in real time. A parent class called `VillageResident` will be used in this example to create child inhabitants with innumerable variations, giving each child object a copy of its own information.

The `VillageResident` class will be packaged in a self-contained AS3 document called `VillageResident.as`. The residents of this village are visual constructs, meaning they are also display objects. As display objects, they will be based on a `MovieClip` symbol in the Library containing an Export Linkage ID named `VillageResident`. Both the `MovieClip` symbol and the AS3 class document will be used to construct a display object that features programmable data attributes representing a given village resident.

The abstract data representation for a given village resident in this example is structured using the following physical and mental data attributes:

- Wisdom
- Ferocity
- Social status
- Health

As shown in Figure 9-1, the parent `VillageResident` class is used to create countless child residents with varying degrees of wisdom, ferocity, social status, and health. In the AS3 class file, the child object applies the specific values to the physical and mental property constructs it has inherited from its parent.

Parent class

Child objects

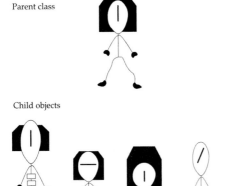

I FIGURE 9-1 Parent class and children objects.

Solution

The name of the AS3 file that represents the `VillageResident` class will be `VillageResident.as`. The class and constructor function within this document must also be named `VillageResident`.

The constructor function performs two main tasks: It assigns specific values to the data attributes inherited from the parent class and it uses these values to modify the display object so that its properties correspond to its intended mental and physical prowess.

Lines 6–9: The data attributes are made `private`. This specification makes them unavailable to code outside the `VillageResident` class document. The keyword `private` will be explored in more detail in the next section.

Line 11: A constructor for a class must be declared as public.

VillageResident.as

```
1  package {
2      import flash.display.*;
3
4      public class VillageResident extends MovieClip {
5          //DATA ATTRIBUES OF A VILLAGE RESIDENT
6          private var wisdom:int;
7          private var ferocity:int;
```

```
8        private var socialStatus:int;
9        private var health:int;
10
11       public function VillageResident () {
12          //TASK 1: INITIALIZE THE RESIDENT'S ATTRIBUTES
13          wisdom = int (Math.random() * 180);
14          ferocity = int (Math.random() * 50);
15          socialStatus = int (Math.random() * 20) + 1;
16          health = int (Math.random() * 30);
17
18          //TASK 2: USE ATTRIBUTES TO MODIFY THE DISPLAY OBJECT
19          //A. MODIFY EYE ACCORDING TO WISDOM
20          this.Eye.rotation+=wisdom;
21          this.Eye.width+=wisdom * 3;
22
23          //B. MODIFY BODY SIZE ACCORDING TO FEROCITY
24          this.Body.width+=ferocity;
25
26          //C. MODIFY CLOTHING ACCORDING TO SOCIAL STATUS
27          this.Body.gotoAndStop(socialStatus);
28
29          //D. MODIFY HAIR ACCORDING TO HEALTH
30          this.Hair.y-=health;
31          this.Hair.width += health;
32       }
33    }
34 }
```

Note

Note the usage of the reserved word this. The mechanism this is used in classes to identify an individual instance. In AS3 it is especially useful for accessing the attributes inherited from the DisplayObject class. This keyword is discussed in more detail in Section 9.1.5.

The AS3 file for the main application might be coded as follows.

mainApp.as

```
1  package {
2     import flash.display.*;
3     import flash.events.*;
4
5     public class mainApp extends MovieClip {
6
7        function mainApp() {
8           var citizenAnna:VillageResident = new VillageResident();
9           citizenAnna.x = 100;
10          citizenAnna.y = 100;
```

```
11              addChild(citizenAnna);
12        }
13    }
14 }
```

Lines 7–11: The variable `citizenAnna` is a member of the `VillageResident` class, which also embodies the `VillageResident` `MovieClip` symbol in the Library. These instructions place a display object on the Stage representing an instance of `VillageResident` named `citizenAnna`.

Example 3 A class for representing an animated cube

Consider a Flash application in which rotating cubes of a fixed size, such as those shown in Figure 9-2, are generated in real time. In addition to the rotating behavior for a given cube, its volume and area will be provided as methods and made accessible to outside document files.

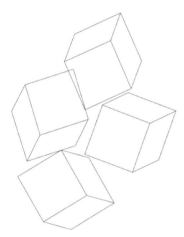

▌ FIGURE 9-2 Animated cubes generated from a `Cube` class.

Solution

The name of the AS3 file that represents the `Cube` class will be `Cube.as`. The class and constructor function within this document must also be named `Cube`.

Aside from the fixed `Width` attribute, the `Cube` class will provide three methods, or operations:

`rotateMe()`: forces the cube instance to automatically rotate.

`cubeArea()`: computes and returns the area of the cube.

`cubeVolume()`: computes and returns the volume of the cube.

The AS3 file bearing the name `Cube.as` might be coded as follows.

Cube.as

```
1  package {
2      import flash.display.*;
3      import flash.events.*;
4
5      public class Cube extends MovieClip {
6          //CLASS DATA ATTRIBUTES
7          private var Width:Number;
8          private var cube:Sprite;
9
10         //CUBE CLASS CONSTRUCTOR
11         public function Cube() {
12             //INITIALIZES CUBE WIDTH TO A FIXED VALUE OF 100
13             Width = 100;
14
15             //DRAWS THE CUBE AS A SPRITE
16             cube = new Sprite();
17             cube.graphics.lineStyle(1,0xFF0000);
18             cube.graphics.moveTo(40,0);
19             cube.graphics.lineTo(140,0);
20             cube.graphics.lineTo(140,100);
21             cube.graphics.lineTo(100,140);
22             cube.graphics.lineTo(0,140);
23             cube.graphics.lineTo(0,40);
24             cube.graphics.lineTo(100,40);
25             cube.graphics.lineTo(140,0);
26             cube.graphics.moveTo(0,40);
27             cube.graphics.lineTo(40,0);
28             cube.graphics.moveTo(100,40);
29             cube.graphics.lineTo(100,140);
30             addChild(cube);
31             this.addEventListener(Event.ENTER_FRAME, rotateMe);
32         }
33
34         //METHOD: ANIMATES THE CUBE
35         private function rotateMe (event:Event) {
36             this.rotation++;
37         }
38         //METHOD: COMPUTES THE AREA OF THE CUBE
39         public function cubeArea():Number {
40             return Width * Width * 6;
41         }
42         //METHOD: COMPUTES THE VOLUME OF THE CUBE
43         public function cubeVolume():Number {
44             return Width * Width * Width;
45         }
46     }
47 }
```

Line 35: The method `rotateMe()` is made `private`. Code outside the `Cube` class will not be able to alter this function or prevent it from executing.

Line 39–45: The member functions `cubeArea()` and `cubeVolume()` are called by the main application document. To be made available to code outside `Cube`, these class methods are declared as `public`.

The AS3 file for the main application might be coded as follows.

mainApp.as

```
1    package {
2        import flash.display.*;
3
4        public class mainApp extends MovieClip {
5
6            function mainApp() {
7                var cube1:Cube = new Cube();
8                addChild(cube1);
9
10               trace ("The area of cube1 is " + cube1.cubeArea());
11               trace ("The volume of cube1 is " + cube1.cubeVolume());
12           }
13       }
14   }
```

Lines 7–8: The variable `cube1`, an instance of the `Cube` class, is constructed and placed on the Stage.

Line 10–11: `cube1` calls its `public` `cubeArea()` and `cubeVolume()` methods to compute its area and volume.

9.1.3 `public`, `private`, and `static` Access Modifiers

As shown in the previous examples, class implementation consists of `public` or `private` elements. The AS3 keywords `public` and `private` are called **access modifiers**.

In the `Cube` class example, the two member functions `cubeArea()` and `cubeVolume()` were declared as `public`, while the attribute `Width` was declared as `private`. Data attributes can be declared as `public`, but are more often given `private` access. Class elements that are identified as `public` can be accessed anywhere within the scope of a given class. In other words, the value of a `public` attribute can be modified and `public` member functions can be called from outside the class.

A class element that has been declared as `private` has restricted accessibility, making it reachable only by member functions defined for the class. A benefit of `private` access is data security. Often a class can be implemented in such a way that it restricts access to the internal structure of the data, such that only the methods in that class can process an object's internal data. This concept is called **information hiding**.

With information hiding, there is a binding relationship between the information and the operations that are performed on that information. The `public` elements are accessible outside the class, and the `private` elements provide the information that is accessible only from within the class itself. Only the member functions declared for the class can operate on the `private` class members. Thus the `private` elements of the class provide the information hiding capabilities.

Another access modifier for a method type is `static`. `static` methods can be called directly from the class itself. In other words, it is not necessary to create a class instance to use a class's `static` methods. Such methods are not accessible as members of an instance of that class, but rather are called by the class itself. A good example of `static` methods is found in the `Math` class. The methods in the `Math` class, such as `Math.sqrt()` and `Math.random()`, are accessible without requiring the creation of an object.

Consider the following three examples.

Example 1

This example illustrates a class called `Temperature` that uses `static` access to `public` functions. The class definition is simply a library containing functions that are related in some way to heat and temperature.

The class `Temperature` is packaged with two member functions, `FahrenheitToCelsius()` and `CelsiusToFahrenheit()`. Both methods are `public` and `static`, which makes them available without the use of a created object. Because this class is not used to create an object, a constructor function is not required.

The second file, the main document class named `mainApp.as`, is used to call the member functions in the `Temperature` class.

Termperature.as

```
1   package {
2       import flash.display.*;
3
4       public class Temperature extends MovieClip {
5
6           public static function FahrenheitToCelsius(temp:Number):Number {
7               return (temp - 32.0) / 1.8;
8           }
9
10          public static function CelsiusToFahrenheit(temp:Number):Number {
11              return temp * 1.8 + 32.0;
12          }
13      }
14  }
```

mainApp.as

```
1   package {
2       import flash.display.*;
3
4       public class mainApp extends MovieClip {
5
6           function mainApp() {
7               var temp:Number = Temperature.FahrenheitToCelsius(212);
8               trace ("The Celsius temperature of Fahrenheit 212 is " , temp);
9
10              temp = Temperature.CelsiusToFahrenheit(100);
11              trace ("The Fahrenheit temperature of Celsius 100 is " , temp);
12          }
13      }
14  }
```

Evaluation

The static methods `FahrenheitToCelsius()` and `CelsiusToFahrenheit()` are called by the file `mainApp.as` on lines 7 and 10. The syntax for these calls requires the class name in which the static function resides, followed by the dot notation and the name of the static function. In addition, both function calls supply an argument.

The output produced is

```
The Celsius temperature of Fahrenheit 212 is 100
The Fahrenheit temperature of Celsius 100 is 212
```

Constructing a library class of static elements can be a time-saving approach when you are building large and complex applications. As shown in this example, a class can serve as a library that provides an organized collection of functions that are commonly needed.

Example 2

In the first code file, the class `Nonsense` is defined with three data attributes, a constructor function, and a member function called `doSomething()`. This class definition illustrates the restricted access provided to `private` class elements and the full access provided to `public` elements. The second file is the main document class, named `mainApp.as`.

Nonsense.as

```
1   package {
2       import flash.display.*;
3
4       public class Nonsense extends MovieClip {
```

```
5         public var A:Number;
6         public var B:Number;
7         private var C:Number;
8
9         public function Nonsense ():void {
10            A=2;
11            B=3;
12            C=4;
13            }
14        public function doSomething():void {
15            trace("A is ", A);
16            trace("B is ", B);
17            trace("C is ", C);
18            }
19        }
20  }
```

mainApp.as

```
1  package {
2     import flash.display.*;
3
4     public class mainApp extends MovieClip {
5
6        function mainApp() {
7            var obj:Nonsense = new Nonsense();
8            obj.doSomething();
9            trace("obj.A is ", obj.A);
10           trace("obj.B is ", obj.B);
11           }
12        }
13  }
```

Evaluation

In the first file Nonsense.as, the data attributes A and B (lines 5 and 6) are identified as public and, therefore, are accessible to the second file mainApp.as. The third attribute, C (line 7), is private and accessible only to the elements within the class that created it. The method doSomething() within the class is public and, therefore, is accessible outside the class.

The output produced by these two files is

```
A is  2
B is  3
C is  4
obj.A is  2
obj.B is  3
```

Example 3

In the first code file, the class Nonsense is defined with one data attribute and a constructor function. This example illustrates a common error attributed to restricted access to private class elements. Private elements are not accessible outside the scope of the file in which they are defined. The second file is the main document class, named mainApp.as.

Nonsense.as

```
1   package {
2      import flash.display.*;
3
4      public class Nonsense extends MovieClip {
5         private var C:Number;
6
7         public function Nonsense ():void {
8            C=4;
9         }
10
11     }
12  }
13
14
```

mainApp.as

```
1   package {
2      import flash.display.*;
3
4      public class mainApp extends MovieClip {
5
6         function mainApp() {
7            var obj:Nonsense = new Nonsense();
8            trace("obj.C is ", obj.C);
9         }
10     }
11  }
```

Evaluation

In the first file Nonsense.as, the data attribute C (line 5) is private and accessible only to the elements within the class that created it.

The output produced is

mainApp.as, Line 8:Attempted access of inaccessible property C

9.1.4 Class Constructors

A class constructor is a function that is used to automatically initialize an object once it has been defined. Constructors are not methods, but they share some similarities with methods, although they also differ in some ways.

As we saw in applications given earlier in this textbook, the advantage of using a constructor is that the constructor function is called automatically when an object is defined. When used in a document class, the constructor begins the program.

Although a constructor is a function, it is often used to allocate memory and generally get an object ready for execution.

Here are some general rules governing the creation and use of constructors:

1. The name of the constructor must be the same as the name of the class and the name of the file.

2. The constructor must be a `public` access method.

3. The constructor cannot have a `return` statement or a `void` return class.

4. The constructor can have parameters. A class cannot have more than one constructor.

5. Constructors should not be designed for tasks other than initializing an object for execution.

Consider the following three examples.

Example 1

The original `Cube` class, constructed in Example 3 in Section 9.1.2, assigned a fixed value to the `Width` attribute of `Cube`. This example illustrates the usage of a class that employs a constructor with a parameter. Like any other function, a class constructor can have parameters. If invalid values are passed as parameters to the constructor, the program must include a way to detect this error and respond appropriately.

On line 10 of the following `Cube.as` code, a value stored in the parameter n is received by the constructor. On line 12, this parameter is used to assign the `Width` attribute.

Cube.as

```
1  package {
2      import flash.display.*;
3
4      public class Cube extends MovieClip {
5          //CLASS DATA ATTRIBUTES
6          private var Width:Number;
7          private var cube:Sprite;
```

```
8
9      //CUBE CLASS CONSTRUCTOR
10     public function Cube(n:Number) {
11         //INITIALIZES CUBE WIDTH
12         Width = n;
13
14         //DRAWS THE CUBE AS A SPRITE
15         cube = new Sprite();
16         cube.graphics.lineStyle(1,0x000000);
17         cube.graphics.moveTo(Width * .4,0);
18         cube.graphics.lineTo(Width + Width * .4,0);
19         cube.graphics.lineTo(Width + Width * .4,Width);
20         cube.graphics.lineTo(Width,Width + Width * .4);
21         cube.graphics.lineTo(0,Width + Width * .4);
22         cube.graphics.lineTo(0,Width * .4);
23         cube.graphics.lineTo(Width,Width * .4);
24         cube.graphics.lineTo(Width + Width * .4,0);
25         cube.graphics.moveTo(0,Width * .4);
26         cube.graphics.lineTo(Width * .4,0);
27         cube.graphics.moveTo(Width,Width * .4);
28         cube.graphics.lineTo(Width,Width + Width * .4);
29         addChild(cube);
30     }
31  }
32 }
```

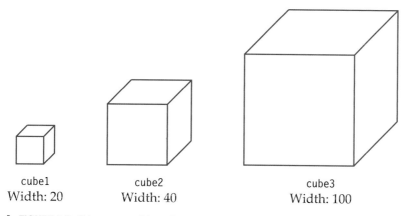

cube1   cube2   cube3
Width: 20   Width: 40   Width: 100

❙ FIGURE 9-3 Objects created from the same constructor with different Width values.

In the mainApp.as document, three instantiations of a Cube are created: cube1, cube2, and cube3. As shown in Figure 9-3, each Cube object is constructed with a different Width.

mainApp.as

```
1   package {
2       import flash.display.*;
3
4       public class mainApp extends MovieClip {
5
6           function mainApp() {
7               var cube1:Cube = new Cube(20);
8               addChild(cube1);
9               cube1.x = 10;
10              cube1.y = 100;
11
12              var cube2:Cube = new Cube(40);
13              addChild(cube2);
14              cube2.x = 100;
15              cube2.y = 100;
16
17              var cube3:Cube = new Cube(100);
18              addChild(cube3);
19              cube3.x = 250;
20              cube3.y = 100;
21          }
22      }
23  }
```

Example 2

The class called Flower is used to build the two complete flowers shown in Figure 9-4. As with the previous example, this class employs a constructor that uses a parameter—in this case, to specify the number of petals in the flower. This example illustrates data validation performed in such a constructor. If invalid parameters are passed to the constructor, the program must include a way to detect this error and respond appropriately.

Petal

I **FIGURE 9-4** Flowers created from the same class constructor with validation.

The document `Flower.as` provides the complete definition for the `Flower` class. This class also uses a `MovieClip` symbol in the Library, representing a single flower petal with the linkage identifier `Petal`.

`Flower` instances can be built with a varied number of petals, with this number being passed as a parameter to the class constructor. As shown on lines 8 and 9, the only data attributes specified for this class are the number of petals, `nPetals`, that make up the `Flower` object and the flower sprite.

The class constructor uses the parameter n to assign the `nPetals` attribute on lines 13–20. Note that the value of `nPetals` will never be less than 6 or more than 30. In this way, the constructor stipulates that a valid `Flower` consists of 6 to 30 petals. When an invalid number is passed to the constructor, it responds by assigning the closest valid number to `nPetals`.

Flower.as

```
1   package {
2       import flash.display.*;
3
4       public const DEGREES_IN_CIRCLE:int = 360;
5
6       public class Flower extends MovieClip {
7           //CLASS ATTRIBUTES
8           private var nPetals:int;      //NUMBER OF PETALS
9           private var flower:Sprite;    //DISPLAY OBJECT
10
11          //CLASS CONSTRUCTOR: RECEIVED NUMBER OF PETALS
12          public function Flower(n:int):void {
13              //VALIDATE NUMBER OF PETALS SPECIFIED
14              if (n >= 6 && n <= 30) {
15                  nPetals = n;
16              }else if (n <6){
17                  nPetals = 6;
18              } else {
19                  nPetals = 30;
20              }
21
22              //CREATE THE FLOWER SPRITE
23              flower = new Sprite();
24              addChild(flower);
25
26              //CONSTRUCT THE FLOWER USING A VALID nPetals
27              var petalRotate:int=DEGREES_IN_CIRCLE / nPetals;
28              var petalWidth:int=petalRotate;
29
30              for (var i:int = 1; i <= nPetals; i++) {
31                  var petalObj:Petal=new Petal;
32                  petalObj.width=petalWidth;
```

```
33                petalObj.rotation=petalRotate *i;
34                petalObj.x=petalObj.y=100;
35                addChild(petalObj);
36                flower.addChild(petalObj);
37            }
38          }
39        }
40  }
```

In the `mainApp.as` document, two instances of the class `Flower` are created, `flower1` and `flower2`, each with a different number of petals. As Figure 9-4 shows, the first `Flower` object is constructed with 6 petals, after rejecting the invalid parameter value of -1, and the second with a valid 12 petals.

mainApp.as

```
1   package {
2       import flash.display.*;
3       public class mainApp extends MovieClip {
4           public function mainApp ():void {
5               var flower1:Flower=new Flower(-1);
6               flower1.x=60;
7               flower1.y=65;
8               addChild(flower1);
9
10              var flower2:Flower=new Flower(12);
11              flower2.x=350;
12              flower2.y=65;
13              addChild(flower2);
14          }
15      }
16  }
```

9.1.5 The this Mechanism

As a member function of a class, a method can directly access the data properties of that class for a given object. Often it is necessary for a method function to refer to the object as a whole, rather than the object's individual data elements. In OOP languages, every object of a class maintains a reference to itself. The name of this reference is `this`, which is a reserved word in AS3. When an object invokes a method function, the function identifies the reference `this` of the object.

When an instance of a class is created, ActionScript 3.0 calls the constructor for that class. By using the keyword `this`, the unique object can be referenced and initialized. To facilitate an object's ability to reference itself, it is especially useful for classes to implement the `this` keyword for member functions.

The next two examples illustrate the use of the `this` mechanism.

Example 1

This example shows how the `this` mechanism works in a constructor. Consider two clouds placed on the Stage, as shown in Figure 9-5. Both instances in this figure are defined by the `Cloud` class, which is packaged in the document class `Cloud.as`. The first instance, named `c1`, is much smaller in scale than the second, named `c2`. In addition, the clouds are located in different positions on the Stage.

By using the ActionScript 3.0 keyword `this`, the constructor is able to identify the exact instance being referenced and assign specific values to its `x`, `y`, `width`, and `height` properties. The `this` keyword acts as a pointer to the current object.

On lines 27, 28, and 31, the `this` keyword is used to identify a specific instance to access its inherited display object properties. Note that a `MovieClip` symbol located in the Flash Library contains an image of a cloud and is defined with a linkage ID of `Cloud`.

`Cloud.as`

```
1   package {
2       import flash.display.*;
3
4       public class Cloud extends MovieClip {
5           //DATA ATTRIBUTES FOR THE CLOUD CLASS
6           private var xPosition:int;
7           private var size :int;
8
9           public function Cloud (l:int, s:int):void {
10              //TASK 1: INITIALIZE xPosition PROPERTY
11              if (l >= 10 && l <= 400) {
12                  xPosition = l;
13              }else if (l < 10) {
14                  xPosition = 10;
15              }else {
16                  xPosition = 400;
17              }
18              //TASK 2: INITIALIZE size PROPERTY
19              if (s >= 20 && s <= 100) {
20                  size = s;
21              }else if (s < 20) {
22                  size = 20;
23              }else {
24                  size = 100;
25              }
26              //TASK 3: INITIALIZE THE LOCATION OF THE CLOUD
27              this.x = xPosition;
```

```
28            this.y = 400;
29
30            //TASK 4: INITIALIZE THE SIZE OF THE CLOUD
31            this.width = this.height = size;
32        }
33     }
34 }
```

The statements in lines 1–4 declare the Cloud objects c1 and c2. The first argument in the Cloud declaration is the location along the *x*-axis; the second argument is the size of Cloud.

```
1   var c1: Cloud = new Cloud (100,20);
2   addChild(c1);
3   var c2: Cloud = new Cloud (200,100);
4   addChild(c2);
```

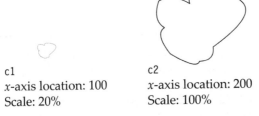

c1
x-axis location: 100
Scale: 20%

c2
x-axis location: 200
Scale: 100%

❙ FIGURE 9-5 Two instances of the Cloud class.

Example 2

This example illustrates the use of the this mechanism to communicate with objects in multiple class applications. Communication between objects occurs when messages are sent from one object to another, asking the recipient object to apply a method on itself. To express that an object should perform a set of tasks, a method function is always specified using dot notation. To facilitate an object's ability to identify itself, AS3 implements the this keyword for all member functions and acts as a reference point to the current object.

Figure 9-6 shows a Ball object, ball1, created from the Ball class. The object ball1 has inherited interactive spinning capabilities, spinMe(), from its parent class Ball.

```
1   var ball1:Ball = new Ball();
2   addChild(ball1);
3   ball1.spinMe();
```

In lines 1–2 the instance ball is created from the Ball class constructor. In line 3, the method spinMe() is used to animate the ball by spinning it as shown in Figure 9-6.

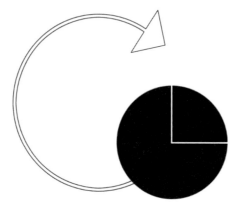

▌ FIGURE 9-6 The Ball object with the spinMe() method activated.

The class constructor for the Ball class will construct a ball with a specified radius. When invoking the public method spinMe(), it is immediately evident which object is referenced. A timer object is used by this method to control the animation.

Ball.as

```
1   package {
2       import flash.display.*;
3       import flash.events.*;
4       import flash.utils.*;
5
6       public class Ball extends MovieClip {
7           //CONSTANT FOR FRICTION
8           private const FRICTION:Number=.75;
9
10          //CLASS DATA ATTRIBUTES
11          private var radius:Number=100;
12          private var ball:Sprite;
13          private var velocity:Number;
14
15          //BALL CLASS CONSTRUCTOR
16          public function Ball(r:Number):void {
17              //INITIALIZE THE RADIUS OF THE BALL TO A VALID NUMBER
18              if (r>=10&&r<=300) {
19                  radius=r;
20              }
21
```

```
22        //DRAWS THE BALL AS A SPRITE
23        ball=new Sprite();
24        ball.graphics.beginFill(0x000000);
25        ball.graphics.lineStyle(1, 0xFFFFFF);
26        ball.graphics.drawCircle(radius, radius, radius);
27
28        ball.graphics.moveTo(radius, radius);
29        ball.graphics.lineTo(radius , radius*2);
30        ball.graphics.moveTo(radius, radius);
31        ball.graphics.lineTo(radius*2 , radius);
32        addChild(ball);
33      }
34
35    //METHOD: CREATE A TIMER EVENT LISTENER TO SPIN THE BALL OBJECT
36    public function spinMe():void {
37        var atimer:Timer=new Timer(150,20);
38        velocity=Math.random()*25+75;
39        atimer.addEventListener(TimerEvent.TIMER, spinInterval);
40        atimer.start();
41      }
42
43    //METHOD: THE TIMER EVENT THAT SPINS THE BALL OBJECT
44    private function spinInterval(event:TimerEvent):void {
45        this.rotation+=velocity;
46        velocity*=FRICTION;
47      }
48    }
49 }
```

9.2 Case Study 1: The Bird Class

Problem and Analysis

Bird baths are enormously popular among all kinds of birds, oftentimes attracting more species of birds than feeders would. This case study looks at the construction of an application representing an interactive atrium containing a bird bath. When the application is first launched, the atrium is devoid of birds. Users can add birds, using an interactive button, which will appear in different sizes with various hovering speeds. All birds arrive on the Stage clean but accumulate dirt as they fly around the atrium. At that point they head to the bird bath and become clean again. The water source in this application is invariable—it does not move or evaporate.

This application can be constructed by using two class documents: a Bird class and a main application program that drives the environment. The Bird class is an actual representation of an abstract data type. It provides implementation details for

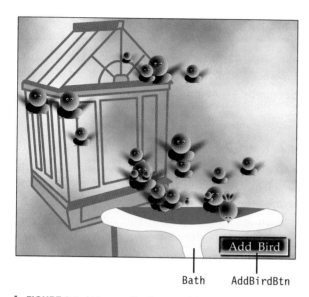

I **FIGURE 9-7** Atrium application containing multiple instances of the Bird class.

the data structure used to define a bird and the operations that govern its behavior. The Bird class in this example encapsulates the attributes and functionality of an imaginary bird. The main application program uses the Bird class to add birds to the environment.

Visual Design

The bird bath and button are the only interactive display objects placed directly on the Stage. The bird bath is given the name Bath and the button is named AddBirdBtn, as shown in Figure 9-7. In addition to the decorative elements that exist in this application, a Bird MovieClip is used for the visual template of all birds added to the atrium. The timeline will require a single frame, as shown in Figure 9-8.

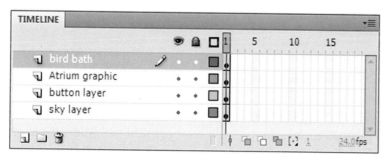

I **FIGURE 9-8** Atrium timeline design.

Program Design

The AS3 code for this application consists of two files: `Bird.as`, the class declaration for all birds in the atrium, and `AtriumApp.as`, which represents the document class file and main application program. We begin by examining the `Bird` class.

Bird Class Design

Because a `Bird` on stage is immediately associated with a graphic image of a bird, the `Bird` class will work with an exported `MovieClip` symbol in the Library. This is accomplished by using the same class name as the linkage ID, which allows both the document class and the `MovieClip` symbol to work in unison.

Consider that all birds in the atrium are either flying or bathing. To render this behavior, the timeline for `Bird` `MovieClip` will consist of two frames. The first frame represents a bird in flight and the second represents a bird bathing. Figure 9-9 shows the timeline and the two representations, with the `Bird` `MovieClip` built in multiple components.

Frame 1:
Bird in flight

Frame 2:
Bird drinking or bathing

| FIGURE 9-9 Timeline construction for the `Bird` exported `MovieClip`.

Bird Properties   A bird has a great number of attributes that would be overwhelming to incorporate in a program such as this one. It is most practical to consider the needs specific to the application. Because the goal of this case study is to create birds that simply bathe and explore their surroundings, only a small number of `Bird` properties are required. The `Bird` properties, shown Table 9-1, are based on the following needs:

Bird's current condition: A bird is either flying or bathing, but its level of dirtiness governs when it bathes and when it flies. A third condition, in which the bird is too dirty to fly, will be added to this list. These three possible conditions for a given Bird will be non-inclusive and describe its current state at any given moment. These three conditions are non-inclusive.

Bird's honing velocity: Birds, like all animals, are born with different athletic abilities. In this case, when a Bird is "born," it is assigned a random velocity. Flying entails a direction and speed. To control the bird's motion as it eases into its target, a distance can be computed and divided by the bird's velocity. Hence, a Bird with a high-velocity assignment will move in small increments, making it travel slowly toward its target.

Dirty bird: Birds acquire dirt every moment they exist. At some point they accumulate so much dirt that it triggers the need to take a bath.

Bathing area: The fresh water in a bird bath is typically large enough to accommodate many birds. In a virtual application, it is important that not all of them pick the exact same spot in which to bathe. In this application, the water in the bath is subdivided into multiple zones. A Bird's bathing zone is computed once a Bird is dirty and represents where the Bird can seek out a bath.

Point of interest: A point of interest represents a changeable location in the atrium that the Bird will explore. It will hover around this spot, simply passing time, until it accumulates enough dirt and decides it needs another bath.

TABLE 9-1 Properties for the Bird Class.

Property Name	Access	Data Type	Description
myCondition	private	int	Holds one of three conditions (isDIRTY, isBATHING, and isFLYING) that describe a Bird at a given moment
velocity	private	Number	Randomly assigned velocity at which a given Bird normally flies
dirtLevel	private	Number	Amount of dirt on the Bird's feathers
bathX	private	Number	Location along the x-axis of the bathing area
bathY	private	Number	Location along the y-axis of the bathing area
interestX	private	Number	The x location of a changing point of interest to the Bird in the atrium
interestY	private	Number	The y location of a changing point of interest to the Bird in the atrium

Bird Functions   Six basic functions, listed in Table 9-2, are required for the Bird class: the constructor, Bird(), and a collection of methods that correspond to the Bird's behavior. Just as there are a large number of properties associated with a bird, so the same goes for Bird behavior. A bird has many instincts, too many to catalog. In this case study, we consider only those behaviors associated with bathing and exploring.

TABLE 9-2 Member Functions Used by the Bird Class

Member Function	Description	Details
Bird()	The constructor function. Initializes the properties of the Bird class and registers an ENTER_FRAME event to drive the functionality of the Bird.	public constructor
living()	The general engine behind the Bird's behavior. This event handler responds to an ENTER_FRAME event; it continually monitors the condition of an individual Bird and decides how it will behave based on its condition.	private event handler (ENTER_FRAME)
explore()	The member function that allows a Bird to explore a point of interest in which to pass its time and accumulate dirt.	private method
findBath()	A member function that locates a specific bathing zone. This method is also responsible for identifying when a bird bath is found and then setting a timer event for a quick 2-second bath.	private method
doneBathing()	A timer event handler that performs the behavior associated with the completion of a bath. This behavior entails tasks such as setting the Bird level to clean and embarking on a new flight around the atrium seeking out a point of interest.	private event handler (timer)
setBathLocation()	A public access method that sets the location of the bath for all birds in the atrium to locate. This function uses two parameters—an x and a y value that identify the bath's position on the Stage.	public Method

Bird Constants   The constants for the Bird class revolve around the Bird's cleanliness and its possible conditions. All Birds are initialized to CLEAN. As time passes, a Bird's dirt level increases. Once the level reaches a value referred to by the constant FILTHY, it needs a bath. The three indicators of a Bird's condition are isBATHING, isFLYING, and isDIRTY. These constants are given private access.

Bird.as   The complete document class for the Bird class is as follows:

```
1   package {
2       import flash.display.*;
3       import flash.events.*;
4       import flash.utils.*;
5
6       public class Bird extends MovieClip {
7           //BIRD CONSTANTS
8           private const CLEAN:Number=0;
9           private const FILTHY:Number=10;
10          private const isBATHING:int=1;
11          private const isFLYING:int=2;
12          private const isDIRTY:int=3
13
14          //BIRD PROPERTIES
15          //a. THE BIRD's CURRENT CONDITION
16          private var myCondition:int;
17
18          //b. SPEED AT WHICH BIRD TRAVELS AND ACQUIRES DIRT
19          private var velocity:Number;
20
21          //c. DIRT LEVEL THAT TRIGGERS WHEN THE BIRD TAKES A BATH
22          private var dirtLevel:Number
23
24          //d. THE BATHING ZONE
25          private var bathX:Number;
26          private var bathY:Number;
27
28          //e. PLACES OF INTEREST TO FLY TO AND DISTANCE TO THEM
29          private var interestX:Number;
30          private var interestY:Number;
31
32          public function Bird():void {
33              //TASK 1: INITIALIZE THE BATHING ZONE
34              this.gotoAndStop(1);
35              bathX=0;
36              bathY=0;
37
38              //TASK 2: INITIALIZE BIRD ATTRIBUTES
39              this.x=10;
40              this.y=10;
41              this.scaleX=Math.random()+.3;
42              this.scaleY=this.scaleX;
43              interestX=200;
44              interestY=50;
```

```
45        velocity=Math.random()*10+4;//BIRD'S NORMAL TRAVELING VELOCITY
46        dirtLevel=CLEAN;//AMOUNT OF DIRT ON BIRD'S BODY
47        myCondition=isFLYING;
48
49        //TASK 3: SET A LISTENER EVENT FOR A FRAME LOOP
50        this.addEventListener(Event.ENTER_FRAME,living);
51     }
52     public function setBathLocation(locationX:Number,
53                               locationY:Number):void {
54        bathX=locationX-100+Math.floor(Math.random()*200);
55        bathY=locationY;
56     }
57
58     private function living(event:Event):void {
59        //TASK : EXAMINE THREE CONDITIONS: isBATHING, isFLYING, isDIRTY
60        switch (myCondition) {
61           case isFLYING :
62              explore();
63              break;
64           case isDIRTY :
65              findBath();
66              break;
67           case isBATHING :
68              //BATHE FOR 2 SECONDS
69              var timer:Timer=new Timer(1000,1);
70              timer.addEventListener(TimerEvent.TIMER, doneBathing);
71              this.gotoAndPlay(2);
72              timer.start();
73        }
74     }
75     private function explore():void {
76        var xDist:Number;
77        var yDist:Number;
78        dirtLevel++;
79        //TASK 1: FLY TO PLACE OF INTEREST
80        xDist=interestX-this.x;
81        yDist=interestY-this.y;
82        this.x+=xDist/velocity;
83        this.y+=yDist/velocity;
84        //TASK 2: CHECK IF FILTHY
85        if (dirtLevel>=FILTHY) {
86           myCondition=isDIRTY;
87        }
88     }
89     private function findBath():void {
90        var xDist:Number;
91        var yDist:Number;
92        //TASK 1: FLY TO BATHING ZONE
93        xDist=bathX-this.x;
```

```
94          yDist=bathY-this.y;
95          this.x+=xDist/velocity;
96          this.y+=yDist/velocity;
97          //TASK 2: CHECK IF BATHING ZONE IS LOCATED
98          if (xDist<10&&yDist<3) {
99              myCondition=isBATHING;
100         }
101     }
102
103     private function doneBathing(event:TimerEvent)void {
104         dirtLevel=CLEAN;
105         this.gotoAndStop(1);
106         myCondition=isFLYING;
107         //TASK: COMPUTE A NEW POINT OF INTEREST TO FLY TO
108         interestX=Math.random()*stage.stageWidth*3-stage.stageWidth;
109         interestY=Math.random()*400-100;
110     }
111   }
112 }
```

atriumApp.as: The Main Document Class Design

The AS3 file `atriumApp.as` is the main document class for this application. It contains two functions: the constructor and the event handler function `addBird()`, which adds a `Bird` from the `Bird` class to the atrium each time the user clicks the button on the Stage. These functions are outlined in Table 9-3.

A global variable array is the most suitable structure for keeping track of all the birds in the atrium. This case study is rather simple and the collection of `Bird` objects will not need additional processing. However, for future reference to these `Birds`, this global array is mandatory.

TABLE 9-3 `birdAtrium.as` Application Progam

Function Name	Description/Tasks
`atriumApp()`	The class constructor for the main document class.
	Task 1: The `atriumApp()` function is the constructor and main function of the program. It executes once the application launches.
	Task 2: This function registers an event listener for a click of the button `AddBirdBtn`. Once this event is triggered, the event handler `addBird()` is called to respond by adding a bird, from the `Bird` class, to the atrium.
`addBird()`	An event handler triggered by the `MouseEvent CLICK`.
	Task 1: This event handler function begins by generating a `Bird` child from the `Bird` class and adding it to the Stage (the atrium).
	Task 2: The collection of `Birds` is stored in a global array, and the new Bird is pushed onto this array.

atriumApp.as

```
1   package {
2       import flash.display.*;
3       import flash.events.*;
4
5       public class atriumApp extends MovieClip {
6           //THE ATRIUM GLOBAL VARIABLES
7           var allBirds:Array = new Array();
8
9
10          //THE APPLICATION CONSTRUCTOR
11          function atriumApp():void {
12              AddBirdBtn.addEventListener(MouseEvent.CLICK, addBird);
13          }
14
15          //THE BUTTON CLICK EVENT HANDLER
16          //ADDS A BIRD TO THE ATRIUM
17          function addBird(event:MouseEvent):void {
18              var birdObj:Bird;
19              birdObj = new Bird();
20              birdObj.setBathLocation(Bath.x, Bath.y);
21              addChild(birdObj);
22              allBirds.push(birdObj);
23          }
24      }
25  }
```

■ 9.3 Inheritance, the IS-A Relationship, and the extends Keyword

An important topic in object-oriented programming is **inheritance**. Inheritance is a feature through which new classes are derived from existing ones. As a result, classes can be related to each other to create a hierarchy of classes. This allows new applications to "inherit" or **extend** code from existing applications, thereby making the chore of programming much more productive.

We have already experienced inheritance in display objects. For example, a MovieClip can be thought of as a derived class. While it has its own structure and behavior, it also shares structural and behavioral elements of the DisplayObject class, which is its base class.

The real world is full of inheritance that we can see firsthand. All living things inherit the characteristics, or traits, of their ancestors. Although we may be different in many ways from our parents, we are also the same in many ways because of the genetic traits that we inherit from them. Similarly, object-oriented programming allows newly created classes to inherit members from existing classes.

Newly derived classes will include both their own members and members inherited from the base class. Thus we can view a collection of classes with common inherited members as a family of classes. Classes are related to one another through inheritance, which in turn creates a class hierarchy. The main reason to use inheritance in complex AS3 applications is to capitalize on this intrinsic mechanism for building a hierarchy among classes.

In inheritance, the important link between a derived class and its base class is the **IS-A** relationship, which is identified in AS3 code using the keyword extends. For example, Figure 9-10 shows the hierarchy of individual members at a college campus. Campus members are subdivided into two categories: students and employees. Both students and employees can be derived from a general member of the college community. Furthermore, an undergraduate student is an extension of a student, as is a graduate student. A faculty member is an extension of an employee, and a student and an employee are both extensions of a college community member. The classes that are most commonly inherited are at the top of the hierarchy.

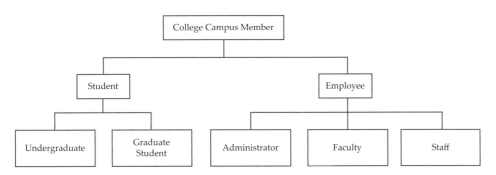

| FIGURE 9-10 Hierarchical structure of a college campus community.

The IS-A link must always be considered in inheritance. For example, Undergraduate **IS-A** Student because Undergraduate can be derived from Student. The OOP AS3 class definition that describes this relationship begins with the header definition

```
public class Undergraduate extends Student {
```

The parent class is Student, which is also called the base class. Undergraduate is the child class, which is also referred to as a **derived** class.

A collection of classes with common inherited members is called a **family** of classes.

9.3.1 protected and private Members of a Derived Class

A derived class is best declared within its own AS3 file. It uses the keyword extends to identify it as being derived from a given base class.

The private data members of a base class cannot be directly referenced from a derived class. For example, if the data in Employee is declared private, a very restricted encapsulation is adhered to and is a clear hindrance when trying to access frequently used data. A derived class should be able to access frequently used and modified data members of a base class easily and directly.

A less restrictive type of encapsulation can be achieved by using the access modifier protected for appropriate data and member functions. A data or function member of a class is considered a protected member if it is accessible to a derived class, but is not visible to any other part of a program. Thus protected members behave like public members for derived classes, but like private members for any other classes outside the class family.

Derived classes use the following program format:

```
package{
    public class derivedClass extends baseClass{
            list of derivedClass properties
            //CLASS CONSTRUCTOR
            public function derivedClass () {

                    .

                    .

                    .

            }
            list of derivedClass methods(){
            }
    }
}
```

Example

Let a base class named Ball be assigned a fixed velocity and weight and the resulting ball be drawn with a white interior. The class FireBall is extended by Ball; hence it is derived from Ball. Figure 9-11 illustrates the relationship between these two classes. The use of protected access ensures that the properties of the parent class Ball are passed along to its derived class FireBall.

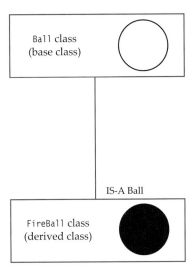

FIGURE 9-11 Hierarchical structure of Ball and FireBall objects.

A FireBall instance is structured to weigh the same as an instance from the Ball class, but both its velocity and the color of its ball sprite are assigned different values. FireBall is designed with a heat property, which is not found in the Ball class. Figure 9-12 shows instances of both classes.

Ball.as

```
1   package {
2       import flash.display.*;
3       public class Ball extends MovieClip {
4           //CLASS DATA ATTRIBUTES
5           protected var ball:Sprite;
6           protected var velocity:int;
7           protected var weight:int;
8
9           //BALL CLASS CONSTRUCTOR
10          public function Ball():void {
11              velocity=11;
12              weight=30;
13              ball=new Sprite();
14              ball.graphics.beginFill(0xFFFFFF);
15              ball.graphics.lineStyle(1, 0x000000);
16              ball.graphics.drawCircle(0, 0, 50);
17              addChild(ball);
18          }
19      }
20  }
```

FireBall.as

```
1   package {
2      import flash.display.*;
3      import flash.geom.ColorTransform;
4
5      public class FireBall extends Ball {
6         //CLASS DATA ATTRIBUTE
7         private var heat:Number;
8
9         //FIREBALL CLASS CONSTRUCTOR
10        public function FireBall():void {
11           heat=37;
12           velocity=2;
13           var newTint:ColorTransform=new ColorTransform(0,0,0,1,0,0,0);
14           ball.transform.colorTransform=newTint;
15           ball.scaleX=scaleY=.75;
16        }
17     }
18  }
```

In the main document class of the application test.as, one Ball object and five FireBall instances are created and placed on the Stage. The output is shown in Figure 9-12.

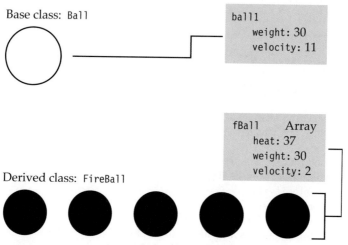

| FIGURE 9-12 An instance of Ball and an array of derived FireBall instances.

test.as

```
1   package {
2      import flash.display.*;
3      public class test extends MovieClip {
4         function test () {
```

```
5        //ADD A BALL INSTANCE
6        var ball1:Ball=new Ball();
7        addChild(ball1);
8        ball1.x=ball1.y=100;
9
10       //ADD FIVE FIREBALL INSTANCES
11       var fBallArray:Array=new Array();
12       for (var i=0; i < 5; i++) {
13           fBallArray[i]=new FireBall();
14           addChild(fBallArray[i]);
15           fBallArray[i].x=i*80 + 50;
16           fBallArray[i].y=300;
17       }
18   }
19  }
20 }
```

■ 9.4 Case Study 2: Birds of a Feather—Sparrows and Parrots

Problem and Analysis

The atrium in this case study deviates from the previous one, in that it is populated with two types of birds: parrots and sparrows (as shown in Figure 9-13). The first task required for building this application is the development of a family of classes representing the birds. Three classes are needed.

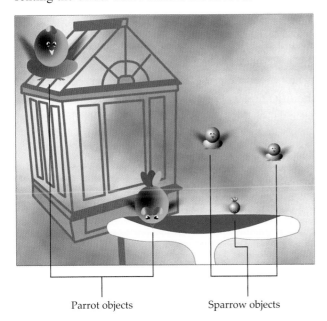

Parrot objects   Sparrow objects

❘ FIGURE 9-13 An atrium with Sparrow and Parrot instances.

The first class, Bird, is used as the base class to define the characteristics that are common to all birds in the atrium. This class was created in Case Study 1.

The second class defines a Parrot and the third defines a Sparrow. Both of these classes are derived from the Bird class. The Parrot and Sparrow birds inherit the traits peculiar to their bird type as well as characteristics from the more general Bird class from which they were derived.

The three AS3 files required for the family of classes are Bird.as, Parrot.as, and Sparrow.as. As Figure 9-14 illustrates, the Bird class, as the parent, is at the top of the class family hierarchy.

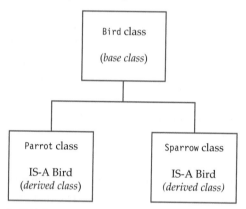

FIGURE 9-14 Hierarchical structure of birds.

Bird Class Design

As the base class for the entire family, Bird contains attribute data and methods that are common to all types of birds. The structure of this class is the same as the previous Bird class with one exception: The property representing velocity is given protected access, making it available for modification by the derived classes Parrot and Sparrow. All other data properties and methods for the Bird.as file remain exactly the same as in Case Study 1.

Bird Data Properties

```
private var myCondition:int;
protected var velocity:Number;
private var dirtLevel:Number;
private var bathX:Number;
private var bathY:Number;
private var interestX:Number;
private var interestY:Number;
```

Bird Methods

```
Bird()
living()
explore()
findBath()
doneBathing()
setBathLocation()
```

Parrot Class Design

The parrots in this case study are designed as generally larger birds with a slower hovering velocity. Visually they are painted with bright greens, reds, and blues. The unique MovieClip symbol used to represent a parrot requires the export linkage name Parrot, which is the same as the class name.

The document class for Parrot packages the constructor, but no other member functions. The constructor assigns a velocity within a slow range and sets the scale of the display object to no less than its original size. In addition to having a varied size, a Parrot object is not necessarily proportional.

Parrot.as

```
1  package{
2     public class Parrot extends Bird{
3        public function Parrot():void {
4           velocity=Math.random() * 20 + 15;
5           this.scaleX+=Math.random();
6           this.scaleY+=Math.random();
7        }
8     }
9  }
```

Sparrow Class Design

The sparrows in the atrium are small, round, grayish-brown birds with short tails. The sparrow class constructor structures them as proportional in width and height, with a faster hovering velocity than a general bird in the atrium. The MovieClip symbol used to represent a sparrow requires the export linkage name Sparrow, the same name given to the class.

Sparrow.as

```
1  package{
2     public class Sparrow extends Bird{
3        public function Sparrow():void {
4           velocity = Math.random() * 5 + 7;
```

```
5              this.scaleX = Math.random() + .4;
6              this.scaleY = this.scaleX;
7          }
8      }
9  }
```

atriumApp.as: The Main Document Class Design

As in Case Study 1, atriumApp.as is the main document class for this application; it serves mainly to test the class declarations. All birds added to the atrium, whether they are Parrot or Sparrow instances, are stored in the array allBirds[]. The code for this AS3 file follows.

atriumApp.as

```
1  package {
2      import flash.display.*;
3      import flash.events.*;
4
5      public class atriumApp extends MovieClip {
6          //CREATE AN ARRAY TO STORE ALL BIRDS IN THE ATRIUM
7          var allBirds:Array = new Array();
8
9          function atriumApp() {
10             //VARIABLES FOR THE TWO TYPES OF BIRDS IN THE ATRIUM
11             var sparrowObj:Sparrow;
12             var parrotObj:Parrot;
13
14             //TASK 1: CREATE 3 SPARROWS AND ADD THEM TO THE ARRAY
15             for (var i:uint = 1; i< 4; i++) {
16                 sparrowObj = new Sparrow();
17                 sparrowObj.setBathLocation(Bath.x, Bath.y);
18                 addChild(sparrowObj);
19                 allBirds.push(sparrowObj);
20             }
21             //TASK 2: CREATE 2 PARROTS AND ADD THEM TO THE ARRAY
22             for (i = 1; i< 3; i++) {
23                 parrotObj = new Parrot();
24                 parrotObj.setBathLocation(Bath.x, Bath.y);
25                 addChild(parrotObj);
26                 allBirds.push(parrotObj);
27             }
28         }
29     }
30 }
```

9.5 Composition and the HAS-A Relationship

The idea of composition is not entirely new to Flash users. For example, MovieClip symbols are typically made from other MovieClip symbols. The **HAS-A**, or **HAS-Many**, relationship is essential to composition. A class can have several components, each a class in itself. The first example shown in Figure 9-15 illustrates a MovieClip symbol of a VillageResident constructed from other MovieClip symbols such as those for a face, hair, and body. In addition, the face is composed of eyes and a nose. The second example in Figure 9-15 shows the composite nature of a Flower class, which HAS-Many versions of the Petal class. In the last example of Figure 9-15, a class called DeckCards consists of many cards—specifically, 52.

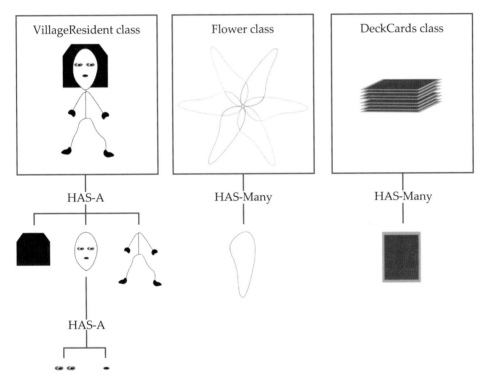

| FIGURE 9-15 Composite class examples.

In class composition, a class can use the data and behavior of another class indirectly by containing an object of that class as a data member. The containing class thus HAS-A class within it. Composition, like inheritance, offers several obvious advantages to Flash developers and AS3 programmers:

- Graphics can be shared among many `MovieClips`.
- Code can be shared among many classes.
- `MovieClips` can be extended.
- Classes can be extended.

All of these advantages are really aspects of the same thing: the reuse of elements. In programming, composition is a way to reuse an existing class, thereby relating these classes. To reuse a class means to create one class object based on another.

A good example of the advantage of class composition is a dust storm. Consider a class called `Dust` that represents a cloud of dust. Now consider an object of the `Dust` class that is composed of hundreds of dirt specks. Each speck of dirt in a dust cloud is individual in its behavior and may vary only slightly in its appearance; each speck of dirt is also an object and a member of a `dirtSpeck` class. In this way, the composite `Dust` object reuses all of the attributes and methods of the dirt specks it is composed of.

■ 9.6 Case Study 3: Food Composition in a Fish Tank

Problem and Analysis

Fish in a tank are often fed by pinching a small amount of food and dropping it into the tank (Figure 9-16). This is a good example of composition. A pinch of food consists of multiple individual food specks, which we will call nibblets. Each nibblet in the pinch of food has its own individual characteristics, such as a variation in size and velocity at which it falls to the bottom of the tank. The environment for this application is considered dynamic in the sense that the fish food can spoil and will eventually be removed from the tank.

The key to solving this problem is to recognize the objects in the fish tank and the operations conducted on those objects. Applications are designed with the future in mind, which means that often we must arrange attributes and operations for these objects.

In this application, objects are constructed representing a pinch of food tossed into the tank. A pinch of food is not a predefined type; hence, a `FoodPinch` class is used to implement its attributes and behavior. In addition, a `FoodPinch` object is defined as exactly three nibblets. A `Nibblet` class provides a way to implement the attributes and behavior for an individual `Nibblet` object.

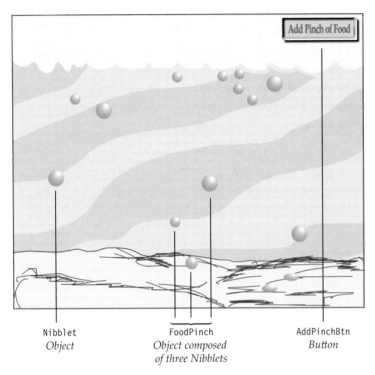

Nibblet   FoodPinch   AddPinchBtn
Object   *Object composed*   *Button*
                           of three Nibblets

❙ FIGURE 9-16 Food instances in an animated fish tank environment.

As shown in Figure 9-17, the containing class is the FoodPinch class, which in turn has a Nibblet class within it. In other words, the FoodPinch class can use the data and behavior of the Nibblet class indirectly.

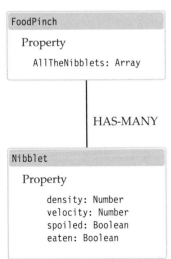

❙ FIGURE 9-17 Hierarchy of containment for the fish tank food element.

Visual Design

The visual side of this application requires a single frame in the Timeline construction. Because the water layer remains the background, it is located on the bottom of the list of layers, followed by the sand layer. The AddPinchBtn button is the only interactive display object on the Stage. All non-interactive elements are merely provided as decoration.

Program Design

In addition to the FoodPinch and Nibblet classes, an AS3 file named fishTankApp.as is used as the main application program and document class. We begin by looking at the Nibblet class.

Nibblet Class Design

Because a nibble of food on the Stage is immediately associated with a graphic image, we must design the Nibblet class to work with an exported Nibblet MovieClip stored in the Library. It is important that the linkage identifier name be the same as the class name, Nibblet.

Understanding how a Nibblet object will behave and be represented is essential to structuring its design. The following definitions are used to characterize a Nibblet:

1. Density. The density attribute for an individual Nibblet varies and is used to determine how quickly a Nibblet falls to the bottom of the tank. In addition, a denser Nibblet is larger in size.

2. Velocity. Not all Nibblets fall to the bottom of the fish tank at the same rate. Some Nibblets are heavier as well as denser, so they fall more rapidly than their counterparts. The velocity is computed based on the Nibblet's density.

3. Has the Nibblet spoiled? It is important to identify the condition of a given Nibblet. Once a Nibblet has perished, it must be physically removed from the tank. The spoiled factor is represented by a property containing a true or false value.

4. Has the Nibblet been eaten? Once a Nibblet has been consumed, it should be removed from the tank. A public property holding a true or false value can be used in a later application to identify if the Nibblet has been consumed by a fish in the tank.

A Nibblet object uses four data attributes: density, velocity, spoiled, and eaten.

Aside from the class constructor, a private utility method is packaged in the class to animate and control the Nibblet as it falls to the bottom of the tank. Table 9-4 outlines both functions.

TABLE 9-4 Nibblet Class Functions

Function Name	Description	Type
Nibblet()	The constructor function initializes the properties of a new Nibblet object. In addition, an ENTER_FRAME event is registered to create an animation in which the Nibblet falls to the bottom of the tank.	public constructor void function
fallToTankFloor()	This event handler is essentially the engine behind the Nibblet's animated fall to the bottom of the tank. It responds to an ENTER_FRAME event and moves the Nibblet to the bottom of the tank. Once it reaches the bottom, it begins to spoil, whereupon it diminishes in height. Once the height reaches a negligible stage, the Nibblet is considered spoiled.	private utility method void function

Nibblet.as

```
1    package {
2        import flash.display.*;
3        import flash.events.*;
4
5        public class Nibblet extends MovieClip {
6            //PROPERTIES FOR A SINGLE NIBBLET
7            public var density:Number;
8            public var velocity:Number;
9            public var spoiled:Boolean;
10           public var eaten:Boolean;
11
12           //FISH TANK PROPERTIES
13           private const TANK_BOTTOM:Number = 490;
14
15           public function Nibblet():void {
16               //TASK 1: INITIALIZE SEVERAL ATTRIBUTES OF A NIBBLET
17               spoiled = false;
18               eaten = false;
19               this.x = Math.random() * 600;
20               this.y = 10;
21
22               //TASK 2: REGISTER AN EVENT LISTENER FOR THIS NIBBLET
23               //        CREATE MOVEMENT FOR NIBBLET DROPPING TO FLOOR
24               this.addEventListener(Event.ENTER_FRAME,fallToTankFloor);
25           }
26
```

```
27        private function fallToTankFloor(event:Event):void {
28            //TASK 1: MOVE TOWARD THE FLOOR AT A SPECIFIED VELOCITY
29            this.y += velocity;
30
31            //TASK 2: CHECK IF NIBBLET IS AT BOTTOM OF THE TANK
32            if (this.y >= TANK_BOTTOM ) {
33                //TASK 3: REDUCE THE HEIGHT OF NIBBLET AS IT SPOILS
34                this.height -= .5;
35                velocity = 0;
36                //TASK 4: CHECK IF NIBBLET IS DONE SPOILING
37                if (this.height < 1){
38                    spoiled = true;
39                }
40            }
41        }
42    }
43 }
```

FoodPinch Class Design

When the user adds a pinch of food to the fish tank, three Nibblet objects appear at the top of the Stage and begin to float toward the bottom of the tank. In other words, a FoodPinch object is composed of exactly three Nibblet objects. The most efficient way to store these Nibblet objects is in an array. This array will be the sole data attribute required by the FoodPinch class. As the containing class, FoodPinch uses the attributes in the Nibblet class.

Aside from the constructor function, an additional public method, checkEatenOr-Spoiled(), is provided as a utility function that corresponds to factors associated with food spoilage. This function checks whether a single Nibblet in the array has perished and, if so, removes it from the fish tank floor.

FoodPinch.as

```
1  package {
2      import flash.display.*;
3
4      public class FoodPinch extends MovieClip {
5          //USE A PUBLIC ARRAY TO HOLD ALL THE NIBBLETS
6          public var AllTheNibblets:Array = new Array();
7
8          public function FoodPinch():void {
9              //TASK: CREATE THREE NIBBLETS AND PLACE IN THE ARRAY
10             for (var i:uint = 1; i <= 3; i++) {
11                 //TASK 1: CONSTRUCT THE NIBBLET OBJECT
12                 var nibbletObj:Nibblet = new Nibblet();
13
```

```
14          //TASK 2: SET THE DENSITY, VELOCITY, AND SCALE OF NIBBLET OBJECT
15          nibbletObj.density = Math.random() * 6 + 2;
16          nibbletObj.velocity = nibbletObj.density / 2;
17          nibbletObj.scaleX = nibbletObj.scaleY = nibbletObj.density * .4;
18
19          //TASK 3: ADD NIBBLET OBJECT TO STAGE AND ARRAY
20          addChild(nibbletObj);
21          AllTheNibblets.push(nibbletObj);
22       }
23    }
24    public function checkEatenOrSpoiled():void {
25       //TASK: CHECK IF A NIBBLET HAS SPOILED OR BEEN EATEN
26       if (AllTheNibblets.length>0) {
27          if (AllTheNibblets[0].spoiled ||AllTheNibblets[0].eaten) {
28             //TASK : REMOVE THE NIBBLET AT THE FRONT OF THE QUEUE
29             removeChild(AllTheNibblets[0]);
30             AllTheNibblets.shift();
31          }
32       }
33    }
34 }
35 }
```

fishTank.as: The Main Document Class Design

fishTank.as is the main document class for the fishTank application. It is designed to work with the FoodPinch class and serves as a means for testing the composition class definitions. This class uses a private, and global, variable for creating a generic pinch of food. In addition to the global variable, this document contains three functions: the constructor and two event handlers. The first event handler is addPinchOFood(), which adds food from the FoodPinch class to the fish tank each time the user clicks the AddPinchBtn button on the Stage. The second event handler routinely checks whether any existing food in the tank has spoiled; any such food is then removed from the Stage.

fishTank.as

```
1  package {
2     import flash.display.*;
3     import flash.events.*;
4
5     public class fishTank extends MovieClip {
6
7        //VARIABLE HOLDING A PINCH OF FOOD
8        private var foodPinchObj:FoodPinch = new FoodPinch();
9
10       public function fishTank():void {
```

```
11        //TASK 1: REGISTER THE LISTENER EVENT FOR THE BUTTON
12        AddPinchBtn.addEventListener(MouseEvent.CLICK, addPinchOFood);
13        //TASK 2: REGISTER AN ENTER_FRAME LISTENER EVENT FOR FOOD SPOILAGE
14        addEventListener(Event.ENTER_FRAME,checkIfFoodSpoiled);
15      }
16
17      private function addPinchOFood (event:MouseEvent):void {
18        //TASK: ADD A PINCH OF FOOD TO THE FISH TANK
19        foodPinchObj = new FoodPinch();
20        addChild(foodPinchObj);
21      }
22
23      private function checkIfFoodSpoiled (event:Event):void {
24        //TASK: CHECK IF NIBBLETS IN THE PINCH OF FOOD HAVE PERISHED
25        foodPinchObj. checkEatenOrSpoiled ();
26      }
27    }
28  }
```

■ 9.7 Polymorphism and the override Access Modifier

Polymorphism, the third principle of object-oriented programming, provides the mechanism for using the same function name to denote different operations. The term "polymorphic" is of Greek origin and means "of many forms." In AS3, polymorphism is associated with functions. A polymorphic function is one that has the same name for different classes in the same family, but different implementations for the various classes.

Polymorphism allows functions with the same name to behave differently within a class family. The advantage of this approach is that it provides an identical function interface for a different implementation in each class. In effect, we can hide alternative operations behind a common interface.

The following example illustrates the concept of polymorphism.

Example

Consider a parent class named Vehicle. This class represents the basic elements of a generic vehicle object on the road. It contains three data characteristics: the color of the vehicle, its main transport purpose, and the number of people the vehicle seats. Each of these attributes is given protected access so that it is accessible to any derived class.

In addition to the data attributes, the Vehicle class contains two public method functions: setTo() resets the data attribute values and displayInfo() outputs the values stored in the data attributes.

Also consider the Bus class, derived from the Vehicle class. Figure 9-18 shows the structure of the Vehicle family hierarchy. As a derived class, Bus is an extension of the Vehicle class. In this example, Bus makes use of the setTo() function from its parent class but uses its own displayInfo() method function. In other words, this polymorphic function overrides displayInfo() within the Vehicle class.

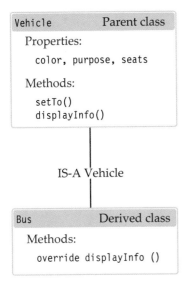

| FIGURE 9-18 The Vehicle family.

Three AS3 files are used in this example:

• Vehicle.as—the parent class definition for Vehicle

• Bus.as—the derived class definition for Bus

• mainApp.as—the document class for the Flash application and the tester program

Vehicle.as (Parent Class)

```
1   package {
2      public class Vehicle {
3         //VEHICLE DATA PROPERTIES
4         protected var color:String;
5         protected var purpose:String;
6         protected var seats:Number;
7         public function setTo(c:String, p:String, s:Number):void {
8            //TASK: USE PARAMETER LIST TO SET THE VEHICLE DATA ATTRIBUTES
9            color=c;
10           purpose=p;
```

```
11              seats=s;
12          }
13          public function displayInfo():void {
14              //TASK: DISPLAY THE DATA ATTRIBUTES IN TRACE STATEMENTS
15              trace("This vehicle is ", color, " in color.");
16              trace("The main purpose of the vehicle is ", purpose, ".");
17              trace("It seats ", seats, " people.\n");
18          }
19      }
20  }
```

Bus.as (Derived from the Vehicle Class)

```
1   package {
2       public class Bus extends Vehicle {
3           public function Bus(s:Number):void {
4               // THE CONSTRUCTOR FUNCTION
5               //TASK 1: ASSIGN A FIXED COLOR AND PURPOSE
6               color="Yellow";
7               purpose="to deliver children to school.";
8               //TASK 2: ASSIGN NUMBER OF SEATS FROM THE PARAMETER
9               seats=s;
10          }
11          override public function displayInfo():void {
12              //TASK : DISPLAY SPECIFIC BUS INFORMATION
13              trace("This school bus is ", color, " in color.");
14              trace("This chauffeured vehicle is used to ", purpose);
15              trace("It seats ", seats, " people.\n");
16          }
17      }
18  }
```

In mainApp.as, two objects are created: a Vehicle and a Bus that is derived from a Vehicle. Attribute values are assigned to each of these objects using the method function setTo() from the Vehicle class.

Polymorphism provides flexibility in program implementation by allowing a different version of an overridden method of an object to be called. When truck, a Vehicle object, is used to call the displayInfo() method, the version in the Vehicle class is the one that is executed. When athleteBus, a Bus object, is used to call the displayInfo() method, the overriding version in the Bus class is the one that is executed.

mainApp.as

```
1  package {
2      import flash.display.*;
3      public class mainApp extends MovieClip {
4          function mainApp() {
5              //TASK 1: CREATE VEHICLE OBJECT, SET ITS ATTRIBUTES AND DISPLAY
6              var truck:Vehicle = new Vehicle();
7              truck.setTo("Black", "recreation", 3);
8              truck.displayInfo();
9              //TASK 2: THE SECOND OBJECT IS A BUS DERIVED FROM A VEHICLE
10             // SET ITS ATTRIBUTES AND DISPLAY
11             var athleteBus:Bus=new Bus(30);
12             athleteBus.displayInfo();
13             athleteBus.setTo("maroon and gray", "transport athletes.", 20);
14             athleteBus.displayInfo();
15         }
16     }
17 }
```

The output produced by these files is

This vehicle is Black in color.

The main purpose of the vehicle is recreation.

It seats 3 people.

This school bus is Yellow in color.

The main purpose of this chauffeured vehicle is to deliver children to school.

It seats 30 people.

This school bus is maroon and gray in color.

This chauffeured vehicle is used to transport athletes.

It seats 20 people.

9.8 Case Study 4: A Complete Fish Tank

Problem and Analysis

This case study examines a dynamic aquarium that contains multiple fish, each characterized in a slightly different way. The final application illustrates the use of all three OOP principles: encapsulation, composition and inheritance, and polymorphism.

AddFoodBtn   AddBrownBtn   AddRedBtn

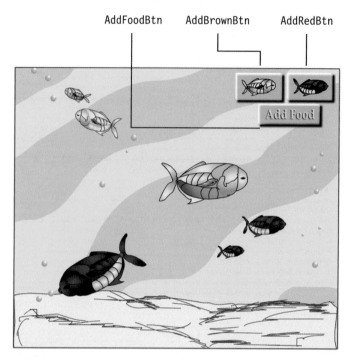

I FIGURE 9-19 An application demonstrating all three OOP principles.

As shown in Figure 9-19, this aquarium allows users to interactively add two general types of fish, both of which are derived from a `Fish` parent class. The first derived `Fish` class represents a brightly colored red fish, aptly named `RedFish`. The second `Fish` class is named `BrownFish`. Besides the variation in color, these two types of `Fish` differ in the speed at which they travel and in their behavior when hungry. `RedFish` are faster and need less food to survive; `BrownFish` require frequent feedings and turn a shade of blue when they become hungry. Both the `BrownFish` and `RedFish` classes are extensions of the `Fish` class, which defines the main characteristics and basic behavior of a given fish. The `Fish` family hierarchy is shown in Figure 9-20.

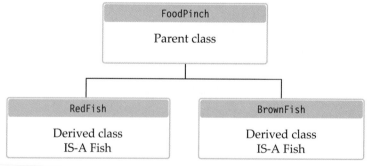

I FIGURE 9-20 The family of classes representing `Fish` in the aquarium application.

In addition to adding Fish, users can interactively drop a pinch of food into the aquarium, then stand back and watch as the Fish eat. As in the previous case study, food is represented by the Nibblet class and its container class FoodPinch.

Six AS3 code files are used for this application:

Fish Representation

```
Fish.as
BrownFish.as
RedFish.as
```

Food Representation

```
FoodPinch.as
Nibblet.as
```

Main Document Class

```
FishTank.as
```

The first task required for solving this problem is the development of a family of classes to represent the fish: Fish, RedFish, and BrownFish.

Algorithm Design for Fish Representation

We begin with the parent class, Fish, which encapsulates the data properties of a generic fish and drives its behavior.

Fish Class

The attributes of all fish in this aquarium will be kept simple: Fish will explore their surroundings until they become hungry, at which point they will search for food to eat. The possible conditions for a given Fish at any moment in time can be identified by one of the following constants: isHUNGRY, isSWIMMING, or isDONE_EATING. The six data properties that describe a generic fish in the tank are outlined in Table 9-5. The first three properties—myCondition, velocity, and stomachCapacity—are given protected status so that they can be accessed by the two derived Fish classes.

TABLE 9-5 Properties of a Fish Object

Property Name	Access	Data type	Description
myCondition	protected	uint	Holds one of three possible conditions for the Fish.
velocity	protected	uint	The velocity at which the given Fish normally swims.
stomachCapacity	protected	uint	The amount of food the fish's stomach holds. This value varies for each Fish.
inStomach	private	int	The amount of food/fuel in a given Fish. This value is used to determine the condition of the Fish.
exploreX	private	Number	The x location of a random spot to be explored by a given Fish.
exploreY	private	Number	The y location of a random exploration spot.

Four basic operations need to be performed on a Fish object:

1. Set the initial information for a Fish
2. Swim in the tank and explore a random spot of interest
3. Locate food when hungry
4. Eat food when hungry until the stomach is satisfied

The complete set of methods for the Fish class is outlined in Table 9-6.

TABLE 9-6 Fish Class Methods

Method Name	Description	Type of Method
Fish()	The constructor function initializes the properties of a new Fish object.	public constructor
moveFish(foodList)	Examines the three possible conditions of the Fish: • isSWIMMING • isHUNGRY • isDONE_EATING Responds by directing a call to the appropriate behavior method function. When a Fish is recognized as isHUNGRY, the incoming parameter foodList array is used to identify the food currently available in the tank.	public method void function

TABLE 9-6 Fish Class Methods (continued)

Method Name	Description	Type of Method
swim()	This function is called when the condition of the Fish is isSWIMMING. When it executes, the Fish burns a calorie by decrementing the value in inStomach. This function also computes the distance to a point of interest to be explored. It examines the value in inStomach, which triggers the new condition isHUNGRY if the stomach is nearly empty.	protected utility method void function
findEatFood(foodList)	Locates a fresh Nibblet of food from the incoming parameter, foodList array, and moves the Fish toward it. If the distance between the Nibblet and the Fish is negligible, the Fish consumes the Nibblet and its condition is set to isDONE_EATING.	protected utility method void function
doneEating()	Sets the Fish's condition to isSWIMMING. Computes a random point of interest in the aquarium for the Fish to explore. Turns the Fish so that it is facing the exploration spot.	protected utility method void function
turnFish()	Given a location to swim to, the Fish is physically turned using the scaleX property so that it faces the location it is swimming toward.	private utility method void function

Next, we discuss the design of the RedFish and BrownFish extended classes.

RedFish Class

The RedFish class is derived from the parent Fish class but varies in minor ways from the base class. The characteristic differences between a RedFish and other Fish in the tank simply revolve around speed and the number of feedings required. RedFish are designed to be the fastest Fish in the tank and can store a large amount of food, meaning they have a larger interval of time between feedings. In terms of other behavior, RedFish conduct themselves in exactly the same manner as any other Fish.

The sole operation to be performed by an object of the type RedFish is the setting of the speed to FAST and the stomach size to LARGE.

As for the visual appearance of a RedFish, it is composed of an animated tail and fin, as shown in Figure 9-21. The name RedFish is also used for the export linkage of this MovieClip.

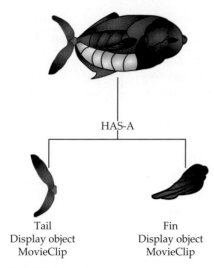

HAS-A

Tail
Display object
MovieClip

Fin
Display object
MovieClip

▌ FIGURE 9-21 The RedFish visual design.

BrownFish Class

The BrownFish class describes a slower Fish with a smaller stomach. In addition to these attributes, this Fish has minor behavioral differences. When it is hungry, it takes on a bluish tint; when not hungry, it becomes a golden brown. To achieve this effect, the MovieClip BrownFish is composed of a MovieClip instance in a top layer, named Golden, that can be made transparent when hungry. This appearance is illustrated in Figure 9-22. The name BrownFish is also used for the export linkage of this MovieClip.

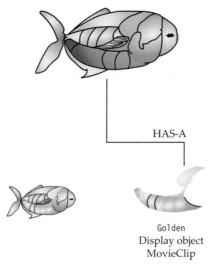

HAS-A

Golden
Display object
MovieClip

▌ FIGURE 9-22 The BrownFish visual design.

Two operations are performed by an object of the type BrownFish. The first operation is executed by the constructor function, which sets the BrownFish's swimming speed to SLOW and its stomach size to SMALL. The second operation is accomplished by a polymorphic function, moveFish(foodList), which is also used by the parent Fish class. In this overriding function of the same name, the BrownFish object alters its color in response to its current condition.

The following AS3 files define the three classes representing fish in the aquarium.

Fish.as

```
1   package {
2       import flash.display.*;
3
4       public class Fish extends MovieClip {
5           //POSSIBLE CONDITIONS OF THE FISH
6           protected const isHUNGRY:uint=1;
7           protected const isSWIMMING:uint=2;
8           protected const isDONE_EATING:uint=3;
9
10  //CONSTANTS DESCRIBING THE SPEED AND STOMACH SIZE OF A FISH OBJECT
11          protected const FAST:uint=50;
12          protected const SLOW:uint=90;
13          protected const LARGE:uint=400;
14          protected const SMALL:uint=200;
15
16          //CONSTANTS FOR TURNING THE FISH IN THE CORRECT DIRECTION
17          protected const FACE_RIGHT:uint=1;
18          protected const FACE_LEFT:int=-1;
19          protected const TURN:int=-1;
20
21          //FISH PROPERTIES
22          protected var myCondition:uint; //CURRENT CONDITION OF THE FISH
23          protected var velocity:uint; //TRAVELING SPEED OF THE FISH
24          protected var stomachCapacity:uint;
25          private var inStomach:int;   //AMOUNT OF FOOD IN STOMACH
26          private var exploreX:Number; //X-AXIS LOCATION TO RELAX AND SWIM
27          private var exploreY:Number; //Y-AXIS LOCATION TO RELAX AND SWIM
28
29          public function Fish():void {
30              //TASK: INITIALIZE FISH ATTRIBUTES
31              this.x=0;       //FISH ARRIVES OFFSTAGE
32              this.y=0;
33              exploreX=Math.random()*stage.stageWidth; //SWIMS TOWARD THIS POINT
34              exploreY=Math.random()*stage.stageHeight;
35              inStomach=200;       // BIT OF FOOD IN STOMACH
36          }
```

```
37
38          public function moveFish(foodList):void {
39             // EXAMINE POSSIBLE CONDITIONS: isSWIMMING, isHUNGRY, isDONE_EATING
40             switch (myCondition) {
41                case isSWIMMING :
42                   swim();
43                   break;
44                case isHUNGRY :
45                   findEatFood(foodList);
46                   break;
47                case isDONE_EATING :
48                   doneEating();
49                   break;
50             }
51          }
52
53          protected function swim():void {
54             //TASK 1: BURN A CALORIE OF FOOD
55             inStomach-;
56
57             //TASK 2: SWIM TOWARD A POINT OF INTEREST
58             var xDist:Number=exploreX-this.x;
59             var yDist:Number=exploreY-this.y;
60             this.x+=xDist/velocity;
61             this.y+=yDist/velocity;
62
63             //TASK 3: DETERMINE IF STOMACH IS NEAR EMPTY/HUNGRY
64             if (inStomach<10) {
65                myCondition=isHUNGRY;
66             }
67          }
68          protected function findEatFood(foodList):void {
69             //LOCATE THE FIRST NIBBLET OF FOOD FROM THE FOODLIST ARRAY
70             if (foodList.length>0) {
71                //TASK 1: FIND DISTANCE TO NIBBLET IN FOODLIST
72                var xDist:Number=foodList [0].x-this.x;
73                var yDist:Number=foodList [0].y-this.y;
74
75                //TASK 2: TURN FISH IN DIRECTION OF NIBBLET IN FOODLIST
76                turnFish(foodList[0].x);
77
78                //TASK 3: MOVE FISH TOWARD A NIBBLET
79                this.x+=xDist/(velocity*.5);
80                this.y+=yDist/(velocity*.5);
81                //TASK 4: IF FISH IS CLOSE TO FOOD, EAT NIBBLET AND BECOME FULL
82                if (Math.abs(this.x- foodList[0].x<30 &&
83                   Math.abs(this.y- foodList[0].y<30) {
```

```
84              this.x=foodList[0].x;
85              this.y=foodList[0].y;
86              foodList[0].eaten=true;
87              myCondition=isDONE_EATING;
88              inStomach= stomachCapacity;
89           }
90        }
91     }
92
93     protected function doneEating():void {
94        //TASK 1: CONDITION IS SWIMMING
95        myCondition=isSWIMMING;
96
97        //TASK 2: IDENTIFY A POINT IN THE AQUARIUM TO EXPLORE
98        exploreX=Math.random()*stage.stageWidth;
99        exploreY=Math.random()*stage.stageHeight;
100
101        //TASK 3: TURN FISH IN DIRECTION OF EXPLORATION
102        turnFish(exploreX);
103     }
104
105     private function turnFish(newLocation):void {
106        if (newLocation<this.x&&this.scaleX==FACE_RIGHT) {
107           this.scaleX=TURN;
108        } else if (newLocation > this.x && this.scaleX == FACE_LEFT) {
109           this.scaleX=FACE_RIGHT;
110        }
111     }
112   }
113 }
```

RedFish.as

```
1  package {
2     public class RedFish extends Fish {
3        public function RedFish():void {
4           //TASK: ASSIGN A SLOW VELOCITY AND SET STOMACH CAPACITY
5           velocity=Math.random() * 10 + FAST;
6           stomachCapacity=LARGE;
7        }
8     }
9  }
```

BrownFish.as

```
1  package {
2     public class BrownFish extends Fish {
3        public function BrownFish():void {
```

```
4          //TASK: ASSIGN A SLOW VELOCITY AND SET STOMACH CAPACITY
5          velocity=Math.random()*10+SLOW;
6          stomachCapacity=SMALL;
7      }
8
9      override public function moveFish(foodList):void {
10         //TASK : EXAMINE THE POSSIBLE CONDITIONS OF THE BROWN FISH
11         switch(myCondition) {
12            case isSWIMMING :
13               this.Golden.alpha=1;
14               swim();
15               break;
16            case isHUNGRY :
17               this.Golden.alpha=0;
18               findEatFood(foodList);
19               break;
20            case isDONE_EATING :
21               this.Golden.alpha=1;
22               doneEating();
23               break;
24         }
25      }
26   }
27 }
```

Algorithm Design for Food Representation

As in the previous case study, the food in this aquarium is represented by the flexible Nibblet class and its container class FoodPinch. There are no differences in the behavior related to food, so the two classes will not be altered in any way.

See Case Study 3 for information on FoodPinch.as and Nibblet.as.

Main Document Class Design

The main application program uses the Fish, RedFish, BrownFish, FoodPinch, and Nibblet classes. The collection of Fish and uneaten and unspoiled food occupy global arrays. The basic operations of this program are as follows:

1. Respond to buttons for adding fish and food.
2. Monitor the spoilage of food.

fishTank.as

```
1 package {
2    import flash.display.*;
3    import flash.events.*;
```

```
4
5      public class fishTank extends MovieClip {
6         // GLOBAL ARRAYS HOLDING ALL FISH AND ALL FOOD
7         private var AllTheFishes = new Array();
8         private var foodPinchObj:FoodPinch = new FoodPinch();
9
10        public function fishTank():void {
11           //TASK 1: REGISTER A MOUSE EVENT FOR EACH BUTTON ON STAGE
12           AddFoodBtn.addEventListener(MouseEvent.CLICK, addPinchOFood);
13           AddBrownBtn.addEventListener(MouseEvent.CLICK, addBrownFish);
14           AddRedBtn.addEventListener(MouseEvent.CLICK, addRedFish);
15
16           //TASK 2: REGISTER ENTER_FRAME LISTENER EVENT FOR FOOD SPOILAGE
17           addEventListener(Event.ENTER_FRAME,monitorFoodSpoilage);
18        }
19
20        private function addPinchOFood(event:MouseEvent):void {
21           //TASK: ADD A PINCH OF FOOD TO THE FISH TANK
22           foodPinchObj = new FoodPinch();
23           addChild(foodPinchObj);
24        }
25
26        private function addBrownFish(event:MouseEvent):void {
27           //TASK: ADD A BROWNFISH OBJECT TO THE STAGE AND FISH ARRAY
28           var brownfishObj:BrownFish = new BrownFish();
29           addChild(brownfishObj);
30           AllTheFishes.push(brownfishObj);
31        }
32
33        private function addRedFish(event:MouseEvent):void {
34           //TASK: ADD A REDFISH OBJECT TO THE STAGE AND FISH ARRAY
35           var redfishObj:RedFish = new RedFish();
36           addChild(redfishObj);
37           AllTheFishes.push(redfishObj);
38        }
39
40        private function monitorFoodSpoilage(event:Event):void {
41           //TASK 1: CHECK AND REMOVE SPOILED FOOD
42           foodPinchObj.checkEatenOrSpoiled();
43           //TASK 2: INFORM FISH OF FRESH FOOD
44           for (var i:int = 0; i < AllTheFishes.length; i++) {
45              AllTheFishes[i].moveFish(foodPinchObj.AllTheNibblets);
46           }
47        }
48     }
49  }
```

■ Review Questions

1. What are class attributes?

2. What are class methods?

3. What is the main difference between a class attribute and a class method?

4. Explain the concept of data abstraction.

5. Explain the concept of encapsulation.

6. What is the difference between an object and a class?

7. Identify the access modifiers. Explain their differences.

8. Explain how the keyword this is used in a class.

9. Explain the differences between inheritance and composition.

10. Give an example of inheritance from everyday life.

11. Give two examples of composition from everyday life.

12. What is meant by protected access?

13. What is a base class?

■ Programming Exercises

1. Create a Monster class consisting of the speed at which a monster travels, the monster's age, and its level of animosity.

2. Create a Car class consisting of the health of a vehicle and its average traveling speed.

3. Create a member function for the Car class created in Exercise 2 that moves the car across the Stage once it is constructed. Force the car to stop moving once it reaches the edge of the Stage.

4. Add four balls to the billiards game from Chapter 6, Case Study 4. Construct each ball as a member of a Ball class and add member functions to control the collisions (see Figure 9-23).

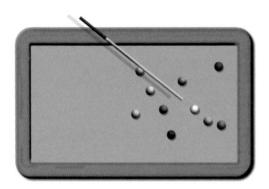

I FIGURE 9-23 Billiards with a `Ball` class and member functions.

5. Create a game of dodgeball that allows the user to move a character on the Stage to dodge balls falling from the top of the Stage (see Figure 9-24).

I FIGURE 9-24 Dodgeball application designed with OOP.

Index